rk St

Managing Innovation and Change

The Open University Business School

The Open University Business School offers a three-tier ladder of opportunity for managers at different stages of their careers: the Professional Certificate in Management; the Professional Diploma in Management; and the Masters Programme.

This Reader is a prescribed Course Reader for the Creativity, Innovation and Change Module (B822) which is part of the Masters in Business Administration at The Open University Business School. Opinions expressed in this Reader are not necessarily those of the Course Team or of The Open University.

Further information on Open University Business School courses and qualifications may be obtained from The Open University Business School, PO Box 197, Walton Hall, Milton Keynes, MK7 6BJ, United Kingdom; tel. OU Business School Information Line: +44 (0) 8700 100311.

Alternatively, much useful course information can be obtained from the Open University Business School's website at http://www.oubs.open.ac.uk

Managing Innovation and Change

Third Edition

Edited by David Mayle

SAGE Publications
London • Thousand Oaks • New Delhi

OU Business School

First edition published 1991. Second edition published 2002.
This third edition published 2006

SAGE Publications Ltd
1 Oliver's Yard
55 City Road
London EC1Y 1SP

SAGE Publications Inc.
2455 Teller Road
Thousand Oaks, California 91320

SAGE Publications India Pvt Ltd
B-42, Panchsheel Enclave
Post Box 4109
New Delhi 110 017

British Library Cataloguing in Publication data

A catalogue record for this book is available
from the British Library

ISBN-10 1-4129-2249-6   ISBN-13 978-1-4129-2249-4
ISBN-10 1-4129-2250-X   ISBN-13 978-1-4129-2250-0 (pbk)

Library of Congress Control Number: 2006922479

Typeset by C&M Digitals (P) Ltd, Chennai, India
Printed on paper from sustainable resources
Printed and bound in Great Britain by Cromwell Press Ltd

Contents

Contents

Contributors

Robert J. Allio is a contributing editor for *Strategy & Leadership*.

Maria Stuttaford (formerly Allison) is a lecturer at the University of St Andrews.

Scott D. Anthony is a Partner at Innosight, a consultancy and education company in Massachusetts.

Amit Baghel is at Concordia University, Montreal.

John Bessant is Professor of Innovation and Technology Management at Imperial College, London.

Nadia Bhuiyan is Associate Director, Concordia Institute for Aerospace and Design Innovation in Montreal.

David E. Bowen is Professor of Management at Thunderbird – The Garvin School of International Management in Arizona.

Henry Chesbrough is Executive Director, Center for Open Innovation at the Haas School of Business, University of California at Berkeley.

Clayton M. Christensen is Professor of Business Administration at Harvard Business School.

Jim Collins runs a management learning laboratory in Boulder, Colorado.

Barrie Dale is Professor of Quality Management at Manchester School of Management.

Bruce Einhorn is a correspondent in *Business Week*'s Hong Kong bureau.

Caroline Emberson researches at the Open University Business School.

Pete Engardio is Senior News Editor, International, for *Business Week*.

Richard Farson is President of the Western Behavioral Sciences Institute in California.

Dave Francis is Senior Research Fellow and Deputy Head of CENTRIM at the University of Brighton.

Paul Geroski was Professor of Economics at London Business School.

Jody Hoffer Gittell is Assistant Professor at Brandeis University in Massachusetts.

Jean Hartley is Professor of Organizational Analysis at Warwick Business School.

Peter Hines is Professor of Supply Chain Management at Cardiff Business School.

Matthias Holweg is Senior Lecturer in Operations Management at the Judge Business School, Cambridge.

Ralph Keyes is a professional author based in Ohio.

Simon Knox is Professor of Brand Marketing at Cranfield School of Management.

Edward E. Lawler III is Distinguished Professor of Business, Marshall School of Business, University of Southern California.

Stan Maklan is a visiting fellow at Cranfield School of Management.

Costas Markides is Professor of Strategic Leadership at London Business School.

Ray Oakey is Professor of Business Development at Manchester Business School.

Charles O'Reilly is Professor of Human Resources Management and Organizational Behavior at Stanford Graduate School of Business.

David Reade researches at the Open University Business School.

Nick Rich is a Director of Cardiff University's Innovative Manufacturing Research Centre.

Karl Schultz is Director of Energy Edge Ltd, a UK-based strategic global energy consultancy.

John Storey is Professor of Human Resource Management at the Open University Business School.

Michael Tushman is Professor of Business Administration at Harvard University.

A. van der Wiele is at the Rotterdam School of Management.

Roger Williams is Professor of Business and Organisation at Erasmus University Rotterdam.

Peter Williamson is Affiliate Professor of Asian Business and International Management at INSEAD.

Ian Wilson is principal of Wolf Enterprises, a strategic management consultancy based in California.

Mohammed Zairi is Professor of Best Practice Management at Bradford University School of Management.

Acknowledgements

Grateful acknowledgement is made to the following sources for permission to reproduce material in this book.

1 *Gaining Competitive Advantage in a Carbon-constrained World: Strategies for European Business*
   K. Schultz and P. Williamson (2005) *European Management Journal*, 23 (4): 383–91.
   © 2005, with permission from Elsevier.

2 *Corporate Social Responsibility: Moving Beyond Investment Towards Measuring Outcomes*
   S. Knox and S. Maklan (2004) *European Management Journal*, 22 (5): 508–16. © 2004, with permission from Elsevier.

3 *Outsourcing Innovation*
   P. Engardio and B. Einhorn (2005) *Business Week*: 21 March.
   Reproduced by permission of Business Week magazine.

4 *From Scenario Thinking to Strategic Action*
   I. Wilson (2000) *Technological Forecasting and Social Change*, 65 (1): 23–9. © 2000, with permission from Elsevier.

5 *Quality is Dead in Europe: Long Live Excellence. True or False?*
   B.G. Dale, M. Zairi, A. van der Wiele and A.R.T. Williams (2000) *Measuring Business Excellence*, 4 (3): 4–10. Republished with permission, Emerald Group Publishing Ltd.

6 *An Overview of Continuous Improvement: From the Past to the Present*
   N. Bhuiyan and A. Baghel (2005) *Management Decision*, 43 (5): 761–71. Republished with permission, Emerald Group Publishing Ltd.

7 *Learning to Evolve: A Review of Contemporary Lean Thinking*
   P. Hines, M. Holweg and N. Rich (2004) *International Journal of Operations and Production Management*, 24 (10): 994–1011. Republished with permission, Emerald Group Publishing Ltd.

8   *The Barriers to Customer Responsive Supply Chain Management*
    J. Storey, C. Emberson and D. Reade (2005) *International Journal of Operations and Production Management*, 25 (3): 242–60. Republished with permission, Emerald Group Publishing Ltd.

9   *Ackoff on Innovation*
    R.J. Allio (2003) *Strategy and Leadership*, 31 (3): 19–26. Republished with permission, Emerald Group Publishing Ltd.

10 *How you can Benefit by Predicting Change*
    S.D. Anthony and C.M. Christensen (2005) *Financial Executive*, 21 (2): 36–41. © 2005, Financial Executives International, 200 Campus Drive, Florham Park, NJ 07932–0674; www.fei.org. Reprinted with permission.

11 *The Era of Open Innovation*
    H. Chesbrough (2003) *MIT Sloan Management Review*, 44 (3): 35–41. © 2004 by Massachusetts Institute of Technology. All rights reserved. Distributed by Tribune Media Services.

12 *The Innovator's Prescription: The Art of Scale*
    C. Markides and P. Geroski (2004) *Strategy and Business*, 35: 2–10. Reprinted with permission from strategy+business, the award-winning management quarterly published by Booz Allen Hamilton www.strategy-business.com

13 *The Empowement of Service Workers: What, Why, How, and When*
    D.E. Bowen and E.E. Lawler III (1992) *Sloan Management Review*, 33 (3): 31–9. © 1992 by Massachusetts Institute of Technology. All rights reserved. Distributed by Tribune Media Services.

14 *Ambidextrous Organizations: Managing Evolutionary and Revolutionary Change*
    M.L. Tushman and C.A. O'Reilly III (1996) *California Management Review*, 38 (4): 8–30. © 1996 by The Regents of the University of California. Reprinted by permission of The Regents and the authors.

15 *Technical Entrepreneurship in High Technology Small Firms: Some Observations on the Implications for Management*
    R.P. Oakey (2003) *Technovation*, 23: 679–88. © 2003, with permission of Elsevier.

16 *Targeting Innovation and Implications for Capability Development*
    D. Francis and J. Bessant (2005) *Technovation*, 25: 171–83. © 2005, with permission from Elsevier.

17 *The Role of Leadership in the Modernization and Improvement of Public Services*
    J. Hartley and M. Allison (2000) *Public Money and Management*, 20 (2): 35–40. Reproduced with permission from Blackwell Publishing.

Introduction

In the period that has elapsed since the second edition, the world has moved on. Technology continues to offer possibilities that most of us can only barely grasp; in many applications the shortfall is not in technological capability but in the human imagination to exploit it. The potential for imminent and irreversible environmental damage is now recognized by *almost* everybody, but the political will to act on this understanding still lags behind. With the accelerating emergence of such economies as India and China, globalization is no longer an academic discipline or a fringe movement, but a business imperative. In the aftermath of Enron and WorldCom, business ethics is no longer regarded as an oxymoron, but, according to some, a growing crisis of capitalism.

So what are we to make of all this? As with all such scenarios, the response is crucial. If we throw up our hands in horror and bemoan the ways of the world, we will become complicit in our own downfall. If we accept the challenge, we can yet exert influence for the good; the seeds are visible.

If the twentieth century was an era of the large corporation, with Fordist organization required to achieve economies of scale and output of any colour 'as long as it's black', there is evidence from the closing decade at least that enterprise is now more manageable in scope, even as it grows in scale.

With the prospect of many lower-skilled jobs being increasingly 'off-shored' by the so-called developed nations to the emerging economies of Asia, it is not too outrageous to suggest that the jobs that then remain will, of necessity, be rather more knowledge-based than previously. And knowledge-based work is different; it is intrinsically much less amenable to supervision and involves hearts and minds, rather than just brains and brawn. The relationship between employer and employee is becoming slightly more equal than has previously been the norm. The employer wants access to the talents, as before, but the nature of the relationship is increasingly different; the employee is growing accustomed to having rather more say in things than hitherto.

A major thread in the second edition, to a much larger extent than its predecessor, was the growth of empowerment. Many years ago, the irrepressible Robert Townsend argued[1] that decisions concerning how work was best conducted should be devolved to the person with most to lose if it was wrong, usually the person actually doing the job. The empowerment movement has flourished in the intervening period, and the notion of giving people a say in the organization of their work is now pretty non-controversial. The consequences of this are indeed significant, once let out of the bottle, the genie is in no mood to re-enter. Key workers are now likely to demand not just local control over the day-to-day operations, but increasingly an input into the wider business strategy. Should an organization not measure up to their expectations, not only in terms of conditions of employment and the organization of their work but also in terms of the sphere of activity and policy towards the wider environment, then they will be increasingly inclined to look for something more congenial. In any form of enterprise, people matter.

When discussing the need for new and/or improved products/processes/systems, I get frequent exhortations from both students and clients to help them and their organizations to 'think outside the box'. My long answer is usually to emphasize that having the novel idea is only one part of the problem; once you think you have found the solution, its realization into practice is inevitably a less-than-trivial exercise. Refinement, improvement, implementation and re-iteration may be less glamorous brethren to 'innovation' but they are no less crucial to successful enterprise (and may require different but complementary skills). Nevertheless, I do usually end up spending time helping them to come up with more innovative, original or sometimes unconventional ideas than they previously thought possible. So clearly, innovation matters too.

Ultimately, you may argue, it is people that come up with new/imaginative ideas. Well, yes, and different folk do indeed have different strengths and weaknesses when it comes to solving 'problems', but the circumstances in which people find themselves have a major bearing on their capacity (and indeed inclination) to contribute to the process of innovation.

The structure of this Reader is partly an attempt to produce a coherent and helpful progression of ideas and concepts, and partly an attempt to showcase articles that I felt had something particularly important to say in the context of the management of innovation and change. On that basis, the articles are grouped into five themes as follows.

Part 1, **Environments**, is an attempt to portray the increasing diversity of pressures to which modern enterprise is subjected. As well as the now predictable imperative that business conducts itself with respect for the physical environment, the social and cultural environment, and for individual and organizational stakeholders, we further have to recognize that globalization implies more than just outsourcing the routine aspects of an operation to somewhere with a lower cost-base.

In the second Part, entitled **Approaches**, we essay a brief review of some of the more persistent TLAs (Three Letter Acronyms) to which the art of management is increasingly prone, and try to recognize some of the more fundamental issues that underpin the effective improvement of an organization and the processes that it comprises.

Part 3 is explicitly about **Innovation** *per se*. The nature of innovation, types of innovation, models of innovation management, and the successful exploitation of innovation.

The next Part is labelled **Change**, but in truth it probably offers a wider range of perspectives than might be inferred by the title alone, encompassing empowerment, change-management, entrepreneurship, cross-cultural management and capability development.

The final Part is about **Leadership**. The intention here is not to make some mystical appeal for great leaders (who sadly are often only observable in retrospect), but to begin to understand what attributes of leadership are consistent with the successful management of innovation and change.

Collectively the chapters encompass a world-view that those of us in the Creative Management Group at the Open University Business School regard as consistent with the effective management of creativity, innovation and change. Some of them may cover familiar territory, others will hopefully be new to many readers in terms of topic or of treatment. Although many of the chapters are relatively recent, some date back to the early part of the decade; one or two even hark back to the previous millennium! For this I offer no apology, referring instead to an old adage that *There are two kinds of fool. One says, 'This is old, and therefore good.' And one says, 'This is new, and therefore better'.*[2] One of the joys of innovation and change, is that ideas are entertained on their merits rather than their provenance. On that basis, the articles that form this Reader have been quite deliberately drawn from a diversity of sources. Academic journals, practitioner publications and the business press, European as much as American. Some of the offerings are relatively straightforward, some are more radical, some are even deliberately provocative. All are offered, together with their own references, with a view to demonstrating the art of the possible and thereby encouraging people to contribute to the situations in which they find themselves.

Managing Innovation and Change forms part of the Open University Business School's MBA course in Creativity, Innovation and Change, as does the associated Reader *Creative Management and Development* (third edition, 2006) by Jane Henry.

The author would like to take this opportunity to thank his colleagues and his students, without whose awkward questions he may not have discovered much of what is included here.

David Mayle
Open University Business School
2006
d.t.mayle@open.ac.uk

Notes

1 Townsend, R. (1970) *Up the Organization*. London: Michael Joseph.
2 Brunner, J. (1975) *The Shockwave Rider*. London: HarperCollins.

Part 1

Environments

All organizations are subject to an increasing number of constraints on the way in which they conduct their business. By and large, this is not a wilfully perverse excess of totally unnecessary red tape (although small businesses in particular may justifiably bemoan the cost and complexity of compliance), but an attempt to codify the interests of the increasing number of stakeholders who may reasonably claim an interest in a given enterprise. Collectively these stakeholders comprise an organization's environment.

When used with a capital E, Environment has come to be interpreted as synonymous with our stewardship of the planet, a growing awareness that physical resources are effectively held in stewardship for future generations and are not ours to consume with no thought for the consequences. In the first article, by **Schultz and Williamson**, the authors set out a consideration of the possible impact of carbon-trading following ratification of the Kyoto protocol. The article is not a simple read, but its value lies in a treatment of emissions reduction in a strategic and purely business-like fashion. Firstly, regulation of this type is here to stay; many would argue that it can only get more stringent as the magnitude of the environmental changes already in train becomes undeniable. As we noted above, regulation in general is not new; the ability to achieve regulatory compliance effectively and efficiently has long been the hallmark of the successful enterprise. Secondly, the future will be different, the world will be a different place and therefore customers, suppliers and markets will all change to accommodate the new conditions. Again this is hardly revelatory, few organizations exist in a static equilibrium. Thirdly, in an age where brand value embraces public perception as a major intangible, getting the wrong reputation can have a serious impact on the accountants' 'bottom line'. Therefore, the authors argue, business must accept the reality of the situation and start planning now; only by careful and detailed consideration of a range of possible responses can organizations hope to create new (or maintain existing) competitive advantage in a carbon-constrained future. It is not just altruism.

The name of Enron has etched itself into public consciousness, above and beyond the plethora of Business School case studies it continues to generate. The post-Enron world seems likely to be further regulated in the domain of Business Ethics. The article by **Knox and Maklan** addresses the current state of Corporate Social Responsibility (CSR) reporting in the UK and concludes that investment in CSR activity (or perhaps more correctly the prospects for growth in CSR activity) is potentially vulnerable due to the inability of existing systems to show a positive contribution to the 'bottom line'. Now this argument is interesting; given the growing clamour for 'Responsible Business' (following what seems to be an accelerating incidence of episodes of unsavoury ethical behaviour), how should we view the future of CSR reporting? On the one hand, should we feel comforted that firms are prepared to engage in, and report, their performance on such dimensions? Or, on the other hand, should we feel concerned lest, once the current spate of mischief is seen to have abated (possibly due to *reduced* reporting?), a cynical capitalism will only do what it is required to do by either shareholders or governments? The answer probably comes down to an article of faith on the nature of business. Ever the optimist, I lean towards a belief that business will increasingly need to look 'beyond the bottom line' – but that doesn't mean that individuals and lobby groups can afford to relax!

The article by **Engardio and Einhorn** is a quite deliberately provocative piece, included here to provide a cautionary note concerning commonly held notions about globalization. Conventional wisdom still has it that even though your Mobile Phone/Digital Camera/DVD player or what-have-you was manufactured in (say) China, this is fine in the general scheme of things because over here in the West we can retain the knowledge-work aspects, and that will sustain our economies, won't it? Well, perhaps not, as these authors take pains to point out. The concept that the so-called 'Developed West' can retain the brain work while emerging economies get their hands dirty with the more straightforward parts of the supply chain is looking increasingly suspect. It seems that the internet is capable of aiding and abetting the spread of technological design capability rather more quickly than growth in social infrastructure is inflating the local cost-base. Did we really believe that proximity to the process technology of manufacture, coupled with effective systems of education, would not prove to be a potent combination? Be afraid, be very afraid.

Scenario Planning first entered the manager's toolkit in 1985 with the publication of a seminal pair of articles by Pierre Wack[1] based on his experiences as Head of Business Environment at Royal Dutch/Shell Group Planning. For all its undoubted power, however, Scenario Planning seems to have struggled to achieve widespread usage. Part of the problem could be that too many consultants have peddled so many different versions that the underlying principles and any generalizable wisdom fail to shine through. The problem may be compounded by the fact that much of Scenario

Planning is about dealing with uncertainty, pondering the unknown, and therefore may sit a little uncomfortably with the 'tendency for action' that lies at the heart of so much traditional management thinking. The article by **Wilson** builds upon such concerns and offers a pragmatic user guide with the intention of assisting would-be users of the technique as they climb the learning curve of Scenario Planning. The author's emphasis on linking scenarios through strategy development into effective action should help to disarm the critique that scenarios are just 'thinking about the future'.

Note

1   Wack, P., (1985) 'Scenarios: uncharted waters ahead', *Harvard Business Review*, September/ October, pp. 73–79, and 'Scenarios: shooting the rapids', *Harvard Business Review,* November/ December, pp. 139–150.

1

Gaining Competitive Advantage in a Carbon-constrained World: Strategies for European Business

Karl Schultz and Peter Williamson

Climate Change: A Strategic Issue

The earth is getting warmer, and weather patterns are becoming more erratic. The reason, most climate scientists believe, is because concentrations of "greenhouse gases" have been rising in the atmosphere. The most important of these gases is carbon dioxide, which is emitted when fossil fuels, such as oil, natural gas, and coal are burned. So far, temperatures have increased by an average of about 1 degree centigrade. Projections of future warming are for temperatures to increase by an additional 2 to 5 degrees in the next century – even with measures taken to reduce emissions.

The impacts of this climate change will vary by region. Sea levels are projected to rise by 0.3 to 0.8 metres this century. Some regions will experience more droughts, while others more floods. One leading concern for Europe is that the Gulf Stream, that currently warms Europe, will cease, leaving the continent with a climate similar to Labrador's. Storms are expected to be more severe, as more energy is in the atmosphere.

Since the late 1980's the prominence of climate change as an environmental issue (and by extension, an energy issue) has skyrocketed. Many in the policy arena consider it the greatest long-term environmental challenge facing the earth. Some consider it the greatest challenge facing humanity.

Today European businesses may be exposed to climate change in up to three broad ways. First, governments are imposing limits on greenhouse gas emissions. Secondly, some of the impacts of climate change will directly impact the business environment. And finally, public perceptions of corporate behaviour have the potential to impact the bottom line. Before turning to the impacts on corporate strategies and possible sources of competitive advantage, it is worth briefly elaborating each of these drivers of increased business exposure to climate change in turn.

Source: K. Schultz and P. Williamson (2005) *European Management Journal*, 23 (4): 383–91.

Regulatory Actions

The Kyoto Protocol, which was negotiated in 1997 and has been ratified by 134 nations, invokes binding limits on emissions. With Russia's ratification, the treaty went into force on 6th February of 2005. Kyoto's limits are generally viewed as just a small step towards stabilizing atmospheric concentrations of greenhouse gases at a level that will have acceptably manageable consequences on the global environment, human health, natural resources and physical infrastructure.

The European Union is taking a leading position in limiting its greenhouse gas emissions. Starting in 2005 approximately 12,000 industrial facilities were granted allowances to emit carbon dioxide into the atmosphere. Total allocations are designed to create a shortage of allowances in order to stimulate companies to reduce emissions. The total real shortage is debatable, but current estimates place the EU-wide shortage at around 50 million tonnes of carbon dioxide pollution per year. If companies are not able to reduce their own emissions cost-effectively, they have the option to purchase allowances from other facilities that have sufficient allowances, or to purchase project-based credits from other countries throughout the world (Kruger and Pizer, 2004).

It is also important to note that the EU Emissions Trading Scheme (EU ETS) is only a part of the necessary steps that European nations must take in order to comply with their targets under the Kyoto Protocol. In 2008 phase two of the Scheme starts, and it is expected that allocations will be further limited, new industries will face caps on emissions, and additional greenhouse gases, such as methane, will be incorporated into the Scheme. Nations are also developing emissions credit purchasing pools to pay for project-based emissions reductions developed outside of the EU. And additional policies are being implemented, such as carbon taxes and renewable energy purchase requirements.

Overall, the Kyoto target for Europe is estimated to result in an annual shortage of carbon dioxide allowances of over 300 millions tonnes. At a cost to comply with Kyoto estimated at roughly €10 per allowance, the total cost/year may amount to approximately €3 billion. But since trading in allowances began, prices have risen steadily (as evident from the trading data in Exhibit 1) and some observers put the cost burden at between €6 billion and €9 billion. European companies will pay for most of these costs, either directly or indirectly.

But while limits on greenhouse gas emissions set by Kyoto will have significant impacts on industry, it will not even come close to solving the problem of climate change. A drastic reduction in global emissions is necessary to stabilize concentrations in the atmosphere at what will be considered an acceptable level. Kyoto only limits industrialized nations' emissions at approximately 5.2% below 1990 levels in the period 2008–2012. World-wide cuts of between 15 and 50% below 1990 levels are necessary to stabilize concentrations at manageable levels and European nations are expected to have to reduce their emissions by even more in order to make this happen. Discussions are already underway to consider next steps beyond Kyoto's period of 2008–2012 (Pearce).

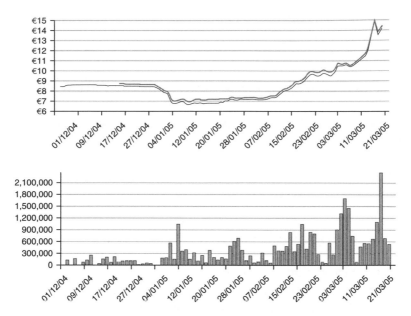

Exhibit 1   *Daily Prices and Trading Volumes of Carbon credits*
(*Source*: Point Carbon)

Business Impacts of Climate Change

The costs of climate change to EU industry will not all stem from regulations. The direct impacts of climate change on infrastructure, agricultural production, and human health will be varied but very real. Those companies involved in developing countries are likely to be even more exposed, as many of the most severe impacts will face these nations. The U.S. Pentagon prepared a report on the impacts of climate change on international security. It states, "warfare may again come to define human life ... As the planet's carrying capacity shrinks, an ancient pattern re-emerges: the eruption of desperate, all-out wars over food, water, and energy supplies" (Schwartz and Randall, 2003).

> Climate change is a phenomenon that is starting to have a major impact on Swiss Re, its partners, and our clients. The question is no longer whether global warming is happening, but how it's going to affect our business.
>
> John Coomber, CEO, Swiss Re

The industries most exposed to climate change are not always the obvious, heavy energy users. In fact, one of the industries most likely to be impacted is insurance. A recent study by Swiss Re, the world's second largest re-insurer, estimated that the costs of claims to insurers from climate change related weather events will be between $30 and $40 billion per year in ten years (Swiss Re, 2004).

Depending on the industry and company, the exposure to climate change will be positive or negative, and may include:

- Access to water resources.
- Supply chain challenges caused by weather, infrastructure strains (shipping, inventory).
- Risks to capital stock from sea level rise and weather (infrastructure).
- Changes in customer needs (caused, for instance, by changes in economies, product demand related to weather, resource availability, etc.).
- Country investment risk caused by changes in national political and security conditions.

The Public Perception Effect

A study of the impacts of the oil giant Exxon Mobil's stance on climate change, which generally is viewed as less interested in mitigating its greenhouse gas emissions than its peers, BP and Shell, indicated that the company may face a number of risks, including a hit on its brand value [in excess of $2 billion], and problems with staff retention, recruitment, and political access amounting to between $10–$50 billion. In addition, its exposure to litigation risk from the damage of climate change could potentially exceed $100 billion. Each year at Exxon's annual shareholder meeting a resolution, most recently supported by 20% of votes, is proposed that demands justification for the company's position (Exxon Mobil Corporation, 2004).

Different companies will face varying degrees of exposure to public perceptions. Some companies will benefit by being seen as contributing to solving the climate problem, such as renewable energy producers, while others will face inherent criticism because of the product that they produce – however necessary it is for the economy to function. Also, those companies with strong brand names and a significant retail component to their sales will be more exposed than companies that sell to industry. As such, coal companies, whose principal customer base are electric-power producers, will be less exposed (at least to public perceptions) than oil companies, that sell petrol to consumers directly.

Threat or Opportunity?

The total costs of these impacts to a business will differ markedly depending on whether a company's exposure derives from its direct emissions, indirect emissions (such as its purchase of electricity from a carbon emitting utility or from sale of a product that results in emissions, like coal or automobiles), or from the impacts of climate change on the business (as we saw above). The challenge for management lies in reducing the totality of these costs and the associated risks including handling the possibility of a shortage of emissions allowances, managing the risks to the company's credit rating, and re-thinking the optimal portfolio of energy sources in a carbon-constrained world. This means developing a broad and comprehensive strategy for managing the new environment. Perhaps most interesting of all, it means looking for new opportunities to gain competitive advantage in a carbon constrained world. As we will see below, if handled correctly, climate change can be an opportunity to steal a march on rivals, not just an unwelcome problem to be dealt with.

But are European businesses approaching the issue strategically? A recent survey by Price Waterhouse Coopers suggested not. Among 75 major European utilities, one of the most exposed of industries, less than half have a climate change strategy (Point Carbon, 2004). Yet a parallel study of U.S. electric utilities exposure to greenhouse gas emissions constraints concluded that between 10 and 35% of the total market capitalization was at risk (CERES 2003). This level of exposure obviously demands top management attention. But from a competitive advantage standpoint, its relative exposure that counts. Here the results look even more startling: another respected study found that the value at risk because of climate change varied between companies by a factor of nearly 60 times (Innovest Strategic Value Advisors 2002).

Opportunities in Managing Carbon Constraints

While most European businesses will face additional costs associated with carbon constraints, there are three areas of opportunity to gain competitive advantage:

1. By minimising the additional costs more effectively than competitors.
2. Differentiating your product by bundling carbon credits into your offering.
3. Turning your capacity to supply carbon credits into a profit centre.

Each is worth consideration in turn.

Minimising the Additional Costs

While the market price of emissions constraints is dependent on many factors outside the control of most companies, like weather and fuel prices, the strategic company will be able to both reduce its own costs and adapt to changes by taking a number of measures that may include:

- Diversifying your fuel consumption to allow for flexibility to exploit to divergent price trends that competitors that are locked in to one fuel source cannot enjoy.
- Active carbon asset management to reduce potential exposure to carbon price fluctuations.
- Public/shareholder public relations: enhance sales or share price.

Product Differentiation Through Bundling

There are a number of opportunities for companies to gain competitive advantage by understanding the carbon constraints throughout their supply chain and customer base, and thus anticipating and reacting strategically to these needs. For example, a fuel supplier might be able to secure low cost carbon credits and offer electric utilities short on allowances a combination fuel and credit product that matches its customer's allowance needs. Likewise a bank or insurance company may through its contacts with energy companies producing credits be able to offer a package of finance/insurance and carbon credits to offset emissions from new build. A manufacturer with caps on its emissions who is able to chose different fuels to supply production would be able to track the energy and allowance prices to come up with the lowest production costs.

Turning Carbon Credit Supply into a Profit Centre

Many European companies will also be in a strong position to supply credits for what is likely to be a growing market. Some companies will find that emissions reductions at their facilities are significantly less costly than the price of a traded allowance. Others will be in a position to source emissions credits from projects specifically designed to offer low cost reductions, in developing countries and economies in transition. For instance, a power generator with skills in producing power from methane that would otherwise be emitted to the atmosphere may be able to develop projects, create carbon credits, and then use these to either offset its own emissions or sell the credits – possibly to strategic partners or electricity customers who have a choice of power supplies.

The opportunities are not limited to heavy industry. Some traders speculate that the carbon credit market may become the largest traded commodity in the world. Investors, traders, insurance companies and of course consultants all may benefit from the creation, supply and transaction of emissions credits.

From Strategy to Action

To turn these strategic ideas into an action plan companies will need to follow the rigorous, five-step process outlined below.

Assess Your Carbon Exposure

For those companies with caps placed on their emissions, this may at first glance seem to be a simple issue. However, for all companies the uncertainties in future policies, climate change patterns, and public sentiment mean that this task is not straightforward.

The first step for companies is to understand what their emissions are, both direct and indirect. As we have already noted, a distinction has to be made between a company's direct emissions, and indirect emissions, from, for instance, purchase of electricity from a carbon emitting utility on one side, or from sale of a product that results in emissions, such as an energy resource like coal or automobiles. Corporate emissions inventory guidelines have been developed for most industries. (For instance, corporate inventory guidelines prepared by the World Resources Institute. See www.wri.org.) And those

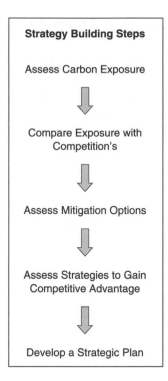

companies already facing caps their historical, direct emissions already have a starting point to which an estimate of their indirect emissions needs to be added. It is also important to divide these emissions by type of greenhouse gas (because methane, for example, is weighted at 15 times carbon dioxide), by facility, and by risk depending on whether emissions are currently capped, are likely to be capped, or are likely not to be capped.

Once the emissions are accounted for, it is next important to quantify in financial terms the current and future carbon liabilities. A reasonable assumption for companies facing caps on their emissions is to use the current European Allowance price and the expected shortage (or surplus) of allowances that the company holds. Preparing different scenarios for future prices and expected shortages will also be important.

The company will also need to estimate the financial impact of its indirect exposure to climate change regulations. These may include increases in power prices, and the ability for companies to switch fuels between lower and higher greenhouse emitting fuels. The company's demand for other commodities facing carbon exposure, such as cement and steel, will also be important to calculate.

As with greenhouse gas regulatory exposure, it will also be important to consider the exposure to climate change events. Are corporate assets vulnerable to any of the expected climate change impacts? Are customers likely to face changes in their purchasing habits because of climate change?

Finally, to complete a thorough audit of a company's carbon exposure, it is critical to gauge customer and shareholder sentiment. Do customers view the company as environmentally responsible? How do existing and potential shareholders, especially large institutional investors, rate the company's activities?

Compare Your Exposure with Competitors

Because the carbon issues are ultimately about impacts on a company's competitive advantage, the second key step will be to benchmark a company's exposures with those of its rivals. Although it may not be possible to quantify these as easily as its own, and although it cannot know what strategies its competition may be taking to reduce their own exposure, a general idea will be available than can result in a comparison of the various exposures, and thus help guide strategies to differentiate itself and become more competitive. It is also important to consider substitutes to its product that may be more or less competitive in a carbon constrained market, which will guide the creation of strategies to either defend market share (if a company is more exposed to carbon constraints), or take market share from other industries.

Assess Your Options to Mitigate Carbon Exposure

There are a number of options available to most industries to reduce or at least manage their carbon exposure. These include:

- Investing in plant retrofits or new investments to reduce emissions.
- Investing in projects to offset emissions.
- Purchasing allowances from the emissions market hedges or other risk management tools.
- Divesting from business activities with too much current or potential carbon exposure.
- Lobbying government to influence decisions on future emissions limits.
- Communicating corporate greenhouse-friendly actions with shareholders and the public.

For each of these options, a reasonable assessment of the marginal costs of each action, adjusted for risk, will be useful to decide the most effective strategy.

It is possible that some companies may find that a "do nothing, but watch" strategy is most appropriate. This is probably only applicable for those companies whose overall exposure is minimal, however, and the hidden indirect impacts of the carbon constrained market need to be identified and evaluated before coming to this decision.

Assess Your Opportunities to Gain Competitive Advantage in the New, Carbon Constrained Environment

Companies in all industries will have the potential to differentiate themselves from competitors based on the assessment of future climate change regulations, direct impacts, and public perceptions.

Companies will in most instances also be able to identify actions and investments that will be more profitable in a carbon constrained business environment. By identifying the company's natural strengths (such as relations with companies that have low cost emission reduction potential), or a customer base faced with very significant carbon exposure (such as electric utilities), managers will be able to develop strategies that differentiate them from their competitors. For instance, fuel suppliers may be in a position to either change their supply to be less carbon intensive than their competitors. This could be direct by producing more greenhouse friendly fuels such as shifting from coal to natural gas, or it could be by securing emissions credits at low cost and then bundling these credits with a fuel sales agreement to meet a customer's emissions allowance needs. As we noted above, it is worth considering the potential of turning the supply of carbon credits into a profit centre.

Develop a Strategic Plan

Once the strategic options are identified, it will be important to create a plan that integrates the various steps and creates clear management of some or all of the following areas:

- Investments
- Divestments
- Purchases
- Hedging strategies
- Sales Strategy
- Public Relations.

Putting the Strategic Approach into Practice

Each industry, and each individual company will have a unique set of carbon exposures and different strategies available to maintain or create competitive advantage in Europe's carbon constrained economy. To better understand some of the basic nuances, and the process to create a corporate carbon strategy, we take the examples of two companies in very different industries, a small cement company and a multinational bank.

The Cement Maker

Following the five-step model, the first task was to assess the company's carbon exposure.

Assessing its Carbon Exposure

Cement making is very carbon intensive. In our example, a Portland Cement company with two separate facilities produces a total of 1.8 million tonnes of cement per year, the direct greenhouse gas emissions are calculated for both emissions by identifying accurate emissions factors for its direct fuel consumption of coal, natural gas, propane and diesel, and emissions from the processing of raw materials into cement. The fuel consumption emissions are estimated to be 220 thousand tonnes of carbon dioxide, and the process emissions are 350 thousand tonnes, for a total of 570,000 tonnes.

Indirect emissions from the consumption of electricity are calculated based on an emissions factor for the power grid in its region. These emissions are estimated to be 25,000 tonnes. The cement maker also considers the emissions from its suppliers (production of limestone, shale, clay, sand and iron) and estimates that the production and transport of these emissions result in an additional 85,000 tonnes of emissions. It then considers the emissions from distributing its cement, and estimates these emissions at 25,000 tonnes.

Finally, it considers the indirect emissions created by its customers. This is a difficult issue to weigh, and it had to consider if substitutes to Portland Cement might be higher or lower in their contribution to greenhouse gas emissions. Its preliminary research indicates that less carbon intensive substitutes, such as use of fly ash in concrete might be favoured in the future, but questions the consistency of resource supply.

It then looked at its overall market value and determined that at an emissions allowance price of €8/tonne, then 570,000 tonnes of direct emissions each year represent a total potential asset value of €4.56 million. However, the manufacturer has been given 520,000 allowances so it is short 50,000 tonnes at a price of €400,000. On the other hand, it expects demand to increase for its product, so the likely exposure is greater. Without changes in its process, it expects to be short 150,000 tonnes in 2007 at an expected value of €1,200,000 and it expects during the second phase of the trading scheme that this shortage will increase. With net revenues of €2.5 million, its exposure is significant.

Looking to the future, the company examined a different set of scenarios for what their allocations are likely to be like starting in 2008. Considering that the allocations are going to be less and allowance prices greater, it assumed for a mid-case scenario that its allocation will drop from 2008–2012, resulting in a shortage valued at 2.5 million, or equal to its current net revenues.

The cement manufacturer then looked at the impacts of carbon constraints on the price of its energy. It assumed that power prices would go up, increasing its costs, and that gas prices would also rise as demand for gas, a less emitting fuel, would go up. Coal prices it assumed would average the same as before the emissions trading scheme, but that the price volatility may increase.

Since its facilities are not very vulnerable to more severe weather, it assumed that this would not be an important issue, but did assume that demand for concrete may increase as the need for new build for sea level rise might increase.

It also considered if its customers would consider the company's position on climate change as an issue, and decided probably, but not to a great extent.

Estimating its Competitors' Carbon Exposure

Ninety five per cent of the cement company's product is sold onto the national market. As such, it looked at each of the top national cement companies, and also looked at the possible competition from brick making and asphalt production. It also looked at the possibility of foreign companies being less exposed, and thus able to enter the national market. In this case, the cement maker determined that there was little differentiation in the national market, but that cement makers in one neighbouring country may have a favourable allocation of allowances, whereas in another the shortage was greater, making its companies less competitive. However, because of the higher transport costs it became less clear if these differences would amount to anything.

Developing its Options to Mitigate Exposure

Based on the above analysis of its exposure, the cement company then ran through a series of options to mitigate its exposure.

Because it will face a shortage of allowances, it decided to analyse the marginal costs of reducing its direct emissions. It found that it could reduce emissions through a number of investments and changes in purchase decisions, including:

- Increasing its use of gas. However, for this scenario it also looked at projected gas prices and determined that a likely switch may not be cost effective, even with the lowered emissions. However, from 2008 on this scenario becomes economic.
- Alternative energy inputs. It identified biomass fuel as being economic if its price didn't increase. However, an analysis of biomass demand suggested that the company wait before deciding on this option.
- Energy efficiency improvements. It identified six different measures, and found that two were cost effective starting now, and two additional would be economic after 2008. A government grant might help finance four of these measures.
- Supplementary cementing materials. It found that it could input fly ash into its process and indirectly reduce emissions. However, it found there was no current means that this would reduce its direct emissions. Nonetheless, because it had a potential supply at a comparable price to its current inputs, it decides to undertake this to show it is doing what it can to indirectly reduce emissions.

The cement company also approached a developer of a project to reduce methane emissions in Vietnam. It found that this project could generate emissions reductions at lower price than the allowance price. However, it is concerned that this project exceeds its typical investment risk threshold.

The company also discussed the option of purchasing futures contracts with an emissions broker. This option would reduce its exposure risk as the price of acquiring its allowances would be fixed.

The company considered a sales push in a neighbouring country with tighter emissions caps on its cement industry. This option was analysed, and the company calculated that it would be competitive on costs. However, there were additional marketing costs and plans to enter this market were postponed until the (probably more stringent) allocations under Phase II announced in 2007.

The company also is a member of its trade association, and could join a working group that would track greenhouse emissions issues.

The company also considered preparing a public relations campaign. Recognising that the company is not particularly large nor is public visibility particularly related to sales, it calculated that this would be a relatively costly option.

Assembling a Strategy for Competitive Advantage

The cement company then took all the options available to it, and prepared a decision model for how to move forward, and when various emissions allowance, energy, and cement prices would warrant taking different steps.

It discovered that the options it identified would likely result in a significantly reduced exposure to greenhouse gas limits, and suspected that its competitors were not looking at all their options as carefully. As such, it thinks it will be able to increase its market share, and even with emissions constraints be in a stronger position.

A Multinational Bank

Assessing its Carbon Exposure

A London-based bank, with offices in Europe and throughout the world, faced no direct caps on its emissions. However, it is a highly visible company with customer perceptions important for its business and it also finances a diverse set of industries, many of which face direct caps on their emissions. Additional investments may be even costlier to cover.

Direct emissions for this company are relatively small, however these are carefully included in the bank's annual corporate social responsibility reports. CO_2 emissions were divided into energy use (indirect electricity consumption) and travel (car, rail, and air travel).

Seventy per cent of the bank's investments are in Europe, and 50% of its investments are in the industrial sectors facing emissions caps. The bank reviewed the exposure of its clients to emissions caps, and also the likely impact different investments would have on future exposure. It found that it had invested in a disproportionately high percentage of companies with heavy exposure, including a number of manufacturing facilities dependent on coal-fired facilities for production. It also had some investments in tourism and port facilities that had the potential to be impacted by changing temperatures and sea-level rise.

Of the non-European investments, it calculated that 30% of these were in countries where caps on emissions already existed or were likely as these countries had Kyoto targets. Twenty per cent of the remaining investments were in the United States and Australia, countries not ratifying Kyoto, but with some State government programs capping emissions. Investments in these countries were viewed as being relatively unexposed to carbon, but facing a higher degree of long term regulatory uncertainty. The remaining 50% of investments outside of Europe were in countries without Kyoto targets, but nearly one third of these investments could generate emissions reduction credits.

Estimating its Competitors' Carbon Exposure

A careful analysis of the competition showed that this bank is moderately exposed. While it has invested a higher percentage into heavily exposed industries than the average, its investments overseas that could generate emissions credits mitigates this somewhat.

Developing its Options to Mitigate Exposure

The bank considered the following options:

- Do nothing. This was rejected because although it had no direct exposure, its indirect investment exposure was significant.
- Augment is sustainable development investment criteria to include a demand for quantification of emissions exposure, and proposed means of minimizing these exposures.
- Undertake a progressive divestment strategy from some of the most exposed and at risk industries – in particular coal fired power in Europe, and some climate sensitive infrastructure and service investments.
- Serve as an important facilitator and financier of emissions credit creation, and supply these credits (through a separately regulated subsidiary) to many of its European clients short on allowances. It was in a position to implement this strategy because of its strong position in overseas emissions generation.
- Strengthen its corporate sustainability message to include a climate change policy. This was viewed as important to maintain good customer relations.

Assembling a Strategy for Competitive Advantage

As the result of adopting a number of these varied measures the bank has significantly lowered risk of its investment portfolio, and created a stronger retail banking image. The emission generation and trading arm also created a new profit centre for the bank.

Conclusion

Managers and boards in most industries are only beginning to come to terms with the new realities of a carbon-constrained economy. Our key message in this article is the need to take a strategic approach. First, to ensure that your company looks beyond its direct emissions to properly assess the exposure both to indirect emissions and to the impacts climate change itself will have on your business. Second, to make sure you unearth opportunities to gain competitive advantage over your rivals by developing strategies to creatively minimize the additional costs, differentiate your product by bundling in carbon credits, and turning the capacity to supply carbon credits into a profit centre for your company. The bottom line is that carbon, just like capital, human resources and products, is now a strategic part of the new competitive game.

References

CERES (2003) Electric power, investors, and climate change: A call to Action. CERES, September (2002).

Exxon Mobil Corporation (2004) Shareholder Resolution on climate Data or Exxon Mobil Corporation, Annual shareholders Meeting, May 26, Dallas, Texas.

Innovest Strategic Value Advisors (2002) Value-at-Risk: Climate change and the Future of Governance, Innovest Strategic Value Advisors, April.

Kruger and Pizer (2004) Greenhouse gas trading in Europe, *Environment*, 46, 8. pp. 8–23, October.

Point Carbon (2004) PWC Corporate Emissions Strategy Survey, *Point Carbon*, 31 March (www.pointcarbon.com).

Pearce, F., Kyoto protocol is just the beginning, *newscientist.com*.

Schwartz, P. and Randall, D. (2003) An abrupt climate change scenario and its implications for US National Security. Report for the US Department of Defense, October.

Swiss Re (2004) Natural catastrophes and man-made disasters in 2003: many fatalities, comparatively modest insured losses, *Sigma*, no. 1.

Corporate Social Responsibility: Moving Beyond Investment Towards Measuring Outcomes

Simon Knox and Stan Maklan

Introduction

At a recent conference in London the CEO of Sustainability, a widely-respected authority on Corporate Social Responsibility (CSR) reporting, offered a stark critique of management practices. His research suggests that the number of firms engaged in social reporting is increasing, as is the average length of these reports. However, despite a widening recognition amongst business leaders of the need to accept a broader responsibility than short term profits, the quality of their company's CSR reporting has hardly improved in the last 5 years (Elkington, 2003). At the same conference, Simon Zadek of Accountability, reporting on his research (Zadek, 2002), concludes that these social reports are not having a significant impact on managerial decision making.

In this paper, we report on an empirical study of CSR policy and practices amongst a number of leading multinationals to explore some of the underlying reasons why CSR reporting seems to have evolved with such low impact on business decision making. In addition, we propose a framework developed during the study which clearly links CSR to both business and social outcomes. In concluding the paper, we highlight some of the policy and practice issues which need to be resolved if the general perception of CSR reporting is to change from being seen as an expensive exercise in compliance.

In the next section, we explore the growing impact of CSR on business as viewed by differing interest groups.

The Growing Impact of Corporate Responsibility on Businesses

Over thirty years ago, Milton Friedman wrote in the *New York Times* that the social responsibility of a business was to increase its profits. Any diversion of company

Source: S. Knox and S. Maklan (2004) *European Management Journal,* 22(5): 508–16.

resources to social programmes, charity and other non-profit generating activities, the Nobel Laureate argues, represents a tax on consumers and investors (Friedman, 1970). Such a tax reduces society's total wealth and satisfaction. His position, based upon sound free-market ideology, has come under increasing attack since time of writing and can no longer provide the business leader with an erudite means of avoiding the issue. Corporate Social Responsibility (CSR) is something that every Board must now address in some form. Ironically, it is arguably the triumph of free-market ideology over regulated economies which has foisted new responsibilities on increasingly powerful multinational companies. Globalisation strategies provides businesses with unprecedented access to markets and ever-lower production costs (Day and Montgomery, 1999), it has also brought closer to reality the concept of the global village first discussed in the 1960s. Business practices, even those conducted a very long way from their home markets, can be subject to intense scrutiny and comment by customers, employees, suppliers, shareholders and governments, as well as other groups upon whose support the business relies. One such group, Non-Governmental Organisations (NGOs), has become more and more powerful in recent years, calling business to account for policies in the areas of fair trade, human rights, workers rights, environmental impact, financial probity and corporate governance. In an ever more cynical world, where society is much less inclined to trust their governments and businesses, NGOs retain high levels of trust across a broad spectrum of society.

Whilst it is true that in certain circumstances powerful multinational companies can impose trading conditions on the less powerful, such as non-unionised workers, commodity producers in developing countries and Third World labourers (Klein, 1999), the idea that modern companies must commit themselves to effectively address poverty and environmental degradation must surely be an overstatement. This discussion between advocates of Milton Friedman's position—limiting responsibility to maximising profit—and NGO activists who regard firms being primarily instruments of social policy represents the extreme ends of the debate. Many academics writing in the field of CSR are cognisant of these extremes and seek to establish a middle ground.

Wood (1991) suggests that the public responsibility of business is divided into areas of social involvement directly related to their business activities and competencies, with secondary areas of involvement relating to its primary activities. For example, an auto maker might reasonably be expected to deal with vehicle safety and the environment but not low-income housing or adult illiteracy. Clarkson's long-term study of corporate behaviour (Clarkson, 1995) indicates that companies deal with stakeholders, not society, and that CSR must distinguish between stakeholder needs and social issues; managers can address stakeholder requirements but not abstract social policy. Carroll (1979) suggests corporate responsibility has different layers: economic, legal, ethical and discretionary categories of business performance and that business leaders must decide the layer at which they choose to operate.

Similarly, the UK Government wishes to establish a middle ground in this debate, with the Prime Minister suggesting that, "we must ensure that economic growth contributes to our quality of life, rather than degrading it. And we can all share the benefits" (DTI, 2001).

Finally, although business leaders themselves acknowledge that their firms are socially created and "licensed", most would argue they were created primarily as economic agents to provide the goods and services society wants at the right price, quality and availability. As such, their firms' competencies are built around their commercial activities. For example, one thousand software firms tackling global poverty through a myriad of small initiatives is laudable but likely to be ineffective. With the exception of a handful of businesses, such as the Body Shop and the Coop Bank who have developed strong CSR policies as a basis for growth, it would, arguably, be more effective—and efficient—for governments to tax these firms and give the money to multinational agencies that are competent in the field.

On balance, it would be most unlikely to find a consensus between the various stakeholders, particularly as CSR is a relatively new and emergent business responsibility. However, in establishing our research objectives, we sought to identify received wisdom about the business case for CSR activities in general, and linkages between these activities and business or social outcomes in particular. In both cases, we found the arguments presented and claims made about the positive impact of CSR on business to be highly assumptive and lacking in empiricism. These assumptions are presented next and our questioning of these beliefs forms the background to our research objectives.

Assertions and Beliefs about the Business Case for CSR

In reviewing the arguments that "you do well by doing good", we can readily identify five commonly-held beliefs which seem to be largely anecdotal and, as such, highly questionable:

- Consumer preferences will increasingly favour products and services from socially responsible, transparent and trustworthy firms (Willmott, 2001 and Mitchell, 2001).

  - The assertion that consumer behaviour will shift to reward social responsibility is grounded in surveys of attitudes and trade-off analysis, not observed behaviour. Attitude-behaviour correspondence seems to lack empirical grounding and is not obviously evident when researched (Knox and Walker, 2001, 2003).

- Investors will increasingly favour responsible companies and irresponsible companies will find their cost of borrowing rises (Accountability, 2002).

  - Zadek (2002) acknowledges that only 4% of the total funds available for stock market investment are governed by CSR principles, therefore, most firms judged not to be socially responsible still have full access to equity funding.

- Potential employees will be attracted only to responsible companies and others risk skill shortages (Department of Trade and Industry, 2001: Citing the 1998 McKinsey Study, "The War for Talent" and MORI research).

- Arguments about competing for talent also appear to be based upon stated intention and not observed behaviour. Citied studies were concluded during the last long period of uninterrupted economic growth and may be cyclical. This link between employee motivations, customer retention and shareholder value has been made separately from CSR theory (Reichheld, 1996).

- Engaging with stakeholders encourages innovation. DTI case studies (2001, 2002) and Kong *et al*. (2002) cite examples of cost saving and revenue growth through fairer supplier policies.

  - von Hippel (1986, 1989) has been presenting these arguments and case-studies for over 20 years without reference to CSR practices.

- Being trusted by stakeholders and pursuing socially responsible policies reduces risks arising from safety issues (consumer, employee and community), potential boycotts and loss of corporate reputation.

  - Clearly, concern for safety and building trust is paramount to the firm's reputation management and future sales but cannot be exclusively associated with CSR policies. In fact, it's just good business practice to pursue both with vigour.

In essence, whilst the above arguments for CSR are intuitively appealing, many researchers admit the links between business performance and the implementation of CSR policy are difficult, if not impossible, to prove (Wood and Jones, 1995).

Against this background, we set our research objectives, design and protocol. These are discussed next.

Research Objectives, Design and Protocol

Since our research objectives are exploratory in nature, we anticipate that our study will contribute to the development of CSR as an instrumental theory. The three specific objectives of our research are:

- To explore how and how strongly CSR investment is linked to business and social outcomes among mainstream business.
- To develop a framework for linking CSR to performance.
- To identify the consistencies (and inconsistencies) among CSR policy makers and how their CSR programmes are implemented.

Clarkson (1995) identified numerous problems encountered by researchers working towards similar objectives. In a landmark, 10-year study, he concludes that researchers should concentrate on how firms actually manage their stakeholders rather than upon empirically validating inherently untestable frameworks of social responsiveness. Consequently, we felt it necessary to look at CSR practice in developing a framework for linking CSR investments to performance.

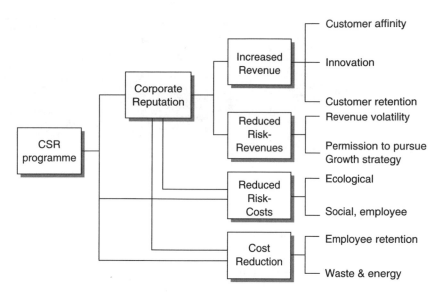

Figure 2.1 *CSR Link to Corporate Reputation and Business Performance*

Research Design and Protocol

Content analysis of the CSR, customer and reputation management literature identified the assertions made about the link between CSR and business and social outcomes. These relationships are illustrated in our prototype framework (Figure 2.1) and suggest that CSR programmes affect stakeholders' cognitions which then change their behaviours in ways sympathetic to the company's commercial interests.

To understand if firms do conceive of the linkage between CSR and performance in this manner, the researchers interviewed the CSR leaders of six multinational companies who are among the global market leaders in their fields. Purposeful sampling (Eisenhardt, 1989) was employed to eliminate firms facing acute CSR issues, such as extraction or tobacco companies, who are judged by the researchers as being unrepresentative of typical businesses.

The selected firms were: Orange (UK), Diageo PLC, Pilkington PLC, Unisys, Company X and Company Y. [Both Company X and Company Y opted to remain anonymous by name but we can report they are a global software vendor and an IT service provider respectively]. All six firms had a readily identifiable executive responsible for CSR. This person normally reported into the Main Boards of their companies through the Corporate Affairs function. Two of the interviewees, Diageo and Pilkington, are responsible for their firm's global CSR policies, one (Unisys) responsible for Europe – Middle East – Africa and the other three responsible for the UK. However, the true power of these individuals within their firm and, hence, their ability to provide accurate data as to how CSR policy influences decision making, cannot readily be assessed by the researchers. We acknowledge this as a limitation of our methodology.

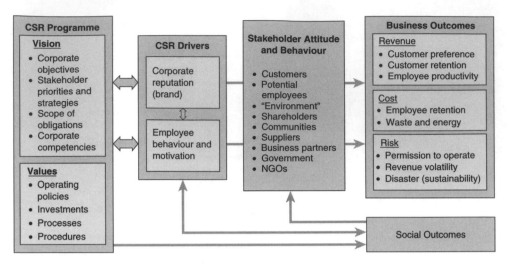

Figure 2.2 *Framework Linking CSR with Outcomes*

Empirical evidence was gathered in semi-structured interviews with these CSR leaders and, whilst the literature identifies a wide variety of definitions of "CSR investments", we allowed the participating companies to determine how they defined CSR rather than impose a definition upon them. Towards the end of the interview and before sighting our prototype framework (Figure 2.1), interviewees were asked to create their own framework illustrating the links between their CSR programmes and outcomes. They were then asked to assess our prototype framework and contrast this with what they had just drawn. As suggested by Eisenhardt (1989), we modified our prototype framework through successive interviews and, after 2 or 3 iterations, the revised framework remained largely unaltered and could be used in the final interviews to guide discussions. Interviews lasted between 2 and 3 hours and each of the respondents agreed to clarify any remaining issues as necessary post interview. Finally, all the interviewees agreed to read and modify a draft of a commercial report we produced (Maklan and Knox, 2003) to ensure that they concurred both with our revised framework (Figure 2.2) and our other findings. This report was unanimously endorsed by our respondents and in the next section, we report on this empirical framework and key findings.

Research Framework and Findings

Since our research framework has been validated by each of our six respondents on behalf of their respective companies, if is both convenient and instructive to present our research findings against this framework:

We found for most respondents that the common starting point of their CSR programmes was the company's vision and values which had usually developed on a normative basis. Whilst none of the respondents would claim to have such a formalised or, indeed, instrumental framework as we offer here, each recognised that their corporate vision and values co-evolved with corporate reputation (sometimes referred to as brand [Davidson, 2002]) and the behaviours of its employees. At the same time, there was full agreement that CSR programmes favourably enhance corporate reputation and to some extent could influence employee behaviour. Thus, it was felt that once CSR is "embedded" in their employees' attitudes to stakeholders and through listening and responding to stakeholder concerns, their business would automatically act more responsibly, have a greater understanding of the risks in its environment and strengthen its corporate reputation:

> "… CSR drives good corporate governance. It comes before the paraphernalia of good governance, and is more integral to the way we operate, the way we behave, the way we treat other people, the way the company is protected." Orange CSR spokesperson.
>
> "Every employee is empowered to do the right, responsive thing and their performance is reviewed in terms of what was achieved and how, based upon our values of integrity, honesty, being open and respectful with others." Company X CSR spokesperson.

With the exception of Diageo which does adopt a shareholder value approach to its CSR polices and practices (i.e. programmes to outcomes directly [Figure 2.2]), the remaining companies tend to measure at the left-hand side of Figure 2.2; setting CSR objectives, identifying their primary stakeholder(s), scoping obligations and, perhaps, developing some measure of employee awareness and their buy-in towards such programmes.

With such strong normative positions linking CSR programmes to the company vision, values and reputation, it is understandable why "hard-edged" business cases do not always accompany CSR programmes since, for most, embracing CSR is intuitive. Whilst this enables rapid CSR adoption in our respondent companies, it fails to address some of the more fundamental questions about their policy and practices regarding CSR programmes. For instance, such policy questions as:

- For what and to whom are we to be held responsible?
- How do we manage the conflicting demands amongst our stakeholders and how should our CSR programmes reflect the way we prioritise their interests?
- How much should we invest in CSR and how does the company assess successful outcomes so that we can continuously improve?

Next, we turn to our findings in which we report shortcomings in CSR policy issues across our sample companies before reporting on their practices which, in a similar way, seem to fall short on best practice examples.

CSR Policy: Findings and Discussion

Referring back to Figure 2.2, we report on our CSR policy findings which relate both to visioning (the scoping of social obligations and the challenge of prioritising stakeholders) and to the assessment of social outcomes. Turning first to the scooping of social obligations:

- **Companies feel responsible for communities impacted by their core business operations**

All respondents interviewed felt that their companies should comply fully both with regulatory (and legislative) demands as well as industry norms and expectations. The key reference point for most companies was their industry, rather than an idealised gold standard of corporate responsibility:

> "We are proud of our brands, and proud of how we lead our industry in social responsibility." Diageo CSR spokesperson.

> "We are an increasingly grown-up business … we understand our impact on the industry, our customers and partners … all stakeholders. We must provide responsible leadership commensurate with our position." Company X CSR spokesperson.

Those with the most articulated positions on what they wish to be held accountable for used the following criteria for this assessment:

- Their social responsibilities should leverage their unique core competencies so as to make a contribution others cannot match.

  For instance, Company X's policy goal is to empower the digitally disadvantaged; addressing the "digital divide" between the I.T. haves and have-nots.

- Their investment should have a great impact on society.

  > "We are world leaders in glass, with manufacturing operations in 25 countries and are major contributors to the local communities where we are located." Pilkington, CEO.

- Their social programmes should have a direct relationship to the industry in which they operate.

For instance, responsible alcohol consumption has been central to Diageo's CSR programme since it was formed out of United Distillers and Grand Metropolitan over 5 years ago. Its central corporate citizenship group manages a number of global initiatives as well as providing seed capital and management expertise to local business units engaged in "alcohol in society" initiatives.

Orange, in addition to consulting and responding to stakeholders on mobile masts, invests in the promotion of better communications between people. It believes the cause is relevant to its business, leverages its corporate competencies and is of importance to its employees.

What was evident to us from this finding was that each company had clearly scoped out their CSR policy around the impact of their operations or brands and seem to conform to Wood's (1991) view about engaging in social involvement directly related to business activities and competencies. By adopting such a normative approach, the unanswered questions here are:

How do these companies know how much to invest in CSR versus the other demands for resources?

What is the extent of their CSR obligations and should they be conditioned by market position?

- **Companies are clear on their most important stakeholders but are less able to set priorities among the rest**

In response to the question posed earlier "to whom are we to be held responsible?" most respondent firms have a flat list of stakeholders beyond their priority stakeholders (normally customers). These include: Government, NGOs, suppliers, employees and communities. There is no consistent approach to prioritising their secondary stakeholders. We offer three possible explanations for this:

1. Companies tend to treat all secondary stakeholders equally.
2. They do not manage secondary stakeholders actively.
3. Most likely, stakeholder differentiation needs to be developed further.

Our research identifies a mechanism for this differentiation based upon Mitchell *et al.* (1997) model which classifies stakeholders into one of seven types according to the urgency, power and legitimacy of their claims over the company. This issue of stakeholder prioritisation is of vital importance to the effective management of CSR and seems to be largely absent in policy decision making amongst the firms interviewed.

- **Social outcomes need more formal assessment**

We define social outcomes to mean the results of CSR programmes, such as the value of the philanthropy (e.g. curing a disease), positive impact on entire eco-systems, reduction in poverty and the increased participation in society by socially disadvantaged groups.

Diageo stands alone in publishing an analysis of social outcomes as well as calculating the Economic Value Added (EVA) it creates in local markets through its activities and tax revenue generated for host governments. The other firms face commercially difficult choices against their policy decision making discussed above since, without a mechanism for prioritising stakeholders for CSR purposes and with no substantive means of measuring successful outcomes, how do senior management make these choices? Is a philanthropic investment decision or a scheme borne out of an appreciation of areas of employees' concern a legitimate CSR programme? Whilst vision and values drive CSR policy making in our framework (Figure 2.2), social outcomes linked to a particular

CSR programme need to have clear metrics established, as does any area of business investment which is predicated by the achievement of targeted outcomes such as brand share, profit and revenue growth.

CSR Practices: Findings and Discussion

Of the three main findings reported here as CSR practices, both risk and stakeholder behaviours are highlighted in our framework (Figure 2.1). Attitudes to CSR reporting, however, are outside the framework and in presenting this finding, we highlight a major paradox. First, we look at business risk:

- **Risk management is not fully integrated with business activities**

A consistent theme throughout the management literature and our interviews was the belief that effective CSR programmes reduce a firm's exposure to rare, but catastrophic risk of the Brent-Spar, Bhopal and Andersen Consulting magnitude:

> "If you truly engage all stakeholders in policy making, then the chances of being blind-sided by a Brent-Spar must be greatly reduced." Unisys CSR spokesperson.

Whilst such corporate disasters are very rare events, each respondent confirmed that their companies had a risk management practice which attempts to identify all potential risks (events) to the business through a systematic and transparent process. This process generally involves assessing the potential impact of each event and assigning a probability of occurrence. Summing up the risks as a weighted average of events and outcomes provides some measure of the total risk facing the company.

In Diageo, the External Affairs function applies this process for the firm and has been able to positively correlate its evolving CSR programme with a year-on-year reduction in weighted-average risk facing the company. This has been achieved by better assessment of the risks, improved contingency planning and stronger relationships with relevant stakeholders through their CSR programmes.

However, in most of our respondent companies, risk is managed separately by the finance department and is not fully integrated with CSR. Each respondent confirmed that finance undertakes formal risk assessment and that neither the process nor the management actions arising from it are managed within the CSR function.

We would suggest, therefore, that there may be a mismatch between where the process for risk assessment resides (Finance) and where the competency for risk management exists (CSR function).

- **Stakeholder behaviours, not only attitudes, count to drive revenue and costs**

Companies appear to be managing the left-hand side of Figure 2.2 more than the right-hand side. Generally, respondents confirmed that their firms develop CSR programmes which are consistent with their core vision and values, manage it through employees and corporate branding and measure stakeholder perceptions of the business. They also confirmed that this does not usually carry through to a robust analysis of stakeholder behaviours and business outcomes.

Firms are measuring what is relatively easy for them to measure i.e. attitudes. As discussed earlier, attitude-behaviour correspondence is often difficult to reconcile (Oliver, 1997). However, it is not for lack of effort or awareness that this situation exists:

"We have been involved with benchmarking groups trying to isolate the impact of CSR upon behaviour from everything else going on ... but it does not seem possible" Diageo CSR spokesperson.

The problem of measuring behaviours transfers into problems of measuring business outcomes, as discussed previously, and attributing some portion of these outcomes to CSR investments and programmes.

The business case logic outlined in the flow of Figure 2.2 is based upon responsibility leading to increased customer expenditure, higher productivity, improved contribution from suppliers and reduced employee turnover. With the exception of risk, they all require some understanding of behaviours and not just attitudes. If firms do not overtly link CSR to changing stakeholder behaviours (and to business outcomes), expenditures on CSR are likely to become more and more vulnerable to criticism over time.

- **Business attitude to CSR reporting is paradoxical**

All respondent companies claim to have conducted a broad and deep scan of the NGO and stakeholder environment relevant to their business operations. Most engage stakeholders and NGOs formally in order to understand and assess the claims being made upon them. Equally, all are comfortable with their understanding of CSR reporting, yet are fierce in their criticisms.

Each respondent totally rejects the ideas of standardised reporting as not being suitable to their own industry (or firm). They listen to the points of view of NGOs and social auditors but reserve the right to report on what they feel is most relevant to their situation. CSR and financial managers feel inundated with requests for information from NGOs and ethical investment analysts, each addressing similar issues with different information demands. One respondent referred to "questionnaire fatigue" in reference to this proliferation of social and environmental assessments. They consider these demands difficult to meet as the data is not always at hand or accumulated according to the definitions of the particular requester. Many respondents were very wary of *de facto* social and environmental legislation being made through NGOs and international humanitarian organisations. One respondent referred to this as "mission creep".

Across all the firms we interviewed (except Pilkington), social and environmental reporting was managed and communicated to stakeholders separately from their financial reports.

We sense a real paradox here of companies wanting standardisation of the information required of them but vociferously rejecting a "one size fits all" approach to CSR measurement and reporting. If the core idea of the triple bottom line of company reporting (improved financial, social and environmental transparency) is to be achieved, then an integrated approach to such reporting and communications across the three areas is required.

Moving Forward with CSR

If our research is any guideline, it seems to us that businesses are facing a number of challenges in their approach to CSR. The argument that a firm has social responsibilities has been accepted. It is our contention, however, that the lack of a systematic framework linking investment in these responsibilities to social or business outcomes could well be inhibiting the development of CSR.

In essence, the framework proposed here calls for a number of CSR policy and practices to be fundamentally re-evaluated. From a policy perspective, we propose that CSR leaders and other management need to build a consensus behind a CSR vision of what and to whom they wish to be responsible and how they wish to measure and report on their performance against the vision. That process will force senior management to consider their company's unique competencies and determine how they can be leveraged to differing social and financial ends. Implementation of that vision through best practices requires measurement of stakeholder behaviours, more integrated risk management and formal assessment of social outcomes.

Recent scandals have demonstrated that the reporting of financial results is problematic, despite standard reports and external verification. Social reporting is even more problematic as it requires verifiable assessments of complex social processes, such as stakeholder dialogue, responsiveness and attitudes. The campaign for global standards is led by a limited number of groups with strong links to the social responsibility community,

If business is unhappy with the plethora of reporting demanded by NGOs, then it will have to find a collective voice and create implementable reporting structures that can secure broad social support.

Acknowledgement

Our thanks to Edelman (London) for sponsoring our research and for facilitating some client contacts.

References

Accountability (2002) *Accountability Printer: Socially responsible investment.* http://www.accountability. org.uk/uploadstore/cms/docs/sociallyresponsibleinvestment.pdf

Carroll, A. (1979) A three-dimensional model of corporate performance. *Academy of Management Review* 4(4), 497–505.

Clarkson, M. (1995) A stakeholder framework for analyzing and evaluating corporate social performace. *Academy of Management Review* 20(1), 92–117.

Davidson, H. (2002) *The Committed Enterprise*. ButterworthHeinemann, Oxford.

Day, G. and Montgomery, D.B. (1999) Charting new directions for marketing. *Journal of Marketing* 63(special edition), 3–13.

Department of Trade and Industry (2001) *Business and Society: developing corporate social responsibility in the UK*. HMSO, UK.

Department of Trade and Industry (2002) *Business and Society: corporate social responsibility 2002*. HMSO, UK.

Eisenhardt, K. (1989) Building theories from case study research. *Academy of Management Review* 14(2), 532–555.

Elkington, J. (2003) *Lauch of AA1000 Conference*. London. *Accountability.org.uk*.

Friedman, M. (1970). The social responsibility of business is to increase its profits. *New York Times Magazine* 32–33 and 122–126. New York.

von Hippel, E. (1986) Lead users: a source of novel product concepts. *Management Science* 34(7), 791–805.

von Hippel, E. (1989) New product ideas from lead users. *Research Technology Management* 32(3), 24–28.

Klein, N. (1999) *No Logo: Taking Aim at the Brand Bullies*. Picador, New York.

Knox, S.D. and Walker, D. (2001) Measuring and Managing Brand Loyalty. *Journal of Strategic Marketing* 9(2), 111–128.

Knox, S.D. and Walker, D. (2003) Empirical developments in the measurement of involvement, brand loyalty and their relationship in grocery markets. *Journal of Strategic Marketing* 11(7), 271–286.

Kong, N., Salzmann, O., Steger, U. and Ionescu-Somers, A. (2002) Moving Business/Industry Towards Sustainable Consumption: The Role of NGOs. *European Management Journal* 20(2), 109–127.

Maklan, S. and Knox, S.D. (2003) *CSR at the Crossroads*. Edelman, London.

Mitchell, A. (2001) *Right Side Up*. Harper Collins Business, London.

Mitchell, R., Agle, B. and Wood, D. (1997) Toward a theory of stakeholder identification and salience: defining the principle of who and what really counts. *Academy of Management Review* 22(4), 853–886.

Oliver, R. (1997) *Satisfaction*. McGraw-Hill Companies Inc, New York.

Reichheld, F. (1996) *The Loyalty Effect*. Harvard Business School Press, Boston, MA.

Willmott, M. (2001) *Citizen Brands*. John Wiley & Sons Ltd, Chichester.

Wood, D. (1991) Corporate social performance revisited. *Academy of Management Review* 16(4), 691–718.

Wood, D. and Jones, R. (1995) Stakeholder mismatching: a theoretical problem in empirical research on corporate social performance. *The International Journal of Organizational Analysis* 3(3), 229–267.

Zadek, S. (2002) *3rd Generation Corporate Citizenship*. <http://www.accountability.org.uk/uploadstore/cms/docs/3rdgencorpcitizenzip.pdf>

Outsourcing Innovation

Pete Engardio and Bruce Einhorn[1]

First came manufacturing. Now companies are farming out R&D to cut costs and get new products to market faster. Are they going too far?

As the Mediterranean sun bathed the festive cafés and shops of the Côte d'Azur town of Cannes, banners with the logos of Motorola, Royal Philips Electronics, palmOne, and Samsung fluttered from the masts of plush yachts moored in the harbor. On board, top execs hosted non-stop sales meetings during the day and champagne dinners at night to push their latest wireless gadgets. Outside the city's convention hall, carnival barkers, clowns on stilts, and vivacious models with bright red wigs lured passersby into flashy exhibits. For anyone in the telecom industry wanting to shout their achievements to the world, there was no more glamorous spot than the sprawling 3GSM World Congress in Southern France in February.

Yet many of the most intriguing product launches in Cannes took place far from the limelight. HTC Corp., a red-hot developer of multimedia handsets, didn't even have its own booth. Instead, the Taiwanese company showed off its latest wireless devices alongside partners that sell HTC's models under their own brand names. Flextronics Corp. demonstrated several concept phones exclusively behind closed doors. And Cellon International rented a discrete three-room apartment across from the convention center to unveil its new devices to a steady stream of telecom executives. The new offerings included the C8000, featuring eye-popping software. Cradle the device to your ear and it goes into telephone mode. Peer through the viewfinder and it automatically shifts into camera mode. Hold the end of the device to your eye and it morphs into a videocam.

HTC? Flextronics? Cellon? There's a good reason these are hardly household names. The multimedia devices produced from their prototypes will end up on retail shelves under the brands of companies that don't want you to know who designs their products. Yet these and other little-known companies, with names such as Quanta

---

Source: P. Engardio and B. Einhorn (2005) *Business Week*: 21 March.

Computer, Premier Imaging, Wipro Technologies, and Compal Electronics, are fast emerging as hidden powers of the technology industry.

They are the vanguard of the next step in outsourcing – of innovation itself. When Western corporations began selling their factories and farming out manufacturing in the 1980s and 1990s to boost efficiency and focus their energies, most insisted all the important research and development would remain in-house.

But that Pledge is now passé. Today, the likes of Dell, Motorola, and Philips are buying complete designs of some digital devices from Asian developers, tweaking them to their own specifications, and slapping on their own brand names. It's not just cell phones. Asian contract manufacturers and independent design houses have become forces in nearly every tech device, from laptops and high-definition TVs to MP3 music players and digital cameras. "Customers used to participate in design two or three years back," says Jack Hsieh, vice-president for finance at Taiwan's Premier Imaging Technology Corp., a major supplier of digital cameras to leading U.S. and Japanese brands. "But starting last year, many just take our product. Because of price competition, they have to."

While the electronics sector is furthest down this road, the search for offshore help with innovation is spreading to nearly every corner of the economy. On February 8 [2005], Boeing Co. said it is working with India's HCL Technologies to co-develop software for everything from the navigation systems and landing gear to the cockpit controls for its upcoming 7E7 Dreamliner jet. Pharmaceutical giants such as GlaxoSmithKline and Eli Lilly are teaming up with Asian biotech research companies in a bid to cut the average $500 million cost of bringing a new drug to market. And Procter & Gamble Co. says it wants half of its new product ideas to be generated from outside by 2010, compared with 20% now.

Competitive Dangers

Underlying this trend is a growing consensus that more innovation is vital – but that current R&D spending isn't yielding enough bang for the buck. After spending years squeezing costs out of the factory floor, back office, and warehouse, CEOs are asking tough questions about their once-cloistered R&D operations: Why are so few hit products making it out of the labs into the market? How many of those pricey engineers are really creating game-changing products or technology breakthroughs? "R&D is the biggest single remaining controllable expense to work on," says Allen J. Delattre, head of Accenture Ltd.'s high-tech consulting practice. "Companies either will have to cut costs or increase R&D productivity."

The result is a rethinking of the structure of the modern corporation. What, specifically, has to be done in-house anymore? At a minimum, most leading Western companies are turning toward a new model of innovation, one that employs global networks of partners. These can include U.S. chipmakers, Taiwanese engineers, Indian software developers, and Chinese factories. IBM is even offering the smarts of its famed research labs and a new global team of 1,200 engineers to help customers develop future products using next-generation technologies. When the whole chain works in sync, there can be a dramatic leap in the speed and efficiency of product development.

The downside of getting the balance wrong, however, can be steep. Start with the danger of fostering new competitors. Motorola hired Taiwan's BenQ Corp. to design and manufacture millions of mobile phones. But then BenQ began selling phones last year in the prized China market under its own brand. That prompted Motorola to pull its contract. Another risk is that brand-name companies will lose the incentive to keep investing in new technology. "It is a slippery slope," says Boston Consulting Group Senior Vice-President Jim Andrew. "If the innovation starts residing in the suppliers, you could incrementalize yourself to the point where there isn't much left."

Such perceptions are a big reason even companies that outsource heavily refuse to discuss what hardware designs they buy from whom and impose strict confidentiality on suppliers. "It is still taboo to talk openly about outsourced design," says Forrester Research Inc. consultant Navi Radjou, an expert on corporate innovation.

The concerns also explain why different companies are adopting widely varying approaches to this new paradigm. Dell, for example, does little of its own design for notebook PCs, digital TVs, or other products. Hewlett-Packard Co. says it contributes key technology and at least some design input to all its products but relies on outside partners to co-develop everything from servers to printers. Motorola buys complete designs for its cheapest phones but controls all of the development of high-end handsets like its hot-selling Razr. The key, execs say, is to guard some sustainable competitive advantage, whether it's control over the latest technologies, the look and feel of new products, or the customer relationship. "You have to draw a line," says Motorola CEO Edward J. Zander. At Motorola, "core intellectual property is above it, and commodity technology is below."

Wherever companies draw the line, there's no question that the demarcation between mission-critical R&D and commodity work is sliding year by year. The implications for the global economy are immense. Countries such as India and China, where wages remain low and new engineering graduates are abundant, likely will continue to be the biggest gainers in tech employment and become increasingly important suppliers of intellectual property. Some analysts even see a new global division of labor emerging: The rich West will focus on the highest levels of product creation, and all the jobs of turning concepts into actual products or services can be shipped out. Consultant Daniel H. Pink, author of the new book *A Whole New Mind,* argues that the "left brain" intellectual tasks that "are routine, computer-like, and can be boiled down to a spec sheet are migrating to where it is cheaper, thanks to Asia's rising economies and the miracle of cyberspace." The U.S. will remain strong in "right brain" work that entails "artistry, creativity, and empathy with the customer that requires being physically close to the market."

You can see this great divide already taking shape in global electronics. The process started in the 1990s when Taiwan emerged as the capital of PC design, largely because the critical technology was standardized, on Microsoft Corp.'s operating system software and Intel Corp.'s microprocessor. Today, Taiwanese "original-design manufacturers", so named because they both design and assemble products for others, supply some 65% of the world's notebook PCs. Quanta Computer Inc. alone expects to churn out 16 million notebook PCs this year in 50 different models for buyers that include Dell, Apple Computer, and Sony.

Now, Taiwanese ODMs and other outside designers are forces in nearly every digital device on the market. Of the 700 million mobile phones expected to be sold worldwide this year, up to 20% will be the work of ODMs, estimates senior analyst Adam Pick of the El Segundo (Calif.) market research firm iSuppli Corp. About 30% of digital cameras are produced by ODMs, 65% of MP3 players, and roughly 70% of personal digital assistants (PDAs). Building on their experience with PCs, they're increasingly creating recipes for their own gizmos, blending the latest advances in custom chips, specialized software, and state-of-the-art digital components. "There is a lot of great capability that has grown in Asia to develop complete products," says Doug Rasor, worldwide strategic marketing manager at chipmaker Texas Instruments Inc. TI often supplies core chips, along with rudimentary designs, and the ODMs take it from there. "They can do the system integration, the plastics, the industrial design, and the low-cost manufacturing, and they are happy to put Dell's name on it. That is a megatrend in the industry," says Rasor.

Taiwan's ODMs clearly don't regard themselves as mere job shops. Just ask the top brass at HTC, which creates and manufactures smart phones for such wireless service providers as Vodafone and Cingular as well as equipment makes it doesn't identify. "We know this kind of product category a lot better than our customers do," says HTC President Peter Chou. "We have capability to integrate all the latest technologies. We do everything except the Microsoft operating system."

Or stop in to Quanta's headquarters in the Huaya Technology Park outside Taipei. Workers are finishing a dazzling structure the size of several football fields, with a series of wide steps leading past white columns supporting a towering Teflon-and-glass canopy. It will serve as Quanta's R&D headquarters, with thousands of engineers working on next-generation displays, digital home networking appliances, and multimedia players. This year, Quanta is doubling its engineering staff, to 7,000 and its R&D spending, to $200 million.

Why? To improve its shrinking profit margins – and because foreign clients are demanding it. "What has changed is that more customers need us to design the whole product," says Chairman Barry Lam. For future products, in fact, "it's now difficult to get good ideas from our customers. We have to innovate ourselves."

Sweeping Overhaul

India is emerging as a heavyweight in design, too. The top players in making the country world-class in software development, including HCL and Wipro, are expected to help India boost its contract R&D revenues from $1 billion a year now to $8 billion in three years. One of Wipro's many labs is in a modest office off dusty, congested Hosur Road in Bangalore. There, 1,000 young engineers partitioned into brightly lit pods jammed with circuit boards, chips, and steel housings hunch over 26 development projects. Among them is a hands-free telephone system that attaches to the visor of a European sports car. At another pod, designers tinker with a full dashboard embedded with a satellite navigation system. Inside other Wipro labs in Bangalore, engineers are designing prototypes for everything from high-definition TVs to satellite set-top boxes.

Perhaps the most ambitious new entrant in design is Flextronics. The manufacturing behemoth already builds networking gear, printers, game consoles, and other hardware for the likes of Nortel Networks, Xerox, HP, Motorola, and Casio Computer. But three years ago, it started losing big cell-phone and PDA orders to Taiwanese ODMs. Since then, CEO Michael E. Marks has shelled out more than $800 million on acquisitions to build a 7,000-engineer force of software, chip, telecom, and mechanical designers scattered from India and Singapore to France and Ukraine. Marks's splashiest move was to pay an estimated $30 million for Frog Design Inc., the pioneering Sunnyvale (Calif.) firm that helped design such Information Age icons as Apple Computer Inc.'s original Mac in 1984. So far, Flextronics has developed its own basic platforms for cell phones, routers, digital cameras, and imaging devices. His goal is to make Flextronics a low-cost, soup-to-nuts developer of consumer-electronics and tech gear.

Marks has an especially radical take on where all this is headed: He believes Western tech conglomerates are on the cusp of a sweeping overhaul of R&D that will rival the offshore shift of manufacturing. In the 1990s, companies like Flextronics "completely restructured the world's electronics manufacturing," says Marks. "Now we will completely restructure design." When you get down to it, he argues, some 80% of engineers in product development do tasks that can easily be outsourced – like translating prototypes into workable designs, upgrading mature products, testing quality, writing user manuals, and qualifying parts vendors. What's more, most of the core technologies in today's digital gadgets are available to anyone. And circuit boards for everything from cameras to network switches are becoming simpler because more functions are embedded on semiconductors. The "really hard technology work" is migrating to chipmakers such as Texas Instruments, Qualcomm, Philips, Intel, and Broadcom, Marks says. "All electronics are on the same trajectory of becoming silicon surrounded by plastic."

Why then, Marks asks, should Nokia, Motorola, Sony-Ericsson, Alcatel, Siemens, Samsung, and other brand-name companies all largely duplicate one another's efforts? Why should each spend $30 million to develop a new smartphone or $200 million on a cellular base station when they can just buy the hardware designs? The ultimate result, he says: Some electronics giants will shrink their R&D forces from several thousand to a few hundred, concentrating on proprietary architecture, setting key specifications, and managing global R&D teams. "There is no doubt the product companies are going to have fewer people design stuff," Marks predicts. "It's going to get ugly."

Granted, Marks's vision is more than a tad extreme. True, despite the tech recovery, many corporate R&D budgets have been tightening. HP's R&D spending long hovered around 6% of sales, but it's down to 4.4% now. Cisco Systems' R&D budget has dropped from its old average of 17% to 14.5%. The numbers also are falling at

Motorola, Lucent Technologies, and Ericsson. In November, Nokia Corp. said it aims to trim R&D spending from 12.8% of sales in 2004 to under 10% by the end of 2006.

Close to the Heart

Still, most companies insist they will continue to do most of the critical design work – and have no plans to take a meat axe to R&D. A Motorola spokesman says it plans to keep R&D spending at around 10% for the long term. Lucent says its R&D staff should remain at about 9,000, after several years of deep cuts. And while many Western companies are downsizing at home, they are boosting hiring at their own labs in India, China, and Eastern Europe. "Companies realize if they want a sustainable competitive advantage, they will not get it from outsourcing," says President Frank M. Armbrecht of the Industrial Research Institute, which tracks corporate R&D spending.

Companies also worry about the message they send investors. Outsourcing manufacturing, tech support, and back-office work makes clear financial sense. But ownership of design strikes close to the heart of a corporation's intrinsic value. If a company depends on outsiders for design, investors might ask, how much intellectual property does it really own, and how much of the profit from a hit product flows back into its own coffers, rather than being paid out in licensing fees? That's one reason Apple Computer lets the world know it develops its hit products in-house, to the point of etching "Designed by Apple in California" on the back of each iPod.

Yet some outsourcing holdouts are changing their tune. Nokia long prided itself on developing almost everything itself – to the point of designing its own chips. No longer. Given the complexities of today's technologies and supply chains, "nobody can master it all," says Chief Technology Officer Pertti Korhonen. "You have to figure out what is core and what is context." Lucent says outsourcing some development makes sense so that its engineers can concentrate on next-generation technologies. "This frees up talent to work on new product lines," says Dave Ayers, vice-president for platforms and engineering. "Outsourcing isn't about moving jobs. It's about the flexibility to put resources in the right places at the right time."

It's also about brutal economics and the relentless demands of consumers. To get shelf space at a Best Buy or Circuit City often means brand-name companies need a full range of models, from a $100 point-and-shoot digital camera with 2 megapixels, say, to a $700 8-megapixel model that doubles as a videocam and is equipped with a powerful zoom lens. On top of this, superheated competition can reduce hit products to cheap commodities within months. So they must get out the door fast to earn a decent margin. "Consumer electronics have become almost like produce," says Michael E. Fawkes, senior vice-president of HP's Imaging Products Div. "They always have to be fresh."

Such pressures explain outsourcing's growing allure. Take cell phones, which are becoming akin to fashion items. Using a predesigned platform can shave 70% of development costs off a new model, estimates William S. Wong, a senior vice-president for marketing at Cellon. That can be a huge saving. As a rule of thumb, it takes around $10 million and up to 150 engineers to develop a new cell phone from scratch. If

Motorola or Nokia guess wrong about the market trends a year into the future, they can lose big. So they must develop several versions.

With most of its 800 engineers in China and France, Cellon creates several basic designs each year and spreads the costs among many buyers. It also has the technical expertise to morph that basic phone into a bewildering array of models. Want a 2-megapixel camera module instead of 1-megapixel? Want to include a music player, or change the style from a gray clamshell to a flaming-red candy-bar shape? No problem: Cellon engineers can whip up a prototype, run all the tests, and get it into mass production in a Chinese factory in months.

Moving Up the Food Chain

Companies are still figuring out exactly what to outsource. PalmOne Inc.'s collaboration with Taiwan's HTC on its popular Treo 650 smart phone illustrates one approach. Palm has long hired contractors to assemble hardware from its own industrial designs. But in 2001, it decided to focus on software and shifted hardware production to Taiwanese ODMs. PalmOne designers still determine the look and feel of the product, pick key components like the display and core chips, and specify performance requirements. But HTC does much of the mechanical and electrical design. "Without a doubt, they've become a part of the innovation process," says Angel L. Mendez, senior global operations vice-president at PalmOne. "It's less about outsourcing and more about the collaborative way in which design comes together." The result: PalmOne has cut months off of development times, reduced defects by 50% and boosted gross margins by around 20%.

Hewlett-Packard, a company with such a proud history of innovation that its advertising tag line is simply "invent," also works with design partners on all the hardware it outsources. "Our strategy is now to work with global networks to leverage the best technologies on the planet," says Dick Conrad, HP's senior vice-president for global operations. According to iSuppli, HP is getting design help from Taiwan's Quanta and Hon Hai Precision for PCs, Lite-On for printers, Inventec for servers and MP3 players, and Altek for digital cameras. HP won't identify specific suppliers, but it says the strategy has brought benefits. Conrad says it now takes 60% less time to get a new concept to market. Plus, the company can "redeploy our assets and resources to higher value-added products" such as advanced printer inks and sophisticated corporate software, he says.

How far can outsourced design go? When does it get to the point where ODMs start driving truly breakthrough concepts and core technologies? It's not here yet. Distance is one barrier. "To be a successful product company requires intimacy with the customer," says Azim H. Premji, chairman of India's Wipro. "That is very hard to offshore in fast-changing markets." Another hurdle is that R&D spending by ODMs remains relatively low. Even though Premier develops most of its own cameras and video projectors, "the really core technology," such as the digital signal processors, is invented in the U.S., says vice-president Hsieh. Premier's latest wallet-size video projector, for example, was based on a rough design by Texas Instruments, developer of the core chip. With margins shrinking fast in the ODM business, however, Premier and other Taiwanese companies know they need to move up the innovation food chain to reap higher profits.

That's where Flextronics and its design acquisitions could get interesting. Inside frog's hip Sunnyvale office, designers are working to create a radically new multimedia, device, for an unnamed corporate client, that won't hit the market until 2007. The plan, says Patricia Roller, frog's co-CEO, is to use Flextronics software engineers in Ukraine or India to develop innovative applications, and for Flextronics engineers to design the working prototype. Flextronics then would mass-produce the gadgets, probably in China.

Who will ultimately profit most from the outsourcing of innovation isn't clear. The early evidence suggests that today's Western titans can remain leaders by orchestrating global innovation networks. Yet if they lose their technology edge and their touch with customers, they could be tomorrow's great shrinking conglomerates. Contractors like Quanta and Flextronics that are moving up the innovation ladder, meanwhile, have a shot at joining the world's leading industrial players. What is clear is that an army of in-house engineers no longer means a company can control its fate. Instead, the winners will be those most adept at marshaling the creativity and skills of workers around the world.

Note

1   With Manjeet Kripalani in Bangalore, Andy Reinhardt in Cannes, Bruce Nussbaum in Somers, N.Y., and Peter Burrows in San Mateo, Calif.

From Scenario Thinking
to Strategic Action

Ian Wilson

Introduction

One day in the fall of 1976 I arranged a meeting between Pierre Wack, who at that time headed Royal Dutch/Shell's Business Environment component, and some of my colleagues in General Electric's strategic planning staff. The focus of our discussion was to be the role of scenarios in corporate planning.

At that time, GE had, arguably, the most elaborate and sophisticated strategic planning system in the corporate world, and Shell was enjoying an international reputation for its pioneering scenarios work. Yet in each case something was missing. Wack was convinced that his scenarios needed a tighter linkage to strategic planning and decision making if they were ever to engage operations managers seriously and continuously. And GE, still shaken and puzzled by the fallout from the first "oil shock," needed to ground its strategy in an assessment of the future that acknowledged, more explicitly, the inherent uncertainties that then marked the future business environment. The two parties thus came to this discussion from differing points of view, but focused on the same central need: linking perceptions about the future to current decisions.

This meeting marked a turning point in my recognition of the critical importance of strengthening the connection between scenario development and strategic action. From this point forward I recognized that, although developing coherent, imaginative and useful scenarios is certainly important, translating the implications of the scenarios into executive decisions and, ultimately, into strategic action was the ultimate reason and justification for the exercise.

Cultural Barriers to Implementation

Scenarios are not an end in themselves. They are a management tool to improve the quality of executive decision making. Yet experience shows that actually using scenarios for this purpose turns out to be a more perplexing problem than the scenario development process itself. As in the larger domain of strategy, implementation—execution—turns out to be the crucial issue.

Source: I. Wilson (2000) *Technological Forecasting and Social Change*, 65 (1): 23–9.

The causes of this implementation problem, in part practical and procedural, are still largely cultural and psychological. The planning culture in most corporations is still heavily biased toward single-point forecasting. In such a context, the managers' premise is, "Tell me what the future will be; then I can make my decision." So their initial reaction, when confronted with the apparent emphasis in scenarios on "multipoint forecasting," is likely to be one of confusion and disbelief, complaining that three (or four) "forecasts" are more confusing, and less helpful, than one. The fact that this is a misperception of the nature and role of scenarios does not in any way lessen the implementation problem.

However, the major cultural barrier to scenario implementation stems from the way we define managerial competence. Good managers, we say, *know* where they are, where they're going, and how they'll get there. *We equate managerial competence with "knowing,"* and assume that decisions depend on facts about the present and about the future. Of course, the reality is that *we have no facts about the future*. In a 1975 presentation to the American Association for the Advancement of Science (AAAS), I highlighted this problem in the following way: "However good our futures research may be, we shall never be able to escape from the ultimate dilemma that all our knowledge is about the past, and all our decisions are about the future."

Scenarios face up to this dilemma, confronting us with the need to acknowledge that we do not, and cannot, know the future. In the most fundamental way, scenarios seek, as Pierre Wack put it, to change our "mental maps" of the future. But, in doing so, scenarios also may seem to challenge the way we define managerial competence. That is, by acknowledging uncertainty, scenarios underscore the fact that we cannot know the future, and so we perceive them as challenges to our presumptions of "knowing," and thus of managerial competence. And because few, if any, corporate cultures reward incompetence, managers have a vested interest in not acknowledging their ignorance, and so in resisting the intrusion of scenario planning into traditional forms of executive decision making.

Dealing with the Dilemma

A starting point for dealing with this dilemma is to establish a clear-cut "decision focus" for every set of scenarios. At SRI International, we insisted that the first step in the scenario process was *not* a review of the changing forces affecting the business environment, but rather agreement on the strategic decision(s) that the scenarios should be designed to illuminate. While it is true that scenarios can also be used as a learning tool to explore general areas of risk and opportunity, this use normally leads to the development of more focused scenarios before decisions are taken. This crucial step establishes, at the outset, that the ultimate purpose of the scenarios is not just to develop plausible descriptions of alternative futures—not even to redraw our mental maps of the future, important as that is—but rather to help executives make better, more resilient strategic decisions. By tying scenarios to needed decisions, we effectively link them to specific planning needs, and prevent the process from straying off into overly broad generalizations about the future of society or the global economy.

Usually, the right decisions on which to focus decisions are strategic rather than tactical. This is because scenarios normally deal more with longer term trends and uncertainties, often with a 5- to 10-year time horizon, rather than short-term developments. Virtually any decision or area of strategic concern in which external factors are complex, changing, and uncertain is a suitable target for the scenario process. However, I have found that the narrower the scope of the decision or strategy (a specific investment or market entry decision, for example), the easier the scenario construction—and interpretation—will be. Developing scenarios for broad strategic concerns—the long-range positioning of a diversified business portfolio, for example—is more difficult.

A word of caution is needed at this point. While clarifying the strategic focus of the scenarios is a critical first step, it is equally important to note that this is not the time for strategizing. Decision makers, particularly senior executives, have a natural impatience with analysis and a tendency to want to "cut to the chase." On many occasions I have had to check this otherwise praiseworthy tendency toward action so that the context for action—the scenarios themselves—can first be established. Once executives see that the process *both begins and ends* with an emphasis on action, they are more easily persuaded of the true value of scenario planning.

What *Not* to Do

Agreeing that the usefulness of scenarios depends upon their ability to influence executive action is a good first step because at least it focuses attention on what would otherwise be a potential problem. However, it leaves unanswered the questions: What do we do with scenarios once we have developed them? How do we translate what we learn from them into action? Before attempting to answer these questions, there are two things that we should *not* do.

First, we do *not* develop a complete strategy for each of the scenarios, and then by some means—maybe by applying the test of discounted cash value—select the one that appears to give the greatest promise of success and profitability. I know of no management team that would willingly undertake to go through a full-blown strategy development exercise two or three or four times (however, many scenarios have been developed). Such a course would more likely lead to "paralysis by analysis" than to constructive action. And, in any case, it would be based on a further misunderstanding of scenario planning: the real aim is to develop a resilient strategy within the framework of alternative futures provided by the scenarios.

Before proceeding, a word of explanation—and caution—is needed at this point. In a number of places in this article I refer to the objective of scenario planning as being the development of a resilient strategy. Now, it should be obvious that resilience is not the only quality to be sought in a strategy; and, taken to an extreme, resilience could mean little more than the lowest common denominator of scenario-specific strategies. At a time that calls for bold, even radical, action in many markets, such an interpretation would be a prescription for mediocrity at best, extinction at worst. My point is, rather, that, before taking bold steps, the strategy should be tested against a variety of scenarios so that the management team is forewarned of potential vulnerabilities. Resilience can then be built into the strategy, *not* by reducing its force or boldness, but rather by "hedging" or contingency planning.

The second thing that we do not do is assign probabilities to the scenarios and then develop a strategy for the "most probable" one. Of course, in saying this, I am taking a controversial position; however, please take confidence from the fact that it is a position that Pierre Wack shared. Probability has more to do with forecasts than with scenarios; and scenarios are not forecasts, for one cannot, reasonably and at the same time, "forecast" three or four quite different futures. Scenarios, as a collection of futures, are intended to establish the boundaries of our uncertainty and the limits to plausible futures.

However, I recognize that there is a very powerful human tendency, born of past experience and culture, to assign probabilities at the end of the scenario process. Every individual ends up with his or her own private assessment of probability; and it is almost certainly better to bring these assessments out into the open for group discussion than to leave them suppressed in individual minds. Indeed, doing this usually serves to underscore the wide diversity of opinions—and the consequent foolishness of trying to reach some sort of consensus on this matter. However, whichever course of action one elects—to engage in this group assessment or not—the critical point is to avoid playing the probabilities game to the point of focusing on one "most probable" scenario to the exclusion of the others. To do so would negate the whole value of the scenario planning exercise.

What to Do

Using scenarios to make strategic decisions requires considerable skill and sophistication; and these qualities take time to acquire. Initially, therefore, any organization experimenting with scenario planning needs some sort of a template, a primer, or step-by-step approach to moving from scenarios to strategy. Some critics will protest that this approach trivializes strategy development, substituting analytical structure for intuitive insight. However, in defense of this utilitarian approach, consider the analogy of learning to play the piano. The beginner has to learn the notes, practice scales, and play rhythmically, paced by a metronome. Only after mastering technique can the piano player perform with feeling and insight. So, too, the beginning scenario player needs to learn some basic techniques that will help to bridge the gap between scenarios and strategy before graduating to a more sophisticated approach.

In this spirit, I offer the following primer of four approaches to this problem, ranging from the most elemental to the more sophisticated.

Sensitivity/Risk Assessment

This approach can be used to evaluate a specific strategic decision such as a major plant investment or a new business development drive. Here, the need for the decision is known beforehand: the question, therefore, is simply whether or not to proceed, after assessing the strategy's resilience or vulnerability in different business conditions.

A step-by-step approach first identifies the key conditions (such as market growth rate, changes in regulatory climate, technological developments) that the future market or industry environment would have to meet to justify a "go" decision, and then assesses the state of these conditions in each scenario. It is then possible to compare the scenario conditions with the desired future conditions, and to assess how successful and how resilient or vulnerable, a "go" decision would be in each scenario. Finally, it is possible to assess the overall resilience of a decision to proceed with the proposed strategy, and to consider the need or desirability of "hedging" or modifying the original decision in some way in order to increase its resilience.

This approach provides a relatively straightforward application of scenarios to decision making, using a series of descriptive and judgmental steps. However, it depends on having a very clear and specific decision focus, one which lends itself to a "go/no go" decision.

An illustration of this approach was provided by a paper company confronted with a decision on whether or not to invest $600 million in a new paper-making facility. The company did not normally use scenarios in its strategic planning, but decided that they would be useful here, given the long life span (30–35 years) of the plant and the corresponding range of uncertainties regarding future electronic technology development, consumer values and time use, prospects for advertising, and general economic conditions.

The scenarios showed, as one might expect, vastly different levels of demand growth, but similar patterns of eventual decline, with the timing of key threats remaining a critical uncertainty. Playing out the investment decision in these different environments suggested that only in the most optimistic conditions would the company meet its "hurdle rate" for return on investment. As a result, the executives decided on a more incremental approach to the investment, significantly scaling down the initial plant size.

Strategy Evaluation

Another relatively straightforward role for scenarios is to act as "test beds" to evaluate the viability of an existing strategy, usually one that derives from traditional single-point forecasting. By playing a companywide or business unit strategy against the scenarios it is possible to gain some insight into the strategy's effectiveness in a range of business conditions, and so to identify modifications and/or contingency planning that require attention.

First, it is necessary to disaggregate the strategy into its specific thrusts (e.g., "Focus on upscale consumer market segments," "Diversify into related services areas") and spell out its goals and objectives. Then it is possible to assess the relevance and likely success (in terms of meeting the desired objectives) of these thrusts in the diverse conditions of the scenarios. Assessing the results of this impact analysis should then enable the management team to identify: (a) opportunities that the strategy addresses and those that it misses; (b) threats/risks that the analysis has foreseen or overlooked; and (c) comparative competitive success or failure.

At this point, it is possible to identify options for changes in strategy and the need for contingency planning.

This approach offers a natural and relatively simple first use of scenarios in a corporate strategic planning system. Assessing an existing strategy requires less sophistication than developing a new strategy; nevertheless, assessment provides a quick demonstration of the utility of scenarios in executive decision making by identifying important "bottom-line" issues that require immediate attention.

A large department-store chain introduced scenarios this way into its strategic exploration of future patterns of change in the economy, consumer values, life styles, and the structure and operations of the retail industry. The company used these scenarios in three distinct ways: (1) evaluate the likely payoff from its current strategy; (2) assess and compare the strategies of key competitors (note: this was an interesting—and useful—application of scenario planning, assessing the competitors' as well as one's own strategy); and (3) analyze retail strategy options to identify the most resilient ones for possible inclusion in the company's strategy (the company did, in fact, expand greatly into speciality stores as a result of this exercise).

Strategy Development (Using a "Planning-Focus" Scenario)

This approach is an attempt to bridge the "culture gap" between traditional planning that relies on single-point forecasting and scenario planning. Basically, it consists of selecting one of the scenarios as a starting point and focus for strategy development, and then using the other scenarios to test the strategy's resilience and assess the need for modification, "hedging" or contingency planning.

The steps involved in this approach are as follows: (a) review the scenarios to identify the key opportunities and threats for the business, looking at each scenario in turn and then looking across all scenarios (to identify common opportunities and threats); (b) determine, based on this review, what the company should do, and should not do, in any case; (c) select a "planning focus" scenario (usually the "most probable" one); (d) integrate the strategic elements identified in step b into a coherent strategy for the "planning focus" scenario; (e) test this strategy against the remaining scenarios to assess its resilience or vulnerability; and (f) review the results of this test to determine the need for strategy modification, "hedging," and contingency planning.

It should be obvious that this approach flies in the face of my earlier assertion that scenarios should not deal in probabilities. And, while the other scenarios are not discarded, there is still the danger that this approach may close executives' minds to "unlikely" (which often means "unpleasant") scenarios and so limits their search for strategy options. However, the approach can be justified as a useful intermediate step (between traditional and scenario planning) in weaning executives away from their reliance on single-point forecasting. It does not commit the ultimate sin of disregarding the other scenarios entirely; and, in its step-by-step process, it does address many of the key questions that scenario-based strategy should ask.

Shell Canada used this approach when it introduced scenarios into its strategic planning system in the early 1980s. As a member of the Royal/Dutch Shell Group, its executives were well aware of the strict interpretation of scenario-based planning, but felt that this modified approach would help the company ease into the new process by making this concession to traditional thinking. In fact, the discussion of probabilities revealed so much uncertainty in executive opinion about future trends, that two scenarios—each with dramatically different drivers—were selected as the "planning focus." The company then proceeded to structure its strategic positioning in answer to three questions: (1) What strategies should we pursue no matter which scenario materializes? (2) What strategies should we pursue if either of the "planning focus" scenarios materializes? (3) How sensitive are base strategies to variations in assumptions under contingent conditions?

In fact, in the end, Shell Canada did succeed, both in bridging the gap between the old and new approaches to strategy development and in preserving the value of considering, and planning for, different business conditions.

Strategy Development (Without Using a "Planning-Focus" Scenario)

In this approach, executives take all scenarios at face value without judging probabilities, and aim for the development of a resilient strategy that can deal with wide variations in business conditions. The step-by-step process in this approach considers: (1) identifying the key elements of a successful strategy (such as geographic scope, market focus, product range, basis of competition); (2) analyzing each scenario to determine the optimal setting for each strategy element (e.g., what would be the best marketing strategy for Scenario A? for Scenario B?); (3) reviewing these scenario-specific settings to determine the most resilient option for each strategy element; and (4) integrating these strategy options into an overall, coordinated business strategy.

Without doubt, this is the most sophisticated—and demanding—approach, one that most closely approximates the goal of strategizing within the scenarios framework, and that makes optimal use of the scenarios in strategy development. It provides management with the maximum feasible range of choice, and forces careful evaluation of these options against differing assumptions about the future. It does, however, demand effort, patience, and sophistication, and works best when the decision makers participate directly throughout the process.

This was the case with a large European financial-services company in which the senior management team was, in effect, both the scenario- and the strategy-development team. After structuring scenarios around their perceptions of the critical uncertainties facing the business, they first identified the strategic opportunities and threats arising from these scenarios. They then used this framework to assess the company's current competitive position and prospective vulnerability. Their approach to strategy development then led them to the following steps: (1) first, to single out 11 key elements of a well-rounded strategy (e.g., product scope, alliances, distribution/delivery, technology); (2) second, to identify the optimal strategic option for each of these 11 elements in each of the four scenarios; and (3) finally, to select the most resilient option for each element, and to integrate the options into a coherent strategy for the company.

Conclusion

I have chosen to emphasize this one aspect of scenario planning—moving from the scenarios themselves to strategy development to action—because, in my experience, it is perhaps the most critical phase of the scenario process. More scenario projects fail because they have no impact on strategy and management decisions rather than because they were unimaginative or poorly constructed.

Moving from traditional planning to scenario-based strategic planning requires a transformation of corporate culture. Scenario planning is not merely a new planning tool, but rather a new way of thinking. Using scenarios on a one-shot basis requires much less investment than instituting them as an integral part of corporate planning. Many, perhaps most, of the problems in introducing scenario planning into an organization stem from a failure to recognize the magnitude and duration of the implementation effort that is required to use this technology to change the prevailing management assumptions.

Like scenarios themselves, this effort has to be tailored to the needs of the organization, but some requirements are constant: senior management commitment, communications, education and guidance, and practice, practice, practice. Like the piano player, the scenarios user will be able to progress from beginning exercises, as outlined here, to intuitive and insightful action only with time, patience, and practice.

Part 2

Approaches

In this Part, the intention is to offer a review of some of the more robust methodologies that have emerged in recent years, particularly those that have now been largely accepted into mainstream thinking. The problem with all such initiatives is that one's experience of them is often largely determined by personal experience, irrespective of whether that experience reflected a well designed, effectively implemented and successful undertaking, or a misunderstood, poorly executed failure. Even the more ephemeral of management fads usually have *something* to recommend them, most of them have after all been successfully trialled in other organizations. So perhaps the saddest outcome is where a perfectly viable methodology fails because it has not been done properly. The best defence against being taken wherever the consultant wants to lead is inevitably a detailed examination of what is being proposed, what it can or cannot do, and what is required to make it work.

The somewhat polemical piece by **Dale et al**. represents an attempt by a group of authors prominent in the field of 'Quality' to reclaim a territory. They argue that the so-called 'Excellence Model' has emerged, evolved and, somewhere along the way, lost sight of the basics. At least part of the discussion devolves to the question of vocabulary, but the thrust of the argument is actually much deeper. Management has long been concerned with performance indicators as an 'instrument panel' to help keep the show on the road, but managing the performance indicators is emphatically not the same as managing the business. Worse, unless those indicators are periodically re-assessed for their continued scope and relevance, it is often possible to satisfy them while the business is in serious decline. Notwithstanding their obvious dissatisfaction with some of the trends as they see them, the authors conclude that there is still hope for Quality (or Excellence, or

Six-Sigma or whatever term gains currency) as long as the focus is more on the attitudes and behaviours of the people involved, and less on ticking boxes.

The topic of attitudes and behaviours figures strongly in the **Bhuiyan and Baghel** review of Continuous Improvement (CI). In this article, the authors argue for CI as the antecedent for a long list of more recent methodologies such as Total Quality Management (TQM), Lean, the Balanced Scorecard and Six-Sigma. While there are many who would argue the point, the similarities do bear scrutiny; a focus on improvement (largely at the expense of radical innovation), an emphasis on learning (such that mistakes are not repeated) and, perhaps fundamentally, the need to engage the hearts and minds of *everyone* in the organization. It is probably this latter aspect that ultimately characterizes the class of methodologies that forms this particular tributary of management thinking; although the commitment of top management is (as ever) required – most notably in terms of behaving in a manner consistent with the ideals espoused and providing the necessary resources – this type of approach cannot be imposed on a workforce, but must rather be encouraged to evolve. As long as management are prepared to 'walk the talk', the promise of CI should be realizable without the danger of it being labelled a fad.

The article by **Hines et al.** provides a more in-depth analysis on the topic of lean thinking. Again the authors aim for a fairly all-embracing definition of just what constitutes Lean, and implicitly argue that the methodology is capable of operating alongside the familiar range of CI/TQM approaches. However, having traced the movement from its origins on the Toyota shop floor, the authors are somewhat reticent about extending it away from its manufacturing base. Waste is waste and exists everywhere. Indeed, the definition offered in the previous article by Bhuiyan and Baghel ('anything for which the customer is not willing to pay') can readily find application in almost any field, and could even be cited as the driving force behind Business Process Re-engineering (BPR). Perhaps the most cogent example is the Direct Line insurance phenomenon that has revolutionized the insurance industry. Without necessarily arguing that the changes effected here were conceived in the name of either Lean or BPR, there seems little doubt that a desire to only do that for which the customer *was* prepared to pay played a crucial role in terms of designing a system to deliver customer value.

The article by **Storey et al.** is long but justifies its inclusion on two counts. First, it starts with a more than useful review of the supply chain management literature, tracing its origins back to the lean and agile movements as well as noting the evolution of supply logistics towards a nominally less adversarial norm. Second, it offers a wonderfully messy case-study, wherein large and reasonably successful organizations indulge in highly non-rational behaviour. That this latter is possible should come to no surprise to folk who have worked in any organization, and yet so much of management theory seems to be predicated upon organizations behaving logically in pursuit of explicit goals. In fact, decisions seem almost to have been made to maximize benefit to the decision taker and have been pursued in almost complete ignorance of the wider issues involved. On the one hand the case could be regarded as a cautionary tale about the perils of systems sub-optimization and non-congruent reward systems; on the other hand it certainly constitutes a salutary lesson about the need for improvement initiatives to be effectively embedded into an organization's culture.

Quality is Dead in Europe – Long Live Excellence: True or False?

B.G. Dale, M. Zairi, A. van der Wiele
and A.R.T. Williams

In many circles total quality management (TQM) is regarded as a "fallen star". Senior managers have tried to introduce it into their organization, often at great expense, and have found it unequal to its initial promise and their expectations. In direct contrast, other companies are still working according to TQM principles and practices. Meanwhile, a third group of companies is making their businesses more efficient by using a set of management initiatives without any over-arching theme, but with a close similarity to TQM.

In our opinion, the lack of success of TQM is not due to the concept but rather the way it has been introduced into an organization and used by managers. It is surprising how many fundamental mistakes are made by senior managers and their advisers in relation to issues such as communication, training, infrastructure, teams and projects, involvement, problem solving, and measurement. In addition, there is a fundamental failure of management to stick to the basics.

It is unclear where the drive came to change from quality and TQM to excellence. We believe it originated from the European Foundation for Quality Management (EFQM) and certain management consultancies. The EFQM acted in response to the perceived tarnished image of TQM, whilst the consultancies sought to address the diminishing demand and increasing competition for their services. In response to the "fallen star" image the EFQM, in its excellence model, has progressively stripped out references to TQM and quality. In the 1999 version of the model, the members of the steering group responsible for the development of the revised model appear to be proud of this. Describing the move from quality management to organizational excellence, Nabitz *et al.* (1999) point out that "The word 'quality' does not appear in either the sub-criteria or the areas to address" and "in the new model, the switch from total

---

Source: B.G. Dale, M. Zairi, A. van der Wiele and A.R.T. Williams (2000) *Measuring Business Excellence*, 4 (3): 4–10. Edited version.

quality management to organizational excellence is a fact." This development has, in turn, been followed by national quality bodies such as the British Quality Foundation (BQF).

It is ironic that at the same time as the EFQM is distancing itself from TQM as a term the Japanese are apparently giving it increased emphasis, as a development from their total quality control (TQC) approach. For example, the theme of the 68th QC Symposium of the Union of Japanese Scientists and Engineers (JUSE), held in June 1999, was "TQM for creating a new Japanese". In addition, there has been no change in the early survey evidence (for example, see McKinsey and Co., 1989) that the quality of Japanese products is superior to that of American products, which in turn is superior to that of the Europeans. This was one of the motivating factors for the establishment of the EFQM, back in 1988.

The Japanese experience of TQC, company-wide quality control (CWQC) or TQM, in respect of the effort spent to develop these and related concepts, shows the inadvisability of tampering with things that work well. Within Japanese business there is a conviction that TQM pays off and considerable belief in, and respect for, what quality can do for the individual, the organization and the government as a whole.

The EFQM was launched in 1988 to encourage European business competitiveness through the use of TQM. Its main mission was, and still is, to create awareness amongst business people of the power of TQM and to demonstrate the benefits of its use and application. A decade or more of sustained effort has seen significant growth of TQM in Europe, in terms of awareness, buy-in and wider application. EFQM case studies confirm many successes across most European countries.

There is therefore no justification for the EFQM to have tampered with the model in the manner described above, particularly at a time when even cynics have started to believe in its value and have started to understand how to use it to best advantage.

The EFQM must answer the following questions for itself, but these should have been considered before stripping out "quality" and "TQM" from the model's criteria and replacing them with "excellence":

- What is wrong with the term TQM? Are people embarrassed about what the model is called? It must be remembered that the customer will continue to demand improvements in quality standards and performance, be it services, product-related or on other dimensions. Quality is not going to go away. The customer will continue to use the concept and insist on tangible evidence that performance is based on quality.
- It is ironic that, for a long time, organizations such as EFQM have accused academics and experts of spending far too much time on jargon building rather than dealing with real substance. Who is guilty now? Who is reminding whom?
- The EFQM should be concerned with the spread of the TQM concept rather than cosmetic and peripheral changes to the excellence model. Positive comments abound about the RADAR (results, approach, deployment, assessment and review) logic, and assessment, review and learning are important in the scoring but these changes are never going to push back the boundaries of quality or excellence. It

appears the effort, resources and energy are spent on "politicizing" the quality movement in Europe rather than ensuring that it works efficiently and effectively. Is the EFQM therefore failing the very business and institutions it is supposed to serve and represent?

- If one looks at the EFQM track record, what has been achieved? There is the model itself with the annual and most prestigious event being the award ceremony. There are conferences, seminars, publicity, networking, benchmarking and learning materials. More efforts should be devoted to learning and understanding how to make TQM work better, how to quantify is benefits in a more meaningful way, how to convince financial institutions and investors of the value of quality, how to introduce TQM at society level – in schools, within the community, and so on. The EFQM should be encouraged to channel its resources to emulate in Europe the good examples from Japan, which can lead to sustainable competitiveness, a long-term perspective on managing businesses and a true belief of the power and importance of quality at all levels and in all fields.

Academics need to challenge the form of term replacement alluded to above and its rationale, "quality and TQM are apparently unpopular, so scrap them and replace with excellence." As veterans of the quality movement – and contributors to the development of the EFQM – we feel it their duty to air the issues surrounding this development and to challenge what has happened. By taking up the theme of excellence, the newcomers to the quality movement are perhaps forgetting or failing to understand what has gone before and the heritage of the quality luminaries. This leads to the second issue that is contributing to the death of quality – the shift away from the quality management basics to a point-scoring mentality.

[...]

Mixed Language

A crucial issue for any organization is clear and good communication. Terms such as "quality", "continuous improvement" and "TQM" should be defined in language which is easily understood by everyone in an organization, and (where feasible) their suppliers and customers – "tabloid newspaper-style" language. Despite the definitions provided by ISO 8402, in 1994 and more recently by ISO 9000:2000 – there is considerable confusion over the use of these terms. As a consequence, there are not only numerous interpretations and definitions but also a variety of concepts, instruments and organizational arrangements, and tools and techniques which underpin TQM. An interesting test for anyone involved in a site visit for an EFQM excellence model assessment is to ask the employees they interview to define "excellence".

It has taken some considerable time to get across to employees within an organization and to the general public the importance of quality, its management and improvement. This form of term replacement not only marginalizes quality but also reinforces the belief that TQM is a fad and quality is no longer an important issue for European business.

Will a new set of terms undermine the undoubted progress which has been made in quality during the last two decades in the western world? Whatever sceptics may think about TQM, continuous improvement, quality assurance or whatsoever approach, however termed, there have been considerable improvements in the products and services which are used in everyday life. According to Cole (1999), "[the quality movement] left in its wake a greatly expanded infrastructure, a partial adaptation of a variety of quality methodologies, and a renewed focus on how to serve customers better and how to use business processes to improve competitive performance".

In terms of the EFQM model, the words "business excellence" (and latterly "excellence") have been in regular use for at least three years but it was only in the 1999 guidelines that a definition was put forward and the principles outlined. There is no rigorous definition of "excellence" or how it differs from "business excellence". This suggests it is just a play on words.

The Origins of Excellence

In the EFQM guidelines for 1999, "excellence" is defined as "Outstanding practice in managing the organization and achieving results, all based on a set of eight fundamental concepts". These fundamental concepts of excellence are "Results orientation; customer focus; leadership and constancy of purpose; management by processes and facts; people development and involvement; continuous learning, innovation and improvement; partnership development; and public responsibility" (EFQM, 1999).

In the draft revision of the ISO 9000 series, the principles of quality management are defined in ISO 9000:2000 as "Customer focus; leadership; involvement of people; process approach; system approach to management; continual improvement; factual approach to decision making and mutually beneficial supplier relationship." Allowing for interpretation of these individual principles it can be seen that there is little or no difference between quality management and excellence. This lack of clear water in definitions is confirmed when comparison is made with the ten- and 14-point cluster summaries of the teachings of Crosby, Deming, Feigenbaum and Juran and with what writers (e.g. Dale, 1999) outline as the elements and practices of TQM. Nor is there any attempt to define excellence in ISO 9000:2000.

All this raises the question as to how the principles of excellence have been selected. Has the TQM literature been trawled and appropriate principles selected and modified by the team responsible for its development to suit the excellence concept? And how has the model been subsequently tested within the EFQM membership?

[...]

There is no firm grounding on which the "principles of excellence" have been developed. The origins seem to be associated with the work of Peters and Waterman (1982) and Peters and Austin (1985). The basis on which the word "excellence" is used by these authors includes some of the following challenges for senior management teams:

- a bias for action;
- getting closer to the customer:
- entrepreneurship and innovation;
- people-based productivity;
- management commitment through hands-on involvement;
- business focus;
- streamlined processes and operations;
- team-based work environment which is driven by shared values; and
- process-based culture.

These so-called prerequisites for excellence are all key ingredients of the TQM philosophy. Are we to conclude that the insistence on excellence is to achieve and establish these objectives? If this is the case, then TQM and excellence are synonymous expressions, so why bother with the change other than for political reasons and to appease those lobbying for the change?

Uppermost in the hearts and minds of most senior managers are survival, improvement and effective competition. Senior managers engage in the marketplace using all their core capabilities to succeed and remain viable, solvent and healthy. Excellence is not necessarily at the core of their actions. Furthermore, believing that excellence can be achieved may encourage complacency and "arrogance" – encouraging companies described as excellent to believe that they have achieved the pinnacle of success. This may partly explain the fall from grace of some of the companies named as "excellent" by Peters and Waterman (1982) and Peters and Austin (1985).

In their haste to embrace the excellence concept, many less mature organizations have skipped over some of the basic and key elements of TQM and have been very selective in what has been adopted, resulting in a highly diluted TQM. An example is the behaviour witnessed in companies aiming for ISO 9000 series certification of their quality management system and in organizations that are aiming to win a quality or excellence award without having in place the basics of the quality management philosophy. Consequently, their approach to the management of the business does not embrace the fundamentals of continuous improvement and they become focused on how many points they have scored or are likely to score against the criteria of the model.

Is TQM Considered Mundane?

One of the simplest excuses for not developing and advancing TQM is to say there is something wrong with the terminology. Studying organizations that have resisted the introduction of a TQM-based change or those that have failed to capitalize on their TQM investment, the same comments and themes reoccur. These include:

- "We couldn't sell it to our senior management team because it is too fluffy and jargonistic."
- "Our culture cannot identify with this terminology. We need to call it something else."
- "We will drive investors away if there is any reference to TQM. We have a serious business to run here and competition is really cut-throat."
- "TQM does not work. The literature says so."
- "TQM is not for us. We haven't got time for it; we need to survive and that is the most important business imperative."

The following are two examples of business leaders who did appreciate the value of TQM. One of them, the current chairman of IBM (a computer manufacturer), who, following the blip that the company had in the early 1990s, said "Thank God for quality; otherwise IBM would not have survived." Whilst the cynics were waiting for IBM to axe wasteful initiatives (and TQM was considered to be the main one), IBM in fact intensified its efforts in this area and became profitable again. Sir Dennis Henderson, ex-chairman of ICI – a coatings, chemicals and materials company – said, "My only regret is that I never got involved in the implementation of TQM at ICI. Although I did not interfere with what my colleagues were doing, I was convinced that the concept [TQM] itself was right for ICI." There are other testimonies from many business leaders who also appreciate what TQM has done for their businesses – many were cynical at first but went on to learn and appreciate the power of TQM.

Another group of commentators is those who continuously make feeble attempts at arguing that TQM is long overdue as a concept and they promise the reader that there is something else instead but never deliver. This includes writers such as Lister, who, in an article entitled "Beyond TQM" wrote: "TQM has not proved to be the panacea for troubled service industries ... Most businesses spend significant amounts ... If an organization's going to embark on a new strategic approach, such as the adoption of service excellence, then it is essential to have the correct process, incremental change process, and customer service management process." Isn't this TQM through the backdoor?

Very often, difficulties associated with the introduction of TQM are to do with resources (Mckowski, 1994), leadership and strategy (Shields, 1994), commitment of senior managers (Evans, 1995), resistance to change (Walsh, 1994), quantification of benefits (Zairi *et al.*, 1994) and lack of systematic methodology (Babbar and Aspelin, 1994).

The Shift from Quality Fundamentals to Points Scoring

The top performing organizations have always undertaken an effective evaluation of their performance to identify what is going well and what needs to be improved. The EFQM has provided a holistic model to facilitate such measurement. The model and the associated self-assessment process have given new direction to the quality movement and have driven deep and lasting changes into organizations. This has helped TQM to "fit" into organizational practice (Van der Wiele, 1998).

Practitioners and academics should continue to support the model and the self-assessment process but there are a number of issues which need to be aired:

- There is a danger that the EFQM and the various national bodies which promote the model are putting all their eggs in one basket and are becoming a "one product" organization.
- The way in which the model is used by some organizations (in the form of a "tick-box" mentality) is resulting in an almost standard method of managing quality and its improvement. In this situation, with the emphasis on detail, on understanding what particular criteria and areas to address are applied to an individual organization, and how to apply the RADAR logic, there is lack of innovation in facilitating systematic process transformation. This shortfall is witnessed both in organizations and in those management consultancies advising businesses in the use of the model.
- There is much well-documented experience and evidence of organizations where the business excellence chanting mantra is rife but those doing the chanting do not have any effective understanding of the major underlying principles of improvement.
- The electronics and automotive industries are most advanced in terms of TQM, at least in the western world. From the 1970s onwards they needed to meet the Japanese quality challenge or go out of business, so they were early adopters of TQM. Non-manufacturing industries only started to consider a TQM approach in the mid-1980s. This pattern of development is not reflected in the profile of organizations which are finalists and winners in the award ceremonies underpinned by the excellence model. This suggests that there is a set of factors in play which are not fully considered by the model and, in addition, there is an assumption that "one size fits all", as far as the weighting of the criteria is concerned. These factors could include strong trade union and labour laws, regulatory controls, process control complexity, supplier and customer interfaces which are out of an individual organization's control, and a range of issues associated with innovation, speed, design and flexibility pressures. Scanning such lists also suggests that some types of organizations are more likely to be award contenders than others. Therefore, the environment in which an organization operates appears to be a key factor on the points scored against the model's criteria.
- The hype surrounding an award event is considerable, despite consoling words from award organizers. Winning an award can be habitual and obsessive. Consequently, some organizations spend considerable time preparing *par excellence* application documents, and resort to ruses and camouflage measures in assessment site visits. This type of displacement activity would be better directed to putting in place improvements which are often self-evident, without resorting to assessment against the excellence model.

- In scoring application award documents, the authors have identified a number of line managers and EFQM-trained assessors who know all the assessment-related language and can put forward well reasoned arguments why a sub-criterion should be scored at 45 per cent rather than 50, but lack deep understanding of TQM and continuous improvement. This leads one to believe that a – very expensive – game is being played.
- Some organizations have spent huge amounts of money on activities relating to self-assessment against the model. In a variety of European settings, senior managers are increasingly raising questions about the value – or lack of it – of this investment. Even when an assessment is complete the organization needs to work out what it should do to get better.

The emphasis of many organizations (mainly those with a lack of experience of continuous improvement) is now on scoring points against the criteria of award models and away from the fundamental basics of the technical essence of quality. Quality management, TQM, business excellence, or excellence – or whatever you want to badge it – has become yet another organizational control system which has to be manipulated and beaten, with high scores attained and improved upon.

How has this state of affairs occurred? The EFQM is run by senior managers to appeal to senior managers. Senior executives appear to like the term excellence, in preference to TQM, and the measures which it brings. It is an easily-sold concept – what self-respecting senior manager does not wish to be associated with excellence? However, it is a different case at middle management level, where commitment is vital to getting the improvements into place. Middle managers like to have something relevant and useful to solve their immediate problems and not to add to them as, for example, improving their scores every year on an EFQM model assessment.

Conclusions

The replacement of quality and TQM by business excellence and excellence poses a question of what terms will be in vogue in 2001 and beyond. We have already seen, within a relatively short period of time, the replacement of business excellence by excellence. The swapping and replacement of terms in response to the perceived tarnished image of TQM does not lead to stability and understanding of quality-related business issues.

The term "excellence" has already started to become subject to ridicule. *The Sunday Times* (Williams, 2000) comments, "When you find people in the public sector using words like 'excellence' they don't mean excellence. They mean saving money." If this theme gets taken up, excellence could be tarnished with the same organizational downsizing brush as business process re-engineering. Whilst term replacement might be OK for quality foundations, management consultancies and businesses, it does not help in the education process of the next generation of managers in the university system. This was one of the original objectives of the EFQM. In the teaching environment, with respect to the EFQM model, lecturers are resorting to the tactic, "for business excellence and excellence read total quality management". One wonders what message is being sent to tomorrow's managers.

Does any of this really matter? Yes it does, for a number of reasons. The situation now, if anything, is worse than when EFQM was founded. The original EFQM was set up to improve European quality in the face of strong Japanese competition. Undoubtedly, as already mentioned in this paper, European quality has improved over the last decade. Also, unfortunately, both Japan and the USA have continued to improve. The urgency is, if anything, even more important in 2000 than it was when the EFQM was founded.

What other basis for competition do we in Europe have? We cannot be the cheapest with our large overhead costs from national and European social programmes. The USA has leapt ahead in hi-tech innovation and in entrepreneurial activity as it has always enjoyed a far better infrastructure. In financing, Europe has always had the advantage of longer-term investors (for example, banks in Germany and investment companies in southern Europe). But now there is a rush to the Anglo-Saxon model of raising money through the US stock market – and, as a consequence, concentration on short-term quarterly results – so that advantage is being steadily eroded. Maybe in design Europe has a chance – but organizations still need to bring designs successfully to the market on time. Business-to-business on the Internet is rapidly becoming central to the majority of sales and purchasing contracting in many business areas. Two essential aspects of being able to buy and sell through the Internet are having well-managed core processes and having a collaborative culture, both of which are areas that a classic TQM approach can help to develop.

Is there hope? Yes, maybe. Although the patient "quality" and "TQM" is being helped – some might say, being pushed – to die. But maybe there is a wonder drug at hand. Classic quality has been reborn in the USA under another new guise. Another new name – not "excellence" this time, but "six sigma". Six sigma is just classic quality engineering stressing lots of the basics, tied into continuous improvement, teamwork and project management. It is put together in an attractive new package and linked to a very powerful organizational change programme. What is good for General Electric must be good for America – and for Europe?

It is important that European business gets back to quality engineering and quality management basics and starts to place less emphasis on scoring points and playing games. The need is urgent because quality engineering skills are not in abundant supply and these can be perceived as non-essential in the excellence era.

It is right and proper to raise the issue of tampering with a concept that has wider implications if not treated seriously. It is important to convey the message that there is nothing wrong with the quality and TQM concept jargon; we have to stop politicizing it and we must devote more time to making it work better. Cosmetics will not make quality sustainable and will not transform society. A re-visit of the purpose of the EFQM and its main mission is urgent. This paper is intended to be the trigger.

References

Babbar, S. and Aspelin, D.J. (1994), "TQM? As easy as ABC", *The TQM Magazine* Vol. 6 No. 3, pp. 32–8.

Cole, R.E. (1999), *Managing Quality Fads,* Oxford University Press, New York, NY.

Dale, B.G. (1999), *Managing Quality,* 3rd ed., Blackwell Publishers, Oxford.

European Foundation for Quality Management (1999), *Assessing for Excellence: A Practical Guide for Self-Assessment,* EFQM, Brussels.

European Quality (2000), Vol. 7 No. 1, February.

Evans, R. (1995), "In defence of TQM", *The TQM Magazine,* Vol. 7 No. 1, pp. 5–6.

Lister, R. (nd), "Beyond TQM", *Management Services,* Vol. 38 No. 5, pp. 8-20.

Nabitz, U., Quaglia, G. and Wangen, P. (1999), "EFQM's new excellence model", *Quality Progress,* October, pp. 118-20.

McKinsey and Company (1989), "Management of quality: the single most important challenge for Europe", *European Quality Management Forum,* Montreux, Switzerland, October.

Mckowski, S.J. (1994), "Quality management: a bitter pill to swallow or a panacea for our pains?", *The TQM Magazine,* Vol. 6 No. 5, pp. 5–6.

Oakland, J.S. (1993), *Total Quality Management: The Route to Imporving Performance,* 2nd ed., Butterworth-Heinemann, London.

Peters, T. and Austin, N. (1985), *A passion for Excellence,* Collins, London.

Peters, T. and Waterman, R.H. (1982), *In Search of Excellence,* Harper & Row, London.

Shields, M. (1994), "Total quality management: another mast to tie your flag to, or a means to change a company's culture?", *The TQM Magazine,* Vol. 6 No. 5, pp. 45–6.

Van der Wiele, A. (1998), *Beyond Fads: Management Fads and Organizational Change with Reference to Quality Management,* Eburon Publishers.

Walsh, P. (1994), "Overcoming TQM fatigue", *The TQM Magazine,* Vol. 6 No. 5, pp. 58–64.

Williams, N. (2000), "They play games, and then they sack you", *The Sunday Times,* 6 February, p. 5.3.

Zairi *et al.* (1994), "Does TQM impact on bottom line results?", *The TQM Magazine,* Vol. 6 No. 1, pp. 38–43.

6

An Overview of Continuous Improvement: From the Past to the Present

Nadia Bhuiyan and Amit Baghel

Introduction

Continuous improvement (CI) is a philosophy that Deming described simply as consisting of "Improvement initiatives that increase successes and reduce failures" (Juergensen, 2000). Another definition of CI is "a company-wide process of focused and continuous incremental innovation" (Bessant *et al.*, 1994). Yet others view CI as either as an offshoot of existing quality initiatives like total quality management (TQM) or as a completely new approach of enhancing creativity and achieving competitive excellence in today's market (Oakland, 1999; Caffyn, 1999; Gallagher *et al.*, 1997). According to Kossoff (1993), total quality can be achieved by constantly pursuing CI through the involvement of people from all organizational levels.

We define CI more generally as a culture of sustained improvement targeting the elimination of waste in all systems and processes of an organization. It involves everyone working together to make improvements without necessarily making huge capital investments. CI can occur through evolutionary improvement, in which case improvements are incremental, or though radical changes that take place as a result of an innovative idea or new technology. Often, major improvements take place over time as a result of numerous incremental improvements. On any scale, improvement is achieved through the use of a number of tools and techniques dedicated to searching for sources of problems, waste, and variation, and finding ways to minimize them.

Over the past decades, CI has been studied from many perspectives. In this paper, our objective is to present the history and evolution of CI, from its early beginnings to sophisticated CI methodologies that are widely used in practice in quality management programs today. We start by discussing the origins of CI, followed by a description of the methodologies that have evolved over the years, and we trace how organizations have used various tools and techniques to address the need for improvement on various levels. The paper also presents research conducted in this field. Through a literature review, we describe the existing research on CI in order to gain an understanding

Source: N. Bhuiyan and A. Baghel (2005) *Management Decision*, 43 (5): 761–71. Edited version.

of how the use of CI has had an impact on organizations, the tools and techniques that are needed to achieve an ongoing cycle of improvement, and the relation of CI to quality and the organization.

History and Evolution of CI

The roots of modern improvement programs can be traced back to initiatives undertaken in several companies in the 1800s, where management encouraged employee-driven improvements, and incentive programs were set in place to reward employees that brought about positive changes in the organization (Schroeder and Robinson, 1991). In 1894, National Cash Register's program included reward schemes, employee development opportunities, and improving labour-management relationships. During the late 1800s and early 1900s, much attention was given to scientific management; this involved developing methods to help managers analyze and solve production problems using scientific methods based on tightly controlled time-trials to achieve proper piece rates and labour standards. The US government then set up the "Training Within Industry" service during the Second World War to enhance the industrial output on a national scale. This included job method training, a program designed to educate supervisors on the importance and techniques of CI methods. This program was later introduced in Japan by management experts like Deming, Juran, and Gilbreth, and by the US forces present there after the end of the Second World War (Robinson, 1990). Eventually, the Japanese developed their own ideas, and quality control, which was used initially in the manufacturing process, had evolved into a much broader term, growing into a management tool for ongoing improvement involving everyone in an organization (Imai, 1986).

While CI initiatives in the past reflected the use of various principles related to work improvement, modern day CI is associated with organized and comprehensive methodologies. These CI programs, in which typically the overall organization, or a large part of it, is involved in change, are also more popularly associated with the introduction of the TQM movement, which also gained leverage in Japan thanks to Edwards Deming.

CI Methodologies

Over the decades, as the need to continuously improve on a larger scale within the organization became an imperative, a number of CI methodologies have developed based on a basic concept of quality or process improvement, or both, in order to reduce waste, simplify the production line and improve quality. The best known of them are: lean manufacturing, six sigma, the balanced scorecard, and lean six sigma.

Lean Manufacturing

Henry Ford systemized lean manufacturing during the early nineteenth century when he established the concept of mass production in his factories. The Japanese adopted lean manufacturing and improved it. This methodology is a systematic approach to identifying and eliminating waste through CI by following the product at the pull of the customer in pursuit of perfection.

In the 1950s, the Toyota Motor Company first implemented Quality Circles within the production process itself. As the Second World War came to an end, Taiichi Ohno, former executive vice president of Toyota, was given the task of developing an efficient production system for the manufacture of automobiles in Japan. Learning a great deal from Henry Ford's assembly lines, and customizing a production process to suit the needs of the Japanese markets, which called for lower volumes of cars, Ohno pioneered and developed the world renowned Toyota production system (TPS), also known as lean manufacturing and now used throughout the world (Womack *et al.,* 1990). The methodology is designed to maintain a continuous flow of products in factories in order to flexibly adjust to changes in demand. The basis of such a flow is called just-in-time (JIT) production, where, through systematic techniques designed to minimize scrap and inventory, and essentially, all forms of waste, quality and productivity are increased, and costs are decreased.

The aim of lean manufacturing is the elimination of waste in every area of production and includes customer relations, product design, supplier networks, and factory management. Womack and Jones (1996) describe lean thinking as the "antidote" to *muda,* the Japanese term for waste. Its goal is to incorporate less human effort, less inventory, less time to develop products, and less space in order to become highly responsive to customer demand while producing top quality products in the most efficient and economical manner possible. Waste is defined as anything for which the customer is not willing to pay. Lean manufacturing, if applied correctly, results in the ability of an organization to learn. Mistakes in the organization are not generally repeated because this in itself is a form of waste that the lean philosophy seeks to eliminate (Robinson, 1990). The lean toolbox is used to eliminate anything that does not add value to a process. According to the $US5 million study done by Womack and Jones, the Japanese manufacturers were twice as effective as their US and other Western counterparts. They determined that the three principles of lean manufacturing are: improve flow of material and information across business function; focus on pull by the customer; commitment of organizations to CI (Womack *et al.,* 1990; Womack and Jones, 1996).

Six Sigma

More recently, six sigma began to gain popularity in the USA in 1986, when Motorola Inc. introduced it as a means of measuring process quality using statistical process control. Motorola went about on a mission to improve its services and products considerably in a span of five years, and to achieve its goal, the six sigma program was launched in 1987. Six sigma has been defined as "an organized and systematic method for strategic process improvement and new product and service development that relies on statistical methods and the scientific method to make dramatic reductions in the customer defined defect rates" (Linderman *et al.,* 2003). Minimizing defects to the level of accepting close to zero was at the heart of the methodology, and focuses on reducing variation in all the processes of the organization. To achieve this, the DMAIC model was developed, i.e. define opportunities, measure performance, analyze opportunities, improve performance, and control performance. Six sigma provides quality measurement that can be used throughout an organization – not only in manufacturing but also in design, administrative, and service areas.

Motorola achieved amazing results through the application of six sigma, from 1987 to 1997, achieving a total savings of $US14 billion while sales enjoyed a fivefold growth during the same period (Klefsjö et al., 2001). Investing in six sigma programs is increasingly considered a mission-critical best practice, even among mid-sized and smaller firms. After the evolution of lean manufacturing, other pioneers have used the six-sigma process to achieve their company's unprecedented goal of a hundred-fold improvement in quality within five years. Top organizations such as GE, ABB, Honeywell, Sony, Honda, and Ford have followed Motorola's lead and have been using six sigma to achieve business excellence.

Balanced Scorecard

In the early 1990s, Robert Kaplan and David Norton developed a methodology that translates the objectives of the organizations into measures, goals and initiatives in four different perspectives, namely financial, customer, internal business process and learning and growth. This methodology came to be known as the balanced scorecard. A balanced scorecard is generally used to clarify and update the business strategy, link the objectives of the organization to the annual budgets, allow organizational change, and increase the understanding of the company vision and mission statements across the organization. A balanced scorecard can be used to translate an organization's mission and vision statements into a broad set of objectives and performance measures that can be quantified and appraised, and measures whether management is achieving desired results. About 50 per cent of the *Fortune* 1,000 companies have a balanced scorecard system in place (Kaplan and Norton, 1996). Niven (2002) refers to the balanced scorecard as a combination of a measurement system, a strategic management system, and a communication tool:

- *Measurement system.* The balanced scorecard helps the organization translate its vision and strategy through the objectives and measures defined rather than stressing on financial measures which provide little guidance. According to Gaplin (1997) "measurable goals and objectives" is one of the most important factors to a successful strategy.
- *Strategic management system.* The balanced scorecard helps organizations align short-term actions with their strategy and thus removes barriers towards organizations strategic implementation in the long term.
- *Communication tool.* The balanced scorecard describes the organizations strategy clarifies and brings it to the average employee. Employees, once aware of the organizations strategies, can contribute towards the overall goal (Niven, 2002).

Deming believed that traditional quality assurance methods, such as product inspection after manufacture, were inefficient at finding the source of variations, which occurred throughout the production process. He pointed out that all business processes had to be considered and that they all needed feedback loops in order to improve. The balanced scorecard considers feedback not only in process outputs, but also in business strategy outputs. Rather than improving the performance of existing processes, the emphasis needs to be placed on processes that must be executed successfully for an organization's strategy to succeed. A balanced scorecard consists of managerial tools used for performance evaluation and the types of feedback it considers provide the guidance needed to continuously improve.

Hybrid Methodology

While individual CI programs help to improve organizational operations in many aspects, they are not necessarily effective at solving all issues. To overcome the weaknesses of one program or another, more recently, a number of companies have merged different CI initiatives together, resulting in a combined CI program that is more far reaching than any one individually. Lean six sigma is the most well-known hybrid methodology, a combination of six sigma and lean manufacturing. The evolution of this hybrid has taken place since maintaining high production rates and high quality, or producing less waste, simply does not address enough areas that require improvement. For example, lean cannot bring a process under statistical control and six sigma alone cannot dramatically improve process speed or reduce invested capital. So the benefits of both six sigma and lean manufacturing were combined. As another example, TQM was being used as the primary quality initiative by the manufacturing organizations, but with TQM there is no clear way of prioritizing which quality project should receive the highest priority, and projects are carried out irrespective of the cost to the corporation. This was one of the reasons for the advent of six sigma. Six sigma is quite explicit about the financial benefits expected from each and every effort. According to six sigma, each and every black belt and champion are expected to contribute between $100,000 and $250,000 of incremental profit every year (George, 2002). However, Tatham and Mackertich (2003) state that while six sigma can be beneficial, it is not appropriate for widespread use.

Lean six sigma

After the apparent benefits of lean and six sigma were brought to the attention of the business world, there were a number of big conglomerates that had implemented both lean and six sigma to attain business excellence. To get a bigger share of the market, they developed a new methodology called lean six sigma. Since lean six sigma is a relatively new methodology, and as such, has not been studied in great detail. Some organizations have been using both methodologies in parallel to each other for years, while some have focused on just lean six sigma as a single methodology for improvement. Lean manufacturing and six sigma individually cannot achieve the required improvements at the rate at which lean six sigma can. Lean six sigma maximizes shareholders value by achieving the fastest rate of improvement in customer satisfaction, cost, quality, process speed and invested capital (George, 2002). Using a combination of lean and six sigma, greater value to the customer can be provided. While lean seeks to eliminate waste, six sigma seeks to reduce variation. By combining the two, waste is first removed, which then allows for variations to be spotted more easily. Lean six sigma also addresses important issues that are overlooked by six sigma and lean manufacturing individually: the steps in the process that should be first tackled; the order in which they should be applied and to what extent and the ways in which significant improvements can be made in terms of cost, quality and lead times. The fusion of the two helps organizations maximize their potential for improvement.

Existing Research

The literature shows that there exists no theoretical basis for CI (Savolainen, 1998). CI tends to be used as a general term that has acquired many of its attributes from other quality initiatives such as TQM and lean manufacturing. While valuable research has been conducted on CI (Bessant *et al.*, 1994; Bessant and Caffyn, 1997), more perspectives are required (Gilmore, 1999).

Lillrank and Kano (1989) refer to CI, or *kaizen,* the Japanese term for CI, as the "principle of improvement"; however, the Japanese Union for Scientists and Engineers (JUSE) literature does not clearly define *kaizen,* but uses it to define other concepts. While the term *kaizen* is often considered synonymous with CI, Imai (1986) proposes that there exist at least three types of *kaizen:* management-, group-, and individual-oriented *kaizen.* Management-oriented *kaizen* is considered to be the most important one as it focuses on the company strategy and involves everyone in the company. Group-oriented *kaizen* is best represented by quality circles, which require employees to form a team or a circle with the goal of finding and solving problems faced during their day-to-day work without any interference from management. Individual-oriented *kaizen* is derived from the concept of bottom-up design, in which the worker makes a recommendation to the problem faced. This has been very successful in the Japanese industry since it is the worker who is on the shop floor and typically knows the best solution to an existing problem. Certain industries even have incentive programs where, depending on the problem and the solution provided, the worker is rewarded, thus encouraging the workers to concentrate on problem areas and find the best solution.

Jha *et al.* (1996) have found that there exists a close link between CI and quality in their survey of the literature. Imai (1986) defines total quality control (TQC) as "organized *kaizen* activities involving everyone in a company- managers and workers, in a totally integrated effort toward improving performance at every level". The link between CI and quality has been expressed by Berger (1996), who asserts that CI "should rightfully be regarded as a general development perspective, applicable with or without the context of TQM". However, from the large number of researchers who associate CI with quality, and from the mere implication that CI seeks to improve, it appears that there exists a link between the two, in some form or another.

CI programs were initially developed in organizations with product-focused processes or repetitive processes, i.e. with relatively high standardization of products and processes.

Special teams were organized to work on improvement tasks, which were separate from their typical organizational tasks. Berger (1997) suggests that improvement tasks can be integrated into the regular work of individual employees, and that depending on product design and process choice, CI must be adapted to the degree of standardization involved. The implication is that CI programs can be applied to different types of work environments. The author presents a typology of organizational designs for CI based on two dimensions: basic task design (where the two forms of this dimension are individual vs group tasks), and improvement task (parallel vs integrated). Basic task design is reliant on the work process and product standardization: within this dimension, group tasks are more common in places with a low degree of standardization whereas individual tasks are prevalent in places that have high product standardization systems. In a highly standardized production system, the improvement task is the responsibility of an individual who might be a professional from engineering, quality, etc., and is qualified and trained in the improvement activities. In the case of production systems with a low degree of standardization, there is no resident expert who takes care of improvement, but teams consisting of ordinary employees try to carry out improvement activities within their work groups. An improvement task deals with the different levels of integration in which improvement activities are separated from ordinary work and they run parallel to each other, also known as parallel tasks. An integrated task is one in which improvement activities are embedded as part of the everyday activities of the employee.

Berger's typology presents five organizational designs based on the two dimensions:

(1) *Quality control circles:* a group of people in the staff who meet regularly to discuss problems and issues related to quality so that they may examine them and come up with solutions.
(2) *Wide-focus CI*: a blend of organic CI and expert task force CI (described below). It is used for temporary operations and for CI in self-managed work groups by combining continuous improvement process teams.
(3) *Organic CI:* multifunctional work groups are integrated with improvement activities. Organic CI is different from other CI models since the improvement activities are not left to the experts for design and planning and the decision-making is not left to the authorities outside the group.
(4) *Expert task force CI:* this form of CI is based on the reliance on temporary expert task force consisting of professionals from quality, engineering and maintenance and therefore the span of improvement tasks requires considerable time and investment.
(5) *Individual CI:* improvements are set off by individuals and generally organized in the form of a suggestion system. Individuals come up with ideas and the implementation of the ideas is left to the specialists.

Lindberg and Berger (1997) have studied the applicability of CI in various types of organizations. The authors found that a number of Swedish organizations with a relatively low degree of standardization of products and processes had successfully integrated CI in work teams. The main thrust of the study was to emphasize the fact that in the traditional Japanese industries, *kaizen* improvements were being achieved by running the *kaizen* activities parallel to the regular work of the employees, which was in total contrast to the concept followed by organizations in Sweden, where CI was integrated into the regular work routines. The parallel structure does have some advantage as it leads to interdepartmental collaboration but it also leads to higher administrative costs (Krishnan *et al.*, 1993).

The CI capability model (Bessant and Caffyn, 1997), developed at CENTRIM at the University of Brighton in the UK, provides a powerful outline and arrangement for evaluating the usefulness of CI implementation. The authors present a framework with suggested routines and behaviours needed to successfully implement CI, and the characteristics needed by companies to develop CI capability. According to Caffyn (1999), CI capability can be defined as "the ability of an organization to gain strategic advantage by extending involvement in innovation to a significant proportion of its members". It comprises a set of ten generic CI behaviours that are seen as essential fundamentals in organizations of all types and sizes:

(1) employee demonstrates awareness and understanding of the organization's aims and objectives;
(2) individual groups use the organization's strategic goals and objectives to focus and prioritize their improvement activity;
(3) the enabling mechanisms (e.g. training, teamwork) used to encourage involvement in CI are monitored and developed;
(4) ongoing assessment ensures that the organization's structure, systems and procedures, and the approach and mechanism used to develop CI, constantly reinforce and support each other;
(5) managers at all levels display active commitment to, and leadership of, CI;
(6) throughout the organization people engage proactively in incremental improvement;
(7) there is effective working across internal and external boundaries at all levels;
(8) people learn from their own and from other's experience, both positive and negative;
(9) the learning of individuals and groups is captured and deployed; and
(10) people are guided by a shared set of cultural value underpinning CI as they go about their everyday work.

It has been found that some of these behaviours might be difficult to practice because firms might find it difficult to break the traditional mindset and encourage their employees to adapt to these new mindsets. However, in order to sustain such behaviour amongst all employees, this model identifies the requirements for a set of CI enablers such as facilitators, recognition systems or company procedures and company policies, which are meant to advance the required CI behaviour, but need to be monitored and developed over a period of time.

Jha *et al.* (1996) state that a better understanding of how CI contributes to an organization's mission and strategy will increase the chances of success. They have also found that there exist distinct elements of CI that revolve around problem solving and make use of problem-solving tools, namely work processes, work simplification, and performance monitoring.

[...]

Discussion

Continuous improvement programs have evolved from traditional manufacturing-focused systems that concentrate on the production line to reduce waste and improve the product quality, into comprehensive, systematic methodologies that focus on the entire organization, from top management to the workers on the shop floor. More recently, large organizations are developing their own CI methodologies to fit their specific needs by encompassing the various tools and techniques of individual methodologies. This signals the need for hybrid methodologies. While CI has evolved over the decades, the basic underlying factor driving this change has been the endless pursuit of organizations to improve.

[...]

Research shows that CI can take place at three different levels within the organization: at the management, group, and individual levels. At the management level, the implications of CI are on the organization's strategy. Group level CI involves problem-solving tasks at a broad level, while individual level CI deals with improvement on a micro scale, i.e. on low level, day-to-day tasks. In order to reap maximum benefits from a CI program, managers must implement CI at each of these levels. CI programs can be applied to different types of work environments. Managers need to evaluate the product design, process choice, and the degree of standardization involved in the organization, and can then decide upon the appropriate methods to use to best implement improvement practices. Managers can evaluate the usefulness of CI programs by monitoring a set of routines and behaviours that are seen as being essential to organizations of all types for CI implementation. It is clear that CI does not come without hardships and struggles; without the active involvement of everyone in the organization, and the required resources and support from top management, CI in any organization cannot be successful.

[...]

References

Berger, A. (1996), "Perspectives on manufacturing development – discontinuous change and continuous improvement", PhD thesis, Chalmers University of Technology, Göteborg.

Berger, A. (1997), "Continuous improvement and kaizen: standardization and organizational designs", *Journal of Integrated Manufacturing Systems,* Vol. 8 No. 2, pp. 110–7.

Bessant, J. and Caffyn, S. (1997), "High involvement innovation", *International Journal of Technology Management,* Vol. 14 No. 1, pp. 7–28.

Bessant, J., Caffyn, S., Gilbert, J., Harding, R. and Webb, S. (1994), "Rediscovering continuous improvement", *Technovation,* Vol. 14 No. 1, pp. 17–29.

Caffyn, S. (1999), "Development of a continuous improvement self-assessment, tools", *International Journal of Operations & Production Management*, Vol. 19 No. 11, pp. 118–53.

Gallagher, M., Austin, S. and Caffyn, S. (1997), *Continuous Improvement in Action: The Journey of Eight Companies*, Kogan Page, London.

Gaplin, T. (1997), *Making Strategy Work*, Jossey-Bass, San Francisco, CA.

George, M. (2002), *Lean Six Sigma: Combining Six Sigma Quality with Lean Production Speed*, McGraw-Hill, New York, NY.

Gilmore, H. (1999), "Continuous incremental improvement: an operations strategy for higher quality, lower costs, and global competitiveness", in Costin, H. (Ed.), *Strategies for Quality Improvement*, The Dryden Press, Hinsdale, IL, pp. 47–55.

Imai, M. (1986), *Kaizen: The Key to Japan's Competitive Success*, Random House, New York, NY.

Jha, S., Michela, J. and Noori, H. (1996), "The dynamics of continuous improvement: aligning organizational attributes and activities for quality and productivity", *International Journal of Quality Science*, Vol. 1 No. 1, pp. 19–47.

Juergensen, T. (2000), *Continuous Improvement: Mindsets, Capability, Process, Tools and Results*, The Juergensen Consulting Group, Inc., Indianapolis, IN.

Kaplan, R. and Norton, D. (1996), *The Balanced Scorecard: Translating Strategy into Action*, Harvard Business School Press, Cambridge, MA.

Klefsjö, B., Wiklund, H. and Edgeman, R. (2001), "Six sigma as a methodology for total quality management", *Measuring Business Excellence*, Vol. 5 No. 1, pp. 31–5.

Kossoff, L. (1993), "Total quality or total chaos?", *HR Magazine*, Vol. 38 No. 4, pp. 131–4.

Krishnan, R., Shani, A., Grant, R. and Baer, R. (1993), "In search of quality improvement: problems of design and implementation", *Academy of Management Executive*, Vol. 7 No. 4, pp. 7–20.

Lillrank, P. and Kano, N. (1989), *Continuous Improvement: Quality Control Circles in Japanese Industry*, Center for Japanese Studies, University of Michigan, Ann Arbor, MI.

Lindberg, P. and Berger, A. (1997), "Continuous improvement – design, organization and management", *International Journal of Technology Management*, Vol. 14 No. 1, pp. 86–101.

Linderman, K., Schroeder, R., Zaheer, S. and Choo, A. (2003), "Six sigma: a goal – theoretic perspective", *Journal of Operations Management*, Vol. 21 No. 2, pp. 193–203.

Niven, P. (2002), *Balanced Scorecard Step by Step: Maximizing Performance and Maximizing Results*, John Wiley & Sons, New York, NY.

Oakland, J. (1999), *Total Organizational Excellence – Achieving World-Class Performance*, Butterworth-Heinemann, Oxford.

Robinson, A. (1990), *Modern Approaches to Manufacturing Improvement*, Productivity Press, Portland, OR.

Savolainen, T. (1998), "Cycles of continuous improvement, realizing competitive advantages through quality", *International Journal of Operations & Production Management*, Vol. 19 No. 11, pp. 1203–22.

Schroeder, D. and Robinson, A. (1991), "America's most successful export to Japan: continuous improvement programs", *Sloan Management Review*, Vol. 32 No. 3, pp. 67–81.

Tatham, M. and Mackertich, N. (2003), "Is six sigma falling short of expectations", *Optimize*, pp. 19–21.

Womack, J. and Jones, D. (1996), *Lean Thinking*, Simon and Schuster, New York, NY.

Womack, J., Jones, D. and Roos, D. (1990), *The Machine That Changed the World*, Macmillan Publishing, New York, NY.

7

Learning to Evolve: A Review of Contemporary Lean Thinking

Peter Hines, Matthias Holweg and Nick Rich

Introduction

A Brief History of Lean

The origins of lean thinking can be found on the shop-floors of Japanese manufacturers and, in particular, innovations at Toyota Motor Corporation (Shingo, 1981, 1988; Monden, 1983; Ohno, 1988). These innovations, resulting from a scarcity of resources and intense domestic competition in the Japanese market for automobiles, included the just-in-time (JIT) production system, the kanban method of pull production, respect for employees and high levels of employee problem-solving/automated mistake proofing. This lean operations management design approach focused on the elimination of waste and excess from the tactical product flows at Toyota (the Toyota "seven wastes") and represented an alternative model to that of capital-intense mass production (with its large batch sizes, dedicated assets and "hidden wastes"). For a full account of these systems, methods, processes and techniques see Monden (1983). Much of the early work at Toyota was applied under the leadership of Taiichi Ohno to car engine manufacturing during the 1950s, later to vehicle assembly (1960s), and the wider supply chain (1970s). It was only at this latter point that supplier manuals were produced and the "secrets" of this lean approach were shared with companies outside Toyota for the first time. These manuals were written in Japanese, and it took almost another decade before the first English literature was available (e.g. Shingo, 1981; Schonberger, 1982; Hall, 1983; Monden, 1983; Sandras, 1989).

Still, the interest taken in lean by the western manufacturing community was limited until the performance gaps between Toyota and other carmakers were highlighted by the book *The Machine that Changed the World*, which also coined the term "lean production" (or "lean manufacturing") (Womack *et al.*, 1990). The exploration of the enterprise model, the infrastructure and practices that support lean production, promoted explicitly a thesis of "transference" and the ability of non-automotive and

Source: P. Hines, M. Holweg and N. Rich (2004) *International Journal of Operations and Production*, 24 (10): 994–1011. Edited version.

non-Japanese emulation based upon the premise that manufacturing problems and technologies were "universal problems" facing management (Womack *et al.*, 1990). Sparked by the superior performance achieved by lean producers over the performance of traditional mass production system designs, western manufacturers emulated the shop-floor techniques, the structural parts of lean, but often found it difficult to introduce the organisational culture and mindset. So many early lean efforts showed localised impact only, and fell short of their intended impact on the overall system's performance (Holweg and Pil, 2001). In this awareness period (up to 1990), the main weaknesses of lean manufacturing were its automotive manufacturing-based view and limited appreciation of how to handle variability in demand. The implementation was entirely too-focused, and generally neglected the human aspects of the high-performance work system core to the lean manufacturing approach.

After 1990, there was a gradual widening of focus away from the shop-floor, a trend often ignored by omission, error or design by many detractors. This process of "extension" was also accelerated by the promotion of successful western case emulation by businesses in diverse sectors that had adapted their production systems to include a new design based upon "lean principles" (Womack and Jones, 1996). These principles involved the identification of customer value, the management of the value stream, developing the capability to flow production, the use of "pull" mechanisms to support flow of materials at constrained operations and finally the pursuit of perfection through reducing to zero all forms of waste in the production system (see Womack and Jones, 1996). This evolution may be summarised as a focus on quality during the literature of the early 1990s, through quality, cost and delivery (late 1990s), to customer value from 2000 onwards, as shown in Table 7.1.

Also during the mid-1990s, the value stream concept evolved and was seen to extend beyond manufacturing or the single company, and stretch from customer needs right back to raw material sources (Hines and Rich, 1997; Rother and Shook, 1998). This provided the link between lean and the supply chain, as for the first time, the production "pull" was extended beyond the boundary of the single factory to include the up- and downstream partners.

The Relationship Between Value and Cost

A critical point in the lean thinking is the focus on value. Often however, value creation is seen as equal to cost reduction. This represents a common yet critical shortcoming of the understanding of lean. Therefore, let us examine the relationship between customer value and cost in detail.

In 1996, Womack and Jones, crystallised value as the first principle of lean thinking (Womack and Jones, 1996). As such, lean had moved away from a merely "shop-floor-focus" on waste and cost reduction, to an approach that contingently sought to enhance value (or perceived value) to customers by adding product or service features and/or removing wasteful activities.

This was a key development, as value was linked to customer requirements, and no longer was simply define through its opposite, waste, on the shop-floor. Regardless of whether an activity appeared to be wasteful from a shop-floor point of view or be costly, it is the customer that ultimately decides what constitutes muda[1] and what does not.

Table 7.1   *The evolution of lean thinking*

Phases	1980–1990 Awareness	1990–mid 1990 Quality	Mid 1990–2000 Quality, cost and delivery	2000+Value system
Literature theme	Dissemination of shop-floor practices	Best practice movement, benchmarking leading to emulation	Value stream thinking, lean enterprise, collaboration in the supply chain	Capability at system level
Focus	JIT techniques, cost	Cost, training and promotion, TQM, process reengineering	Cost, process-based to support flow	Value and cost, tactical to strategic, integrated to supply chain
Key business process	Manufacturing, shop-floor only	Manufacturing and materials management	Order fulfilment	Integrated processes, such order fulfilment and new product development
Industry sector	Automotive – vehicle assembly	Automotive – vehicle and component assembly	Manufacturing in general – often focused on repetitive manufacturing	High and low volume manufacturing, extension into service sectors
Shingo (1981, 1988)	Shingo (1981, 1988) Schonberger (1982, 1986) Monden (1983) Ohno (1988) Mather (1988)	Womack et al. (1990) Hammer (1990) Stalk and Hout (1990) Harrison (1992) Anderson Consulting (1993, 1994)	Lamming (1993) MacBeth and Ferguson (1994) Womack and Jones (1994, 1996) Rother and Shook (1998)	Bateman (2000) Hines and Taylor (2000) Holweg and Pil (2001) Abbas et al. (2001) Hines et al. (2002)

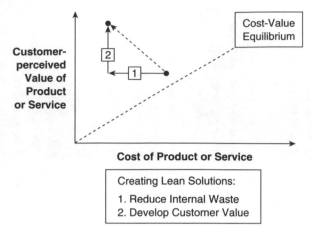

Figure 7.1 *Relation of value, cost and waste*

Figure 7.1 highlights the relationship between value and cost, and shows how products or services can be plotted with regards to their relative cost-value proposition to the customer. The further above the cost-value equilibrium a product/service can be positioned, the more attractive proposition it is to the customers. The cost-value equilibrium denotes the situation whereby the product provides exactly as much value, which the customer is willing to pay for, as the product costs. This migration from a mere waste reduction focus to a customer value focus opens essentially a second avenue of value creation:

- Value is created if internal waste is reduced, as the wasteful activities and the associated costs are reduced, increasing the overall value proposition for the customer.
- Value is also increased, if additional features or services are offered, which are valued by the customer. This could entail a shorter delivery cycle or smaller delivery batches, which might not add additional cost, yet add customer value.

Objectives

Lean as a concept has evolved over time, and will continue to do so. As a result of this development, significant confusion about what is lean, and what is not has arisen – a fact clearly observable at both academic and practitioner conferences in logistics and operations management. The key objective of this paper is therefore to provide a framework that explains the developments of the lean concept over time. The questions we seek to answer are:

- What are the key stages of the lean evolution?
- Within these stages, what are the key criticisms? And subsequently;
- Are these criticisms justified?

Overall, we seek to set a vision to help companies to see where they can evolve to in their lean thinking, as well as developing a framework to understanding this using organisational learning theoretical underpinning, in particular the framework suggested by McGill and Slocum (1993).

Criticism of Lean

Introduction

In its development over time, critics either from within or outside the lean movement have rightly pointed to various gaps in lean thinking. As lean thinking evolved however, these gaps changed. Table 7.2 gives a summary of the gaps in lean thinking and its main critics over time.

This evolution is largely driven because of the shortcomings of lean that surfaced as organisations progressed on their learning curve, as well as the extension of lean thinking into new sectors with different settings and constraints. Key aspects of this criticism are the lack of contingency and ability to cope with variability, the lack of consideration of human aspects, and the narrow operational focus on the shop-floor. Let us examine these in more detail.

Lack of Contingency

There is still a general misunderstanding of the contingent nature required to apply lean thinking. Indeed, the otherwise excellent *Learning to See* publication from the Lean Enterprise Institute (LEI) failed in its first incarnation to have an appropriate focus on demand variability and quality issues (Rother and Shook, 1998). However, this lesson had been learnt by the time that the extension *Seeing the Whole* was published in 2002 (Jones and Womack, 2002).

This having been said, for many companies the major focus of lean implementation is still the shop floor and their search for competitive advantage has yet to rely on the more recent lean integrative approaches. Indeed, the car industry, the "mother of lean thinking", is still largely in this shop-floor dimension and has focused largely on optimising the car assembler and first tier supplier tier (Holweg and Jones, 2001). The paradoxical situation of piecemeal lean application is that the most productive car plants in Europe produce into the highest level of finished stocks in Europe.

What is needed in the car industry is an aligned supply that provides strategic value to the customer, by building cars to customer order (Holweg and Pil, 2001). Interestingly, this is a conclusion reached by Monden, who codified the Toyota production system in 1983. However, even Toyota in Japan has so far failed to produce more than two-thirds of their cars to real customer order.[2] The result of this "build-to-forecast" approach across Europe is that there are currently $18bn of unsold vehicles held in European markets, and 350,000 units in UK alone (see Fisher, 1997; Holweg and Jones, 2001; Holweg and Pil, 2001; Holweg, 2003 for more detail).

Table 7.2   *The main gaps and criticisms of lean thinking*

	1980–1990	1990–mid 1990	Mid 1990–1999	2000+
Key gaps	Outside shop-floor Inter-company aspects Systemic thinking Auto assembly only	Mainly auto Human resources, exploitation of workers Supply chain aspects System dynamics aspects	Coping with variability Integration of processes Inter-company relationships Still mainly auto Integrating industries	Global aspects Understanding customer value Low volume industries Strategic integration E-business
Main critics	Carlisle and Parker (1989) Fucini and Fucini (1990)	Williams *et al.* (1992) Garrahan and Stewart (1992) Rineheart *et al.* (1993)	Davidow and Malone (1992) Cusumano (1994) Goldman *et al.* (1995) Harrison *et al.* (1999) Suri (1999) Schonberger and Knod (1997)	Bateman (2000) Christopher and Towill (2001) van Hoek *et al.* (2001)

Human Aspects

A further aspect that has attracted criticism is that lean production systems could be viewed through a Marxist lens as being exploitative and high pressure to the shop floor workers. Chief among the critics in this area are Garrahan and Stewart (1992) in their studies of the UK Nissan facility, a site that repeatedly has achieved the highest output of cars per worker in Europe.[3] In a similar vein, Williams *et al.* (1992) suggest that lean production is de-humanising and exploitative. Although such left-wing authors have failed to gain widespread support for their views, they have however raised an important point for those academics and practitioners interested in applying lean thinking, namely that lean should be regarded as more than a set of mechanistic hard tools and techniques and the human dimensions of motivation, empowerment and respect for people are very important. Indeed, the present authors would argue that these elements are key to the long-term sustainability of any lean programme, regardless of the industry sector.

Scope and Lack of Strategic Perspective

Linked to this last criticism is the almost complete lack of discussion of strategic level thinking in lean programmes as opposed to discussions of how to apply a series of different tools and techniques until quite recently. Again the current authors would argue that this gap has led to a lack of sustainability of many lean transformation programmes. In particular, the use of policy deployment and other strategy formation and deployment tools is of central importance (see for instance, Hines and Taylor, 2000; Hines *et al.*, 2002). Earlier references to such strategic thinking are either consigned to isolated academic papers (such as Tennant and Roberts, 2001) or Japanese texts (such as Akao, 1991), neither of which reached a mainstream lean readership.

Coping with Variability

Another focal point of the criticism was the ability of lean production systems and supply chains to cope with variability, a key aspect of the lean approach. Indeed, in order to add value to the customer the lean approach seeks to find ways to manage variability and to create capacity by utilising assets more effectively than in traditional systems.

Various lean approaches, such as mixed model scheduling and level scheduling (also referred to as *heijunka*), had earlier been developed to do this. However, in the case of demand variability, these approaches have sought to flatten or control demand, as the original lean pioneers came from fairly stable demand environments industries, such automotive sector supply chains (at least downstream of the assembler). This high-volume and repetitive demand character suits the application of kanban pull-scheduling. However, such kanban-style solutions can be inflexible and thus have attracted criticism from authors such as Cusumano (1994) and Schonberger and Knod (1997).

As a result, many detractors confused pull and kanban, assuming that the latter tool was the only way of achieving customer-driven scheduling. In many other sectors though, demand variability was a main inhibitor to the implementation of lean in general, and kanban in particular. As a result, various contributors proposed agile solutions (*inter alia:* Goldman *et al.*, 1995, van Hoek *et al.*, 2001). The agile school introduced a greater emphasis on dealing with customer demand variability, flexible assemble-to-order systems, creating virtual supply chains and greater use of IT tools. Some of the main differences are summarised by Christopher *et al.* (1999) in Table 7.3.

Learning Steps – From Prescription to Contingency

Four Stages of Organisational Learning

Lean has evolved considerably over time. The four stages of lean thinking defined here are indeed closely related to the stages of development of organisational learning. This will be demonstrated using McGill and Slocum's (1993) four type classification of organisational learning. The first type of organisation is what McGill and Slocum call the "knowing organisation". This type of organisation, as in the first lean awareness stage, believes that there is a best way of doing things that is well established and is closely associated with the scientific management of the likes of Max Weber (1964) and Frederick W. Taylor (1911). Within this type of organisation efficiency is key and firms tend to be bounded by an underlying philosophy of rationality. In the lean case, this rationality would include the mindset that waste is bad and should be removed, where waste is

Table 7.3 *The main differences between lean and agile*

Lean	Agile
Satisfy the customer by adding value and eliminating waste	Satisfy the customer by configuring to order
Long-term relationships with supplier	"Fluid clusters" of suppliers, virtual supply chains
Measure output-criteria, e.g. quality, cost and delivery (QCD)	Measure customer satisfaction
Smooth workflow	Allow for unpredictability
Plan ahead	Face the unpredictable
Reduce stocks to a minimum throughout	Supply chain stock reduction is not the key

Source: adapted from Christopher *et al.* (1999)

often defined with an introspective engineering definition of value. Such companies may also be described as "adaptive" or "single-loop", and can only be successful if competing in a mature and static environment (Argyris and Schon, 1978).

The evolution of the lean concept can be likened to organisational learning, both for the general lean movement and firms who progress along this four-stage lean maturity matrix. Here, organisational learning may be defined as "the process of improving action through better knowledge and understanding" (Fiol and Lyles, 1985, p. 803). Dodgson (1993, p. 377) describes organisational learning as:

> The ways firms build, supplement and organise knowledge and routines around their activities and within their cultures and adapt and develop organisational efficiency by improving the use of the broad skills of the workforce.

Such learning takes place through a phased process of information acquisition, information distribution, information interpretation and use, knowledge transmission and storage (Huber, 1991; Nevis *et al.*, 1995). The evolution of lean thinking along such a learning organisation spectrum is shown in Table 7.4.

Stage 1 – Cells and Assembly Lines

Turning firstly to the evolution from prescription to contingency, the awareness and quality stages of lean involved the highly prescriptive application of a set of tools and methods. These tools are well documented to include kanban, 5S (housekeeping), "single minute exchanges of dies" (SMED – changeover time reduction) and cellular manufacturing (e.g. Monden, 1983; Schonberger, 1986; Harrison, 1992). However, even at this pre-1995 point in time, arguably the dominant paradigm in the field of organisational design and change had moved to a contingency approach (Child, 1977). Such an approach would suggest that there was no one correct "best practice" approach "that is highly effective for all organisations" (Donaldson, 1996, p. 51).

However, in order to understand what the lean movement was at this point it is important to make reference back to the industries in which lean thinking was primarily being

Table 7.4 *The development of a contingent evolved lean approach*

	1980–1990 Cell and line	1990–mid 1990 Shop-floor	Mid 1990–1999 Value stream	2000+ Value system
Prescription/ contingency	Highly prescriptive tool-based approach	Highly prescriptive best practice approach	Lean principles Value stream mapping Prescriptive "one best way"; "Toyota is best"	Contingency involving: customer value, policy deployment, size industry, technology
Organisational learning	Knowing organisation Single-loop learning Management by objectives	Understanding organisation Single-loop learning Management by objectives	Thinking organisation Single (and some often ineffective double) loop learning Management by fact	Learning organisation Double-loop (and some Deutero learning) Management by fact

deployed, namely the automotive industry and other discrete product or engineering sectors with very similar organisational environments in terms of volume produced, product variety and their nature of component assembly. As such, one might argue that as long as lean thinking was applied within these very similar environments its lack of theoretical contingency was of little importance. However, this view would be contradicted by many, as even this limited but relatively homogeneous range of firms would still face differences in environment (Burns and Stalker, 1961), organisational size (Child, 1975), organisational strategy (Chandler, 1962) and technology (Woodward, 1965).

Stage 2 – Shop-Floor

McGill and Slocum's second type of organisation is the understanding organisation, which may be likened to the second "shop-floor" lean stage. Such organisations are governed by a set of core values and management practices that are designed to clarify, communicate and reinforce the company's culture. In this case, the lean quality stage has firms imbibed in a prescriptive best practice lean approach that is largely centred on the manufacturing area. As such they are often not open to further change and expanding their learning experiences. A typical response when discussing the application of lean with such firms is that "yes, we are doing lean", even if they are only applying it in limited islands of excellence on the shop-floor.

Stage 3 – Value Stream

To counter this prescriptive "one best way" approach advocates of lean thinking in the third quality, cost and delivery (QCD) stage started to re-position lean thinking as based on a set of five key principles that it was claimed could be applied across a wide range of industrial settings (Womack and Jones, 1996). Indeed, a series of cases of this application were provided in this text. However, most of these cases are still drawn from component based manufacturing industries and involved the common application of *kaikaku* (i.e. improvement via breakthrough events, as opposed to *kaizen,* continuous improvement) events deployed by Japanese consultants Shingjutsu and their followers.

In spite of these shortcomings, there was the start of an awareness that individual value streams (or specific supply chains) should be individually mapped and contingent solutions found for their improvement (Hines and Rich, 1997; Rother and Shook, 1998). This having been said there was still a significant focus on the "one best way" which would typically be answered by the question "what would Toyota do?" This still largely prescriptive picture of lean thinking is well summarised in Womack and Jones's framework for the lean leap (Table 7.5) which defines a "one best way" which, although containing a good deal of sensible advice, tends to ignore the various contingent features discussed above.

This third type of organisation is best described as the "thinking organisation", which typically focuses on a set of problem-solving management practices, as in the order fulfilment-focused QCD-stage lean firm. However, as in the thinking organisation, these solutions may be criticised as being piecemeal and providing discrete and identifiable solutions, but generally just within one business process. Typical the use of value stream mapping within the order fulfilment[4] process would be seen here.

Table 7.5 *Time frame for the lean leap*

Phase	Specific steps	Time frame
Get started	Find a change agent Get lean Knowledge Find a lever Map value streams Begin *kaikaku* Expand your scope	First six months
Create a new organization	Reorganize by product family Create a lean function Devise a policy for excess people Devise a growth strategy Remove anchor-draggers Instill a "perfection" mind-set	Six months through year two
Install business systems	Introduce lean accounting Relate pay to firm performance Implement transparency Initiate policy deployment Introduce lean learning Find right-sized tools	Years three and four
Complete the transformation	Apply these steps to your suppliers/customers Develop global strategy Transition from top-down to bottom-up improvement	By the end of year five

Source: Womack and Jones, 1996

However, within this order fulfilment process, there would be a high degree of questioning and challenging of existing practices characterised by double-loop learning (Senge, 1990). Such a lean organisation typically ignores a range of other key processes such as new product development (NPD) and the development of new business opportunities. Such a company would typical rely heavily on a single process diagnostic tool such as Toyota's information and physical flow mapping tool popularised by Rother and Shook (1998).

Such firms also tend to assume that improvements should be based solely on improvements in quality, cost and delivery in the belief that in improving these areas it will create customer value. In some parts of mature industries, such as the automotive supplier sector, this may be a reasonable assumption but the current authors believe this is a dangerous assumption in most other instances. Indeed, in many or most other cases the customer values a wider and more complex range of tangible and intangible attributes such as brand, image, environmental issues and local production. As such, these types of organisation may be criticised for their limited scope and focus. Kiernan (1993) suggests that the linear approach adopted by this type of organisation virtually precludes the ability to step back and ask more fundamental, difficult and useful questions. Such questions may include: "should we be in industry at all?" The result of this often poor strategic alignment is often a "scatter blast" approach of initiatives with many acting in conflict. Such organisations are unlikely to achieve sustainable improvement against customer desired value attributes.

Stage 4 – Value Systems

The fourth value systems stage of lean thinking involves a much greater degree of contingency, as it moves past the rhetoric of customer value to include approaches to the active capture of customer needs such as the value attribute approach described in Hines *et al.* (2002). In addition, this is linked to the active use of contingent strategy deployment using policy deployment (Hines *et al.*, 2000). The application of policy deployment takes into account the various contingent factors impinging on an organisation such as their size, industrial sector, industrial dynamics and technology employed. As such, using this fourth lean value system stage, a unique contingent approach is created using a range of tools drawn from diverse management approaches such as the earlier lean manufacturing, six sigma, marketing, agile manufacturing, system dynamics, theory of constraints, and revenue management.

The last phase of McGill and Slocum's model is the learning organisation, here likened to the lean value system stage. Such organisations seek to maximise the learning opportunities of employees, suppliers, customers and even competitors. However, here each change is viewed as a hypothesis to be tested and by checking the results of the experiment, the learning organisation learns how to undertake the experiment better the next time. Within this context tools such as four fields mapping (see Dimancescu *et al.*, 1997 for details) would be employed within the lean value system firm within its contingently defined key core processes with bottom-up implementation plans validated by the catch balling process with the firms's policy deployment approach (Hines *et al.*, 2000; Hines *et al.*, 2002). Such an approach facilitates learning, and widespread double-loop learning could be expected.

Indeed, the various value stream maps from the different core business processes may also be the basis for what Bateson (1972) calls "deutero-learning" – involving the ability to "learn how to learn". The types of methods and approaches that one would expect to see to illustrate this would include supplier associations (for inter-company or network learning: see Hines and Rich, 1998), real-time strategy formation and policy deployment (for strategic and operational people alignment), attention to a range of key business processes (Dimancescu *et al.*, 1997) and strong evidence of learning by doing activities rather than classroom training. The question that advocates of this level of lean would ask is "what should Toyota do?"

Conclusions and Outlook

[...]

Lean is one of the most influential new paradigms in manufacturing, and has expanded beyond the original application on the shop floor of vehicle manufacturers and component suppliers in the auto industry, ranging from "heavy" industries such as primary metals (notably Alcoa's production system see www.alcoa.com) to aerospace businesses (*Financial Post,* 1999; Womack and Jones, 1996). In particular when applied to sectors outside the high-volume repetitive manufacturing environment, lean production has reached its limitations, and a range of other approaches to counter variability, volatility and variety have been suggested. Here, the often quoted lean-agile debate is applicable, discussing whether an agile or a lean strategy, or even a hybrid approach is most suitable (Naylor *et al.,* 1999; Christopher and Towill, 2001).

[...]

In terms of moving this agenda forward, research is called for that looks at how lean value systems can be created in a "green-field" environment – rather than lean approaches just seeking to rectify the errors of earlier generations. In addition, the application of this approach will clearly require a contingent application, which very likely will be unique both to a particular value system and industrial sector. Further research is called for to see how this may be achieved in under-researched sectors, such as low-volume manufacturing and service environments like health care, which are still in early stages of their lean evolution.

Notes

1. *Muda* is the Japanese word for waste, in the sense of wasted effort or time.
2. The remainder of cars is generally made for export to Europe, the United States or elsewhere, and are used to buffer the build-to-order service to domestic customers.
3. Labour productivity in terms of hours per vehicle, or annual vehicle output per employee are the standard measures used in the auto sector, and were also used by Womack *et al.* (1990).
4. Order Fulfilment refers to the process covering all activities from the receipt of an order, its production scheduling, raw material purchasing, parts delivery, production, storage and distribution to the final customer.

Acknowledgement

The authors would like to acknowledge and thank Niall Piercy and Sharon Williams for their contributions towards this paper.

References

Abbas, Z., Khaswala, N. and Irani, S. (2001), "Value network mapping (VNM): visualization and analysis of multiple flows in value stream maps", paper presented at the Lean Management Solutions Conference, St Louis, MO, September.

Akao, Y. (Ed.) (1991), *Hoshin Kanri: Policy Deployment for Successful TQM,* Productivity Press, Cambridge, MA.

Andersen Consulting (1993), *The Lean Enterprise Benchmarking Report,* Andersen Consulting, London.

Andersen Consulting (1994), *The Second Lean Enterprise Benchmarking Report,* Andersen Consulting, London.

Argyris, C. and Schon, D. (1978), *Organisational Learning: A Theory of Action Perspective*, Addison-Wesley, New York, NY.

Bateman, N. (2000), *Factors Affecting the Sustainability of Process Improvement Activities*, Industry Forum, Birmingham.

Bateson, G. (1972), *Steps to an Ecology of Mind*, cited in Argyris, C. and Schon, D.A. (1996), *Organisational Learning II: Theory, Method and Practice*, Addison-Wesley Publishing, Reading, MA, Chandler Publishing, San Francisco, CA.

Burns, T. and Stalker, G.M. (1961), *The Management of Innovation*, Tavistock, London.

Carlisle, J.A. and Parker, R.C. (1989), *Beyond Negotiation: Redeeming Customer-Supplier Relationships*, Wiley, Chichester.

Chandler, A.D. (1962), *Strategy and Structure: Chapters in the History of the Industrial Enterprise*, MIT Press, Cambridge, MA.

Child, J. (1975), "Managerial and organisational factors associated with company performance, Part 2: A contingency analysis", *Journal of Management Studies*, Vol. 12, pp. 12–27.

Child, J. (1977), "Organisational design and performance: contingency theory and beyond", *Organsiation and Administrative Science*, Vol. 8, pp. 169–83.

Christopher, M., Harrison, A. and van Hoek, R. (1999), "Creating the agile supply chain: issues and challenges", International Symposium on Logistics, Florence, July.

Christopher, M. and Towill, D.R. (2001), "An integrated model for the design of agile supply chains", *International Journal of Physical Distribution & Logistics Management*, Vol. 31 No. 4, pp. 253–46.

Cusumano, M.A. (1994), "The limits of 'lean'", *Sloan Management Review*, Vol. 35 No. 4, pp. 27–35.

Davidow, W. and Malone, M. (1992), *The Virtual Corporation: Structuring and Revitalizing the Corporation for the 21st Century*, Harper Business, New York, NY.

Dimancescu, D., Hines, P. and Rich, N. (1997), *The Lean Enterprise: Designing and Managing Strategic Processes For Customer Winning Performance*, AMACOM, New York, NY.

Dodgson, M. (1993), "Organisational learning: a review of some literature", *Organisation Studies*, Vol. 14 No. 3, pp. 375–94.

Donaldson, L. (1996), "The normal science of structural contingency theory", in Clegg, S.R. and Hardy, C. (Eds), *Studying Organisation: Theory and Method*, Sage Publications, London.

Fiol, C. and Lyles, M. (1985), "Organisational learning", *Academy of Management Review*, Vol. 10 No. 4, pp. 803–13.

Financial Post Canada (1999), "Aerospace industry mimics Toyota", *Financial Post*, 10 March.

Fisher, M.L. (1997), "What is the right supply chain for your product?", *Harvard Business Review*, Vol. 75 No. 2, pp. 105–16.

Fucini, J. and Fucini, S. (1990), *Working for the Japanese*, The Free Press, New York, NY.

Garrahan, P. and Stewart, P. (1992), *The Nissan Enigma: Flexibility at Work in a Local Economy*, Mansell, London.

Goldman, S., Nagel, R. and Preiss, K. (1995), *Agile Competitors and Virtual Organsiations*, van Nostrand Reinhold, New York, NY.

Hall, R. (1983), *Zero Inventories*, Dow Jones-Irwin, Homewood, IL.

Hammer, M. (1990), "Reengineering work: don't automate, obliterate", *Harvard Business Review*, Vol. 68 No. 4, pp. 104–9.

Harrison, A. (1992), *Just-in-Time in Perspective*, Prentice Hall, London.

Harrison, A., Christopher, M. and van Hoek, R. (1999), *Creating the Agile Supply Chain*, Institute of Logistics and Transport Focus, Corby.

Hines, P., Lamming, R., Jones, D., Cousins, P. and Rich, N. (2000), *Value Stream Management: Strategy and Excellence in the Supply Chain*, Financial Times Prentice Hall, Harlow.

Hines, P. and Rich, N. (1997), "The seven value stream mapping tools", *International Journal of Operations & Production Management*, Vol. 17 No. 1, pp. 46–64.

Hines, P. and Rich, N. (1998), "Outsourcing competitive advantage: the use of supplier associations", *International Journal of Physical Distribution & Logistics Management*, Vol. 28 No. 7, pp. 524–46.

Hines, P., Silvi, R. and Bartolini, M. (2002), "Demand chain management: an integrative approach in automotive retailing", *Journal of Operations Management*, Vol. 20 No. 3, pp. 707–28.

Hines, P. and Taylor, D. (2000), *Going Lean – A Guide for Implementation*, Lean Enterprise Research Centre, Cardiff Business School, Cardiff.

Holweg, M. (2003), "The three-day car challenge – investigating the inhibitors of responsive order fulfilment in new vehicle supply systems", *International Journal of Logistics: Research and Applications*, Vol. 6 No. 3, pp. 165–83.

Holweg, M. and Jones, D.T. (2001), "The build-to-order challenge: can current vehicle supply systems cope?", in Taylor, D. and Brunt, D. (Eds), *Manufacturing Operations and Supply Chain Management: The Lean Approach*, Thomson Learning, London, pp. 362–72.

Holweg, M. and Pil, F. (2001), "Successful build-to-order strategies start with the customer", *Sloan Management Review*, Vol. 43 No. 1, pp. 74–83.

Huber, G. (1991), "Organisational learning: the contributing processes and literature", *Organisaion Science*, Vol. 2 No. 1, pp. 88–115.

Jones, D.T. and Womack, J. (2002), *Seeing the Whole: Mapping the Extended Value Stream*, The Lean Enterprise Institute, Brookline, MA.

Kiernan, M. (1993), "The new strategic architecture: learning to compete in the twenty-first century", *Academy of Management Executive*, Vol. 7 No. 1, pp. 7–21.

Lamming, R. (1993), *Beyond Partnership: Strategies for Innovation and Lean Supply*, Prentice Hall, London.

McGill, M.E. and Slocum, J.W. (1993), "Unlearning the organisation", *Organisational Dynamics*, Vol. 22 No. 2, pp. 67–79.

MacBeth, D. and Ferguson, N. (1994), *Partnership Sourcing, an Integrated Supply Chain Approach*, Pitman, London.

Mather, H. (1988), *Competitive Manufacturing*, Prentice Hall, Englewood Cliffs, NJ.

Monden, Y. (1983), *The Toyota Production System*, Productivity Press, Portland, OR.

Naylor, B.J., Naim, M.M. and Berry, D. (1999), "Leagility – integrating the lean and agile manu-facturing paradigms in the total supply chain", *International Journal of Production Economics*, Vol. 62, pp. 107–18.

Nevis, E.C., BiBella, A.J. and Gould, J.M. (1995), "Understanding organisations as learning systems", *Sloan Management Review*, Vol. 36 No. 2, pp. 73–85.

Ohno, T. (1988), *The Toyota Production System: Beyond Large-Scale Production*, Productivity Press, Portland, OR.

Rich, N. and Francis, M. (1998), "Overall supply chain performance measurement: focusing improvements and stimulating change" paper presented at the 2nd Annual Logistics Research Network Conference, Cranfield.

Rineheart, J., Huxley, C. and Robertson, D. (1993), *Just Another Car Factory? Lean Production and its Contents*, Cornell University Press, Ithaca, NY.

Rother, M. and Shook, J. (1998), *Learning To See: Value Stream Mapping to Add Value and Eliminate Muda*, The Lean Enterprise Institute, Brookline, MA.

Sandras, W.A. (1989), *Just-in-Time: Making it Happen. Unleashing the Power of Continuous Improvement*, John Wiley & Sons, New York, NY.

Schonberger, R.J. (1982), *Japanese Manufacturing Techniques*, The Free Press, New York , NY.

Schonberger, R.J. (1986), *World Class Manufacturing – The Lessons of Simplicity Applied*, The Free Press, New York, NY.

Schonberger, R. and Knod, E. (1997), *Operations Management: Customer-Focused Principles*, Irwin/ MacGraw Hill, Boston, MA.

Senge, P. (1990), *The Fifth Discipline: The Art and Practice of the Leaning Organisation*, Doubleday Currency, New York, NY.

Shingo, S. (1981), *Study of the Toyota Production Systems,* Japan Management Association, Tokyo.

Shingo, S. (1988), *Non-Stock Production: The Shingo System for Continuous Improvement,* Productivity Press, Cambridge, MA.

Stalk, G. and Hout, T. (1990), *Competing Against Time: How Time-based Competition is Reshaping Global Markets,* The Free Press, New York, NY.

Suri, R. (1999), *Quick Response Manufacturing,* Productivity Press, Portland, OR.

Taylor, F.W. (1911), *Principles of Scientific Management,* Harper & Row, New York, NY.

Tennant, C. and Roberts, P. (2001), "Hoshin Kanri: implementing the catchball process", *Long Range Planning,* Vol. 34 No. 3, pp. 287–308.

van Hoek, R., Harrison, A. and Christopher, M. (2001), "Measuring agile capabilities in the supply chain", *International Journal of Operations & Production Management,* Vol. 21 No. 1/2, pp. 126–47.

Weber, M. (1964), *The Theory of Social and Economic Organisation,* Collier MacMillan, London.

Williams, K., Harlam, C., Williams, J., Cutler, T., Adcroft, A. and Johal, S. (1992), "Against lean production", *Economy and Society,* Vol. 21 No. 3, pp. 321–54.

Womack, J. and Jones, D.T. (1994), "From lean production to the lean enterprise", *Harvard Business Review,* Vol. 72 No. 2, pp. 93–104.

Womack, J. and Jones, D.T. (1996), *Lean Thinking: Banish Waste and Create Wealth for Your Corporation,* Simon and Schuster, New York, NY.

Womack, J., and Jones, D.T. and Roos, D. (1990), *The Machine That Changed the World,* Rawson Associates, New York, NY.

Woodward, J. (1965), *Industrial Organisation: Theory and Practice,* Oxford University Press, Oxford.

The Barriers to Customer Responsive Supply Chain Management

John Storey, Caroline Emberson and David Reade

Introduction

It has been argued that particular features of the contemporary competitive market environment are making new kinds of demands on suppliers and retailers. Shortened product life cycles, and the fragmentation of formerly standard products, impel a shift towards more "agile" and "customer responsive" behaviour by suppliers of goods and services. These dynamics are especially notable in the context of the fashion industry and clothing retail in general (Sparks and Fernie, 1998; Jones, 2002). Moreover, given the way value chains have been disaggregated in recent years this in turn requires responsiveness throughout the supply-chain (Gattorna, 1998; Pine, 1993; Goldman *et al.*, 1995; Christopher, 1998). And numerous studies have emphasised the importance of integrating suppliers, manufacturers and customers (Frohlich and Westbrook, 2001; Clinton and Closs, 1997).

Most case studies report examples of apparently successful initiatives; but these studies often display certain weaknesses. For example, the time frames they describe are usually too circumscribed, the change agents who were involved often use such opportunities to parade their achievements, and the lessons offered are usually too general to serve as useful points of practical action. In this paper we use a supply chain case study with a time-frame extending over two decades to help reveal some of the barriers to effective customer responsive supply chain management even under very favourable conditions. In high-street fashion, retailing the "need" for such an approach is readily apparent. The fate of this cutting-edge initiative analysed in this paper helps reveal, in sharp form, the deep-seated behavioural and organisational barriers to customer responsive supply chain management.

The purpose of the paper is to critically assess relevant theory and prescription concerning agility, business to business relationships, buyer-supplier relationships and collaborative planning in the light of a detailed case study. The paper presents a number of significant challenges to current theory and it suggests some alternative propositions.

[...]

Source: J. Storey, C. Emberson and D. Reade (2005) *International Journal of Operations and Production*, 25 (3): 242–60. Edited version.

The Customer Responsive Supply Chain Literature

In this section, we examine three major strands of literature in order to help construct an appropriate analytical framework and to derive a set of propositions against which to interpret behaviour among the players we researched. In addition to the lean and agile supply chain literature there has been significant work in retailer-supplier relations and there has been substantial work in the areas of quick response (QR), collaborative planning, forecasting and replenishment (CPFR) and efficient consumer response (ECR). Our research draws upon and contributes to each of these three main strands of literature – though in the main it also presents a critique and challenge to them.

The Lean and Agile Supply Chain Literature

Fast-moving, volatile market conditions with short product life cycles carry far-reaching implications for production processes, for the way companies are organised and for the way their supply chains operate. For example, according to Goldman *et al.* (1995, p. xv), "Agility based competition [...] is destined to displace mass-production-based competition as the norm for global commerce". Agility as here understood, defines a set of interlinked changes in marketing, production, design and organisation. It is normally also understood as requiring new capabilities in managing across organisational boundaries.

The need to cope with volatile demand requires the capability to manage the supply chain in a way that enables quick response (Sabath, 1998). While functional products with predictable demand benefit most from "physically efficient" supply chain processes, innovative and fashion-oriented products demand "market responsive" supply chain processes that are focussed on speed and flexibility rather than on cost (Fisher, 1997; Aitken *et al.*, 2002). The implication is that supply chain management in today's market environment needs to progress beyond the "lean" focus of its initial inception (Christopher and Towill, 2000). The proposed way forward is to reduce the lead-time gap so that the manufacturing cycle is based on a richer picture of known orders and less on forecasts (Christopher and Juttner, 2000; Christopher, 1998). Achieving this would require a special, sustained relationship between retailer and supplier.

The concept of the "lean enterprise" as developed by Womack and Jones (1996) has been stretched by others (e.g. Naylor *et al.*, 1999; Abernathy *et al.*, 2000) to include supply chains that aim to eliminate all wastes so as to achieve a schedule with maximum efficiency. Some observers have suggested that the concept of "leagile" (i.e. lean combined with agile) supply chains can achieve situations where supply chains are able to switch between lean approaches during the early (upstream) production processes and more agile approaches during the later (downstream) processes (Naylor *et al.*, 1999; Bruce *et al.*, 2004). Building for stock in the upstream stages while postponing the finishing touches to customised goods at the downstream stages can achieve this state of affairs. But such "compromise" practices, it is alternatively suggested, do not deliver the full potential of a truly agile supply chain.

True agility requires rapid and appropriate responses to fluctuating consumer demand. This, in turn, requires much greater "visibility" through the supply chain than has conventionally been the norm. Ideally this would enable all players in the supply chain to see from one end of the pipeline to another in as close to real time as possible. These characteristics are also predicated on the full exploitation of information and technology (Harrison and van Hoek, 2002) through inter-organisational collaboration and co-operation.

However, as our case study will starkly reveal, technological capability is by no means sufficient and inter-organisational co-operation can be hard-won. Even when the technology is available, there can be enormous organisational and behavioural barriers to agile or customer responsive behaviour in supply chain situations, which seemingly cry out for such responses (Storey, 2002). These behavioural barriers serve to question the prescriptive and predictive "agility thesis" as well as the contingency theory of Gattorna (1998) and his colleagues (Gattorna and Walters, 1996).

[...]

The Organisational Buyer-Supplier Relationship Literature

Long-term, collaborative relationships with a few trusted suppliers have been described as representing a general trend over the past decade or so (Anderson *et al.*, 1994; Wilkinson and Young, 1995; Ford, 1990; Sheth, 1996; Sheth and Sharma, 1997; and Special Issue of *Industrial Marketing Management*, 2004). There is said to be growing evidence that "firms are moving away from the traditional approach of adversarial relationships with a multitude of suppliers to one of forging longer term relationships with a selected few suppliers" (Kalwani and Narayandas, 1995, p. 1). A similar claim has been made by many others (Dwyer *et al.*, 1987; Spekman, 1988). The International Marketing and Purchasing Group (IMP) has extensively researched business relationships with a comparable idea in mind (Ford, 1990; Hakansson and Snehota, 1995).

[...]

The exploration of "commitment" and "trust" in relationship marketing and buyer-supplier collaboration has been a predominating theme (Morgan and Hunt, 1994; Dwyer *et al.*, 1987; Young and Wilkinson, 1989). Indeed, relationship marketing has largely been defined in these terms. The essential theme of such literature is the co-operative aspects of economic behaviour. Analysts within this mode emphasise and usually extol "norms of sharing and commitment based on trust" (Achrol, 1991, p. 89). The importance of "bonding and commitment" are also stressed (Wilson and Mummalaneni, 1986). Within the relationship marketing literature, commitment and trust are indeed usually claimed to be the key, central, concepts. The parties to the relationship are required to make a trade-off: "In relational markets, both the organisation and the customer concede some control and autonomy in return for assurance of equitable exchange and reduction of risk over the longer term" (Bowen *et al.*, 1989, p. 83). Here we see again the notion being advanced of a rational calculation being undertaken by organisations. Such assumptions are questioned by our research.

The proposition that buying organisations necessarily enter into a rational weighing of costs and benefits is one that we wished to explore in greater depth. In the context of an increasingly global market economy, we suggest that there are limits to the direct transferability of lessons from interpersonal relationships to inter-organisational trading relationships. Moreover, when not assessing buyer-supplier relationships in rational-choice terms, there is another tendency to analyse them in terms of growth, maturation and adaptation (Brennan and Turnbull, 1999). Again, while adaptation and evolution in relationships undoubtedly occur, there can be circumstances in which these relationship-building measures are countermanded by much bigger forces and considerations – especially at strategic level in large international firms. While the literature reviewed in this section focuses on relationship building between buyers and suppliers, there is another relevant segment of literature that attends rather more to modes of collaborative planning. These we term as retail logistics initiatives.

Retail Logistics Initiatives

Various initiatives in retail logistics [...] share some of the characteristics of the collaborative buyer-supplier models discussed above. These movements have been based on the premise that shared benefits can be derived by suppliers and retailers through collaborative action on cost reduction, efficiency savings, and customer service improvements (Giunipero and Brand, 1996; Cooke, 1999; Giunipero and Fiorito, 2001).

[...]

[However], "despite increasing willingness to work together, there remain many attitudes, prejudices and corporate cultures to be changed and hidden agendas to be exposed if the full range of possibilities are to be explored" (Whiteoak, 1994, p. 33).

[...]

To summarise, the concept of "supply chain management" and related concepts of buyer-supplier collaborative behaviour have provoked a large and rapidly expanding body (or rather bodies) of literature. As most reviewers acknowledge, however, the bulk of the literature to date has remained at the prescriptive and speculative level, and these prescriptions tend not to be based on sound empirical research. Equally, another significant gap is that while the organisational and behavioural aspects are widely accepted as critical to the success or failure of supply chain management initiatives, there is a paucity of studies that have grappled with these elements. The issues widely identified as requiring much fuller investigation in supply chain research are the organisational and behavioural factors. As has been noted: "An understanding of human behaviour and its implications for supply chain design and management, form the missing ingredient in contemporary thinking about supply chain strategy" (Gattorna, 1998, p. 1). Hence, a further purpose of this paper to address this challenge.

Research Methods

This case study was constructed from a number of interlocking sources that were cross-checked and used as prompts for further enquiry. The first and most important source was a series of very detailed and extensive semi-structured interviews with key informants from Marks and Spencer (past and present) and their leading suppliers.

Virtually, all of the informants had played active, often indeed the leading, parts in the various initiatives described herein. Their motives and intentions formed key parts of the investigation, as did their analyses of the situation and their readings of the motives, intent and behaviours of other actors. The interviews were tape-recorded and transcribed. Some of the interviews extended for as much as half a day. There were a total of nine detailed interviews of this kind. In addition, a second source of data was round-table meetings at which managers from different companies (including suppliers and retailers together) could compare their interpretations of the events and processes analysed in this account.

A third source of data was derived from internal company documents including reports, memoranda, minutes of meetings, and progress reports and stakeholder analyses. These were unusually detailed and extensive because they often represented the work of the key informants and their close associates. A fourth source was a time-line analysis tracked through documentary sources in the public domain. A great deal of this was derived from the financial press as Marks and Spencer has long enjoyed one of the highest profiles – indeed, stories about the company occur on virtually a daily basis. This secondary source was used as a further cross-check on the prime information supplied through the accounts of the players themselves. The details of the initiative analysed in the main part of this paper was not reported in the media but the surrounding events such as the appointments of consultants or the shift to overseas suppliers were well documented.

The investigation explored the organisational and behavioural dilemmas as they were construed by influential members from the different, interacting, organisations. It was a major advantage to be able to explore the changing relationship from the multiple vantage points of the retailer and the various competing suppliers. The analysis draws on the rich legacy of company histories (Briggs, 1984) and biographies (Bookbinder, 1993). These recount the development of the distinct flavour of Marks and Spencer supplier relationships over the past century, through the Second World War (Bookbinder, 1993) to a contemporary analysis of Marks and Spencer's recent fall (Bevan, 2001) and problematical recovery. The prime focus of the case covers the past decade up to the present day but in addition, accounts of the pattern of buyer-suppliers and supply chain behaviour in the previous decade are also examined. The research tracked the changing nature of supply chain management, the change initiatives, and also sought to analyse their rationale, methods and consequences – both intended and unintended.

The Supplier Initiative: the Launch of Vendor Managed Inventory

The Marks and Spencer supply chain management system was characterised both by a certain formal sophistication and yet also by significant problems. These problems were experienced at the level of the supply chain as a whole but perhaps most acutely by the garment suppliers. This section examines a major initiative launched by Courtaulds, one of the then top four suppliers, as a means of alleviating a particular set of problems. The origins of the initiative are traced and its nature, implementation, operation and its ultimate erosion are explored.

Prior to the initiative to be described below, one main pattern of supply chain management predominated. Marks and Spencer managed their buying activities through a series of stage-gate decision points. Key stages in the contracting process were: the issue of a pre-production contract to the supplier formally authorising raw material purchase; completion of the full contract confirming cost prices; and a series of "alterations to order" (ATOs), which formalised colour and ratio requirements. This "contract management" system was automated and extended to integrate with the product development process during the late 1990s. "Call off" of stock for distribution to stores was managed separately. There was no guarantee that because product had been produced in line with contracts, it would be requested in these same timeframes. Consequently, the supplier took most of the risk and bore the cost of maintaining stock in the warehouse and the cost of discounting or disposing of stock that did not sell. In practical terms, final goods could sit in a warehouse at the expense of the supplier. However, one of the most disturbing problems from a supplier point of view – and the one that prompted action in this case – was the practice whereby Marks and Spencer would, on occasions, suddenly cancel orders on a range of items even though the manufacturer might be in mid-flow of production. This was a relatively common practice. It caused significant problems and involved considerable cost. One of these occasions proved to be the catalyst for the initiative examined here.

Manufacturing companies depend upon efficient operation for their cost effectiveness. One of the biggest costs is triggered by changeovers and resetting of machinery. As one informant from Courtaulds expressed this: "if the manufacturer is normally running at 70 to 80 per cent efficiency this is drastically undercut by every changeover – usually down to about 50 per cent for a number of weeks. It's serious money down the tube". Against this backcloth, the catalyst for change in this instance was a combination of an especially unreasonable shift in demand from a Marks and Spencer merchandiser, and the presence of a person in the supplying company with the capability and commitment to effect a major change to prevent the problem from reoccurring.

One day, a phone call was received from a Marks and Spencer merchandiser announcing that the company would not be requiring any more of a particular range of items. This peremptory announcement occurred while the factory concerned was in the middle of a production season and in the middle of a production run with some 20 people producing 500 dozen items every week. A senior manager in this supplier company reported to us:

> I had to go straight down to the production manager and say "I'm awfully
> sorry but you need to cease production immediately". This surprise news
> caused absolute consternation – there were huge repercussions and we all
> ended up in the managing director's office.

As already indicated, such abrupt cancellations were not unusual, but the scale and impact of this one constituted the proverbial "last straw". It prompted certain players in Courtaulds to look for an alternative way of operating.

The Launch of a New Way, 1991–1992

Out of this crisis came a new initiative. A senior management group talked the problem through and pondered the idea that there had to be a better way to operate in the future. The discussion extended over a few days. The analysis was that the abrupt change in demand was not a function of the marketplace, but rather it was a consequence of the shortcomings of the merchandisers in Marks and Spencer who were showing their incapability to forecast the demand. It was agreed by the supplier's senior management team that one of them would write a proposal to go to Marks and Spencer. The heart of the new proposal was that, in exchange for a continual feed of sales and stock information from Marks and Spencer, the supplier would adjust their production schedules in line with sales and would assume responsibility for replenishment. This was an early instance of vendor-managed inventory (VMI).

The relevant Marks and Spencer merchandiser cautiously agreed to the proposal. On the basis of this, the supplier took a number of styles and built a logic using spreadsheets. The plan depended on an electronic file of sales data sent to the supplier by the merchandiser once per week. This gave transparency in relation to stocks held by the retailer and sales that week in every store both of that supplier's own range and of all other sales of other suppliers of that range of clothing. Real consumer behaviour became far more apparent and, as a consequence, production could be planned much more accurately to reflect the trends and patterns. The actual sales figures were a revelation to the supplier – not least in terms of what they indicated about the misleading translations of them by merchandisers in the past and the consequent wild pattern of orders which used to be placed.

The Golden Era 1992–1996

The new system resulted in real benefits to both supplier and retailer. None the less the new way of operating relied on persuasion and indeed continual re-persuasion of new job incumbents as turnover among merchandisers was quite high. The posture adopted by Marks and Spencer was mainly passive and accepting rather than proactive and championing – a stance which occasioned some resentment among the supplier managers. At the same time, the management of all the spreadsheets was becoming a big administrative job for the supplier to handle. With the assistance of a specialist IT consultancy a tailor-made forecasting package was constructed. This had the ability to import the Marks and Spencer text file that was being sent every Monday morning. An EDI approach that was developed took the level of analysis from individual transactions up to more aggregate bulk reporting levels.

The supplier each Monday morning could run an exception report showing any styles that had not been correctly forecast. The biggest variations were prioritised for attention. Each week a revised forecast based on these analyses of the previous week's sales was produced. Using this method, the company reached a forecast accuracy in the high 90 percentiles.

Further advantages accrued. The production demand emerging from the forecasting package was loaded into an ERP package as a demand on production. Numerous benefits "started to emerge all over the place". For example, because of the frequency of these input adjustments, large costly changes were avoided. There were better sales and lower stocks. Further, the company developed better relations with the merchandisers. The benefits were especially marked in products that allowed long production runs for the product category. Efficiency and margins reached unprecedented heights. There was a 130 per cent return on capital employed in 1995. The stock turn was a record high and the stocks were managed correctly. The kind of abrupt stops and starts that had triggered the initiative in the first place were avoided.

There were also huge gains derived from the fact that as a result of more accurate production planning there was far less discounting of remaindered stock. This had a significant impact on margins. The previous practice would have seen one fifth or one quarter of a total order being discounted at half price. This made a major dent in overall profit margins. The costs of discounting have a hidden, disproportionate, effect on profitability, which is often unrealized by the players involved. But, on the basis of the new system, Marks and Spencer became one of the most profitable and efficient retailers as it rarely had to discount these products.

The new system was delivering many benefits. There were reduced stock levels both in terms of work in progress and finished goods. This resulted from the open information sharing and the ability of the supplier to manage order replenishment directly and in a timely manner. There was improved on-shelf availability and a consequent uplift in total sales. These benefits, in turn meant better availability and far fewer, if any, discount episodes. There were also reduced costs in managing and operating the supply chain. There was less duplication of effort and there was potential for even greater significant reduction through infrastructure reduction – that is the new system would have allowed the elimination of some distribution centers. Meanwhile, manufacturing costs were lower because there was far better factory utilisation arising from improved ability to plan and less exposure to the kind of peremptory and unexpected cancellations of the kind noted at the outset to this case description. The smoother, more accurate production procedures could be transmitted throughout the supply chain to the benefit of all participants. When considered from all angles, the new customer-responsive supply chain arrangements were a resounding success.

Signs of Erosion, 1997

However, in 1997 the new system, despite its numerous advantages, began to unravel. A number of things were responsible for this. Some of these were interlinked, but others can be traced to an unconnected series of events. Together, they were said to have "destroyed the solution" and they highlight variables that the dominant supply chain and buyer-supplier literatures tend to neglect.

First, there was a complete change of organisational structure within Marks and Spencer. A whole new group of people came in and they changed the department structure. Many of the new intake did not like the idea of sharing sales data with suppliers, a practice on which the new system depended. At the same time, Marks and Spencer also changed the method used for generating the daily and weekly sales reports and so the data did not reach the supplier in the way in which it was needed. As a consequence of these two changes the supplier lost access to the weekly feed of sales data.

In addition, Marks and Spencer adopted a merchandising approach based on "collections" – that is groups of products were now to be displayed together and this meant they had to be available together. The focus of the new system on smooth sales forecasting and stock management was less attuned to this new priority. It worked less well for the one-off, co-ordinated launch of complementary products made for the fashion market using the quick sale, discount and clear model.

Then there was a further coincidental factor that intruded. The large supplying company itself was making changes that served to undermine the smooth operation of the supply model. The senior management team devised an internationalising strategy – they insisted that production be placed offshore. There was rapid expansion of production facilities in a number of developing countries – mainly located in South East Asia and North Africa – especially in Morocco. But these facilities were growing too fast and they were found to be not reliable enough to operate the finely adjusted vendor managed inventory method. Their use illustrated the intrusion of a new priority. Further, complementary sets of clothes were sourced in different countries, but it proved hard to ensure that they arrived in a co-ordinated way. There was also an extra six weeks lead time to be factored in. As one manager in the supply company observed

> We returned to the old model. There were immediate negative consequences
> on profits and efficiencies. The degree of profitability reached in 1995 and
> 1996 has never been recaptured.

There was a wholesale destruction of the integrated supply chain. Moreover, the pace of expansion in Morocco meant that the control over materials suffered and production reliability also deteriorated. This had negative consequences on the relationship with Marks and Spencer buying departments. A nadir was reached in 2001. Sales volumes halved and profits were much reduced.

Analysis and Explanation

The preceding narrative describes the sequence of events. It tells a story of crisis in 1991 (with the trigger of sudden full cancellation of an order in mid-production flow) and the consequent launch of a new initiative that delivered dramatic results by 1995. It further reveals how the new arrangement proved to be fragile despite its success and how a series of events led to a rapid unravelling of the painstakingly constructed supply chain arrangements. In this section, we seek to unravel and explain the factors that led to the collapse of a rational functioning system. We believe that the underlying causes of collapse are indicative of the kind of barriers to effective supply chain management that can be found in many other companies and sectors. Further, we contend that the lessons that can be drawn from this experience are highly relevant to the renewed experiments in buyer-supplier relationships being conducted at the present time in Marks and Spencer and in many other companies.

Moreover, the case study also reveals that much of the supply chain literature, which posits an inexorable shift to collaborative transparent relationships underestimate the organisational and behavioural complexities even under the most favourable circum-stances. Above all, the case also reveals that a formal, technically superior system is vulnerable to organisational and behavioural factors. Three factors are immediately apparent. First, the high-performing initiative proved ultimately no match for the affinity of a succession of senior Marks and Spencer managers to traditional practices and assumptions in which they were well schooled. Second, the initiative was vulner-able to the status and reward considerations impelling merchandisers to pursue prior-ities other than forecasting and smooth delivery of stock. Third, and most devastating, senior managers on both sides – within Courtaulds and within Marks and Spencer – were prepared to completely override and disregard this smoothly operating partner-ship arrangement when other (often competing) policy considerations were adopted as "must-be-done at all costs" objectives. In the case of Courtaulds – and to a certain extent in Marks and Spencer – this meant a decisive and radical shift in favour of overseas supply. In the case of Marks and Spencer, the competing policy priority was a total reappraisal of its supply base and the ending of contracts for some long-standing suppliers.

Other factors were simultaneously at play. In 1997, Marks and Spencer's fortunes began to slide in the face of competition and as a result they became less relaxed about releasing their sales figures. There was public criticism of their products and the city became increas-ingly critical. Senior managers at board level entered into a phase of open conflict. In that environment an open, partnership-oriented, approach was not in favour.

It should also be remembered that the vendor managed inventory system, which is described in this case had not been created by Marks and Spencer; one part of the com-pany had simply responded positively to one supplier's initiative. In consequence, the sys-tem, although extremely successful, was neither widely nor deeply embedded in Marks and Spencer. This partial success indicates the severe limits to pan-organisational knowledge transfer within the company. Similarly, while other suppliers were offered the sales data by Marks and Spencer, few were able to take full advantage of it as they had not developed the systems to use it properly.

In due course, after the undoing of the initiative, Marks and Spencer did instigate an investigation of its own into VMI. It engaged consultants to explore and develop the con-cept (alongside some other objectives). This time, because the initiative came from within Marks and Spencer, it had the advantage of top level sponsorship. Despite this, even this version of VMI has so far only experienced partial take-up. We found that many buying departments are still sceptical of its value. The newly created system is, in any case, rather less advanced than the one abandoned a couple of years previously that had been led by one of its suppliers. The new Marks and Spencer system is hosted as a web-based service rather than feeding the data directly to the supplier as previously. Suppliers maintain that to use the data for effective supply chain planning, they need the regular data feed and not simply web-based access to view stocks.

However, Marks and Spencer seem now to be relearning the importance of co-operating with their suppliers. Partnership had been largely abandoned from the late 1990s until 2002. It is now very much a component part of the current recovery strategy. For example, the streaming of strategic sourcing is a joint decision to leverage geographical scale. This to be done in future "in a way that does not shaft the supplier" as one Marks and Spencer manager put it. Such arrangements are being reconstituted alongside other, alternative operating models (However, the practicalities of managing VMI as just one replenishment option within a multi-modal system is producing its own difficulties).

Another explanation of the failure to exploit a change that parties on both sides recognised as producing great benefits stems from the fact that many of the Marks and Spencer merchandisers had "grown complacent". They had become accustomed to being "sold to", they had been "pampered" and they had not had to think through supply issues. They have been "saved from their own mistakes" by suppliers who have helped them out and so avoided exposing their weaknesses in supply chain management. An unintended consequence was that forecasting, resupply and supply chain management more generally did not receive the attention they deserved.

Managers within the company had also become insular. Most were recruited at a young age and did not subsequently work outside Marks and Spencer. Marks and Spencer routines and procedures were deeply embedded. As other recent research within this company has shown (Mellahi *et al.*, 2002), Marks and Spencer staff found it very difficult to accept that change was necessary – or to envision what different approaches might look like. There was a very strong adherence to traditional, tried and trusted, ways that had for such a long time previously brought forth success.

In part, this is further explained by the way these merchandiser positions are staffed and the way merchandisers are motivated. Past practice has been to rotate staff through these positions at regular intervals and this had prevented (it seems purposely) the development of long-term relationships with suppliers. In addition, the recruits to these positions seemed to approach the role with an overconfidence and aggression. Their interests seemed not to rest in forecasting but in other dimensions of purchasing. Because of their short tenure in these assignments, the supplier was faced with a constantly changing "partner" and thus had to keep reselling the counter-cultural idea of shared data again and again. Many of these merchandisers – especially if they came as they often did, from other purchasing areas – were fundamentally sceptical. They started out with the view that "we do not do it this way". They often sought to reverse the process to the erstwhile "normal routine". One of the supplier managers observed that "I always felt that we were holding on to a beachhead. In the end the opposing forces got too strong for us and they pushed us back into the sea".

The case also reveals a surprising resistance to learning by the Marks and Spencer organisation. They currently operate mixed models but they seem not to be actively testing them in the full and open way that would be necessary in order to assess their learning potential across the company as a whole.

The case reveals the importance of converted and committed sponsors. Despite the evident success of the new VMI system, Marks and Spencer had not as a whole fully bought-into or embraced the idea as a general working mode. It was treated as if it were an experiment. As such, when other priorities emerged it was quickly and easily abandoned. Even within the supplying company that had introduced and campaigned for the method, it was precariously positioned. The chief executive of the company had become an enthusiast but the chief executive of the division merely remained passive in relation to it. Hence, even here, when a new apparent priority emerged – the new strategy of outsourcing production to low cost international locations – the commitment to VMI proved to be shallow and was easily pushed aside.

To conceive and launch the initiative required a great deal of creative thinking, technical capability and sheer persistence in constantly selling and promoting the idea through numerous presentations. The idea required extensive internal marketing. The introduction and sustainability of the new VMI system also required a cluster of new capabilities. First, there was a need for a capability to envisage an alternative way of operating. Second, this had to be underpinned by a capability to interpret the nature and source of the problems that were presenting themselves in sudden changes in supply requests. Then, there was also a needed capability to analyse what could be done. This required technical capabilities. There had to be an ability to design the architecture of the new model and the capability to make it run. There was also a simultaneous need to build the relationships required to ensure that the information would be released and delivered regularly. Crucially important too was the energy and capability to champion the idea to internal colleagues and then to the retailer. As the above account reveals, this had to be done time and time again.

Some of the resistance within Marks and Spencer could be traced to the prevailing set of expectations and the culture. The traditional conflictual approach of the merchandisers was underpinned and sustained by the kind of leadership to which they were exposed and to the kind of reward culture within which they operated. Within the Marks and Spencer context of the 1990s, being good at forecasting was not a skill or a priority that was being rewarded or highly regarded. Indeed, the managing director of another one of the clothing suppliers argued:

> Some of the more old fashioned merchandisers in Marks and Spencer rewarded people who were macho with suppliers who missed a target. There was this culture, which is still there to a certain extent, which is a merchandiser should be "tough" and should penalise suppliers for doing things wrong. The behaviours that were rewarded were those associated with being good at negotiating price discounts and brutal in penalising errors. There seemed to be no reward for being very good at forecasting. In that environment merchandisers would feel free to cancel production on stocks they did not want, no matter what consequence down the supply chain that might carry. This kind of behaviour was applauded in that macho culture. This could lead to lots of gameplaying and even falsification of figures on both sides. There was a lack of trust.

The new system, if it was to survive against these forces would have required a shift away from a whole set of long-held and deeply embedded assumptions. These were assumptions about the acceptability of opportunistic behaviour, and an ongoing "win-lose" mentality that, despite the public relations spin, was prevalent within many parts of Marks and Spencer.

Summary and Conclusions

This case has revealed the nature and extent of the gap between the idealized depictions in the prescriptive supply chain management literature and the reality on the ground. That gap is especially significant given the relatively favourable circumstances of a sophisticated and reputable major retailer. The study reveals that a "customer-responsive supply chain" with minimal stock-out events, minimal obsolescence, and prompt response to market fluctuations – is technically feasible. This is an important finding. For a short period at least, and in circumscribed conditions, the concept can deliver huge advantages. But, the study also reveals that even when it does work, this is no guarantee of managerial support for its continuance.

The difficulties described here can be found in even more exaggerated form in many other circumstances. The identification of the nature and importance of these behavioural dynamics helps to correct for the naivety in much of the existing literature about inter-firm "co-operation" and "collaboration".

As already noted, a promising test case was purposely selected. If co-operative supply chain relationships were to encounter difficulties in such circumstances then the challenges can be expected to be much more severe elsewhere. Many of the critical success factors were present. There was a clear business need with a logic compelling collaboration for suppliers and retailer. There was a technical solution and ample resources to install that solution. There was a clear proposition and the advantages for both supplier and retailer were readily apparent. There were common performance measures. And there was even a highly successful demonstration period extending over a period of about three years.

But, there were also critical missing elements. There was less than full commitment by the top team of either company. The concept had not been fully accepted by many managers in Marks and Spencer. This is an important point that needs to be noted in relation to much of the literature on supply chain management and buyer-supplier relationships. These literatures, as described earlier in the paper, tend to treat organisations (business-to-business buyers and sellers) as virtual individuals who make calculated rational choices. Much of the research seeks the nature of the criteria – or variables – which are supposedly weighed by these actors. But, in reality, as we found in this case, and others, supply chain issues and inter-organisational relationships more generally are not salient on corporate agendas. Relationships are built at a more operational level and they therefore, remain vulnerable to changes in corporate policy that intrude upon established, emergent, practices.

The study has generated some important challenges to the now very considerable body of literature on business-to-business buyer-supplier relationships and the literature on supply chain management. The case analysis does not of course mean that the previous literature is "wrong": we agree that collaborative relationships can potentially be beneficial. The analysis reveals the organisational behavioural factors that can impede the realisation of the ideal. There are four main underlying assumptions and claims in those literatures that ought to be re-addressed in the light of this study.

First, there is an assumption underpinning much of the buyer-supplier relationship literature, and the supply chain management literature that firms act in a similar manner as individual decision makers might do in considering and weighing series of options. This is especially evident in the literature built around the idea that buyers spend time calculating which suppliers to develop and which ones merit the investment needed to maintain an ongoing relationships [...]. The study suggests, however, that these calculations, in so far as they do occur, are made rather more at an operational level and that as a result their outcomes can be easily overridden by competing corporate level priorities.

For example, Morgan and Hunt (1994, p. 24) claim that "buyers anticipation of high switching costs gives rise to an interest in maintaining a quality relationship". These two interrelated notions (that buying organisations necessarily enter into rational open debate about such factors, and second, that anticipated costs are rationally weighed against each other) were challenged by the findings of our study. These kinds of issues were not, in practice, openly debated in such terms in any sustained way even in these large sophisticated companies. Rather, the study reveals starkly how alternative corporate strategies and priorities can rudely interrupt and easily brush aside organisational collaborative relationships. The study at Marks and Spencer revealed a more complex and less formally rational pattern of behaviour with non-rational actions.

Second, the study also challenges the notion widely canvassed that buyer-supplier relationships proceed in a number of incremental "stages" [...]. This supposedly rational, process of search and decision in a series of logical phases does not accord with the more tentative and iterative reality that we encountered. Indeed, as the case clearly reveals, much more to the fore was a contrary pattern – one which required champions of the initiative within Courtaulds to continually have to re-convince buyers and merchandisers in Marks and Spencer as they were replaced by new staff.

Third, in the case recounted, there were strong competing ideas flourishing in other parts of both Marks and Spencer and Courtaulds and at higher levels. Hence, the collaborative supply chain initiative, despite its positive financial and technical logic and proven outcomes – continued to be at risk. The arrangement not only had to be regarded as worthwhile under benign conditions, it had also to be sustainable and seen as worth preserving when difficult conditions were encountered. Above all, the converts and enthusiasts on both sides were too few. The idea had not permeated the collaborating companies; it was essentially in the heads and the working practices of just a handful of people. Thus, the idea was always at risk when people moved posts or when alternative priorities swept away the arrangement as a sacrifice on the altar of supposedly "bigger" ideas.

Fourth, the dominant theme in the buyer-supplier relationship literature of "commitment" and "trust" in relationship marketing and buyer-supplier collaboration (Morgan and Hunt, 1994; Dwyer et al., 1987; Young and Wilkinson, 1989) needs reconceptualising. The reason is that this literature is constructed on the basis of organisations operating as unitary (somewhat reified) entities that engage in "trusting" or "committed" relationships depending on known variables. But as our research has shown, organisations labelled as "buyers" or "sellers" in fact contain multiple agents. They are engaged in intra-organisational as well as inter-organisational negotiations. The operational staff who may have built up trust and commitment as a result of interaction are subject to commands and instructions from seniors who have different experiences and other agendas. The essential theme of the trust and commitment literature is the co-operative aspects of economic behaviour. Analysts within this mode emphasise and usually extol "norms of sharing and commitment based on trust" (Achrol, 1991, p. 89). Within the relationship marketing literature, commitment and trust are indeed claimed to be the key concepts but, as our study emphasises, while some actors may build such trust and commitment across organisational boundaries they can be overridden in their decision making by corporate chiefs. It was noted in the literature review that many authors emphasise the importance of building social bonds through repeat trading interactions (Tomkins, 2001). But, as the case reported here demonstrates, while this social bonding occurs at operational levels, there is another more strategic business level in large firms that often remains aloof from these social bonds – or arrives without engagement in that legacy – and as result these ties and obligations can be swept aside with surprising ease in the face of alternative priorities.

One might have expected the clothing manufacturer to be the party to the relationship that would be tempted to reassert standardised manufacturing orientations over service orientations based on intangibles. But, as the case revealed, it was the retailer rather than the manufacturer that was mainly responsible for disrupting the relationship and which de-emphasised the service values. The appealing, logical, notion of "customer-responsive supply chain management", which has been so elegantly described in the normative literature, is thus found in practice to be prone to a number of critical organisational and behavioural barriers to its smooth enactment.

References

Abernathy, F.H., Dunlop, J.T. and Hammond, J. (2000), "Retailing and supply chains in the information age" *Technology in Society*, Vol. 22, pp. 5–31.

Achrol, R. (1991), "Evolution of the marketing organisation: new forms for turbulent environments". *Journal of Marketing*, Vol. 55 No. 4, pp. 77–93.

Aitken, J., Christopher, M. and Towill, D. (2002), "Understanding, implementing and exploiting agility and leaness", *International Journal of Logistics Management*, Vol. 5 No. 1, pp. 59–74.

Anderson, J.C., Hakansson, H. and Johanson, J. (1994), "Dyadic business relationships within a business network context", *Journal of Marketing*, Vol. 58 No. 4, pp. 1–15.

Bevan, J. (2001), *The Rise and Fall of Marks and Spencer*, Profile Books, London.

Bookbinder, P. (1993), *Simon Marks, Retail Revolutionary*, George Weidenfeld and Nicholson, London.

Bowen, D.E., Siehl, C. and Schneider, B. (1989), "A framework for analyzing customer service orientations in manufacturing", *Academy of Management Review*, Vol. 14 No. 1, pp. 75–95.

Brennan, R. and Turnbull, P.W. (1999), "Adaptive behavior in buyer-supplier relationships", *Industrial Marketing Management*, Vol. 28 No. 5, pp. 481–95.

Briggs, A. (1984), *Marks and Spencer 1884–1984*, Octopus Books, London.

Bruce, M., Daly, L. and Towers, N. (2004), "Lean or agile – a solution for supply chain management in the textiles and clothing industry?", *International Journal of Operations & Production Management*, Vol. 24 No. 1/2, pp. 151–70.

Christopher, M. (1998), *Logistics and Supply-Chain Management: Strategies for Reducing Cost and Improving Service*, Prentice-Hall, London.

Christopher, M. and Juttner, U. (2000), "Developing strategic partnerships in the supply chain: a practitioner perspective", *European Journal of Purchasing & Supply Management*. Vol. 6, pp. 117–27.

Christopher, M. and Towill, D.R. (2000), "Supply chain migration from lean and functional to agile and customised", *Supply Chain Management: An International Journal*, Vol. 5 No. 4, pp. 206–13.

Clinton, S.R. and Closs, D.J. (1997), "Logistics strategy; does it exist?", *Journal of Business Logistics*, Vol. 18 No. 1, pp. 19–44.

Cooke, J.A. (1999), "CPFR: the countdown begins", *Logistics Management*, Vol. 59, pp. 16–27.

Dwyer, F.R., Schurr, P. and Sejo, Oh (1987), "Developing buyer-seller relationships", *Journal of Marketing*, Vol. 51, pp. 11–27.

Fisher, M.L. (1997), "What is the right supply-chain for your product?", *Harvard Business Review*, Vol. 75, (March-April), pp. 105–16.

Ford, D. (1990), *Understanding Business Markets: Interaction, Relationships and Networks*, Academic Press, London.

Frohlich, M.T. and Westbrook, R. (2001), "Arcs of integration: an international study of supply chain strategies", *Journal of Operations Management*, Vol. 19 No. 2, pp. 185–200.

Gattorna, J.L. (Ed.) (1998), *Strategic Supply Chain Alignment*, Gower, Aldershot.

Gattorna, J.L. and Walters, D.W. (1996), *Managing the Supply Chain: A Strategic Perspective*, Macmillan, New York, NY.

Giunipero, L.C. and Brand, R. (1996), "Purchasing's role in supply chain management", *International Journal of Logistics Management*, Vol. 7 No. 1, pp. 29–38.

Giunipero, L.C. and Fiorito, S.S. (2001), "The impact of vendor incentives on quick response", *International Review of Retail Distribution & Consumer Research*, Vol. 11 No. 4, pp. 359–77.

Goldman, S., Nagel, R. and Preiss, K. (1995), *Agile Competitors and Virtual organisations: Strategies for Enriching the Customer*, Van Nostrand Reinhold, New York, NY.

Hakansson, H. and Snehota, I. (Eds) (1995), *Developing Relationships in Business Networks*, Routledge, London.

Harrison, A. and van Hoek, R. (2002), *Logistics Management and Strategy*, Pearson Education, Harlow.

Jones, R.M. (2002), *The Apparel Industry*, Blackwell, Oxford.

Kalwani, M. and Narayandas, N. (1995), "Long-term manufacturing-supplier relationships: do they pay-off for supplier firms?", *Journal of Marketing*, Vol. 59 No. 1, pp. 1–16.

Mellahi, K., Jackson, P. and Sparks, L. (2002), "An exploratory study into failure in successful organisations: the case of Marks and Spencer", *British Journal of Management*, Vol. 13 No. 1, pp. 15–29.

Morgan, R.M. and Hunt, S.D. (1994), "The commitment-trust theory of relationship marketing", *Journal of Marketing*, Vol. 58 No. 3, pp. 20–38.

Naylor, J.B., Naim, M.M. and Berry, D. (1999), "Leagility: integrating the lean and agile manufacturing paradigms in the total supply chain", *International Journal of Production Economics*, Vol. 62 , pp. 107–18.

Pine, B.J. (1993), *Mass Customisation: The New Frontier in Business Competition*, Harvard Business School Press, Boston.

Sabath, R. (1998), "Volatile demand calls for quick response", *International Journal of Physical Distribution & Logistics Management*, Vol. 28 No. 9/10, pp. 698–704.

Sheth, J.N. (1973), "A model of industrial buyer behavior", *Journal of Marketing*, Vol. 37, pp. 50–6.

Sheth, J.N. (1996), "Organisational buying behavior: past performance and future expectations", *Journal of Business and Industrial Marketing*, Vol. 11, pp. 7–24.

Sheth, J.N. and Sharma, A. (1997), "Relationship marketing: an agenda for inquiry", *Industrial Marketing Management*, Vol. 26, pp. 91–100.

Sparks, L. and Fernie, J. (Eds) (1998), *Logistics and Retail Management: Insights into Current Practice and Trends from Leading Experts*, Kogan Page, London.

Spekman, R.E. (1998). "Strategic supplier selection: understanding long-term buyer relationships", *Business Horizons*, July/August, pp. 75–81.

Storey, J. (2002) "What are the key general manager issues in 'Supply Chain Management'?", *Journal of General Management*, Vol. 27 No. 4, pp. 15–28.

Tomkins, C. (2001), " Inter-dependencies, trust and information in relationships, alliances and networks", *Accounting Organisations and Society*, Vol. 26 No. 2, pp. 161–91.

Whiteoak, P. (1994), "The realities of quick response in the grocery sector", *International Journal of Physical Distribution & Logistics Management*, Vol. 24 No. 10, pp. 33–40.

Wilkinson, I. and Young, L. (1995), "Business dancing: the nature and role of inter-firm relations in business strategy", *Asia-Australia Marketing Journal*, Vol. 2 No. 1, pp. 67–79.

Wilson, D.T. and Mummalaneni, V. (1986), "Bonding and commitment in buyer-seller relationships: a preliminary conceptualisation", *Industrial Marketing and Purchasing*, Vol. 1 No. 3, pp. 44–58.

Womack, J.P. and Jones, D.J. (1996), *Lean Thinking*, Simon Schuster, New York, NY.

Young, L. and Wilkinson, I. (1989), "The role of trust and cooperation in marketing channels: a preliminary study", *European Journal of Marketing*, Vol. 23 No. 2, pp. 109–22.

Part 3

Innovation

Innovation seems to be *the* business imperative of the twenty-first century, with exhortations to 'innovate or die' now appearing in every part of the literature, but just what do we mean by innovation? By general consensus, two factors initially emerge as crucial: novelty and utility. An innovation is, almost by definition, novel; even if not original in some absolute sense, it must at least represent something unexpected in terms of the particular application to hand. Utility also seems essential; having a good idea is not enough, it needs to be implemented in practice before meriting the name innovation.

The previous Part contained two articles reviewing what are best described as 'improvement' methodologies: Continuous Improvement and Lean. Both are concerned not with some step-function, 'out with the old, in with the new'-style of process redesign, but with the accumulated effects of many small, incremental changes. So should we include such activities within our definition? Arguably no: innovation is more usefully reserved for relatively large, discontinuous change, leaving improvement as the term of choice for smaller, more incremental steps. Nevertheless, we still have to deal with a now venerable body of literature that at best may use terms like 'innovation process' to subsume both elements, and at worst may use the words almost interchangeably. In any form of enterprise, both innovation and improvement have a vital role to play, the perceived glamour of the former should not blind us to the very real benefits of the latter.

For many, Russell Ackoff is regarded as the godfather of the systems movement that still informs much of management thinking. The **Allio** chapter relates a short 2003 interview with the man on the topic of, very loosely, innovation. As would be expected from a self-styled iconoclast, the views expressed are quite deliberately provocative, to the point where Ackoff is effectively advocating a fairly radical reconceptualization of business and management. The salient point, in the context of this Part of this book, is that such a reconceptualization is arguably a necessary precursor to any form of discontinuous change. Indeed the argument could be paraphrased into more familiar language as an argument for managers to 'think outside the box'.

In recent years, Clayton Christensen has been a prolific author on the topic of innovation, perhaps best known for introducing the concept of disruptive innovation. In the article by **Anthony and Christensen** included here, the authors build upon earlier work by using the awareness of said phenomenon to augment the organizational radar. No-one is really going to offer management any form of reliable crystal ball, but there is merit in examining innovation history if only to avoid repeating the same mistakes. Many critical failures arise because a management team has been to some extent 'blind-sided' by developments that simply lie outwith their previous experience. The authors argue that disruptive change needs to be assessed on its own terms, and not dismissed purely because it fails to conform to existing mindsets.

Not too long ago, an organization's commitment to Research and Development was denoted by the proportion of its turnover that was spent on R&D. While this may indeed function as a sign of intent, it remains an input measure. A far more cogent measure would involve some consideration of the value gained from such investment. Now, any examination of such things as the granting of patents, the emergence of new technologies or the evolution of new business models tends to reveal that large organizations often struggle with anything that is radically different, and that small, often new companies are actually quite good at discontinuous change. Eventually, pennies dropped and the problem resolved into how large organizations, with funds and infrastructure at their disposal, could tap in to the innovative potential of smaller companies. This process is a key element of Open Innovation as outlined by Henry **Chesbrough**. In this chapter, Open Innovation arguably starts with the plausible premise that 'not all the smart people work for us'. Given this realization, that the intrinsic value of an idea is of more interest than whence it came, it becomes possible to deconstruct traditional 'closed' models of innovation and re-assemble them in entirely more interesting ways, inevitably involving a network of diverse organizations carrying out different parts of the process.

Until relatively recently the Innovation literature has been largely concerned with the emergence of the product (and in too many instances that meant a physical device rather than even a product/service mix). In many ways this was an understandable corollary of traditional 'closed' models of innovation but times have changed; innovation is now increasingly applied to the exploitation of the product in its wider sense. The chapter by **Markides and Geroski** is entirely concerned with strategies for the innovative exploitation of other folks' ideas. To a very large extent complementing the multiple agency models from the earlier chapters by Anthony and Christensen and by Chesbrough, the authors underscore the creative opportunities open to both existing players and new entrants in evolving markets.

Ackoff on Innovation

Robert J. Allio

Robert J. Allio recently interviewed Russell Ackoff on behalf of Strategy & Leadership *to obtain his specific suggestions for reinventing how managers learn to develop effective strategy and promote innovation.*

Strategy & Leadership: According to your recent indictment in *Strategy & Leadership* of management consultants who aggressively promote themselves as gurus with a prescription for change, most of them have only platitudes or tautologies to offer organizations that seek guidance on strategy. Why is to so easy for purveyors of platitudes to dupe managers?

Russell Ackoff: Because most managers don't have the knowledge and understanding required to deal with complexity, they attempt to reduce complex situations to simple ones. As a result, they tend to look for simple, if not simple-minded, solutions to problems. For this reason managers are susceptible to management gurus pitching panaceas. When a panacea appears to work in one or two prominent business situations, it can quickly become a fad. The consultants relentlessly promote these fads and fantasies because they're sources of business.

S&L: So these consultants simply respond to market demand for solutions?

Ackoff: Yes. There are exceptions of course. In my experience the larger consulting firms are the most guilty of promulgating fantasies like "down sizing", "benchmarking", and "process re-engineering".

S&L: What responsibility do the business schools have for this condition?

Ackoff: A great deal. In general, I find that business schools tend to avoid the important complex strategic problems that corporate management is currently involved with. Not too long ago at a meeting of the deans of business schools I identified the set of six or seven corporate problems on which I was working. I asked them if any of them had courses that addressed such problems – not a single one of them was covered.

S&L: An example of these problems you are working on?

Source: R.J. Allio (2003) *Strategy and Leadership*, 31 (3): 19–26.

Ackoff: One is, "How can you plan to market a truly new product – one the consumer cannot conceptualize?". Another is: "What kind of support is required to enable an organization to learn and adapt effectively to a rapidly changing environment?"

I have "endeared" myself to some faculty and business schools by identifying the three things that business schools do for students. First, they provide students with a vocabulary that enables them to talk with authority about subjects they do *not* understand. Second, they transmit to them a set of principles that have demonstrated an ability to withstand any amount of disconfirming evidence. Third, they provide a ticket of admission to a job where they can learn something about management and business. Around 95 percent of what managers use on the job they learned on the job. The most they get out of business school is connections. Attendance at a business school is justified economically in terms of return on investment, but not in terms of providing an education.

S&L: Let me go back to the search by management for panaceas. Are the corporate managers ignorant, insecure, naïve?

Ackoff: They are not stupid. They are misinformed, incorrectly instructed, and do not understand what fundamental changes are going on their environments. They are products of a defective educational system. Consequently, 50 percent of the corporations in the *Fortune* 500 of 25 years ago no longer exist. The average life of an American corporation is 14.5 years. Out of 23 new corporations created each year, only one survives the first year. We incorrectly characterize the American economy by the successful ones. We ignore the failures. The strength of the American economy lies in the fact that it can survive more inefficiency than any other economy in the world. If any other economy had the number of failures that we've had, it wouldn't survive. We had almost 1,000 bankruptcies last year of major corporations and we are beating that this year so far. Imagine what our performance would be like if that inefficiency were decreased.

S&L: Are you suggesting that this is the consequence of inept management, a Darwinian survival phenomenon?

Ackoff: Yes, I am. Gary Hamel and other management observers identify the numerous failures and look for their causes in faulty management practices. But the one cause that dominates all others is management error.

When I talk to managers, I usually start with a quote from Einstein, "Without changing our pattern of thought, we will not be able to solve the problems we created with our current patterns of thought". Managers always agree with this. But when I ask, "What is our current pattern of thought?" they haven't the foggiest idea. Because of this they cannot understand their failures.

S&L: Are you advocating that we do better research to failures as opposed to successes?

Ackoff: No. We have to educate managers on the nature of the fundamental intellectual changes that are occurring within our culture. These require a change in the way we think and what we think about.

S&L: What are some of the characteristics of this new paradigm?

Ackoff: One of them is the development of *synthetic* thinking, which provides better understanding of complex systems than analytical thinking does. Synthetic thinking is a way of thinking about and designing a system that derives the properties and behavior of its parts from the functions required of the whole. The whole has properties that none of its parts have.

Analysis of a system reveals how it works but synthetic thinking is required to explain why it works the way it does. Systems thinking integrates the two.

Analysis breaks a system down into its parts, tries to explain the behavior of these parts, and then attempts to aggregate this understanding into an understanding of the whole. It cannot succeed because when a system is taken apart it loses all its essential characteristics and so do its parts. A disassembled automobile cannot transport people and a motor taken out of it cannot move anything, even itself.

Analysis, applied to systems, and therefore corporations, can only yield knowledge of how the system works, but never an understanding of why it works the way it does.

S&L: You're making the important distinction between knowing a system and understanding it.

Ackoff: Yes. Knowledge is transmitted through instructions, which are the answers to *how-to* questions. Understanding is transmitted through explanations, which answer the *why* questions. Herein lies a very fundamental difference. Corporations and corporate managers do not understand the importance of this difference. They tend to have a lot of knowledge but little understanding of the complex systems they manage and the environments in which they operate. To echo Peter Drucker, they tend to manage things right rather than manage the right things. The righter (more efficiently) they managed the wrong thing, the wronger (less effective), they become.

S&L: Where can executives get reliable advice on how to run their organizations, if not from consultants or the business schools?

Ackoff: Don't start with books on strategy, with alleged experts, or so-called educators. Instead, start with iconoclasts – individuals who can help others acquire understanding about the changes taking place in the way we think, and what we think about. Once managers understand the changing paradigm, to use your term, then they can ask: "What are the implications of strategic thinking?". The approach I suggest seems terribly complicated compared to what most consultants advise. When someone asked Peter Drucker what he thought of the solutions proposed in the 1990s by Peters and Waterman's best selling book *The Search for Excellence,* he said, "I wish it were that simple". Complex problems do not have simple-minded solutions.

S&L: Can you cite examples of corporations that manage systemically?

Ackoff: Yes, there are a number – Hermann Miller, Fed Ex, Westinghouse Furniture Systems, SAS, and Gore-Tex, to mention a few.

S&L: In order to think systemically, I need to understand the relationship between the parts and the whole. Doesn't that mean I need to have data that show the causal relationship among those parts?

Ackoff: You have to understand how the interactions of the parts, and the parts with the whole and its environment, create the properties of the whole. Cause-effect is about actions, not interactions. Most managers currently manage the actions of their organizations' parts taken separately. This is based on the false assumption that improving the performance of the parts separately necessarily improves the performance of the whole, the corporation. That is a false premise. In fact, you can destroy a corporation by improving its individual parts. Try putting a Rolls Royce engine in a Hyundai.

S&L: So your premise is, if we are going to have more effective corporations, then we need to understand the system that comprises the organization. When you give that prescription to a manager, what are you telling him to do?

Ackoff: He has to re-conceptualize the corporation. The origin of the word "corporation" is "corpus", a body, an organism, biological entity. According to the law a corporation is a person. Organisms, unlike mechanisms, have purposes of their own. But, in an organism, the parts have no purposes of their own. They are mechanisms. It is only the whole that has a purpose. So, the current conception of a corporation involves thinking that its parts exist only to serve the purposes of the whole and the whole has no obligation to serve the purposes of the parts – only to keep them, as organs, healthy and safe. And this is the wrong metaphor for a modern corporation.

We should no longer treat a corporation as a biological system. We should treat it as a social system. A social system has purposes of its own, so do its parts, and so do the systems that contain it and the other systems they contain. A social system floats in a sea of purposes at multiple levels with some purposes incompatible within and between levels; and its management must concern itself with all of these. It is for this reason that we are becoming aware of the need to know how to manage complexity. There is a growing need to think of the corporation as a *community,* not as an organism.

Now, the implications of re-envisioning a corporation as a community are huge. First, ownership becomes irrelevant. This notion that stockholders own a corporation is in decline. They are investors and shouldn't be treated as owners. No one owns a nation, state, city, or neighborhood. But each must take into account the purposes of all its stakeholders.

Communities have an obligation to facilitate the development of its members, to contribute to their quality of life and standard of living, and to enable them to pursue their objectives as well as they know how.

The third fundamental characteristic of a community is that it is not a hierarchy but a "lower-archy". In a community, those in a position of authority are selected by the people below them, not above them. Authority does not flow from the top down as it does in most corporations; it flows from the bottom up, and so do resources. So the task of turning a corporation around into a community and a lower-archy is really huge.

S&L: What about leading such a transition?

Ackoff: This requires more than management; it requires leadership. The thing that leaders do that managers don't is articulate an inspiring vision and guide the formulation of a strategy for its pursuit. Good or bad, you look at a Lenin or a Churchill, and what they did is produce a vision shared by others. In Churchill's case, he produced a vision of victory for the allies and helped formulate a strategy for getting there.

To lead requires different skills than to manage. Some unique individuals combine those two skills, but generally not. Churchill was a magnificent leader in WWII. He was not a good manager, but he had enough sense to pick people who were. He surrounded himself with people who could do what he couldn't do, and who couldn't do what he could.

S&L: Let's talk about how to formulate effective strategy – not by listening to consultants, not by going to business school, but by understanding the system.

Ackoff: First by understanding what's happening inside and outside the organization, then by developing a vision of what the organization could be within the emerging culture and environment. Next by preparing a strategy for reaching or moving closer to that vision.

For example, our healthcare system is a mess. We are the only developed country in the world without universal coverage; about 42 million people are uninsured. It is estimated that excessive testing, excessive surgery, or excessive prescribing of drugs that interact adversely causes at least half of the illness in the US. The federal government recently found that about one million people per year are seriously infected while in hospitals and approximately 100,000 die from these infections. *The fact is that the US doesn't have a healthcare system.* We have an illness and disability care system. Why? We or our surrogates pay the system for taking care of us when we are sick or disabled. Therefore, the greatest threat to the existence of the system is pervasive health! Little wonder that the system accepts and encourages practices that preserve, maintain and create illness and disability.

The time is ripe for somebody to see the real problem and say, "Let's design a healthcare system, one that has incentives for producing and maintaining health, not illness and disabilities".

S&L: Let me ask you to advise the individual who sees such an opportunity and creates a vision. The manager wants to develop a strategy to implement that vision. How does the manager develop effective strategy?

Ackoff: This requires design, and designs that lead require creativity. Creativity involves a three-step process. The first step is to identify assumptions that you make which prevent you from seeing the alternatives to the ones that you currently see. These are self-imposed constraints. The second step is to deny these constraining assumptions. The third is to explore the consequences of the denials. Creativity of individuals can be enhanced by practice, particularly under the guidance of one who is creative.

S&L: As opposed to learning creative strategy from case studies?

Ackoff: Case studies usually provide examples of uncreative solutions to problems. Learning a business principle from a case may help one practice that principle, but it doesn't show you how to creatively solve problems.

S&L: What's a good alternative to the case method?

Ackoff: The best way to learn is through apprenticeship and neither the educational system nor education within corporations is built on apprenticeship.

S&L: How do you implement the concept of apprenticeship in the corporation?

Ackoff: I lived in England for a while and I was tremendously impressed by the concept of a shadow cabinet. Years later, working with the brewing company, Anheuser-Busch, I asked the CEO, August Busch, III, and each member of the executive committee (all 11 vice presidents) to pick one up-and-coming young person to serve on a shadow policy committee for the corporation. Each issue that goes to the top for solution first goes to this group and they make their recommendations to the top group. Members are replaced every few years. They are exposed to a real education and learn how to think strategically through continuous interaction with top management.

In the organizational design called *a circular organization or democratic hierarchy*, every manager has a board consisting of him/herself, his/her immediate subordinates and his/her immediate superior. These boards have responsibilities similar to those of parliament and congress while the manager has those of an executive office. This too has turned out to be a very effective educational process and way to raising morale and productivity. Furthermore, it simplifies succession planning.

S&L: Give me an example of a creative systemic thinking process that resulted in an important new product.

Ackoff: An urban automobile. Before we could start to redesign the automobile for urban use, someone had to ask, "What is the most basic assumption we make that affects the design of our current automobiles?". The answer: we currently design automobiles to serve in a variety of environments, to serve many purposes. Is this a correct assumption? When the automobile was developed it was so expensive relatively that only the most prosperous families could afford one. Therefore, the initial need was for a general-purpose vehicle. But today, most households in the US contain two or more cars, enabling us to divide their use between urban and inter-urban trips and between use at rush hour or off hours. So, this gives us an opportunity to design an urban automobile for workday and work-time use. On the average, how many people ride in an urban automobile? It turns out to be 1.2, more than 80 percent of the cars in the city contain just one or two people. So, we can design a two-passenger automobile for urban use. And what is the speed at which you get the maximum density of people on a highway all moving in the same direction? It turns to be between 35 and 40 mph. So we build the car with a maximum cruising capacity of 40 mph. The car, currently available only through custom production, goes more than 80 miles per gallon, is non polluting, and would, if in general use, eliminate all urban congestion until well into this century.

These examples answer the question you asked earlier: "How do you work out the means strategically?". First, we decided we wanted an automobile that will avoid pollution congestion and maximize comfort and convenience. To design one from scratch creatively we had to identify the assumptions on which the design of the current automobile is based, deny them, and explore the consequences. The need that remains is for a strategy that will lead to progress toward realization of such a vehicle.

S&L: You are describing the process of critical thinking.

Ackoff: It's more than just thinking critically; it's a process of rethinking constructively and creatively.

S&L: So, in the management arena, does research have a role – for example to suggest enduring relationships or natural laws? How would you critique the Boston Consulting Group research on the experience curve that led to the market share hypothesis?

Ackoff: Experience is a dynamic concept, isn't it? Without experience, learning would not be possible. Therefore, to say that experience results in learning is to say nothing. Then to add that performance improves with learning it also a tautology. How could performance improve without learning?

S&L: But it quantifies the impact.

Ackoff: No, it doesn't quantify, it gives you the shape of the curve, and that's trivial. It just says you become more efficient with practice.

S&L: The PIMS research resulted in a multivariate regression equation from which certain conclusions were drawn. The PIMS apostles would argue that those equations could explain profitability.

Ackoff: They're wrong. They don't explain anything. They are not explanatory; they're descriptive. The PIMS model operates on the assumption that regression has something to do with causality and that's absolutely false. The most that regression can do is formulate a causal hypothesis that can be tested. It cannot establish any causal relationships.

S&L: What are some other strategic management "predictors" that are misused or misunderstood?

Ackoff: In his book about corporate longevity, Arie de Geus postulates that all companies that have lived for more than 100 years have certain characteristics. By studying such companies he identified properties to which he attributes their continuing survival. But he didn't show that all the companies that don't live for 100 years don't have those characteristics. His inferences may be correct, but they are not justified by his argument.

S&L: Lack of a "control sample" is also a problem with Jim Collins' research for his influential business books *Good to Great* and *Built to Last: Successful Habits of Visionary Companies,* and many other best sellers too.

Ackoff: But, that's the kind of simple-minded stuff that's being bought.

S&L: What's your advice to a practicing manager on how to become a more effective strategist and leader?

Ackoff: First, to get educated on what's happening in the culture and the new world, to become aware of the nature of the fundamental intellectual transformations taking place and what their implications are for the future of business and management generally. Second, to attach themselves to people who show creative thinking and engage with them in the process of redesigning, from scratch and with no constraints, the systems they manage.

10

How You Can Benefit by Predicting Change

Scott D. Anthony and Clayton M. Christensen

Take a step back to the late 1970s and imagine being Ken Olson, the founder and CEO of Digital Equipment Corp. (DEC), the then world's leading minicomputer manufacturer. You make sophisticated, high-end equipment that is sold to the world's leading corporations, and your company has been phenomenally successful over the past two decades. You observe that a series of entrepreneurs have come up with a simple, low-price computer meant to be used by individuals. What does this mean?

How would you answer that question? The personal computer market doesn't exist, so there's no market research report to turn to. And, your current customers aren't much use. Imagine if you went to them and said, "We're going to sell you a product that is much worse than what you currently use. You won't be able to do much with it, but maybe someday you will." What would you expect them to say — or do? Would they rush to purchase this new product?

In this context, then, it is quite natural that in 1977, Ken Olson famously said, "There is no reason anyone would want a personal computer in their home."

This anecdote isn't meant to single out Olson. Back in the '40s, IBM Corp. CEO Tom Watson said, "I think there is a world market for maybe five computers." Microsoft Corp. Chairman Bill Gates in 1980 said that "640 [kilobytes of memory] ought to be enough for anybody." In the 19th century, the CEO of telegraphy giant Western Union dismissed the telephone as an electrical "toy".

The fact is, across the sweep of history, industry leaders have done a poor job identifying the innovations that ultimately have the most transformational potential.

Indeed, identifying transformational technologies is surprisingly difficult. Our natural instincts are to look for data proving that something critical is going on, but unassailable data only exists about the past. Too often, the data and evidence trickling into a market reflects what has already happened, and sometimes even occurred in the distant past. Waiting for conclusive evidence, therefore, consigns people to take action when it is too late. After all, by the time the writing is on the wall, everyone can read it.

But that is not the only way, as now there are useful tools to help executives and analysts understand what will happen in the future. It is now possible to use "disruptive innovation theory" to spot early signals of industry change, confidently predict how

Source: S.D. Anthony and C.M Christensen (2005) *Financial Executive*, 21 (2): 36–41.

Disruptive Innovation Theory

The disruptive innovation theory holds that existing companies have a high probability of beating entrant attackers when the contest is about sustaining innovations: *radical or incremental improvements that target demanding customers at the high end of the market who are willing to pay premium prices for better products*. Established companies tend to lose to attackers armed with disruptive innovations: cheaper, simpler, more convenient products or services that start by meeting the needs of less-demanding customers.

The figure below illustrates the disruptive innovation theory. The figure has two types of improvement trajectories. The solid lines illustrate company improvement trajectories. They show how products and services get better over time. The dotted line shows a customer demand trajectory — not the quantity customers demand, but the performance they can use. For simplicity, the figure shows a single line, although it shows how in every market there is a distribution of customers based on the performance they demand. As the figure suggests, a customer's needs in a given market application tend to be relatively stable over time.

Sustaining innovations, illustrated by the curved arrows, move companies along established improvement trajectories. They are improvements to existing products on dimensions historically valued by customers. Airplanes that fly farther, computers that process faster, cellular phone batteries that last longer and televisions with incrementally or dramatically clearer images are all sustaining innovations.

Because companies can innovate faster than people's lives change, the pace of sustaining innovation nearly always outstrips the ability of customers to absorb it, opening the door for disruptive developments.

Disruptive products or services initially are inferior to existing offerings, at least along dimensions by which mainstream customers measure value. However, they are typically more affordable and simpler to use than products in the incumbents'

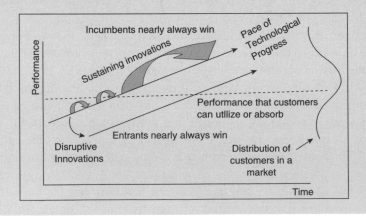

(Continued)

product portfolio. They create growth outside of the core market among customers that are delighted with the product or service despite its limitations.

Some disruptive innovations disrupt an existing market from the low end. Dell Inc.'s direct-to-customer business model, Wal-Mart Stores Inc.'s discount retail store, Nucor Corp.'s steel minimill and The Vanguard Group Inc.'s index mutual funds are all examples of this kind of "low-end" disruption.

Other disruptive innovations create entirely new markets by competing against nonconsumption, eBay Inc. democratized the auction process, seizing it from the domain of the wealthy. Similarly, the personal computer liberated computing from the *cognoscenti* and delivered it to the masses. The Kodak camera, Bell telephone, Sony transistor radio and Xerox photocopier are classic examples of these new-market disruptions.

those signals will unfold and react appropriately. Executives that learn how to spot the signals of disruptive change will have much greater insight into the potential and perils of emerging technologies, improving their ability to make the right strategic decisions.

The "disruptive innovation theory," first described by Clayton Christensen in the 1997 book *The Innovator's Dilemma* (see box), holds that organizations have the best chance of creating new growth by bringing disruptive innovations into a marketplace. These innovations either create new markets or reshape existing markets by delivering a new, highly desired value proposition to customers.

There is a simple, important principle at the core of the disruptive innovation theory: companies innovate faster than customers' lives change. Because of this, companies end up producing products that are too good, and too expensive for many customers. This phenomenon happens for a good reason: good managers are trained to seek higher profits by bringing better products to the most demanding customers in the market place. But in that pursuit of profits, companies end up "overshooting" less-demanding customers who are perfectly willing to take the basics at reasonable prices. And they ignore "nonconsumers" who lack the skills, wealth or ability to consume at all.

For example, in the 1990s, companies continued to invest to produce higher-quality compact disk technology. However, products were already more than good enough for what customers needed. How did companies create new growth? By using a simple, convenient technology called MP3 that actually had lower audio quality than existing solutions but had new benefits related to customizability and convenience. MP3 is a classic disruptive technology.

Even today, it continues to have limitations along important dimensions such as audio quality. However, it is so much more flexible that people can consume music in entirely new ways, using MP3 players as portable jukeboxes. Companies such as Apple Computer Inc. used the simple, convenient technology to create booming growth.

The situation for Sony Corp. was completely different. MP3 technology looked unattractive to engineers who worked on Sony's product lines that competed based on offering superior sound quality. Consider this comment from a Sony engineer in a recent *Wall Street Journal article:* "I don't really like hard disks — they're not Sony technology. As an engineer, they're not interesting."

While Apple's success with the iPod is transforming the company, Sony appeared to drag its heels entering the market, only recently releasing a MP3 player.

Disruption Developments Flower

Disruptive developments are beginning to flower in a number of different industries. For example, in healthcare, companies are introducing quick and convenient diagnostic services delivered by nurse-practitioners in kiosks located in retail stores. The leading example of this emerging model is Minnesota-based MinuteClinic. At MinuteClinic kiosks in Target stores, customers can receive diagnostic tests for about a dozen ailments, such as strep throat. The service is sharply cheaper than going to a general practitioner's office, and service is guaranteed in 15 minutes.

Education is another industry where "consuming" typically requires paying steep fees and going to centralized locations. On-the-job training and online adult education providers are delivering extremely relevant, low-cost education in more convenient ways. For example, the University of Phoenix now educates more than 100,000 students, both on traditional campuses and over the Internet. It explicitly targets adult students who lack the wealth, time or test scores to attend traditional programs.

Additionally, more and more corporations are finding it more valuable to train high-potential managers at internal "universities" (such as General Electric Co.'s Crotonville training center) than to send them to expensive onsite Masters of Business Administration (MBA) programs.

Disruption is also swirling around the telecommunications industry. A technology known as Voice over Internet Protocol (VoIP) now allows companies to offer cheap, customizable telephony service over the Internet. One company following an interesting model using VoIP is Skype Technologies S.A., a peer-to-peer solution created by the duo that introduced Kazaa (the peer-to-peer file swapping software that gives music and film industry executives nightmares). Kazaa is owned by Sharman Networks Ltd. Customers using Skype's program can send and receive calls from their personal computer to other Skype users around the world. The application is simple (and free) to download and install, and calls are high-quality and free.

In aviation, historical industry leaders The Boeing Co. and Airbus S.A.S are obsessed with their fight for the high end of the industry. Airbus recently unveiled its massive A380 super jumbo jet, which can hold up to 600 passengers and can be modified to include services such as a gymnasium. Meanwhile, regional jet manufacturers like

Embraer (Empresa Brasileira de Aeronautica S.A.) and Bombardier Inc. have created big businesses providing smaller planes to regional carriers. And a number of players are racing to create very-low cost airplanes that will enable the birth of a vibrant air taxi industry. Startups such as New Mexico-based Eclipse Aviation Corp. and Colorado-based Adam Aircraft Industries, corporate jet manufacturers such as Cessna Aircraft Co. and automobile manufacturers such as Honda Motor Co. Ltd. are all targeting the space.

These and similar developments, in industries ranging from automotive to financial services to consumer electronics, fit a pattern. A company has found a way to bring a radically different value proposition into an overlooked part of the market. Although these kinds of developments often seem inoffensive at first, as disruptive attackers grow and improve, they often emerge as serious competitive threats. (See box "Seeing What's Next.")

Seeing What's Next
Process Analyzes Industry Change

Seeing What's Next suggests following a three-part process to use the theories of innovation to spot and interpret disruptive developments and predict industry change.

Part 1: *Look for signals of change, for signs of companies emerging to meet the needs of three different customer groups: overshot customers, undershot customers and nonconsuming customers.*

Undershot customers are customers for whom existing solutions are not good enough. Signals of undershot customers include customers eagerly snatching up new products, steady or increasing prices and the struggles of specialists. Undershot customers look for sustaining innovations that close the gap between what is available and the job they are looking to get done.

"Overshot" customers are customers for whom existing solutions are too good. Signals of overshot customers include customer reluctance to purchase new products, declining prices and the emergence of specialists. Overshot customers welcome low-end disruptive innovations that offer good enough technological performance at low prices.

Nonconsumers are customers that lack the skills, wealth or ability to "do it themselves." Signals of nonconsumption includes customers that have to turn to someone with more skills or training in order to consume, a market limited to those with great wealth and the need to go to centralized, inconvenient locations to consume. Nonconsumers welcome new-market disruptive innovations that make it easy for them to do it themselves.

(Continued)

(Continued)

Part 2: *Analyze competitive battles to see which firms are likely to emerge triumphant.* There are two components to this analysis. The first involves identifying each combatant's strengths, weaknesses and blindspots by looking at their resources (what they have), processes (the way they do their business), and values (decision rules that determine how resources get allocated).

The second part requires identifying the company that is taking advantage of "asymmetries," doing what its opponent has neither the skills nor the motivation to do. Pay particular attention to asymmetric processes and values. Whereas resources are extremely flexible, processes and values are inflexible, determining what a company can and cannot and will and will not do.

Part 3: *Look at important strategic choices that can help to determine ultimate winners and losers.* For entrants, start by looking to see if the company is properly preparing for battle by hiring the right management team, instituting an appropriate strategy-making process and receiving funding from investors that will allow the company to follow a disruptive path.

Finally, assess whether an incumbent has developed the capability to capitalize on disruptive trends. Well-schooled incumbents could respond to a disruptive threat by setting up a separate organization or using an established process to parry the disruptive attacker.

Implications

Spotting potentially transformational innovations is one thing. Understanding the implications of those innovations is another. One pressing challenge facing many [...] managers is allocating scarce investment dollars between innovation opportunities. It is, indeed, tough, as opportunities that seem to have a high probability of creating growth often flop. Acquisitions produce frustratingly inconsistent but typically negative returns.

Managers can use the disruptive innovation model in three ways to improve their return on innovation investment. They can: 1) limit investment in overshot dimensions; 2) proactively scan for disruptive developments; and 3) use the model to guide investment decisions. More detail on each follows.

Limit Investment in Overshot Markets

Companies should continually monitor whether they have overshot a customer segment, because further investment in overshot dimensions promises to disappoint. How can you identify an overshot segment? Overshot customers begin to complain that products are too complicated and expensive. They stop using and valuing new features. Importantly, they begin to pay decreasing prices for new innovations. Declining prices and margins in a given market tier are often signs of overshot customers.

For example, there are many signs that enterprise software providers have overshot much of the market. Many customers are growing increasingly unwilling to pay for expensive software up-grades because they find that old versions of software are good enough for their needs. They are increasingly turning to low-cost providers such as Salesforce.com.

A company that invests in improving along overshot dimensions is unlikely to realize the full rewards from its innovation effort because customers will not value the enhancements. These kinds of proposals will usually contain data showing the fantastic returns from historical investments to improve products for this product segment. But that data explains what happened in the past, not what will happen in the future.

Proactively Scan for Disruptive Developments

The model implies that [...] managers make sure that they continuously scan for threats emerging outside of the core market. When companies have to name their most daunting competitor, they often point to the leading incumbent in their marketplace. Thirty years ago, General Motors Corp. (GM) would point to Ford Motor Corp. Twenty years ago DEC would point to Prime Computer Corp., Wang Laboratories and Nixdorf Computer AG. Today, Boeing would point to Airbus; Harvard Business School would point to Stanford Business School.

These are all sustaining rivals, where companies are fighting for existing customers in existing markets. These battles are important, but companies also need to watch for disruptive innovations incubating outside of the core market. Today, GM's largest threat comes from Toyota Motor Corp., which took root in the lowest end of the auto industry in the 1960s. Tomorrow, GM's largest threat will come from an Asian manufacturer that figures out how to make a $2,500 car.

Keeping tabs on sustaining competitors involves watching so-called "lead" customers and carefully analyzing market data. Watching for disruptive developments involves looking for companies targeting the low-end of existing markets and customer groups seemingly in the market's fringe. It involves looking for companies that fit the established pattern of disruptive innovators.

Companies that need to pay particularly close attention to disruption are those that operate in markets where consumption is limited by having particular skills, a degree of wealth or access to a centralized setting. Competitors with disruptive intentions will inevitably find a way to tackle one of those constraints and reach a group of customers historically locked out of the market.

Although it may take a while, you can predict that the company that has democratized a limited market will improve its solution to the point where it can materially affect existing providers.

When companies identify a legitimate disruptive development, they can, of course, invest to create a rival offering. Doing so must be managed quite carefully, however, because the established ways in which the core business operates often get in the way of creating viable disruptive entrants. Alternatively, a company can acquire one of the emerging disruptive attackers to capitalize on its growth potential.

Use the Model to Guide Acquisition Targets

Why a company would ever expect to create profitable growth through acquisitions is a mystery to many academics. Study after study has shown that, on average, acquisitions destroy value — the price paid for the acquisition doesn't justify the subsequent performance of the acquired company.

Many companies find that large acquisitions provide stable but lackluster returns, whereas small acquisitions typically have highly variable outcomes, occasionally producing blockbuster returns. Screening for small targets that match identified disruptive patterns can in essence cut the tail off of the returns distribution curve, allowing companies to capture disruptive growth before it becomes fully understood by the marketplace.

For example, Johnson & Johnson's Medical Device and Diagnostics business unit acquired four separate disruptive businesses in the '80s: Cordis Corp. (stents), Lifescan Inc. (blood glucose monitors), Vistakon (disposable contact lenses) and Ethicon Inc. (endoscopic surgery). Those four acquisitions grew at a compound annual rate of more than 40 percent during the '1990s, accounting for almost all of the division's growth.

Similarly, in the early '1990s, The Washington Post Co. recognized that there were disruptive trends that were poised to change the education industry as education moved beyond the classroom. It acquired Kaplan Inc. and a number of other training companies. The training and education part of The Washington Post Co. now accounts for more than 50 percent of the company's revenue.

Bringing the Future into Focus

Historically, predicting industry change has just seemed to be an impossible task. After all, if the experts get it wrong so frequently, what hope is there for the rest of us?

Using the right theory, however, can help improve our collective ability to see into the future. It can help to separate signal from noise, amplifying the important information that seems to be buried in overwhelming amounts of data. It can help to pinpoint industry-changing firms or business models long before markets and experts recognize that change is afoot. It can help explain who is going to win and who is going to lose when powerful competitors square off. And it can help bring key management decisions into focus, highlighting the levers managers can pull to change competitive actions.

Finally, using the right theory can bring the future into much sharper focus, allowing the senior executive decision-makers to confidently see what's next and act appropriately.

11

The Era of Open Innovation

Henry W. Chesbrough

In the past, internal R&D was a valuable strategic asset, even a formidable barrier to entry by competitors in many markets. Only large corporations like DuPont, IBM and AT&T could compete by doing the most R&D in their respective industries (and subsequently reaping most of the profits as well). Rivals who sought to unseat those powerhouses had to ante up considerable resources to create their own labs, if they were to have any chance of succeeding. These days, however, the leading industrial enterprises of the past have been encountering remarkably strong competition from many upstarts. Surprisingly, these newcomers conduct little or no basic research on their own, but instead get new ideas to market through a different process.

Consider Lucent Technologies, which inherited the lion's share of Bell Laboratories after the breakup of AT&T. In the 20th century, Bell Labs was perhaps the premier industrial research organization and this should have been a decisive strategic weapon for Lucent in the telecommunications equipment market. However, things didn't quite work out that way. Cisco Systems, which lacks anything resembling the deep internal R&D capabilities of Bell Labs, somehow has consistently managed to stay abreast of Lucent, even occasionally beating the company to market. What happened?

Although Lucent and Cisco competed directly in the same industry, the two companies were not innovating in the same manner. Lucent devoted enormous resources to exploring the world of new materials and state-of-the-art components and systems, seeking fundamental discoveries that could fuel future generations of products and services. Cisco, on the other hand, deployed a very different strategy in its battle for innovation leadership. Whatever technology the company needed, it acquired from the outside, usually by partnering or investing in promising startups (some, ironically, founded by ex-Lucent veterans). In this way, Cisco kept up with the R&D output of perhaps the world's finest industrial R&D organization, all without conducting much research of its own.

The story of Lucent and Cisco is hardly an isolated instance. IBM's research prowess in computing provided little protection against Intel and Microsoft in the personal

---

Source: H. Chesbrough (2003) *MIT Sloan Management Review*, 44 (3): 35–41.

computer hardware and software businesses. Similarly, Motorola, Siemens and other industrial titans watched helplessly as Nokia catapulted itself to the forefront of wireless telephony in just 20 years, building on its industrial experience from earlier decades in the low-tech industries of wood pulp and rubber boots. Pharmaceutical giants like Merck and Pfizer have also watched as a number of upstarts, including Genentech, Amgen and Genzyme, has parlayed the research discoveries of others to become major players in the biotechnology industry.

From Closed to Open

Is innovation dead? Hardly, as punctuated by the recent advances in the life sciences, including revolutionary breakthroughs in genomics and cloning. Then why is internal R&D no longer the strategic asset it once was? The answer lies in a fundamental shift in how companies generate new ideas and bring them to market. In the old model of *closed innovation,* firms adhered to the following philosophy: *Successful innovation requires control.* In other words, companies must generate their own ideas that they would then develop, manufacture, market, distribute and service themselves (see "The Closed Innovation Model", Figure 11.1). This approach calls for self-reliance: If you want something done right, you've got to do it yourself.

For years, the logic of closed innovation was tacitly held to be self-evident as the "right way" to bring new ideas to market and successful companies all played by certain implicit rules. They invested more heavily in internal R&D than their competitors and they hired the best and the brightest (to reap the rewards of the industry's smartest people). Thanks to such investments, they were able to discover the best and greatest number of ideas, which allowed them to get to market first. This, in turn, enabled them to reap most of the profits, which they protected by aggressively controlling their intellectual property (IP) to prevent competitors from exploiting it. They could then reinvest the profits in conducting more R&D, which then led to additional breakthrough discoveries, creating a virtuous cycle of innovation.

For most of the 20th century, the model worked — and it worked well. Thanks to it, Thomas Edison was able to invent a number of landmark devices, including the phonograph and the electric light bulb, which paved the way for the establishment of General Electric's famed Global Research Center in Niskayuna, New York. In the chemical industry, companies like DuPont established central research labs to identify and commercialize a stunning variety of new products, such as the synthetic fibers nylon, Kevlar and Lycra. Bell Labs researchers discovered amazing physical phenomena and harnessed those discoveries to create a host of revolutionary products, including transistors and lasers.

Toward the end of the 20th century, through, a number of factors combined to erode the underpinnings of closed innovation in the United States. Perhaps chief among these factors was the dramatic rise in the number and mobility of knowledge workers, making it increasingly difficult for companies to control their proprietary ideas and expertise. Another important factor was the growing availability of private

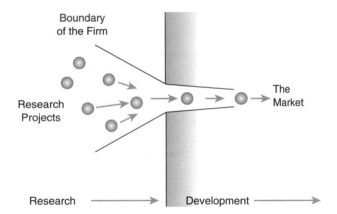

Figure 11.1   *The Closed Innovation Model*

In closed innovation, a company generates, develops and commercializes its own ideas. This philosophy of self-reliance dominated the R&D operations of many leading industrial corporations for most of the 20th century.

venture capital, which has helped to finance new firms and their efforts to commercialize ideas that have spilled outside the silos of corporate research labs.

Such factors have wreaked havoc with the virtuous cycle that sustained closed innovation. Now, when breakthroughs occur, the scientists and engineers who made them have an outside option that they previously lacked. If a company that funded a discovery doesn't pursue it in a timely fashion, the people invloved could pursue it on their own — in a startup financed by venture capital. If that fledgling firm were to become successful, it could gain additional financing through a stock offering or it could be acquired at an attractive price. In either case, the successful startup would generally *not* reinvest in new fundamental discoveries, but instead, like Cisco, it would look outside for another technology to commercialize. Thus, the virtuous cycle of innovation was shattered: The company that orginally funded a breakthrough did not profit from the investment, and the firm that *did* reap the benefits did not reinvest its proceeds to finance the next generation of discoveries.

In this new model of *open innovation,* firms commercialize external (as well as internal) ideas by deploying outside (as well as in-house) pathways to the market. Specifically, companies can commercialize internal ideas through channels outside of their current businesses in order to generate value for the organization. Some vehicles for accomplishing this include startup companies (which might be financed and staffed with some of the company's own personnel) and licensing agreements. In addition, ideas can also originate outside the firm's own labs and be brought inside for commercialization. In other words, the boundary between a firm and its surrounding environment is more porous, enabling innovation to move easily between the two (see "The Open Innovation Model", Figure 11.2).

At its root, open innovation is based on a landscape of abundant knowledge, which must be used readily if it is to provide value for the company that created it. However, an organization should not restrict the knowledge that it uncovers in its research to its internal market pathways, nor should those internal pathways necessarily be constrained to bringing only the company's internal knowledge to market. This perspective suggests some very different rules (see "Contrasting Principles of Closed and Open Innovation," [page 132]. For example, no longer should a company lock up its IP, but instead it should find ways to profit from others' use of that technology through licensing agreements, joint ventures and other arrangements.

One major difference between closed and open innovation lies in how companies screen their ideas. In any R&D process, researchers and their managers must separate the bad proposals from the good ones so that they can discard the former while pursuing and commercializing the latter. Both the closed and open models are adept at weeding out "false positives" (that is, bad ideas that initially look promising), but open innovation also incorporates the ability to rescue "false negatives" (projects that initially seem to lack promise but turn out to be surprisingly valuable). A company that is focused too internally — that is, a firm with a closed innovation approach — is prone to miss a number of those opportunities because many will fall outside the organization's current businesses or will need to be combined with external technologies to unlock their potential. This can be especially painful for corporations that have made substantial long-term investments in research, only to discover later that some of the projects they abandoned had tremendous commercial value.

The classic example is Xerox and its Palo Alto Research Center (PARC). Researchers there developed numerous computer hardware and software technologies — Ethernet and the graphical user interface (GUI) are two such examples. However, these inventions were not viewed as promising businesses for Xerox, which was focused on high-speed copiers and printers. In other words, the technologies were false negatives[1] and they languished inside Xerox, only to be commercialized by other companies that, in the process, reaped tremendous benefits. Apple Computer, for instance, exploited the GUI in its Macintosh operating system while Microsoft did the same in its Windows operating system.

How Prevalent Is Open Innovation?

This is not to argue that all industries have been (or will be) migrating to open innovation. At this point, different businesses can be located on a continuum, from essentially closed to completely open. An example of the former is the nuclear-reactor industry, which depends mainly on internal ideas and has low labor mobility, little venture capital, few (and weak) startups and relatively little research being conducted at universities. Whether this industry will ever migrate towards open innovation is questionable.

At the other extreme, some industries have been innovators for some time now. Consider Hollywood, which for decades has innovated through a network of partnerships and alliances between production studios, directors, talent agencies, actors, scriptwriters, independent producers and specialized subcontractors (such as the

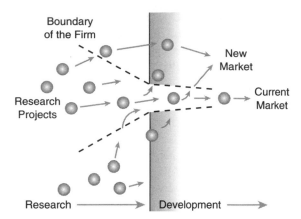

Figure 11.2   *The Open Innovation Model*

In the new model of open innovation, a company commercializes both its own ideas as well as innovations from other firms and seeks ways to bring its in-house ideas to market by deploying pathways outside its current businesses. Note that the boundary between the company and its surrounding environment is porous (represented by a dashed line), enabling innovations to move more easily between the two.

suppliers of special effects). The mobility of this workforce is legendary: Every waitress is a budding actress; every parking attendant has a screenplay he is working on.

Many industries — including copiers, computers, disk drives, semiconductors, telecommunications equipment, pharmaceuticals, biotechnology and even military weapons and communications systems — are currently transitioning from closed to open innovation. For such businesses, a number of critically important innovations have emerged from seemingly unlikely sources. Indeed, the locus of innovation in these industries has migrated beyond the confines of the central R&D laboratories of the largest companies and is now situated among various startups, universities, research consortia and other outside organizations. This trend goes well beyond high technology — other industries such as automotive, health care, banking, insurance and consumer packaged goods have also been leaning toward open innovation.

Consider Procter & Gamble, the consumer-product giant with a long and proud tradition of in-house science behind its many leading brands. P&G has recently changed its approach to innovation, extending its internal R&D to the outside world through the slogan "Connect & Develop."[2] The company has created the position of director of external innovations and has set a goal of sourcing 50% of its innovations from outside the company in five years, up from an estimated 10% this year.[3] This approach is a long way from the "not invented here," or NIH, syndrome that afflicts many large, successful industrial organizations. Recently, P&G scored a huge success with SpinBrush, an electric toothbrush that runs on batteries and sells for $5. The idea for the product, which has quickly become the best-selling toothbrush in the United States, came not from P&G's labs but from four entrepreneurs in Cleveland.

Table 11.1   *Contrasting Principles of Closed and Open Innovation*

Closed Innovation Principles	Open Innovation Principles
The smart people in our field work for us.	Not all of the smart people work for us* so we must find and tap into the knowledge and expertise of bright individuals outside our company.
To profit from R&D, we must discover, develop and ship it ourselves.	External R&D can create significant value: internal R&D is needed to claim some portion of that value.
If we discover it ourselves, we will get it to market first.	We don't have to originate the research in order to profit from it.
If we are the first to commercialize an innovation, we will win.	Building a better business model is better than getting to market first.
If we create the most and best ideas in the industry, we will win.	If we make the best use of internal *and* external ideas, we will win.
We should control our Intellectual property (IP) so that our competitors don't profit from our ideas.	We should profit from others' use of our IP, and we should buy others' IP whenever it advances our own business model.

* This maxim first came to my attention in a talk by Bill Joy of Sun Microsystems over a decade ago. See, for example, A. Lash. "The Joy of Sun," The Standard. June 21, 1999. htttp://rhestandard.net.

P&G also tries to move its own innovations outside. Recently, the company instituted a policy stating that any idea that originates in its labs will be offered to outside firms, even direct competitors, if an internal business does not use the idea within three years.[4] The goal is to prevent promising projects from losing momentum and becoming stuck inside the organization.

The Different Modes of Innovation

Indeed, many companies have been defining new strategies for exploiting the principles of open innovation, exploring ways in which external technologies can fill gaps in their current businesses and looking at how their internal technologies can spawn the seeds of new businesses outside the current organization. In doing so, many firms have focused their activities into one of three primary areas: *funding, generating* or *commercializing innovation.*

Funding Innovation

Two types of organizations — *innovation investors* and *benefactors* — are focused primarily on supplying fuel for the innovation fire. The original *innovation investor* was the corporate R&D budget but now a wide range of other types has emerged, including venture capital (VC) firms, angel investors, corporate VC entities, private equity investors and the Small Business Investment Companies (SBICs), which provide VC to small, independent businesses and are licensed and regulated by the U.S. Small Business Administration. Their capital helps move ideas out of corporations and universities and into the market, typically through the creation of startups. In addition to financing, innovation investors can supply valuable advice for helping startups avoid the common growing pains that afflict many fledgling firms.

With the recent economic downturn and the implosion of numerous dot-com firms, innovation investors have understandably turned somewhat gun-shy. However, though it seems these players are down, they are hardly out. VCs currently have about $250 billion in capital under management, of which $90 billion is idle.[5] When the economy rebounds, innovation investors will likely spot and fund new developments in areas like genomics and nanotechnology, which will likely spur the next economic wave of innovation.

Innovation benefactors provide new sources of research funding. Unlike investors, benefactors focus on the early stages of research discovery. The classic example here is the National Science Foundation (NSF), an independent agency of the U.S. government. Through its awards and grants programs, the NSF provides about 20% of federal support for academic institutions to conduct basic research. The Defense Advanced Research Projects Agency (DARPA) has also been a key benefactor, particularly for the early work in much of the computer industry.

Some companies are devoting a portion of their resources to playing the role of benefactor. By funding promising early-stage work, they get a first look at the ideas and can selectively fund those that seem favorable for their industry. An interesting development with innovation benefactors is the possible rise in philanthropy from private foundations, especially those backed by wealthy individuals. For example, the billionaire Larry Ellison, chairman and CEO of software giant Oracle, has founded an organization that provides about $50 million annually for basic research in cancer, Parkinson's and Alzheimer's diseases as well as other disorders. Interestingly, the foundation was set up specifically for early exploration — research so embryonic that scientists aren't able to obtain funds through traditional grants, such as those awarded by the NSF.

Generating Innovation

There are four types of organizations that primarily generate innovation: *innovation explorers, merchants, architects* and *missionaries. Innovation explorers* specialize in performing the discovery research function that previously took place primarily within corporate R&D laboratories. Interestingly, a number of explorers evolved as spinoffs of laboratories that used to be a part of a larger organization. Just a year ago, for example, PARC became a separate, independent entity from Xerox. Similarly, Telcordia Technologies was formed from the divestiture of the Bell System and is now home to about 400 researchers with a broad range of expertise, from software engineering to optical networking.

An interesting development with explorers has been taking place with the major government labs, such as Sandia National Laboratories, Lawrence Livermore National Laboratory and the MIT Lincoln Laboratory. In the aftermath of the end of the Cold War, these organizations have been seeking new missions for their work and much of their basic research is finding applications in commercial markets. Consider Lincoln Laboratory, which has conducted radar and other defense research since the 1950s. Technology developed there for missile detection has recently been adapted to cancer treatment, enabling microwave energy to be focused more effectively at tumors.

Innovation merchants must also explore, but their activities are focused on a narrow set of technologies that are then codified into intellectual property and aggressively sold to (and brought to market by) others. In other words, innovation merchants will innovate but only with specific commercial goals in mind, whereas explorers tend to innovate for innovation's sake. For the merchants, royalties from their IP enable them to do more research in their areas of focus. Indeed, such companies rise and fall with the strength of their IP portfolios.

One example of an innovation merchant is Qualcomm, which conducts extensive internal research on telecommunications, including code divisions multiple access (CDMA), a standard for wireless technology. Originally, Qualcomm manufactured cellular phones and software products such as the Eudora e-mail program, but today it focuses on licensing its CDMA technology and producing the associated chipsets for use by other cell-phone manufacturers. Qualcomm currently boasts more than 100 licensees, including Motorola, Nokia and Kyocera.

Innovation architects provide a valuable service in complicated technology worlds. In order to create value for their customers, they develop architectures that partition this complexity, enabling numerous other companies to provide pieces of the system, all while ensuring that those parts fit together in a coherent way. Boeing, for example, will engineer the overall design of an aircraft like the 747, after which companies like GE can then develop and manufacture the jet engines and other constituent parts. Innovation architects work in areas that are complex and fast-moving, which disfavors the "do-it-yourself" approach. To be successful, innovation architects must establish their systems solution, communicate it, persuade others to support it and develop it in the future. They must also devise a way to capture some portion of the value they create, otherwise they will find it impossible to sustain and advance their architecture.

For example, the dramatic rise of Nokia in wireless communications has been due, in part, to the strong lead it took in establishing the global system for mobile communication (GSM) technology as a standard for cellular phones. Accomplishing that required working closely with a number of other companies, as well as the governments of many European countries. Specifically, Nokia research helped define the now-accepted standards for moving GSM from a narrow- to broad-bandwidth spectrum and the company pushed hard to establish that technology: It willingly licensed the research to others and partnered with companies (including competitors) to develop the chipsets necessary for implementing the standard.[6] Those efforts have helped Nokia to become the world's dominant supplier of wireless-phone handsets, controlling nearly 40% of the global market.

Innovation missionaries consist of people and organizations that create and advance technologies to serve a cause. Unlike the innovation merchants and architects, they do not seek financial profits from their work. Instead, the mission is what motivates them. This is characteristic of many community-based nonprofits and religious groups but also occurs in the software industry. Here, user groups help define how a particular software program will evolve. These organizations, which include professional programmers as well as hobbyists, not only identify bugs (and possible ways to fix them), but additionally might even create a "wish list" of potential features that the next generation of a software product might include.

The evolution of the computer operating system Linux exemplifies this approach. Originally developed by Linus Torvalds, Linux has advanced over the years thanks to the arduous efforts of an informal network of programmers around the world. The software is freely available to anyone, and it has become a viable alternative to commercial offerings such as Microsoft Windows NT.

Commercializing Innovation

Lastly, two types of organization are focused on bringing innovations to market: *innovation marketers* and *one-stop centers*. *Innovation marketers* often perform at least some of the functions of the other types of organization, but their defining attribute is their keen ability to profitably market ideas, both their own as well as others'. To do so, marketers focus on developing a deep understanding of the current and potential needs in the market and this helps them to identify which outside ideas to bring in-house. Most of the drugs that are currently in Pfizer's pipeline, for instance, originated outside the company.

Another example of an innovation marketer is Intuit, which sells personal financial software products such as the popular Quicken program. For a number of years, Intuit has been able to keep Microsoft at bay — one of the very few companies that can make that claim — by maintaining close and disciplined interactions with its customers to gain in-depth knowledge about their needs. In keeping with the innovation marketer's role, Intuit has become adept at identifying and adapting outside technologies to satisfy those needs. In this way, the company has consistently been able to profit from innovations it did not discover. For example, it acquired two of its popular products — TurboTax (a tax-preparation program) and QuickBooks (small-business accounting software) — from the outside and enhanced both programs to meet its customers' needs.

Innovation one-stop centers provide comprehensive products and services. They take the best ideas (from whatever source) and deliver those offerings to their customers at competitive prices. Like innovation marketers, they thrive by selling others' ideas, but are different in that they typically form unshakable connections to the end users, increasingly managing a customer's resources to his or her specifications. For example, the Web site for Yahoo! enables people to shop, send e-mail, manage their personal finances, hunt for jobs and keep up-to-date on current events.

While Yahoo! targets consumers, other one-stop centers are focused on business-to-business interactions. IBM's Global Services division, for instance, sells IT solutions to other companies, and interestingly, will install and service hardware and software from any vendor, including IBM's competitors. In other words, it will provide the best solution to its customers, regardless of the origin of those products.

Although many companies are focusing on just funding, generating or commercializing innovation, some are continuing to do all three. As mentioned earlier, industrial powerhouses like GE, Dupont and AT&T (with Bell Labs) were the exemplars of this approach in the United States during the 20th century, and the success of those corporations has cast the mold for most central R&D organizations. To this day, a number of companies, called *fully integrated innovators,* continue to espouse the closed innovation credo of "innovating through total control."

IBM in the mainframe computer market is one such example. Thanks to the company's T.J. Watson Research Center and its other internal R&D labs, virtually all of the value-added components inside an IBM mainframe computer come from IBM itself. This includes the semiconductor circuits that power the main processing unit, the disk storage, the high-speed circuitry that routes signals, the tape backup storage, the operating system and the different application programs. To accomplish that, IBM must manage technology advances in both hardware and software within different internal divisions, coordinating future releases of software and new versions of hardware to assure its customers of continued improvements in price and performance.

IBM's mainframe business raises an important point: A corporation can deploy different modes of innovation in different markets. Specifically, IBM is a one-stop center for consulting services and a fully integrated innovator with respect to mainframes. Another important point is that competing modes can coexist in the same industry. In pharmaceuticals, for example, Merck has remained a fully integrated innovator while Pfizer is becoming an innovation marketer. It remains to be seen which of those modes (or perhaps another) will dominate.

All of the different modes will evolve in an open innovation environment, and future ones will probably emerge as well. One possible development is the rise of specialized intermediaries that function as brokers or middlemen to create markets for IP.[7] More than likely, there won't be one "best way" to innovate, although some modes will face greater challenges than others.

Fully integrated innovators, for instance, have become an endangered species in many industries. As ideas spill out of the central R&D labs of large corporations, the other modes of innovation are in a position to profit from them. In fact, these other modes have risen in prominence in response to the perceived limitations of fully integrated innovators. Much of IBM's innovation, for instance, has been migrating from the fully integrated mode toward the one-stop center approach.

The explorer mode depends on external sources of funding because of the considerable resources and uncertainty of conducting long-term research. Outside of the life sciences, this support has dwindled substantially in the past decade, making a number of explorers vulnerable. Recent societal concerns, such as for "homeland security" in the United States, may supply a new impetus for government funding, and already many explorers are making the transition. Sandia National Labs, for instance, is currently developing robots for disabling bombs. It is questionable, however, whether new security research missions will fit with the strengths and abilities of the current explorers or whether a new cadre of them will arise instead.

Innovation merchants also face significant challenges. Although the concept of supplying innovation to a "marketplace for ideas" is attractive in theory, it is devilishly tricky to accomplish. For one thing, merchants must determine how best to gain access to the complementary assets that might be needed to commercialize an innovation. Another issue is that the laws for IP protection are ill-defined at best, making it risky for merchants to limit their revenue stream solely to the marketing of their IP.

Innovation architects encounter a different set of challenges in their roles of organizing and coordinating complex technologies. Although ideas are plentiful, that very abundance can make it extremely difficult to create useful systems. Furthermore, innovation architects, through the harnessing of a broad network of companies, must balance the creation of value with the need to capture a portion of that value. Boeing, for instance, is able to do so by acting as the systems assembler for its aircraft. With other technologies, however, the means by which innovation architects can benefit from their roles is not so straightforward.

Several of the modes of innovation rely on a continued supply of useful ideas and technologies from the outside. Although university research is now more abundant and of higher quality than in the past, the flow of that knowledge into the commercial sector faces several obstacles. Such research is necessarily filtered through the silos of academic departments and that process tends to discourage cross-discipline breakthroughs. In addition, universities are now allowed to patent their discoveries, and although the change has benefited professors (who are able to form their own commercial ventures), it has also taxed the efforts of companies, particularly small firms, to profit from that source of innovation.

Long Live Open Innovation

Today, in many industries, the logic that supports an internally oriented, centralized approach to R&D has become obsolete. Useful knowledge has become widespread and ideas must be used with alacrity. If not, they will be lost. Such factors create a new logic of open innovation that embraces external ideas and knowledge in conjunction with internal R&D. This change offers novel ways to create value — along with new opportunities to claim portions of that value.

However, companies must still perform the difficult and arduous work necessary to convert promising research results into products and services that satisfy customer's needs. Specifically, the role of R&D needs to extend far beyond the boundaries of the firm. Innovators must integrate their ideas, expertise and skills with those of others outside the organization to deliver the result to the marketplace, using the most effective means possible. In short, firms that can harness outside ideas to advance their own businesses while leveraging their internal ideas outside their current operations will likely thrive in this new era of open innovation.

Notes

1. The early work on PARC comes from D.K. Smith and R.C. Alexander, "Fumbling the Future: How Xerox Invented, Then Ignored, the First Personal Computer" (New York: William Morrow & Co., 1988). The story was revisited in M. Hilzik, "Dealers of Lightning" (New York: HarperBusiness, 1999). An alternative perspective — that Xerox managers did not "fumble" these technologies but consciously ushered them out the door — can be found in H. Chesbrough, "Graceful Exists and Foregone Opportunities: Xerox's Management of Its Technology Spinoff Companies," Business History Review 76 (winter 2002): 803–838.
2. N. Sakkab, P&G's senior vice president for R&D for Global Fabric and Home Care, described P&G's new Innovation strategy in an address to the Industrial Research Institute. See N. Sakkab, "Connect & Develop Complements Research & Develop at P&G," Research Technology Management 45 (March-April 2002): 38–45.
3. H. Chesbrough, interview with Larry Huston, August 5, 2002. Huston, director of external innovation at Procter & Gamble, noted as well that the "Connect & Develop" initiative had strong support from P&G's board of directors and that there has been a board subcommittee working on the issue.
4. Sakkab, "Connect & Develop," 38–45.
5. "Too Much Ventured Nothing Gained: VCs Are a Hurting Bunch. New Companies Feel Their Pain," Fortune, November 25, 2002.
6. For an account of Nokia's R&D approach to GSM, see M. Häikiö, "Nokia: The Inside Story" (London: Financial Times Prentice Hall, 2002), 120–121 (in particular).
7. M. Sawhney, E. Prandelli and G.Verona, "The Power of Innomediation," MIT Sloan Management Review 44 (winter 2003): 77–82: and J.D. Wolpert, "Breaking Out of the Innovation Box," Harvard Business Review 80 (August 2002): 76–83.

12

The Innovator's Prescription: The Art of Scale: How to Turn Someone Else's Idea into a Big Business

Costas Markides and Paul Geroski

In October 2003, in a statement issued after the company's annual meeting, Procter & Gamble Chairman and Chief Executive Alan G. Lafley said, "Our vision is that 50 percent of all P&G discovery and invention could come from outside the company." The target was ambitious: In 2002, only one-fifth of new ideas put into development by P&G came from the outside. But the company hoped that if it worked with public companies, startups, and universities, outside innovation would ultimately comprise half its portfolio.

Procter & Gamble's goal is part of the newest wave in management thinking. Thought leaders from academia and inside companies have argued repeatedly in recent years that opening the firm to outside innovation is an important path to sustained growth. Berkeley's Henry Chesbrough calls this model "open innovation." C.K. Prahalad and Venkatram Ramaswamy of the University of Michigan argue that companies and their customers should innovate together, to "co-create value."

This advice differs markedly from conventional thinking about innovation. There has long been a cultural and management bias in favor of discovery, especially discovery that takes place inside the corporate walls. Many of us aspire to become a modern-day Thomas Edison — the pioneer, the inventor, and the founder of a firm that launches the industries of the future. A natural by-product of this bias is that most of the academic research on and guidance given to companies to make them more "innovative" is primarily guidance on how they can become better at "creation" — discovering something new, testing it in the market, and, if successful, creating a new market.

However, successful innovation requires much more than discovering something new. As we all know, the majority of new ideas fail or never grow beyond small and insignificant market niches. To be truly successful, a new idea must ultimately grow and capture a mass market. Our aim is to describe the strategies that a company can use to turn someone else's big idea into a big business.

Source: C. Markides and P. Geroski (2004) *Strategy and Business*, 35: 2–10.

We begin with a radical recommendation: To succeed at scaling up new radical markets, don't even try to create them.

Consolidation is King

In our last article for *strategy + business,* we argued that discovery and scaling up are essentially different activities that do not necessarily have to be performed by the same firm. (See "Colonizers and Consolidators: The Two Cultures of Corporate Strategy," Fall 2003.) In fact, in the majority of cases, the companies that pioneer — or, in our terminology, colonize — new *radical* markets are *not* the ones that ultimately consolidate and take ownership of those markets.

Radical (or disruptive) innovations are those that, like the PDA in the 1990s, the PC in the late 1970s, and the television in the 1950s, introduce major new value propositions that upset existing customer habits and behaviors. Moreover, the markets they create undermine the competencies and complementary assets on which existing competitors have built their success.

We believe that big established firms do not have to be actively involved in both the colonization and the consolidation of new radical markets. Given their skills and attitudes, incumbents will be better off if they stick to consolidation, positioning themselves to exploit the pioneering efforts of others. One primary way established firms can accomplish this is by developing a network of feeder firms and serving as a venture capitalist to them. When a feeder firm has successfully demonstrated the existence of a market for a new product or service, the established firm can use its skills and competencies — in manufacturing, marketing, sales, and management of the extended enterprise — to scale up that market.

Unfortunately, few companies have the courage to do what Procter & Gamble is attempting to do. They fear that by separating discovery from consolidation, they might not be able to take advantage of the market when it grows. They are mistaken. We have recently researched a number of industries to understand how new radical markets are created and how they evolve. The evidence shows that the firms that discover the new market are not the ones that consolidate and conquer it. The evidence also shows that discovery and consolidation are essentially different activities undertaken by different firms.

In industry after industry, we see the same phenomenon: As soon as a new radical market emerges, hundreds of new entrants rush to colonize it. Before long, consolidation takes place and most of the early entrants disappear. A few survive. But even these early survivors usually are not the ones that end up conquering the new market. The true winners are those firms that undertake a series of actions that scales up the new market. How do they do that? We have identified five distinct strategies.

Focus on the Price/Performance Trade-off

The first move for consolidators is to draw the market's attention away from the wonders of technical superiority, to attributes they can exploit, especially the best functionality at the most attractive price.

The early colonizers of new markets tend to stress the *technical* attributes of their product or service. This happens because the entrepreneurs who created the company often are engineers whose technical and engineering skills allowed them to translate a certain technology into a new product. It is the functionality of the product that attracts the first customers.

You see this emphasis on the technical attributes of the product in the early days of most young radical markets. Xerox sold its copiers on the basis of their functionality and the speed at which they made copies; Ampex sold its VCRs on the quality of their recording; Leica sold its cameras on the quality of their lenses; and Apple sold its hand-held computers on their breakthrough handwriting-recognition software.

Putting the spotlight on a product's technical aspects and functionality at this stage is understandable. To begin with, although the product represents the passion of its inventor, it gains the necessary support to enter the development phase only because corporate or private financiers believe it satisfies a certain customer need. Unless it has the necessary technical features to meet this need, early financiers won't back it. Second, the natural inclination of inventor-engineers is to call attention to the things they know and those they believe make their product superior. Third, at the birth of any new market, the performance of early products is still below what the customers ultimately will want. For all these reasons, pioneers battle each other by adding functionality to their products, and competition in the early stages of the market is based on product features and performance.

The efforts of these pioneers create the initial market niche. The customers who rush to purchase the new product tend to be technology enthusiasts or early adopters. They don't particularly mind that the product is flawed or expensive — they just want to get their hands on the new "toy." Of course, early adopters represent only a small fraction of the population; by definition, pioneers are targeting a niche market.

It is at this stage that forward-thinking consolidators can move in and "steal" the market away, by shifting the basis of competition from technical performance to such attributes as quality and price. This makes the product attractive to the mass market and facilitates rapid growth. (See Exhibit 1.)

The evolution of the disposable diaper market in the U.S. illustrates well how price and functionality can drive market consolidation. Chicopee Mills, a unit of Johnson & Johnson, introduced the first disposable diaper, Chux, in 1932. Two other providers, Sears and Montgomery Ward, launched disposable diapers after World War II.

By 1956, disposable diapers accounted for only 1 percent of diaper changes in the U.S. The main reason was their high cost, about 9 cents per unit, which was more than double what laundry service cost (and much more costly than home washing). Another reason was the product's performance: The early diapers' absorbent core was made of several layers of tissue paper, which led to excessive leakage. As a result, consumers treated disposable diapers as a luxury item to be used only on special occasions (such as traveling with babies).

That same year, Procter & Gamble acquired a paper-pulp plant. The company put Victor Mills, a chemical engineer, and his team of engineers, in charge of figuring out what to do with it. A grandfather, Mr. Mills thought about how much he hated to change diapers; it occurred to him that using cellulose fibers instead of paper would vastly improve the performance of the disposable diaper. That involved design and production challenges. The diaper had to be soft enough to be comfortable, yet strong enough not to disintegrate when wet; and the company needed to devise a manufacturing process that would allow it to produce the diaper cheaply enough to attract the average consumer.

After five years of research, Procter & Gamble introduced Pampers in 1961. The initial test was not successful. Although consumers said they liked the product, it was still too expensive for most. Drawing upon its experience in grocery marketing, P&G calculated that a retail price of 6.2 cents per diaper would stimulate mass demand. This meant reducing manufacturing costs to around 3 cents, a figure that entailed significant reductions in raw material costs and a more efficient manufacturing process.

Five years later, P&G finally succeeded in producing the disposable diapers at 3.5 cents a unit. Pampers was rolled out nationally at a retail price of 5.5 cents, and became an instant success. The U.S. disposable diaper market grew from $10 million in 1966 to $370 million by 1973. Pampers' triumph was so overwhelming that the market pioneer, Johnson & Johnson, withdrew Chux and focused on private label production.

Although Procter & Gamble captured the diaper market by improving quality and reducing prices, there are many cases when a late entrant has captured the market even with a product that is inferior to that of pioneers. This is because colonizers, passionate about functionality, often overengineer a product or service, adding features that customers do not need, sinking costs into unnecessary research and development, and missing mass-market price targets. Consolidators can steal the market away by creating a product that might not be as good as the pioneers', but is "good enough." When this is combined with a much lower price, the mass market will switch to the consolidator's "inferior" product.

The story of how Palm conquered the handheld computer market illustrates this point. Apple Computer Inc. created the market by introducing the Newton in August 1993. Palm Inc. followed three months later with the Zoomer. Both products flopped; they had poor handwriting-recognition software, and were expensive, heavy, and overburdened with PC functions (such as spreadsheets) that slowed their performance.

In 1995, Palm was acquired by U.S. Robotics, a larger firm with financial and marketing clout. The following year, the company introduced the Palm Pilot. By just about any technical performance measure, the Palm Pilot was far less sophisticated than Apple's Newton. But that proved to be the foundation of its success; whereas the Newton was a sort of junior PC, the Pilot was conceived as an *accessory to* the PC — an organizer with connectivity. It was also simple and fast and, more important, cheap — $299, compared with $700 for the Zoomer and almost $1,000 for the Newton.

By 2000, Palm controlled more than 70 percent of the market for what became known as personal digital assistants, which had subsumed the existing market for portable organizers that had been dominated by Philips, Casio, and others. In the years that followed the Palm Pilot's introduction, Microsoft developed its own operating system for handheld computers, Windows CE. Yet Microsoft's attempts to make inroads in this market by adding more features and more memory have failed thus far.

Exhibit 1 *Scaling Up a Market by Emphasizing Different Product Attributes*

Industry	Pioneers	Product Attributes Emphasized by Pioneers	Firms Scaling Up the Market	Product Attributes Emphasized by the Scaling-up Firms
Photocopying	[Haloid] Xerox and 3M	Speed and quality of copying	Canon	Price, size, and quality
Handheld computers	Apple and Casio	Writing recognition software and functionality	Palm [3Com]	Price, size, and PC synchronization
Online brokerage	K. Aufhauser, Security APL, and Howe Barnes	Convenience	Chartes Schwab	Price, convenience, and speed of execution
Portable computers	Osborne and Kaypro	Technology and functionality	IBM	Price and size
Video recorders	Ampex	High-quality recording	JVC and Sony	Price, size and weight
Online bookselling	Books.com and clbooks.com	Convenience	Amazon.com	Availability, convenience, and price
Motorcycles	Triumph and Harley-Davidson	Speed and power	Honda	Size and price
35mm cameras	Leica	Quality (of lenses and pictures) and engineering	Canon and Nikon	Price and ease of use

(Continued)

Exhibit 1 *(Continued)*

Industry	Pioneers	Product Attributes Emphasized by Pioneers	Firms Scaling Up the Market	Product Attributes Emphasized by the Scaling-up Firms
Microwave ovens	Tappan Stove Co., Raytheon Co., and Litton	Speed and quality	Panasonic, Sharp, and Samsung	Price
Internet service	CompuServe	Technology, info content, speed, and functionality	America Online	Ease of use and price
Food processors	Cuisinart	Speed, technical features, and quality	Black & Decker	Price
Shaving razors	Cutthroat razors and Autostrop Safety Razor Co.	High-grade steel for lifetime of sharpening	Gillette	Disposable blade, price and ease of use
Pocket calculators	Bowmar	Speed, technical features, and ease of use	Texas Instruments	Price
Disposable diapers	Chicopee Mills [J&J]	Ease of use and quality	Procter & Gamble	Price and ease of use
Fax machines	Xerox	Quality and speed	Sharp	Price and ease of use

Source: Costas Markides and Paul Geroski (2003)

Microsoft's motto of "more is better" has come up against Palm's "smaller, faster, cheaper." So far, Palm is winning.

Get a Bandwagon Rolling

Achieving a price that makes the product attractive to the mass market is only part of the challenge. A second priority for consolidators looking to succeed at scaling a market is to create a consumer bandwagon effect that will establish their design as dominant. There are at least three complementary strategies that history shows are used to bring this about.

Alliance strategies can help a design become dominant. Co-opting rivals or potential entrants by licensing them to manufacture according to your specifications might limit short-term profits, but can accelerate the adoption of a common standard or design. This "open innovation" strategy is the one JVC used to establish its VHS format as the industry standard in the video-cassette recorder market, defeating Sony's technically superior Betamax standard. JVC was quick to form alliances and agree to deals with original equipment manufacturers (OEMs). As part of this process, JVC kept the product design fluid and provided extensive manufacturing and marketing support to its allies. By 1984, JVC had more than 40 partners, and its VHS format had conquered the market.

The importance of an alliance strategy in creating bandwagons is best seen in cases where competitors haven't adopted such a strategy. Consider the brutish six-year life of quadraphonic sound — the four-channel experience — which was designed to liberate long-suffering music lovers from the confines of stereo. By all accounts, it was clearly superior to stereo sound. Yet it failed to get established. Why?

It all started in 1971 when Columbia Records (CBS) introduced its SQ (or "matrix") system. Its first rival was the confusingly labeled QS system championed by Sansui. But its major competitor turned out to be the CD-4 "discrete" system that JVC introduced and RCA records supported. Both systems were superior to stereo, a fact that led Chase Econometrics to predict in 1974: "Quadraphonic sound will eventually replace stereo … by the end of the 1980s."

However, the two systems were incompatible. Instead of cooperating to establish quad as the dominant design over stereo, the two main competitors began pointing out weaknesses and problems in each other's systems. Forced to make a choice, consumers wisely decided to play it safe and stay with stereo; audio dealers refrained from promoting uncertain systems; and artists refused to record using the new technology. By 1976, quad was dead, although mulitchannel surround sound is today becoming dominant thanks to a new product, the DVD.

A second way to speed up a consumer bandwagon is simply to engineer a merger with a major rival, and retire a competing design. Caught in an expensive battle with the British Satellite Broadcasting consortium, Rupert Murdoch's U.K. satellite television service, Sky TV, acquired it in 1990. Today, Sky's dishes are the ones seen all over Britain.

A third way to generate a consumer bandwagon is to use marketing to create the illusion that a design has already become dominant. Hollywood studios do this all the time when they limit the number of screens on which a new release shows, generating crowds at a few theaters. Palm similarly limited the distribution of the original Pilots. Stores began to sell out, creating a reinforcing buzz in the business press about the new product.

Reduce Consumer Risk

The third major strategy that consolidators exploit to scale up new radical markets is to reduce the customers' risk in adopting the new product.

The story of how Henry Heinz built consumer confidence in canned foods and scaled up this market more than 100 years ago provides a fine illustration of the importance of risk insurance to market consolidation. To appreciate the challenge he faced, imagine life back in the middle of the 19th century. Most people lived on or near farms and consumed a steady diet of fresh food. Even urban dwellers were used to purchasing food in an unprocessed form in open markets. Under these circumstances, it's hard to understand why anyone would contemplate consuming food from a can or a box that could not be seen, felt, smelled, tasted, or tested before opening the package.

Henry Heinz confronted this challenge with unlikely ammunition: horseradish. In the 1870s, most bottled horseradish was sold in green or brown bottles to disguise its generally low quality. Heinz started out by selling his horseradish in clear bottles, to signal his confidence in it. He also cultivated local grocers and hoteliers and used them to help certify the quality of his product. Soon, the public began to associate high quality with his name, creating a brand that was effectively an insurance policy for consumers. The brand helped facilitate Heinz's geographic expansion and extension into other products, such as pickles, celery sauce, and other condiments. His deepest geographic penetration was in cities, where resistance to nonfresh food was already low and where housewives often had so many demands on their time that economizing food preparation time was a priority. Moreover, the early products made by Heinz did not compete directly with fresh food but were complements to it.

The Heinz saga highlights the importance of developing customer trust in a new product or service, and thus in the entire market segment itself. A brand is the result of this process, which can include broadcast communication, direct communication with the end consumer, and use of credible experts or allies to spread the word. Indeed, the list of tactics in building customer trust is always evolving. (See "Focus: How eBay Created a Trust Bandwagon".)

A fourth tactic by which consolidators scale up a market is to build the distribution that can reach the masses. This might require setting up a new distribution channel from scratch (as the auto companies did in the early 20th century). But most of the time it requires persuading existing channels to accept the new product.

Focus: How eBay Created a Trust Bandwagon

The online auction site eBay.com has succeeded in persuading millions of rational human beings to send money to total strangers, for goods, sometimes quite expensive goods, they have never seen. The strategy, premised on eBay's ability to use technology to build a trust-based brand, originated with company founder Pierre Omidyar. Believing that democracy should be the core principle of the company, Mr. Omidyar came up with the idea for a "feedback forum" through which individuals (suppliers or purchasers) would earn a reputation based on their trading habits. The concept is simple: If we do business together on eBay and if I am happy with the merchandise that you sold me and you are happy with how rapidly I paid you and how I treated you in the e-mail discussion that we had, then we give good feedback on each other for everyone else to see. This serves to enhance our reputations as users. Too many negative comments and you are banned as an eBay seller forever. The feedback forum is particularly critical for sellers, the vast majority of whom are small retailers or individuals who rely on eBay exclusively.

To ensure even higher professional standards by its sellers, eBay recently announced that it will offer low-cost premium health insurance to "Power Sellers," those who sell at least $2,000 a month via eBay and achieve 98 percent positive feedback ratings. Not every seller on eBay reaches that level; in fact, established companies appear to have the most difficulty meeting the feedback criterion. As of 2003, both IBM and Ritz Camera had positive feedback levels of only 93 percent; Disney's feedback was labeled "private," indicating that bidders could not view comments left by previous buyers. This seems to show that the huge shipping and handling fees and slow turnaround times that go along with many large companies' direct marketing efforts do not work on eBay.

Although eBay relies mainly on buyers and sellers to police themselves, it does investigate fraud claims when required to ensure that confidence and trust in its service is maintained at all times. The company is aware that even a handful of unhappy users could damage its reputation. Although its technology and tactics are specific to its industry, the principle is universal – to scale up a market, consolidators must invest in reducing the customer's perceived or real risk of adopting a new product or service.

— **C.M. and P.G.**

Achieving acceptance by distributors can be extremely difficult. It usually means the would-be consolidator has to use market power or develop an innovative strategy. Golden Wonder, a Scotland-based division of Imperial Tobacco, used both methods to grow the potato chip market in the U.K. sixfold in the 1960s. In the process, it increased its market share from near zero to 40 percent in only 10 years.

Until 1960, potato chips were sold overwhelmingly to men in pubs; the "crisps" complemented beer, and (as publicans and brewers both knew) salt increased drinkers' thirst. Since more than 75 percent of total sales were made through pubs, all main competitors had set up their distribution systems to supply pubs around the country.

Golden Wonder Launched its assault on the market in 1961 by changing its target consumer, and promoting the potato chip as a nourishing snack for women and children. Heavy investments in advertising were made to transform the image of the product and position it for domestic consumption. The company developed competencies for the distribution channel most appropriate for its targeted customers — supermarkets and other retail outlets. It trained a sales force to pursue grocers, gave incentives to independent "merchandising sales cadets" to sell the product to retailers, arranged for shop displays, and provided point-of-sale promotional material. The company also invested heavily in a new production technology to improve the quality of the product, drive down costs, and reduce prices. In the period 1958 to 1969, sales of potato chips in pubs went from 75 percent of the total to 25 percent; sales in supermarkets and other retail stores grew from 25 percent to 65 percent. (Other channels accounted for the remainder.)

Building up distribution to the mass market is not cheap and becomes even more costly when a market is scaling up. During that period, a market figuratively explodes in size, as buying becomes frenzied and sales skyrocket. Companies aspiring to scale a market must be willing to invest financial and managerial resources in setting up the necessary distribution quickly, for a sale lost at this stage will go to a competitor, and a customer may be lost for life. Alliance strategies may be particularly effective for this task.

Support Complementary Products

A fifth strategy a firm can use to scale up markets for new products and services is to support the growth of complementary goods.

Many goods and services are consumed with other goods and services. Indeed, some products have no value in the absence of such complements. Having a car won't get you far if there are no gas stations; CDs do not sound sweet without a CD player and a set of speakers; a DVD player will be an expensive toy without Hollywood movies and video rental shops.

Certainly, the development of an open platform encourages complementary products and services to enter the market. For example, by keeping its design open and encouraging other OEMs to produce that design, JVC quickly established a large customer base for its VCRs, reducing the risk Hollywood studios might have faced in adopting the VHS format for their tapes. When the studios accepted the format, it prompted the emergence of video rental shops.

Trying to keep a proprietary hold on a design is almost certainly more profitable if that design emerges as the dominant design — something that shareholders in Microsoft know — but it lowers the probability that that design will win. By contrast, letting the design become open makes it more likely that it will become dominant, but lowers the profits that the company might accrue from such a strategy.

Other complementarity strategies a company might employ are to provide financial support to makers of corresponding products; develop the complementary goods on its own; sponsor industrywide standards; and use alliances with providers of complementary goods to control choke points on the emerging industry's value chain. It is the responsibility of consolidators to promote the growth of complementary goods. Without them, a market cannot be scaled up.

Research Methodology

We examined the historical evolution of 20 newly created markets from the moment they were created until they grew to mass market. The 20 markets were television, personal computers, scientific instruments, the Internet, super computers, online groceries, cars, beer, Internet service provision, tires, semiconductors, baked beans, genetically modified foods, mobile phones, video recorders, satellite TV, stereo sound, typewriters, computer operating systems, and medical diagnostic imaging.

This helped us understand the difference between creating and consolidating a new market and appreciate that the companies that created new markets were not the ones that scaled them up. We then developed a list of 25 companies that were successful in scaling up new markets and wrote a historical account of how they did it. The insights presented in this paper derive from these 25 cases. Further details of the first part of this research can be found in *The Early Evolution of New Markets* [Oxford University Press, 2003], by Paul Geroski. Our full research findings was published in November 2004 by JosseyBass in *Racing to Be Second: How to Conquer the Industries of the Future*, by Paul Geroski and Costas Markides.

New Music

We started this article by proposing that consolidators should let others create a radical new market and then move in to "steal" the market and scale it up, using the competencies that they already have. As a test case of our consolidation-versus-colonization hypothesis, we suggest you keep your eyes trained on the evolution of the digital music industry. In particular, notice how relative latecomers such as Apple and Dell are now taking the market away from the pioneers.

The $35 billion recorded music industry is still in the early stages of a transition away from CDs to digital downloads, a transformation now widely accepted as inevitable inside and outside the entertainment field. The market for portable MP3 players — a consumer appliance category that didn't exist until the late 1990s — is growing exponentially, and is expected to reach $2.6 billion by 2005, up from $1 billion in 2003.

The current category leader, in terms of both sales and imagination, is Apple Computer. Having introduced the stylish iPod portable player in 2001 and propelled it to an 18 percent market share in the U.S., Apple furthered its leadership claim in April 2003 by unveiling new ultrathin iPods with mass storage capacity, and an Internet-based music store, iTunes. The new Internet store opened after Apple had reached an unprecedented agreement with all the major record labels to allow legal downloading of their music for 99 cents a song. More than 10 million songs were sold in the first four months following the launch of iTunes, while the new and slimmer iPod looked set to completely dominate the portable MP3 players market.

So far, Apple has played the consolidation game brilliantly. The colonizers of the digital music industry included research institutions, such as Germany's Fraunhofer Institute, the inventor of the MP3 format, and startup companies, notably Napster, whose peer-to-peer file-sharing service popularized the format. With that open format already established, Apple followed several of the principles described above, using its talent for design, its entertainment industry networks, its trusted brand, and attractive pricing to dominate the digital download marketplace. But that doesn't mean that Apple will remain a winner forever. A host of new rivals have entered the market, none more formidable than the Dell Computer Corporation.

On October 28, 2003, Dell unveiled its Dell DJ MP3 player. The DJ had three advantages over the iPods then on the market:

1. It was much cheaper. The 15-gigabyte DJ sold for only $249, 38 percent less than the 15-gigabyte iPod. It also offered all the key features of its more expensive and glamorous rival.
2. Dell teamed with music software firm Musicmatch Inc. to create the Dell Music Store, which matches iTunes in price but offers a greater choice of songs. This is because Musicmatch has licensing deals with 30 independent music companies, in addition to the five major record labels, enabling it to offer a larger music library — currently more than 250,000 tracks, with plans to increase its library to more than 500,000 by the end of 2004. As of late 2003, Apple's iTunes had 200,000 tracks.
3. Dell's DJ was easily linkable to PCs. Although Apple introduced a Windows version of iTunes (by bundling Musicmatch's Jukebox software with Apple's iPod), it is still unclear whether the company will be able to win over Windows users in the long term, a task made more difficult by the fact that Microsoft insists that Apple has not licensed its Windows Media technology or its copyright protection software (both of which are used by many of the new iTunes-like services). This means that people who want to access the likes of Musicmatch, Napster 2.0 (Napster's successor), or BuyMusic.com (which offers 79-cent downloads) will not be able to use iPods.

Although it's certainly too soon to tell which company, if any, will dominate the market for MP3 players and services, both Dell and Apple have been enormously innovative in scaling up a market pioneered by others.

And that is exactly the point we want to make to senior executives of modern, major corporations: Most strategists will try to persuade you that discovery is the essence of innovation, the most creative part of business. But don't you believe it. Scaling up a market is not only as innovative — it also creates tremendous value. And it's clearly the area where established firms have an advantage over pioneers because they possess the requisite skills and competencies to convert niche markets into mass markets. Scaling up is the area in which big established firms could make a big difference. This should therefore be the focus of their attention.

References

Costas Markides and Paul Geroski, "Colonizers and Consolidators: The Two Cultures of Corporate Strategy," *s+b*, Fall 2003; www.strategy-business.com/press/article/03306

C.K. Prahalad and Venkatram Ramaswamy, "The Co-Creation Connection," *s+b*, Second Quarter 2002; www.strategy-business.com/press/article/18458

Clayton M. Christensen, Mark W. Johnson, and Darrell K. Rigby, "Foundations for Growth: How to Identify and Build Disruptive New Businesses," *Sloan Management Review*, Spring 2002; smr.mit.edu

Gary Hamel, "Bringing Silicon Valley Inside," *Harvard Business Review*, September/October 1999; www.harvardbusinessonline.com

Constantinos Markides, "Strategic Innovation in Established Companies," *Sloan Management Review*, Spring 1998; smr.mit.edu

James Brain Quinn, "Outsourcing Innovation: The New Engine of Growth," *Sloan Management Review*, Summer 2000; smr.mit.edu

Henry Chesbrough, *Open Innovation: The New Imperative for Creating and Profiting from Technology* (Harvard Business School Press, 2003)

Gary Hamel, *Leading the Revolution* (Harvard Business School Press, 2000)

Richard Leifer, Christopher M. McDermott, Gina Colarelli O'Connor, Lois S. Peters, Mark Rice, and Robert W. Veryzer, *Radical Innovation: How Mature Companies Can Outsmart Upstarts* (Harvard Business School Press, 2000)

Steven P. Schnaars, *Managing Imitation Strategies: How Later Enrants Seize Markets from Pioneers* (Free Press, 1994)

Gerard J. Tellis and Peter N. Golder, *Will and Vision: How Latecomers Grow to Dominate Markets* (McGraw-Hill, 2001)

Part 4

Change

Whether welcome or not, most of us are sooner or later forced to admit that change seems to be here to stay. Products come and go with increasing rapidity; the domestic video tape recorder seems to be entering obsolescence little more than 30 years after its debut. In an earlier chapter, Russell Ackoff pointed out that half of the corporations in the Fortune 500 of 25 years ago no longer exist. There is little evidence that such trends will not continue or even accelerate. Against such a backdrop, managers must perforce become informed consumers of management wisdom. The uncritical acceptance of the latest fad may represent not just a small mistake, but perhaps a fatal error. Given that the stakes are potentially so high, a manager needs to look behind the headlines and fully understand the messy reality behind the deceptively simple prescriptions on offer.

It is probably fair to say that empowerment is also here to stay. In a world where whatever work remains after automation is increasingly less susceptible to supervision, employers will increasingly seek to engage hearts and minds, rather than just brain and brawn. The chapter by **Bowen and Lawler** cogently emphasizes that, for all its undoubted advantages, empowerment not only incurs necessary costs, but also there may be circumstances where those costs actually outweigh the benefits. Properly empowered employees can offer very real benefits in terms of the creation of an organizational capability that is difficult for competitors to copy. Nevertheless, it remains a critical dilemma for managers to achieve an appropriate balance between empowerment and control.

The **Tushman and O'Reilly** chapter starts with a tacit acknowledgment that change comes in many forms. Echoing the work of Chesbrough and of Anthony and

Christensen (as well as the structure of this reader) they draw a key distinction between, in their terminology, incremental and revolutionary change. Although the article has drawn criticism for the 'fuzziness' of its guidelines[1], the basic tenets seem to have borne up well in the ten years since publication. Of particular value is the emphasis on culture; in the words of the authors 'organizational culture is a key to both short term success *and*, unless managed correctly, long-term failure'. The very behaviours, attitudes and mind sets that make an organization what it is today, are likely to contain the seeds of ultimate failure. The messages are ultimately simple; change comes in different forms; get used to it; culture matters. The solutions are necessarily complex.

The chapter by **Oakey** on Technical Entrepreneurship starts with a statement of the seemingly obvious; most technical entrepreneurs are driven (and 'driven' is often the appropriate word) by more than just the prospect of making their fortune. Whether their primary motivation is regarded as freedom (from external control) or the need to themselves take control, such folk may not always follow a strictly rational path towards profit maximization. In particular, the seeming disdain felt by many 'real' scientists for the social sciences in general and management in particular will often lead to a damaging neglect of basic business functions, Following an all-too-believable description of the way in which high-technology small firms operate, key lessons emerge regarding the motivation of the technical entrepreneur; no-one should be surprised that they will behave very differently from their large company cousins and that their organization's culture will necessarily reflect this.

Francis and Bessant start their article with a deliberately inclusive definition of Innovation embracing 'sustaining and disruptive technologies' (after Christensen), improvement *and* radical innovation, and domains comprising Product, Process, Positioning and Paradigm. As with the earlier chapter by Markides and Geroski, the authors are concerned with much more than just the 'better mousetrap' aspect of innovation as they explore a range of possible responses to a perceived 'need for change'. In every case, the same fundamental message emerges; innovation and change, however defined, can only arise if people are prepared to challenge the givens and confront the organizational orthodoxy. After discussing behaviour in each of their four domains, and then illustrating each domain via both 'do better' and 'do different' examples, the authors conclude with a helpful device to assist would-be innovators to explore a range of possibilities for change in their own organizations.

[1] e.g. Stringer, R. (2000) 'How to Manage Radical Innovation', *California Management Review*, 42, 4 (Summer)

The Empowerment of Service Workers: What, Why, How, and When

David E. Bowen and Edward E. Lawler III

In recent years, businesses have rushed to adopt an empowerment approach to service delivery in which employees face customers 'free of rulebooks', encouraged to do whatever is necessary to satisfy them, but that approach may not be right for everyone. Managers need to make sure that there is a good fit between their organizational needs and their approach to front-line employees.

Empowering service workers has acquired almost a 'born again' religious fervour. Tom Peters calls it 'purposeful chaos'. Robert Waterman dubs it 'directed autonomy'. It has also been called the 'art of improvisation'.

Yet in the mid-1970s, the production line approach to service was the darling child of service gurus. They advocated facing the customer with standardized, procedurally driven operations. Should we now abandon this approach in favour of empowerment?

Unfortunately, there is no simple, clear-cut answer. In this article we try to help managers think about the question of whether to empower by clarifying its advantages and disadvantages, describing three forms that empower employees to different degrees and presenting five contingencies that managers can use to determine which approach best fits their situation. We do not intend to debunk empowerment, rather we hope to clarify why to empower (there are costs, as well as benefits), how to empower (there are alternatives) and when to empower (it really does depend on the situation).

The Production Line Approach

In two classic articles, the 'Production-line approach to service' and the 'Industrialization of service', Theodore Levitt described how service operations can be made more efficient by applying manufacturing logic and tactics.[1] He argued:

Source: D.E. Bowen and E.E. Lawler III (1992) *Sloan Management Review*, 33(3): 31–9.

Manufacturing thinks technocratically, and that explains its success. By contrast, service looks for solutions in the performer of the task. This is the paralyzing legacy of our inherited attitudes: the solution to improved service is viewed as being dependent on improvements in the skills and attitudes of the performers of that service.

While it may pain and offend us to say so, thinking in humanistic rather than technocratic terms ensures that the service sector will be forever inefficient and that our satisfactions will be forever marginal.[2]

He recommended (1) simplification of tasks, (2) clear division of labour, (3) substitution of equipment and systems for employees and (4) little decision-making discretion afforded to employees. In short, management designs the system, and employees execute it.

McDonald's is a good example. Workers are taught how to greet customers and ask for their order, including a script for suggesting additional items. They learn a set procedure for assembling the order (for example, cold drinks first, then hot ones), placing items on the tray and placing the tray where customers need not reach for it. There is a script and a procedure for collecting money and giving change. Finally, there is a script for saying thank you and asking the customer to come again.[3] This production line approach makes customer service interactions uniform and gives the organization control over them. It is easily learned; workers can be quickly trained and put to work.

What are the gains from a production line approach? Efficient, low-cost, high-volume service operations, with satisfied customers.

The Empowerment Approach

Ron Zemke and Dick Schaaf, in *The Service Edge: 101 Companies that Profit from Customer Care,* note that empowerment is a common theme running through many, even most, of their excellent service businesses, such as American Airlines, Marriott, American Express and Federal Express. To Zemke and Schaaf, empowerment means 'turning the front line loose', encouraging and rewarding employees to exercise initiative and imagination: 'Empowerment in many ways is the reverse of doing things by the book'.[4]

The humanistic flavour of empowerment pervades the words of advocates such as Tom Peters:

It is necessary to 'dehumiliate' work by eliminating the policies and procedures (almost always tiny) of the organization that demean and belittle human dignity. It is impossible to get people's best efforts, involvement, and caring concern for things you believe important to your customers and the long-term interests of your organization when we write policies and procedures that treat them like thieves and bandits.[5]

And from Jan Carlzon, CEO of Scandinavian Airlines Systems (SAS):

To free someone from rigorous control by instructions, policies, and orders, and to give that person freedom to take responsibility for his ideas, decisions and actions is to release hidden resources that would otherwise remain inaccessible to both the individual and the organization.[6]

In contrast to the industrialization of service, empowerment very much looks to the 'performer of the tasks' for solutions to service problems. Workers are asked to suggest new services and products and to solve problems creatively and effectively.

What, then, does it really mean – beyond the catchy slogans – to empower employees? We define empowerment as sharing with front-line employees four organizational ingredients: (1) information about the organization's performance, (2) rewards based on the organization's performance, (3) knowledge that enables employees to understand and contribute to organizational performance and (4) power to make decisions that influence organizational direction and performance. We will say more about these features later. For now, we can say that with a production line approach, these features tend to be concentrated in the hands of senior management; with an empowerment approach, they tend to be moved downward to frontline employees.

Which Approach is Better?

In 1990, Federal Express became the first service organization to win the Malcolm Baldrige National Quality Award. The company's motto is 'people, service, and profits'. Behind its blue, white and red planes and uniforms are self-managing work teams, gainsharing plans and empowered employees seemingly consumed with providing flexible and creative service to customers with varying needs.

At UPS, referred to as 'Big Brown' by its employees, the philosophy was stated by founder Jim Casey: 'Best service at low rates.' Here, too, we find turned-on people and profits. But we do not find empowerment. Instead we find controls, rules, a detailed union contract and carefully studied work methods. Neither do we find a promise to do all things for customers, such as handling off-schedule pickups and packages that don't fit size and weight limitations. In fact, rigid operational guidelines help guarantee the customer reliable, low-cost service.

Federal Express and UPS present two different faces to the customer and behind these faces are different management philosophies and organizational cultures. Federal Express is a high-involvement, horizontally co-ordinated organization that encourages employees to use their judgement above and beyond the rulebook. UPS is a top-down, traditionally controlled organization, in which employees are directed by policies and procedures based on industrial engineering studies of how all service delivery aspects should be carried out and how long they should take.

Similarly, at Disney theme parks, ride operators are thoroughly scripted on what to say to 'guests', including a list of pre-approved 'ad libs'! At Club Med, however, CEO Jacques Giraud fervently believes that guests must experience real magic and the resorts' GOs (*gentils organisateurs*, 'congenial hosts') are set free spontaneously to create this feeling for their guests. Which is the better approach? Federal Express or UPS? Club Med or Disney?

At a recent executive education seminar on customer service, one of us asked, 'Who thinks that it is important for their business to empower their service personnel as a tool for improving customer service?' All 27 participants enthusiastically raised their hands. Although they represented diverse services – banking, travel, utilities, airlines and shipping – and they disagreed on most points, they all agreed that empowerment is key to customer satisfaction. But is it?

Empowering Service Employees: Why, How, and When

Why Empower: The Benefits

What gains are possible from empowering service employees?

Quicker on-line responses to customer needs during service delivery

Check-in time at the hotel begins at 2pm, but a guest asks the desk clerk if she may check in at 1.30pm. An airline passenger arrives at the gate at 7.30am, Friday, for a 7.45am departure and wants to board the plane with a travel coupon good Monday through Thursday and there are empty seats on the plane. The waitress is taking an order in a modestly priced family restaurant; the menu says no substitutions, but the customer requests one anyway.

The customer wants a quick response. And the employee would often like to be able to respond with something other than: 'No, it is against our rules' or 'I will have to check with my supervisor.' Empowering employees in these situations can lead to the sort of spontaneous, creative rule breaking that can turn a potentially frustrated or angry customer into a satisfied one. This is particularly valuable when there is little time to refer to a higher authority, as when the plane is leaving in 15 minutes. Even before greeting customers, empowered employees are confident that they have all the necessary resources at their command to provide customers with what they need.

Quicker on-line responses to dissatisfied customers during service recovery

Customer service involves both delivering the service, such as checking a guest into a hotel room and recovering from poor service, such as relocating him from a smoking floor to the non-smoking room he originally requested. Although delivering good service may mean different things to different customers, all customers feel that service businesses ought to fix things when service is delivered improperly. Figure 13.1 depicts the relationships among service delivery, recovery and customer satisfaction.

Best outcome	• A good delivery encounter
⬆️ ⬇️	• A poor delivery encounter with complaint elicited and recovery achieved
	• A poor delivery encounter with complaint elicited and recovery not achieved
Worst outcome	• A poor encounter with complaint elicited

Figure 13.1 *Possible outcomes during service delivery and recovery*

Source: Service Breakthroughs: Changing the Rules of the Game by James L. Heskett, W. Earl Sasser, Jr., and Christopher W. L. Hart. Copyright © 1990 by James L. Heskett, W. Earl Sasser, Jr., and Christopher W.L. Hart. Adapted with permission of The Free Press, a Division of Macmillan, Inc.

Fixing something after doing it wrong the first time can turn a dissatisfied customer into a satisfied, even loyal, customer. But service businesses frequently fail in the act of recovery because service employees are not empowered to make the necessary amends with customers. Instead, customers hear employees saying, 'Gee. I wish there was something I could do, but I can't', 'It's not my fault', or 'I could check with my boss, but she's not here today.' These employees lack the power and knowledge to recover, and customers remain dissatisfied.

Employees feel better about their jobs and themselves

Earlier we mentioned Tom Peters' thinking on how strict rules can belittle human dignity. Letting employees call the shots allows them to feel 'ownership' of the job; they feel responsible for it and find the work meaningful. Think of how you treat your car as opposed to a rented one. Have you ever washed a rental car? Decades of job design research show that when employees have a sense of control and of doing meaningful work they are more satisfied. This leads to lower turnover, less absenteeism and fewer union organizing drives.

Employees will interact with customers with more warmth and enthusiasm

Research now supports our long-standing intuition that customers' perceptions of service quality are shaped by the courtesy, empathy and responsiveness of service employees.[7] Customers want employees to appear concerned about their needs. Can empowerment help create this? One of us has done customer service research in branch banks that showed that when the tellers reported feeling good about how they were supervised, trained and rewarded, customers thought more highly of the service they received.[8] In short, when employees felt that management was looking after their needs, they took better care of the customer.

In service encounters, employees' feelings about their jobs will spill over to affect how customers feel about the service they get. This is particularly important when employee attitudes are a key part of the service package. In banking, where the customer receives no tangible benefits in the exchange other than a savings deposit slip, a sour teller can really blemish a customer's feelings about the encounter.

Empowered employees can be a great source of service ideas

Giving front-line employees a voice in 'how we do things around here' can lead to improved service delivery and ideas for new services. The bank study showed that the tellers could accurately report how customers viewed overall service quality and how they saw the branches' service climate (e.g. adequacy of staff and appearance of facilities).[9]

Front-line employees are often ready and willing to offer their opinion. When it comes to market research, imagine the difference in response rates from surveying your employees and surveying your customers.

Great word-of-mouth advertising and customer retention

Nordstrom's advertising budget is 1.5 percent of sales, whereas the industry average is 5 percent. Why? Their satisfied-no-matter-what customers spread the word about their service and become repeat customers.

The costs

What are the costs of empowerment?

A greater dollar investment in selection and training

You cannot hire effective, creative problem solvers on the basis of chance or mere intuition. Too bad, because the systematic methods necessary to screen out those who are not good candidates for empowerment are expensive. For example, Federal Express selects customer agents and couriers on the basis of well-researched profiles of successful performers in those jobs.

Training is an even greater cost. The production line approach trains workers easily and puts them right to work. In contrast, new hires at SAS are formally assigned a mentor to help them learn the ropes; Nordstrom department managers take responsibility for orienting and training new members of the sales team; customer service representatives at Lands' End and L. L. Bean spend a week in training before handling their first call. They receive far more information and knowledge about their company and its products than is the norm.

The more labour intensive the service, the higher these costs. Retail banking, department stores and convenience stores are labour intensive and their training and selection costs can run high. Utilities and airlines are far less labour intensive.

Higher labour costs

Many consumer service organizations, such as department stores, convenience stores, restaurants and banks, rely on large numbers of part-time and seasonal workers to meet their highly variable staffing needs. These employees typically work for short periods of time at low wages. To empower these workers, a company would have to invest heavily in training to try to quickly inculcate the organization's culture and values. This training would probably be unsuccessful and the employees wouldn't be around long enough to provide a return on the investment. Alternatively, the organization could pay higher wages to full-time, permanent employees, but they would be idle when business was slow.

Slower or inconsistent service delivery

Remember the hotel guest wanting to check in early and the airline passenger requesting special treatment at the gate? True, there is a benefit to empowering the employee to bend the rules, but only for the person at the front of the line! Customers at the back of the line are grumbling and checking their watches. They may have the satisfaction of knowing that they too may receive creative problem solving when and if they reach the counter, but it is small consolation if the plane has already left.

Based on our experiences as both researchers and customers, we believe that customers will increasingly value speed in service delivery. Purposeful chaos may work against this. We also believe that many customers value 'no surprises' in service delivery. They like to know what to expect when they revisit a service business or patronize different outlets of a franchise. When service delivery is left to employee discretion, it may be inconsistent.

The research data show that customers perceive reliability – 'doing it right the first time' – as the most important dimension of service quality. It matters more than employees' responsiveness, courtesy or competency or the attractiveness of the service setting.[10] Unfortunately, in the same research, a sample of large, well-known firms was more deficient on reliability than on these other dimensions. Much of the touted appeal of the production line approach was that procedurally and technocratically driven operations could deliver service more reliably and consistently than service operations heavily dependent upon the skills and attitudes of employees. The production line approach was intended to routinize service so that customers would receive the 'best outcome' possible from their service encounters – service delivery with no glitches in the first place.

We feel that service managers need to guard against being seduced into too great a focus on recovery, at the expense of service delivery reliability. We say 'seduced' because it is possible to confuse good service with inspiring stories about empowered employees excelling at the art of recovery. Recovery has more sex appeal than the nitty-gritty detail of building quality into every seemingly mundane aspect of the service delivery system, but an organization that relies on recovery may end up losing out to firms that do it right the first time.

Violations of 'fair play'

A recent study of how service businesses handle customer complaints revealed that customers associate sticking to procedures with being treated fairly.[11] Customers may be more likely to return to a business if they believe that their complaint was handled effectively because of company policies rather than because they were lucky enough to get a particular employee. In other words, customers may prefer procedurally driven acts of recovery. We suspect that customers' notions of fairness may be violated when they see employees cutting special deals with other customers.

Giveaways and bad decisions

Managers are often reluctant to empower their employees for fear they will give too much away to the customer. Perhaps they have heard the story of Willie, the doorman at a Four Seasons Hotel, who left work and took a flight to return a briefcase left behind by a guest. Or they have heard of too many giveaways by empowered Nordstrom employees. For some services, the costs of giveaways are far outweighed by enhanced customer loyalty, but not for others.

Sometimes creative rule breaking can cause a major problem for an organization. There may be a good reason why no substitutions are allowed or why a coupon cannot be used on a certain day (e.g. an international airfare agreement). If so, having an empowered employee break a rule may cause the organization serious problems, of which the employee may not even be aware.

These are some of the costs and benefits of empowerment. We hope this discussion will help service businesses use empowerment knowledgeably, not just because it is a fad. But we must add one more caveat: there is still precious little research on the consequences of empowerment. We have used anecdotal evidence, related research (e.g. in job design) and our work on service. More systematic research must assess whether this array of costs and benefits fully captures the 'whys' (and 'why nots') of empowerment.

How to Empower: Three Options

Empowering service employees is less understood than industrializing service delivery. This is largely because the production line approach is an example of the well-developed control model of organization design and management, whereas empowerment is part of the still evolving 'commitment' or 'involvement' model. The latter assumes that most employees can make good decisions if they are properly socialized, trained and informed. They can be internally motivated to perform effectively and they are capable of self-control and self-direction. This approach also assumes that most employees can produce good ideas for operating the business.[12]

The control and involvement models differ in that four key features are concentrated at the top of the organization in the former and pushed down in the organization in the latter. As we discussed earlier, these features are the following: (1) information about organizational performance (e.g. operating results and competitor performance); (2) rewards based on organizational performance (e.g. profit sharing and stock ownership); (3) knowledge that enables employees to understand and contribute to organizational performance (e.g. problem-solving skills); and (4) power to make decisions that influence work procedures and organizational direction (e.g. through quality circles and self-managing teams).

Three approaches to empowering employees can be identified (see Figure 13.2).[13] They represent increasing degrees of empowerment as additional knowledge, information, power, and rewards are pushed down to the front line.

Empowerment, then, is not an either/or alternative, but rather a choice of three options:

1 *Suggestion involvement* represents a small shift away from the control model. Employees are encouraged to contribute ideas through formal suggestion programmes or quality circles, but their day-to-day work activities do not really change. Also, they are only empowered to recommend; management typically retains the power to decide whether or not to implement.

   Suggestion involvement can produce some empowerment without altering the basic production line approach. McDonald's, for example, listens closely to the front line. The Big Mac, Egg McMuffin and McMDLT were all invented by employees, as was the system of wrapping burgers that avoids leaving a thumbprint in the bun. As another example, Florida Power and Light, which won the Deming quality award, defines empowerment in suggestion involvement terms.

2 *Job involvement* represents a significant departure from the control model because of its dramatic 'opening up' of job content. Jobs are redesigned so that employees use a variety of skills. Employees believe their tasks are significant, they have considerable freedom in deciding how to do the work, they get more feedback and they handle a whole identifiable piece of work. Research shows that many employees find enriched work more motivating and satisfying and they do higher quality work.[14]

   Often job involvement is accomplished through extensive use of teams. Teams are often appropriate in complex service organizations such as hospitals and airlines because individuals cannot offer a whole service or handle a customer from beginning to end of service delivery. Teams can empower back-office workers in banks and insurance companies as well.

   Employees in this environment require training to deal with the added complexity. Supervisors, who now have fewer shots to call, need to be reoriented toward supporting the front line, rather than directing it. Despite the heightened level of empowerment it brings, the job involvement approach does not change higher level strategic decisions concerning organization structure, power and the allocation of rewards. These remain the responsibility of senior management.

3 *High-involvement organizations* give their lowest level employees a sense of involvement not just in how they do their jobs or how effectively their group performs, but in the total organization's performance. Virtually every aspect of the organization is different from that of a control-oriented organization. Business performance information is shared. Employees develop skills in teamwork, problem solving and business operations. They participate in work unit management decisions. There is profit sharing and employee ownership.

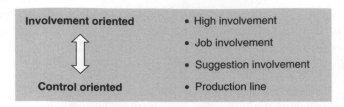

Figure 13.2 *Levels of empowerment*

High-involvement designs may be expensive to implement. Perhaps most troublesome is that these management techniques are relatively undeveloped and untested. People Express tried to operate as a high-involvement airline and the ongoing struggle to learn and develop this new organizational design contributed to its operating problems.

Today, America West is trying to make the high-involvement design work. New hires spend 25 percent of their first year's salary on company stock. All employees receive annual stock options. Flight attendants and pilots develop their own work procedures and schedules. Employees are extensively cross-trained to work where they are needed. Only time will tell if America West can make high-involvement work as it struggles with its financial crisis stemming from high fuel costs and rapid growth.

Federal Express displays many high-involvement features. A couple of years ago, it began a company-wide push to convert to teams, including the back office. It organized its 1000 clerical workers in Memphis into superteams of five to ten people and gave them the authority and training to manage themselves. These terms helped the company cut customer service problems, such as incorrect bills and lost packages, by 13 percent in 1989.

When to Empower: A Contingency Approach

Management thought and practice frequently have been seduced by the search for the 'one best way to manage'. Unfortunately, business does not lend itself to universal truths, only to 'contingency theories' of management. For example, early job enrichment efforts in the 1960s assumed that all employees would prefer more challenging work and more autonomy. By the 1970s it was clear that only those employees who felt the need to grow at work responded positively to job enrichment.[15] As the research on it is still thin, it is at least possible that empowerment is a universal truth, but historical evidence weighs against it being the best way to manage in all situations.

We believe that both the empowerment and production line approaches have their advantages and that each fits certain situations. The key is to choose the management approach that best meets the needs of both employees and customers.

Table 13.1 presents five contingencies that determine which approach to adopt. Each contingency can be rated on a scale of 1 to 5 to diagnose the quality of fit between the overall situation and the alternative approaches. The following propositions suggest how

Table 13.1   *The contingencies of empowerment*

Contingency	Production line approach							Empowerment
Basic business strategy	Low cost, high volume	1	2	3	4	5		Differentiation, customized, personalized
Tie to customer	Transaction short time period	1	2	3	4	5		Relationship, long time period
Technology	Routine, simple	1	2	3	4	5		Non-routine, complex
Business environment	Predictable, few surprises	1	2	3	4	5		Unpredictable, many surprises
Types of people	Theory X managers employees with low growth needs, low social needs, and weak interpersonal skills	1	2	3	4	5		Theory Y managers, employees with high growth needs, high social needs, and strong interpersonal skills

to match situations and approaches. Matching is not an exact science, but the propositions suggest reasonable rules of thumb.

Proposition 1: The higher the rating of each contingency (5 being the highest), the better the fit with an empowerment approach; the lower the rating (1 being the lowest), the better the fit with a production line approach.

Proposition 2: The higher the total score from all five contingencies, the better the fit with an empowerment approach; the lower the total score, the better the fit with a production line approach. A production line approach is a good fit with situations that score in the range of 5 to 10. For empowerment approaches, suggestion involvement is a good fit with situations that score in the range of 11 to 15, job involvement; with scores that range from 16 to 20 and high involvement with scores that range from 21 to 25.

Proposition 3: The higher the total score, the more the benefits of increasing empowerment will outweigh the costs.

We now describe each contingency's implications for a production line or empowerment approach.

Basic business strategy

A production line approach makes the most sense if your core mission is to offer high-volume service at the lowest cost. 'Industrializing' service certainly leverages volume.

The question is what is the value-added from spending the additional dollars on employee selection, training and retention necessary for empowerment? This question is especially compelling in labour-intensive services (e.g. fast food, grocery stores and convenience stores) and those that require part-time or temporary employees.

The answer depends on what customers want from the service firm and what they are willing to pay for. Certain customer segments are just looking for cheap, quick and reliable service. They do want quality – a warm hamburger rather than a cold one. But they are not necessarily expecting tender loving care. Even if they wanted it, they wouldn't pay for it.

These customers prefer a production line approach. A recent study of convenience stores actually found a negative relationship between store sales clerks being friendly with customers.[16] Customers wanted speed and friendly clerks slowed things down. The point is that customers themselves may prefer to be served by a non-empowered employee.

At Taco Bell, counter attendants are expected to be civil but they are not expected or encouraged to be creative problem solvers. Taco Bell wants to serve customers who want low-cost, good-quality, fast food. Interestingly, the company believes that as more chains move to customized, service-oriented operations, it has more opportunities in the fast, low-price market niche.

The production line approach does not rule out suggestion involvement. As mentioned earlier, employees often have ideas even when much of their work is routinized. Quality circles and other approaches can capture and develop them.

An empowerment approach works best with a market segment that wants the tender loving care dimension more than speed and cost. For example, SAS targets frequent business travellers (who do not pay their own way). The SAS strategy was to differentiate itself from other airlines on the basis of personalized service. Consequently, the company looked at every ingredient of its service package to see if it fitted this segment's definition of service quality and, if so, whether or not customers would pay for it.

Tie to customer

Empowerment is the best approach when service delivery involves managing a relationship, as opposed to simply performing a transaction. The service firm may want to establish relationships with customers to build loyalty or to get ideas for improving the service delivery system or offering new services. A flexible, customized approach can help establish the relationship and get the ideas flowing.

The returns on empowerment and relationship building are higher with more sophisticated services and delivery systems. An employee in the international air freight industry is more likely to learn from a customer relationship than is a gasoline station attendant.

The relationship itself can be the principal valued commodity that is delivered in many services. When no tangibles are delivered, as in estate planning or management consulting, the service provider often is the service to the customer and empowerment allows the employee to customize the service to fit the customer's needs.

The more enduring the relationship and the more important it is in the service package, the stronger the case for empowerment. Remember the earlier comparison between Disney, which tightly scripts its ride operators, and Club Med, which encourages its GOs to be spontaneous? Giraud, Club Med's CEO, explains that Disney employees relate to their guests in thousands of brief encounters; GOs have week-long close relationships with a limited number of guests. The valuable service they sell is 'time'.

Technology

It is very difficult to build challenge, feedback and autonomy into a telephone operator's job, given the way the delivery technology has been designed. The same is true of many fast food operations.

In these situations, the technology limits empowerment to only suggestion involvement and ultimately may almost completely remove individuals from the service delivery process, as has happened with ATMs.

When technology constrains empowerment, service managers can still support front-line employees in ways that enhance their satisfaction and the service quality they provide. For example, managers can show employees how much their jobs matter to the organization's success and express more appreciation for the work they do. In other words, managers can do a better job of making the old management model work!

Routine work can be engaging if employees are convinced that it matters. Volunteers will spend hours licking envelopes in a fundraising campaign for their favourite charity. Disney theme park employees do an admirable job of performing repetitive work, partly because they believe in the values, mission and show business magic of Disney.

Business environment

Businesses that operate in unpredictable environments benefit from empowerment. Airlines face many challenges to their operations: bad weather, mechanical breakdowns and competitors' actions. They serve passengers who make a wide variety of special requests. It is simply impossible to anticipate many of the situations that will arise and to 'programme' employees to respond to them. Employees trained in purposeful chaos are appropriate for unpredictable environments.

Fast food restaurants, however, operate in stable environments. Operations are fairly fail-safe; customer expectations are simple and predictable. In this environment, the service business can use a production line approach. The stability allows, even encourages, management with policies and procedures, because managers can predict most events and identify the best responses.

Types of people

Empowerment and production line approaches demand different types of managers and employees. For empowerment to work, particularly in the high-involvement form, the company needs to have Theory Y managers who believe that their employees can act independently to benefit both the organization and its customers. If the management ranks are filled with Theory X types who believe that employees only do their best work when closely supervised, then the production line approach may be the only feasible option unless the organization changes its managers. Good service can still be the outcome. For example, most industry observers would agree that Delta and American Airlines are managed with a control orientation rather than a strong empowerment approach.

Employees will respond positively to empowerment only if they have strong needs to grow and to deepen and test their abilities – at work. Again, a checkered history of job enrichment efforts has taught us not to assume that everyone wants more autonomy, challenge and responsibility at work. Some employees simply prefer a production line approach.

Lastly, empowerment that involves teamwork requires employees who are interested in meeting their social and affiliative needs at work. It also requires that employees have good interpersonal and group process skills.

The Future of Service World

How likely is it that more and more service businesses will choose to face the customer with empowered employees? We would guess that far more service organizations operate at the production line end of our continuum than their business situations call for. A 1989 survey of companies in the Fortune 1000 offers some support for this view.[17] This survey revealed that manufacturing firms tend to use significantly more employee-involvement practices than do service firms. Manufacturing firms use quality circles, participation groups and self-managing work teams far more than service firms.

The intense pressure on the manufacturing sector from global competition has created more dissatisfaction with the old control-oriented way of doing things. Also, it can be easier to see the payoffs from different management practices in manufacturing than in service. Objective measures of productivity can more clearly show profitability than can measures of customer perceptions of service quality. However, these differences are now blurring as service competition increases and service companies become more sophisticated in tracking the benefits of customer service quality.

As service businesses consider empowerment, they can look at high-involvement manufacturing organizations as labs in which the various empowerment approaches have been tested and developed. Many lessons have been learned in manufacturing about how to best use quality circles, enriched jobs and so on. And the added good news is that many service businesses are ideally suited to applying and refining these lessons. Multisite, relatively autonomous service operations afford their managers an opportunity to customize empowerment programmes and then evaluate them.

In summary, the newest approaches to managing the production line can serve as role models for many service businesses, but perhaps not all. Before service organizations rush into empowerment programmes, they need to determine whether and how empowerment fits their situation.

References

1   T. Levitt, 'Production-line approach to service', Harvard Business Review, September-October 1972, pp. 41–52; and T. Levitt, 'Industrialization of service', *Harvard Business Review,* September-October 1976, pp. 63–74.

2   Levitt (1972), op.cit.

3   D. Tansik, ' Managing human resource issues for high-contact service personnel', in *Service Management Effectiveness,* eds D. Bowen, R. Chase and T. Cummings (San Francisco: Jossey-Bass, 1990). [Note: McDonald's staff are now allowed to improvise their greeting.]

4   R. Zemke and D. Schaaf, *The Service Edge: 101 Companies that Profit from Customer Care* (New York: New American Library, 1989), p. 68.

5   As quoted in Zemke and Schaaf (1989), p. 68.

6   J. Carlzon, *Moments of Truth* (New York: Ballinger, 1987).

7   V. Zeithaml, A. Parasuraman and L. L. Berry, *Delivering Quality Service: Balancing Customer Perceptions and Expectations* (New York: Free Press. 1990). See also B. Schneider and D. Bowen, 'Employee and customer perceptions of service in banks: replication and extension', *Journal of Applied Psychology,* 70, 1985, pp. 423–433.

8   Schneider and Bowen (1985).

9   Ibid.

10 Zeithaml, Parasuraman and Berry (1990), op.cit.

11 C. Goodwin and I. Ross, 'Consumer evaluations of responses to complaints: what's fair and why', *Journal of Services Marketing,* 4, 1990, pp. 53–61.

12 See E. E. Lawler III, *High–Involvement Management* (San Francisco: Jossey-Bass, 1986).

13 See E. E. Lawler III, 'Choosing an involvement strategy', *Academy of Management Executive,* 2, 1988, pp. 197–204.

14 See for example J. R. Hackman and G. R. Oldham, Work Redesign (Reading, Massachusetts: Addison-Wesley, 1980).

15 Ibid.

16 R. J. Sutton and A. Rafaeli, "Untangling the relationship between displayed emotions and organizational sales: the case of convenience stores', *Academy of Management Journal,* 31, 1988, pp. 461–468.

17 E. E. Lawler III, G. E. Ledford Jr. and S. A. Mohrman, *Employee Involvement in America. A Study of Contemporary Practice* (Houston: American Productivity & Quality Center, 1989).

Ambidextrous Organizations: Managing Evolutionary and Revolutionary Change

Michael L. Tushman and Charles A. O'Reilly III

All managers face problems in overcoming inertia and implementing innovation and change. But why is this problem such an enduring one? Organizations are filled with sensible people and usually led by smart managers. Why is anything but incremental change often so difficult for the most successful organizations? And why are the patterns of success and failure so prevalent across industries and over time? To remain successful over long periods, managers and organizations must be ambidextrous—able to implement both incremental and revolutionary change.

Patterns in Organization Evolution

Across industries there is a pattern in which success often precedes failure. But industry-level studies aren't very helpful for illustrating what actually went wrong. Why are managers sometimes ineffective in making the transition from strength to strength? To understand this we need to look inside firms and understand the forces impinging on management as they wrestle with managing innovation and change. To do this, let's examine the history of two firms. RCA semiconductors and Seiko watches, as they dealt with the syndrome of success followed by failure.

The stark reality of the challenge of discontinuous change can be seen in Table 14.1. This is a listing of the leading semiconductor firms over a forty-year period. In the mid-1950s, vacuum tubes represented roughly a $700 million market. At this time, the leading firms in the then state-of-the-art technology of vacuum tubes included great technology companies such as RCA, Sylvania, Raytheon, and Westinghouse. Yet between 1955 and 1995, there was almost a complete turnover in industry leadership. With the advent of the transistor, a major technological discontinuity, we see the beginnings of a remarkable shakeout. By 1965, new firms such as Motorola and Texas

Source: M.L. Tushman and C.A. O'Reilly III (1996) *California Mnagement Review*, 38 (4): 8–30. Edited version.

Table 14.1   *Semiconductor Industry 1955–1995*

	1955 (Vacuum Tubes)	1955 (Transistors)	1965 (Semi-conductors)	1975 (Integrated Circuits)	1982 (VLSI)	1995 (Sub-micron)
1.	R.C.A	Hughes	TI	TI	Motorola	Intel
2.	Sylvania	Transitron	Fairchild	Fairchild	TI	NEC
3.	GE	Philco	Motorola	National	NEC	Toshiba
4.	Raytheon	Sylvania	GI	Intel	Hitachi	Hitachi
5.	Westinghouse	TI	GE	Motorola	National	Motorola
6.	Amperex	GE	RCA	Rockwell	Toshiba	Samsung
7.	NationalVideo	RCA	Sprague	GI	Intel	TI
8.	Rawland	Westinghouse	Philco	RCA	Philips	Fujitsu
9.	Eimac	Motorola	Transitron	Philips	Fujitsu	Mitsubishi
10.	Lansdale	Clevite	Raytheon	AMD	Fairchild	Philips

Source: Adapted from R. Foster, *Innovation: The Attacker's Advantage* (New York, NY: Summit Books, 1986).

Instruments had become important players while Sylvania and RCA had begun to fade. Over the next 20 years still other upstart companies like Intel, Toshiba, and Hitachi became the new leaders while Sylvania and RCA exited the product class.

Why should this pattern emerge? Is it that managers and technologists in 1955 in firms like Westinghouse, RCA, and Sylvania didn't understand the technology? This seems implausible. In fact, many vacuum tube producers did enter the transistor market, suggesting that they not only understood the technology, but saw it as important. RCA was initially successful at making the transition. While from the outside it appeared that they had committed themselves to transistors, the inside picture was very different.

Within RCA, there were bitter disputes about whether the company should enter the transistor business and cannibalize their profitable tube business. On one side, there were reasonable arguments that the transistor business was new and the profits uncertain. Others, without knowing whether transistors would be successful, felt that it was too risky not to pursue the new technology. But even if RCA were to enter the solid-state business, there were thorny issues about how to organize it within the company. How could they manage both technologies? Should the solid-state division report to the head of the electronics group, a person steeped in vacuum tube expertise?

With its great wealth of marketing, financial, and technological resources, RCA decided to enter the business. Historically, it is common for successful firms to experiment with new technologies.[1] Xerox, for example, developed user-interface and software technologies, yet left it to Apple and Microsoft to implement them. Western Union developed the technology for telephony and allowed American Bell (AT&T) to capture the benefits. Almost all relatively wealthy firms can afford to explore new technologies. Like many firms before them. RCA management recognized the problems of trying to play two different technological games but were ultimately unable to resolve them. In the absence of a clear strategy and the cultural differences required to compete in both markets, RCA failed.

In his study of this industry, Richard Foster (then a Director at McKinsey & Company) notes, "Of the 10 leaders in vacuum tubes in 1955 only two were left in 1975. There were three variants of error in these case histories. First is the decision not to invest in the new technology. The second is to invest but picking the wrong technology. The third variant is cultural. Companies failed because of their inability to play two games at once: To be both effective defenders of what quickly became old technologies and effective attackers with new technologies."[2] Senior managers in these firms fell victim to their previous success and their inability to play two games simultaneously. New firms, like Intel and Motorola, were not saddled with this internal conflict and inertia. As they grew, they were able to re-create themselves, while other firms remained trapped.

In contrast to RCA, consider Hattori-Seiko's watch business. While Seiko was the dominant Japanese watch producer in the 1960s, they were a small player in global markets (see Table 14.2). Bolstered by an aspiration to be a global leader in the watch business, and informed by internal experimentation between alternative oscillation technologies (quartz, mechanical, and tuning fork). Seiko's senior management team made a bold bet. In the mid-1960s, Seiko transformed itself from being merely a mechanical watch firm into being both a quartz and mechanical watch company. This move into low-cost, high-quality watches triggered wholesale change within Seiko and, in turn, within the world-wide watch industry. As transistors replaced vacuum tubes (to RCA's chagrin), quartz movement watches replaced mechanical watches. Even though the Swiss had invented both the quartz and tuning fork movements, at this juncture in history they moved to reinvest in mechanical movements. As Seiko and other Japanese firms prospered, the Swiss watch industry drastically suffered, By 1980, SSIH, the largest Swiss watch firm, was less than half the size of Seiko. Eventually, SSIH and Asuag, the two largest Swiss firms, went bankrupt. It would not be until after these firms were taken over by the Swiss banks and transformed by Nicholas Hayek that the Swiss would move to recapture the watch market.

The real test of leadership, then, is to be able to compete successfully by both increasing the alignment or fit among strategy, structure, culture, and processes, while simultaneously preparing for the inevitable revolutions required by discontinuous environmental change. This requires organizational and management skills to compete in a mature market (where cost, efficiency, and incremental innovation are key) *and* to develop new products and services (where radical innovation, speed, and flexibility are critical). A focus on either one of these skill sets is conceptually easy. Unfortunately, focusing on only one guarantees short-term success but long-term failure. Managers need to be able to do both at the same time, that is, they need to be ambidextrous. Juggling provides a metaphor. A juggler who is very good at manipulating a single ball is not interesting. It is only when the juggler can handle multiple balls at one time that his or her skill is respected.

These short examples are only two illustrations of the pattern by which organizations evolve: periods of incremental change punctuated by discontinuous or revolutionary change. Long-term success is marked by increasing alignment among strategy, structure, people, and culture through incremental or evolutionary change punctuated by discontinuous or revolutionary change that requires the simultaneous shift in

Table **14.2** *Employment in the Swiss Watch Industry. 1955–1985*

Year	No. of Firms	No. of Employees
1955	2300	70,000
1965	1900	84,000
1970	1600	89,000
1975	1200	63,000
1980	900	47,000
1985	600	32,000

strategy, structure, people, and culture. These discontinuous changes are almost always driven either by organizational performance problems or by major shifts in the organization's environment, such as technological or competitive shifts. Where those less successful firms (e.g., SSIH, RCA) react to environmental jolts, those more successful firms proactively initiate innovations that reshape their market (e.g., Seiko).[3]

What's Happening?
Understanding Patterns of Organizational Evolution

These patterns in organization evolution are not unique. Almost all successful organizations evolve through relatively long periods of incremental change punctuated by environmental shifts and revolutionary change. These discontinuities may be driven by technology, competitors, regulatory events, or significant changes in economic and political conditions. For example, deregulation in the financial services and airline industries led to waves of mergers and failures as firms scrambled to reorient themselves to the new competitive environment. Major political changes in Eastern Europe and South Africa have had a similar impact. The combination of the European Union and the emergence of global competition in the automobile and electronics industries has shifted the basis of competition in these markets. Technological change in microprocessors has altered the face of the computer industry.

The sobering fact is that the cliché about the increasing pace of change seems to be true. Sooner or later, discontinuities upset the congruence that has been a part of the organization's success. Unless their competitive environment remains stable—an increasingly unlikely condition in today's world—firms must confront revolutionary change.

[...]

To succeed over the long haul, firms have to periodically reorient themselves by adopting new strategies and structures that are necessary to accommodate changing environmental conditions. These shifts often occur through discontinuous changes—simultaneous shifts in strategy, structures, skills, and culture. If an environment is stable and changes only gradually, as is the case in industries such as cement, it is possible for an organization to evolve slowly through continuous incremental change. But, many managers have learned (to their stockholders' chagrin) that slow evolutionary change in a fast-changing world is, as it was for the dinosaurs, a path to the boneyard.

Figure 14.1 *Two Invisible Forces: Technology Cycles and Evolution*

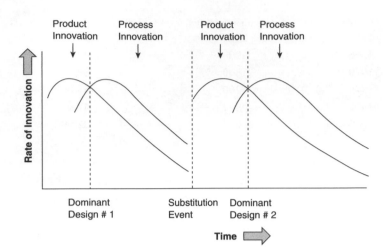

Adapted from J. Utterback, *Mastering the Dyanamics of Innovation* (Boston, MA: Harvard Business School Press, 1994)

Technology Cycles

Although organizational growth by itself can lead to a periodic need for discontinuous change, there is another more fundamental process occurring that results in punctuated change. This is a pervasive phenomenon that occurs across industries and is not widely appreciated by managers. Yet it is critical to understanding when and why revolutionary change is necessary: This is the dynamic of product, service, and process innovation, dominant designs, and substitution events which together make up technology cycles. Figure 14.1 shows the general outline of this process.[4]

In any product or service class (e.g., microprocessors, automobiles, baby diapers, cash management accounts) there is a common pattern of competition that describes the development of the class over time. As shown in Figure 14.1, technology cycles begin with a proliferation of innovation in products or services as the new product or service gains acceptance. Think, for example, of the introduction of VCRs. Initially, only a few customers bought them. Over time, as demand increased, there was increasing competition between Beta and VHS. At some point, a design emerged that became the standard preferred by customers (i.e., VHS). Once this occurred, the basis of competition shifted to price and features, not basic product or service design. The emergence of this *dominant design* transforms competition in the product class.[5] Once it is clear that a dominant design has emerged, the basis of competition shifts to process innovation, driving down costs, and adding features. Instead of competing through product of service innovation, successful strategies now emphasize compatibility with the standard and productivity improvement. This competition continues until there is a major new product, service, or process substitution event and the technology cycle kicks off again as the basis of competition shifts back again to product or service variation (e.g., CDs replacing audio tapes). As technology cycles evolve, bases of competition shift within the market. As organizations change their strategies, they must also realign their organizations to accomplish the new strategic objectives. This usually requires a revolutionary change.

A short illustration from the development of the automobile will help show how dramatic these changes can be for organizations. At the turn of the century, bicycles and horse-driven carriages were threatened by the "horseless carriage," soon to be called the automobile. Early in this new product class there was substantial competition among alternative technologies. For instance, there were several competing alternative energy sources—steam, battery, and internal combustion engines. There were also different steering mechanisms and arrangements for passenger compartments. In a fairly short period of time, however, there emerged a consensus that certain features were to be standard—that is, a dominant design emerged. This consisted of an internal combustion engine, steering wheel on the left (in the U.S.), brake pedal on the right, and clutch on the left (this dominant design was epitomized in the Ford Model T). Once this standard emerged, the basis of competition shifted from variations in what an automobile looked like and how it was powered to features and cost. The new competitive arena emphasized lower prices and differentiated market segments, not product variation. The imperative for managers was to change their strategies and organizations to compete in this market. Those that were unable to manage this transition failed. Similar patterns can be seen in almost all product classes (e.g., computers, telephones, fast foods, retail stores).

With a little imagination, it is easy to feel what the managerial challenges are in this environment. Holding aside the pressures of growth and success, managers must continually readjust their strategies and realign their organizations to reflect the underlying dynamics of technological change in their markets. These changes are not driven by fad or fashion but reflect the imperatives of fundamental change in the technology. This dynamic is a powerful cause of punctuated equilibria and can demand revolutionary rather than incremental change. This pattern occurs across industries as diverse as computers and cement, the only issue is the frequency with which these cycles repeat themselves. Faced with a discontinuity, the option of incremental change is not likely to be viable. The danger is that, facing a discontinuous change, firms that have been successful may suffer from life-threatening inertia—inertia that results from the very congruence that made the firm successful in the first place.

The Success Syndrome: Congruence as a Managerial Trap

Managers, as architects of their organizations, are responsible for designing their units in ways that best fit their strategic challenges. Internal congruence among strategy, structure, culture, and people drives short-term performance.[6] Between 1915 and 1960. General Radio had a strategy of high-quality, high-priced electronic equipment with a loose functional structure, strong internal promotion practices, and engineering dominance in decision making. All these things worked together to provide a highly congruent system and, in turn, a highly successful organization. However, the strategy and organizational congruence that made General Radio a success for 50 years became, in the face of major competitive and technological change, a recipe for failure in the 1960s. It was only after a revolutionary change that included a new strategy and simultaneous shifts in structure, people, and culture that the new company, renamed GenRad, was able to compete again against the likes of Hewlett-Packard and Textronix.[7]

Successful companies learn what works well and incorporate this into their operations. This is what organizational learning is about: using feedback from the market to continually refine the organization to get better and better at accomplishing its mission. A lack of congruence (or internal inconsistency in strategy, structure, culture, and people) is usually associated with a firm's current performance problems. Further, since the fit between strategy, structure, people, and processes is never perfect, achieving congruence is an ongoing process requiring continuous improvement and incremental change. With evolutionary change, managers are able to incrementally alter their organizations. Given that these changes are comparatively small, the incongruence injected by the change is controllable. The process of making incremental changes is well known and the uncertainly created for people affected by such changes is within tolerable limits. The overall system adapts, but it is not transformed.

When done effectively, evolutionary change of this sort is a crucial part of short-term success. But there is a dark side to this success. [...] Older, larger firms develop structural and cultural inertia—the organizational equivalent of high cholesterol. Figure 14.2 shows the paradox of success. As companies grow, they develop structures and systems to handle the increased complexity of the work. These structures and systems are interlinked so that proposed changes become more difficult, more costly, and require more time to implement, especially if they are more than small, incremental modifications. This results in *structural inertia*—a resistance to change rooted in the size, complexity, and inter dependence in the organization's structures, systems, procedures, and processes.

Quite different and significantly more pervasive than structural inertia is the *cultural inertia* that comes from age and success. As organizations get older, part of their learning is embedded in the shared expectations about how things are to be done. These are sometimes seen in the informal norms, values, social networks and in myths, stories and heroes that have evolved over time. The more successful an organization has been, the more institutionalized or ingrained these norms, values, and lessons become. The more institutionalized these norms, values, and stories are, the greater the cultural inertia—the greater the organizational complacency and arrogance. In relatively stable environments, the firm's culture is a critical component of its success. Culture is an effective way of controlling and coordinating people without elaborate and rigid formal control systems. Yet, when confronted with discontinuous change, the very culture that fostered success can quickly become a significant barrier to change. When Lou Gerstner took over as CEO at IBM, he recognized that simply crafting a new strategy was not the solution to IBM's predicament. In his view, "Fixing the culture is the most critical—and the most difficult—part of a corporate transformation."[8] Cultural inertia, because it is so ephemeral and difficult to attack directly, is a key reason managers often fail to successfully introduce revolutionary change—even when they know that it is needed.

The Paradox of Culture

The paradox of culture in helping or hindering companies as they compete can be seen in many ways. [...] The importance of organizational culture transcends country,

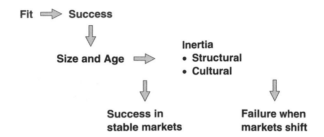

Figure 14.2 *The Success Syndrome*

industry, and firm size. Whether they are electronics giant Samsung, a Hong Kong bank, U.S. conglomerate Allied Signal, a high-tech firm such as Applied Materials or a low-tech company such as Nordstrom, or car manufacturers Nissan, Rover, or General Motors, culture [is often reported to be] a critical factor in the performance of the company. The language used in describing the importance of culture is often similar. Yukata Kume, President of Nissan, observed: "The most challenging task I faced when I became president five years ago was to reform the corporate culture ... I decided that the major reason for our suffering or business predicament lay within Nissan itself."[9] Jack Welch at GE commented on the future demands on organizations: "In the nineties the heroes, the winners, will be entire companies that have developed cultures that instead of fearing the pace of change, relish it."[10]

While news articles about successes and failures are not proof of anything, they offer an interesting window on the concerns of practicing managers and savvy journalists. Whether the issue is can Nike successfully export its "Just do it" culture to help drive global growth, or can Nokia, a Finnish maker of mobile phones, shed its stodgy culture in time to compete in the fast-moving telecommunication market, the managerial challenges are similar: How can managers diagnose and actively shape organizational cultures to both execute today's strategies and create the capabilities to innovate for tomorrow's competitive demands? To help focus and frame the crucial issue of managing culture, let's reflect on a few examples in which organizational culture helped firms succeed or was a significant part of their problem in adapting to new circumstances.

Here's the Good News

First, consider the remarkable transformation of British Airways. In 1981, British Airways lost almost $1 billion. Their customers often referred to the airline's initials "BA" as standing for "Bloody Awful." Ask any frequent flyer for his or her experiences on BA during this period and horror stories will emerge. Even the employees were embarrassed. One employee acknowledged that "I remember going to parties in the late 1970s, and if you wanted to have a civilized conversation, you didn't actually say that you worked for British Airways, because it got you talking about people's last travel experience, which was usually an unpleasant one."[11] When the announcement was made by the British government that the firm was to be privatized, the *Financial Times* newspaper sniffed that it might be that some investors would buy the stock, but only because "every market has a few masochists."

A scant five years later, however, BA's profits were the highest in the industry, 94 percent of its employees bought stock in 1987 when the firm went public, and passengers were making statements like the following: "I can't tell you how my memory of British Airways as a company and the experience I had 10 years ago contrasts with today. The improvement in service is truly remarkable." What accounts for this turnaround? The answer is largely to be found in the cultural revolution engineered by top management, Lord King, and Sir Colin Marshall.

After deciding that they were in the service business rather than the transportation business, British Airways put virtually it's entire 37,000 person work force through a two-day culture change program entitled "Putting People First." Almost all of the 1400 managers went through a five-day version entitled "Managing People First" (MPF). On the surface this program is not conceptually unique. What separates MPF from most management training sessions is its magnitude, the consistency with which it was applied, and the support of top management. Colin Marshall, the Chief Executive Officer, has called it the "single most important program now in operation" at BA and has addressed almost all of the 64 MPF classes.[12]

The emphasis on the culture change effort at BA was on instilling the new culture, establishing an evaluation scheme that measured not only what managers did but how they did it, and a compensation program with bonuses up to 20 percent based on how managers behave. Managers at BA appreciate that any airline can load passengers on a plane and fly them across the Atlantic. BA understands that they are in the service business and any competitive advantage has to be in the service they offer customers. As Bob Nelson, head of the program noted. "The issue with customer service is that you can train monkeys to smile and make eye-contact, but what the hell do you do when you get a nonstandard requirement?"[13]

With essentially the same work force, flying largely the same routes, and using the same technology, British Airways has become one of the world's leading airlines. Its competitive advantage is not in strategy or technology but in a culture shared throughout the organization that provides a level of service that competitors have found difficult to imitate. The lesson that we need to explore is how senior managers were successful in managing the culture to provide competitive advantage. What was it that they did that their competitors have been unable to do?

[...]

Here's the Bad News

[...] There are equally unhappy stories to tell; ones in which the culture of the firm is sometimes linked to failure. And, as suggested earlier, the paradox is often that it is the culture associated with the earlier success of the firm that becomes a part of its downfall. Think briefly about two icons of American business success and the difficulties they currently face: IBM and Sears. (While we use IBM and Sears, the phenomenon is world-wide.)

Between 1990 and 1993, IBM lost a total of $14 billion, with an $8.1 billion loss in 1993 alone. How could this happen? Certainly the computer business is a complex one. IBM was and is a very large firm, which complicates the decision-making process. Nevertheless, numerous presumably smart people were employed specifically to anticipate changes and insure that the firm was prepared to meet them. How, then, can we account for this failure, a failure that has cost almost 200,000 people their jobs and shareholders a loss of billions of dollars? If would be wrong to underestimate the complex difficulties in managing a firm of IBM's size. Certainly the answer must include aspects of strategy, organizational design, technology, and people.

However, perhaps the most important part of the answer to this question, and certainly a part of any solution, is in the culture of IBM; a culture characterized by an inward focus, extensive procedures for resolving issues through consensus and "push back," an arrogance bred by previous success, and a sense of entitlement that guaranteed jobs without a reciprocal *quid pro quo* by some employees. This culture— masquerading under the old IBM basic beliefs in excellence, customer satisfaction, and respect for the individual—was manifest in norms that led to preoccupation with internal procedures rather than understanding the reality of the changing market. In his letter to the shareholders in the 1993 Annual Report, CEO Lou Gerstner states, "We have been too bureaucratic and too preoccupied with our own view of the world." He sees as one of his toughest and most critical tasks to change this entrenched and patriarchical culture into one characterized by a sense of urgency. Without this shift, he believes IBM will continue to squander its talent and technology.

While occurring in a very different industrial context, a similar drama is playing out at Sears, the great American retailer. Again, the picture is a complicated one and it would be wrong to oversimplify it. The broad outlines of the problem are, however, easily visible. Until 1991, Sears was the largest retailer in the U.S. with over 800 stores and 500,000 employees, including over 6,000 at headquarters in the Sears Tower in Chicago. For decades it was the family department store for America, a place where one could buy everything from clothes to tools to kitchen appliances. However, by the mid-1980s, trouble had begun to surface. Market share had fallen 15 percent from its high in the 70s, the stock price had dropped by 40 percent since Edward Brennan had become CEO in 1985, and chronic high costs hindered Sears from matching the prices of competitors such as Wal-Mart, K-mart, Circuit City, the Home Depot, and other low-cost specialty stores.[14]

Under Brennan's leadership, Sears made a number of strategic changes in attempts to halt the slide. Yet the execution of the strategy was dismal. Observers and analysts attributed the failure to Brennan's inability to revamp the old Sears culture that, as one respected analyst noted, was a "culture [...] rooted in a long tradition of dominating the retailing industry ... But this success bred in Sears executives an arrogance and an internal focus that was almost xenophobic." Another observed that "the main problem with Sears is that its managers and executives are 'Sears-ized'—so indoctrinated in the lore of past glories and so entrenched in an overwhelming bureaucracy that they cannot change easily."[15] The old Sears culture, like the old IBM culture, was a product of their success: proud, inward-looking, and resistant to change.

The lesson is a simple one: organizational culture is a key to both short-term success *and*, unless managed correctly, long-term failure. Culture can provide competitive advantage, but as we have seen, it can also create obstacles to the innovation and change necessary to be successful. In the face of significant changes in technology, regulation, or competition, great managers understand this dynamic and effectively manage *both* the short-term demands for increasing congruence and bolstering today's culture *and* the periodic need to transform their organization and re-create their unit's culture. These organizational transformations involve fundamental shifts in the firm's structure and systems as well as in its culture and competencies. Where change in structure and systems is relatively simple, change in culture is not. The issue of actively managing organization cultures that can handle both incremental and discontinuous change is perhaps the most demanding aspect in the management of strategic innovation and change.

Ambidextrous Organizations: Mastering Evolutionary and Revolutionary Change

The dilemma confronting managers and organizations is clear. In the short-run they must constantly increase the fit or alignment of strategy, structure, and culture. This is the world of evolutionary change. But this is not enough for sustained success. In the long-run, managers may be required to destroy the very alignment that has made their organizations successful. For managers, this means operating part of the time in a world characterized by periods of relative stability and incremental innovation, and part of the time in a world characterized by revolutionary change. These contrasting managerial demands require that managers periodically destroy what has been created in order to reconstruct a new organization better suited for the next wave of competition or technology.[16]

Ambidextrous organizations are needed if the success paradox is to be overcome. The ability to simultaneously purse both incremental and discontinuous innovation and change results from hosting multiple contradictory structures, processes, and cultures within the same firm. There are good examples of companies and managers who have succeeded in balancing these tensions. To illustrate more concretely how firms can do this, consider three successful ambidextrous organizations, Hewlett-Packard, Johnson & Johnson, and ABB (Asea Brown Boveri). Each of these has been able to compete in mature market segments through incremental innovation and in emerging markets and technologies through discontinuous innovation. Each has been successful at winning by engaging in both evolutionary and revolutionary change.

[...]

Organizational Architectures

Although the combined size of these three companies represents over 350,000 employees, each has found a common way to remain small by emphasizing autonomous groups. For instance, J&J has over 165 separate operating companies that scramble relentlessly for new products and markets. ABB relies on over 5,000 profit centers with an average of 50 people in each. These centers operate like small businesses. HP has over 50 separate divisions and a policy of splitting divisions whenever a unit gets larger than a thousand or so people. The logic in these organizations is to keep units small and autonomous so that employees feel a sense of ownership and are responsible for their own results. This encourages a culture of autonomy and risk taking that could not exist in a large, centralized organization. In the words of Ralph Larsen, CEO of J&J, this approach "provides a sense of ownership and responsibility for a business you simply cannot get any other way."[17]

But the reliance on small, autonomous units are not gained at the expense of firm size or speed in execution. These companies also retain the benefits of size, especially in marketing and manufacturing. ABB continually reevaluates where it locates its worldwide manufacturing sites. J&J uses its brand name and marketing might to leverage new products and technologies. HP uses its relationships with retailers developed from its printer business to market and distribute its new personal computer line. But these firms accomplish this without the top-heavy staffs found at other firms. Barnevik reduced ABB's hierarchy to four levels and a headquarters staff of 150 and purposely keeps the structure fluid. At J&J headquarters, there are roughly a thousand people, but no strategic planning is done by corporate. The role of the center is to set the vision and review the performance of the 165 operating companies. At HP, the former CEO, John Young, recognized in the early 1990s that the more centralized structure that HP had adopted in the 1980s to coordinate their minicomputer business had resulted in a suffocating bureaucracy that was no longer appropriate. He wiped it out, flattening the hierarchy and dramatically reducing the role of the center.

In these companies, size is used to leverage economies of scale and scope, not to become a checker and controller that slows the organization down. The focus is on keeping decisions as close to the customer or the technology as possible. The role of headquarters is to facilitate operations and make them go faster and better. Staff have only the expertise that the field wants and needs. Reward systems are designed to be appropriate to the nature of the business unit and emphasize results and risk taking. Barnevik characterizes this as his 7–3 formula: better to make decisions quickly and be right seven out of ten times than waste time trying to find a perfect solution. At J&J this is expressed as a tolerance for certain types of failure; a tolerance that extends to congratulating managers who take informed risks, even if they fail. There is a delicate balance among size, autonomy, teamwork, and speed which these ambidextrous organizations are able to engineer. An important part of the solution is massive decentralization of decision making, but with consistency attained through individual accountability, information sharing, and strong financial control. But why doesn't this result in fragmentation and a loss of synergy? The answer is found in the use of social control.

Multiple Cultures

A second commonality across these firms is their reliance on strong social controls.[18] They are simultaneously tight and loose. They are tight in that the corporate culture in each is broadly shared and emphasizes norms critical for innovation such as openness, autonomy, initiative, and risk taking. The culture is loose in that the manner in which these common values are expressed varies according to the type of innovation required. At HP, managers value the openness and consensus needed to develop new technologies. Yet, when implementation is critical, managers recognize that this consensus can be fatal. One senior manager in charge of bringing out a new work station prominently posted a sign saying, "This is not a democracy." At J&J, the emphasis on autonomy allows managers to routinely go against the wishes of senior management, sometimes with big successes and sometimes with failures. Yet, in the changing hospital supply sector of their business, managers recognized that the cherished J&J autonomy was stopping these companies from coordinating the service demanded by their hospital customers. So, in this part of J&J, a decision was made to take away some of the autonomy and centralize services. CEO Larsen refers to this as J&J companies having common standards but unique personalities.

A common overall culture is the glue that holds these companies together. The key in these firms is a reliance on a strong, widely shared corporate culture to promote integration across the company and to encourage identification and sharing of information and resources—something that would never occur without shared values. The culture also provides consistency and promotes trust and predictability; [...] these norms and values provide the glue that keeps these organizations together. Yet, at the same time, individual units entertain widely varying subcultures appropriate to their particular businesses. [...]

This tight-loose aspect of culture is crucial for ambidextrous organizations. It is supported by a common vision and by supportive leaders who both encourage the culture and know enough to allow appropriate variations to occur across business units. These companies promote both local autonomy and risk taking and ensure local responsibility and accountability through strong, consistent financial control systems. Managers aren't second-guessed by headquarters. Strategy flows from the bottom up. [...] On the other hand, in return for the autonomy they are granted, there are strong expectations of performance. Managers who don't deliver are replaced.

Ambidextrous Managers

Managing units that pursue widely different strategies and that have varied structures and cultures is a juggling act not all managers are comfortable with. At ABB, this role is described as "preaching and persuading." At HP, managers are low-key, modest, team players who have learned how to manage this tension over their long tenures with the company. At HP, they also lead by persuasion. "As CEO my job is to encourage people to work together, to experiment, to try things, but I can't order them to do it," says Lew Platt.[19] Larsen at J&J echoes this theme, emphasizing the need for lower level managers to come up with solutions and encouraging reasonable failures. Larsen claims that the role is one of a symphony conductor rather than a general.

One of the explanations for this special ability is the relatively long tenure managers have in these organizations and the continual reinforcement of the social control system. Often, these leaders are low-keyed but embody the culture and act as visible symbols of it. As a group the senior team continually reinforces the core values of autonomy, teamwork, initiative, accountability, and innovation. They ensure that the organization avoids becoming arrogant and remains willing to learn from its competitors. Observers of all three of these companies have commented on their modesty or humility in constantly striving to renew themselves. Rather than becoming complacent, these organizations are guided by leaders who venerate the past but are willing to change continuously to meet the future.

The bottom-line is that ambidextrous organizations learn by the same mechanism that sometimes kills successful firms: variation, selection, and retention. They promote variation through strong efforts to decentralize, to eliminate bureaucracy, to encourage individual autonomy and accountability, and to experiment and take risks. This promotes wide variations in products, technologies, and markets. [...] These firms also select "winners" in markets and technologies by staying close to their customers, by being quick to respond to market signals, and by having clear mechanisms to "kill" products and projects. This selection process allowed the development of computer printers at HP to move from a venture that was begun without formal approval to the point where it now accounts for almost 40% of HP's profits. Finally, technologies, products, markets, and even senior managers are retained by the market, not by a remote, inwardly focused central staff many hierarchical levels removed from real customers. The corporate vision provides the compass by which senior managers can make decisions about which of the many alternative businesses and technologies to invest in, but the market is the ultimate arbiter of the winners and losers. Just as success or failure in the marketplace is Darwinian, so too is the method by which ambidextrous organizations learn. They have figured out how to harness this power within their companies and organize and manage accordingly.

Summary

Managers must be prepared to cannibalize their own business at times of industry transitions. While this is easy in concept, these organizational transitions are quite difficult in practice. Success brings with it inertia and dynamic conservatism. Four hundred years ago, Niccolo Machiavelli noted, "There is no more delicate matter to take in hand, nor more dangerous to conduct, nor more doubtful in its success, than to be a leader in the introduction of changes. For he who innovates will have for enemies all those who are well off under the old order of things, and only lukewarm supporters in those who might be better off under the new."[20]

While there are clear benefits to proactive change, only a small minority of far-sighted firms initiate discontinuous change before a performance decline. Part of this stems from the risks of proactive change. One reason for RCA's failure to compete in the solid-state market or for SSIH's inability to compete in quartz movements came from the divisive internal disputes over the risks of sacrificing a certain revenue stream from vacuum tubes and mechanical watches for the uncertain profits from transistors and quartz watches. However, great managers are willing to take this step. Andy Grove of Intel puts it succinctly. "There is at least one point in the history of any company when you have to change dramatically to rise to the next performance level. Miss the moment and you start to decline."[21]

Notes

1. A. Cooper and C. Smith, "How Established Firms Respond to Threatening Technologies," *Academy of Management Executive*, 16/2 (1992): 92–120.
2. R. Foster, *Innovation: The Attacker's Advantage* (New York, NY: Summit Books. 1986). p. 134.
3. B. Virany, M. Tushman, and E. Romanelli. 'Executive Succession and Organization Outcomes in Turbulent Environments," *Organization Science*, 3 (1992): 72–92; E. Romanelli and M. Tushman, "Organization Transformation as Punctuated Equilibrium," *Academy of Management Journal*, 37 (1994): 1141–1166: M. Tushman and L. Rosenkopf, "On the

Organizational Determinants of Technological Change: Towards a Sociology of Technological Evolution," in B. Staw and L. Cummings, eds., *Research in Organization Behavior*, Vol. 14 (Greenwich. CT: JAI Press, 1992); D. Miller, "The Architecture of Simplicity." *Academy of Management Review*, 18 (1993): 116–138; A. Meyer, G. Brooks, and J. Goes, "Environmental Jolts and Industry Revolutions," *Strategic Management Journal*, 6 (1990): 48–76.

4. M. Tushman and L. Rosenkopf, "On the Organizational Determinants of Technological Change: Towards a Sociology of Technological Evolution," in B. Staw and L. Cummings, *Research in Organization Behavior*, Vol. 14 (Greenwich, CT: JAI Press, 1992): M. Tushman and P. Anderson. "Technological Discontinuities and Organization Environments.' *Administrative Science Quarterly*, 31 (1986): 439–465: W. Abernathy and K. Clark. "Innovation: Maping the Winds of Creative Destruction." *Research Policy*, 1985. pp. 3–22; J. Wade. "Dynamics of Organizational Communities and Technological Bandwagons," *Strategic Management Journal*, 16 (1995): 111–133; J. Baum and H. Korn. "Dominant Designs and Population Dynamics in Telecommunications Services," *Social Science Research*, 24 (1995): 97–135.

5. For a more complete treatment of this subject, see J. Utterback. *Mastering the Dynamics of Innovation* (Boston. MA: Harvard Business School Press, 1994). See also R. Burgelman & A. Grove, "Strategic Dissonance," *California Management Review*, 38/2 (Winter 1996): 8–28.

6. D. Nadler and M. Tushman. *Competing by Design* (New York. NY: Oxford University Press, in press); D. Nadler and M. Tushman. "Beyond Charismatic Leaders: Leadership and Organization Change," *California Management Review*. (Winter 1990): 77–90.

7. See M. Tushman, W. Newman, and E. Romanelli. "Convergence and Upheaval: Managing the Unsteady Pace of Organizational Evolution." *California Management Review*, 29/1 (Fall 1986): 29–44.

8. L. Hays, "Gerstner Is Struggling as He Tries to Change Ingrained IBM Culture," *Wall Street Journal*. May 13, 1994.

9. J. Kotter & N. Rothbard, "Cultural Change at Nissan Motors." *Harvard Business School Case*. #9–491–079, July 28, 1993.

10. "Today's Leaders Look to Tomorrow." *Fortune*, March 26, 1990. p. 31.

11. J. Leahey, "Changing the Culture at British Airways." *Harvard Business School Case*. #9–491–009, 1990.

12 L. Bruce, "British Airways Jolts Staff with a Cultural Revolution." *International Management*, March 7, 1987. pp. 36–38

13. Ibid.

14. See, for example, D. Katz. *The Big Store: Inside the Crisis and Revolution at Sears* (New York, NY: Viking, 1987): S. Caminiti, "Sears' Need: More Speed." Fortune: July 15. 1991. pp. 88–90.

15. S. Strom. "Further Prescriptions for the Convalescent Sears." *New York Times*. October 10, 1992.

16. D. Hurst, *Crisis and Renewal* (Boston, MA: Harvard Business School Press, 1995): R. Burgelman. "Intraorganizational Ecology of Strategy Making and Organizational Adaptation," *Organizational Science*, 2/3 (1991): 239–262: K. Eisenhard and B. Tabrizi, "Acceleration Adaptive Processes," *Administrative Science Quarterly*, 40/1 (1995): 86–110; J. Morone. *Winning in High Tech Markets* (Boston. MA: Harvard Business School Press. 1993); M. Iansiti and K. Clark, "Integration and Dynamic Capability," *Industry and Corporation Change*, 3/3 (1994): 557–606; D. Leonard-Barton, *Wellsprings of Knowledge* (Boston, MA: Harvard Business School Press, 1995).

17. J. Weber, "A Big Company that Works," *Business Week*, May 4, 1992. p. 125.

18. See C. O'Reilly. "Corporations, Culture, and Commitment: Motivation and Social Control in Organizations," *California Management Review*, 31/4 (Summer 1989): 9–25; or C. O'Reilly and J. Chatman, "Culture as Social Control: Corporations, Cults, and Commitment," in B. Staw and L. Cummings, eds., *Research in Organizational Behavior*, Vol. 18 (Greenwich, CT: JAI Press, 1996).

19. A. Deutschman. "How H-P Continues to Grow and Grow." *Fortune*, May 2, 1994, p. 100.

20. N. Machiavelli, *The Prince*, translated by L.P.S. de Alvarez (Dallas, TX: University of Dallas Press, 1974).

21. S. Sherman, "Andy Grove: How Intel Makes Spending Pay Off," *Fortune*, February 22, 1993, p. 58.

Technical Entrepreneurship in High Technology Small Firms: Some Observations on the Implications for Management

R.P. Oakey

Introduction

The technical entrepreneur is an acknowledged key catalyst in the process of industrial formation and growth (Cooper, 1970; Rothwell and Zegveld, 1982; Cardullo, 1999). Commencing in the eighteenth century, the Industrial Revolution was dependant upon technical entrepreneurs who, although originally trained as professional engineers, instinctively taught themselves to become expert business managers (e.g. James Watt; Isambard Kingdom Brunel; Robert Stevenson). Such industrial history confirms that the birth of new industries usually depended upon the revolutionary skills of one or more of these key technical innovators, who make the critical pioneering scientific discoveries (and/or innovations in management) that trigger the birth of new industrial sectors (Schumpeter, 1934; Schmookler, 1966; Freeman, 1982).

However, these powerful historical examples of past success should not obscure the fact that technical entrepreneurship remains important today, and that there is a common heritage shared between the above early entrepreneurs and their modern counterparts. For example, the relatively recent development of the computer industry is an instance of how technical entrepreneurs continue to create new industries. From the initial exploits of Hewlett and Packard, through the contributions of Jobs and Wozniak at Apple Computers, to the software-empire of Bill Gates at Microsoft, it is clear that technical entrepreneurs have played key roles in the birth, growth and consolidation of this new family of software and hardware computer-related activities. Moreover, the computer industry has subsequently delivered "knock on" efficiency gains across a wide range of other industrial and service sector activities (Freeman, 1982). Clearly, technical entrepreneurs continue to be a major force within industry and commerce.

None the less, although technical ability has often provided the scientific knowledge *necessary* for an individual to become a successful technical entrepreneur, it is important to stress that *sufficiency* to ensure success lies in an ability to develop

Source: R.P Oakey (2003) *Technovation*, 23: 679–88.

additional business management skills with which to exploit such expertise. Indeed, there are recent examples of technical entrepreneurs who, although of critical importance in scientific terms to the birth of a new sector, *were not* ultimately successful because they were unable to develop effective management skills. Perhaps the best example of this phenomenon (of key relevance to this paper on high technology technical entrepreneurship) is that of William Shockley, the man generally credited with invention of the point contact transistor, the technical basis for the modern semiconductor industry (Saxenian, 1985). Although forming Shockley Transistor in Palo Alto in the early 1950s, and giving the Silicon Valley industrial complex its core product, he did not instinctively have (nor was he able to develop) the business management skills necessary to allow his company to grow. This led, despite strong technical success, to a break up of his company from which eight engineers, led by Gordon Moore "spun off" in 1957 to form the Fairchild Corporation, and later Intel (Cardullo, 1999). Most significantly, while it might be argued that such a failure is evidence that the management skill components of technical entrepreneurship is instinctive and cannot be taught, this paper will take the counterview that technical entrepreneurs *can* gainfully acquire management skills, principally through management education.

Problems resulting from unbalanced technical and business skills not withstanding, effective technical entrepreneurship, when *balance* is achieved, continues to account for many successful "leading edge" high technology firms (Cooper, 1970; Oakey, 1995). Indeed, such balance is critical because, as noted above, although technical ability alone will rarely deliver commercial success, it is also true that high technology businesses based on entrepreneurs *without* technical skills (i.e. that he or she "buys in") rarely succeed (Rothwell and Zegveld, 1982; Oakey, and Mukhtar, 1999). This is because, in order for entrepreneurs to be fully committed to new technical ideas, ideally they should have *intimate* technical knowledge of the product development concerned, and an almost "evangelical" belief in its market potential (Oakey, 1995). Significantly, this key quality often convinces external investors to invest since, when venture capitalists claim that financial projections are secondary to "the people" involved in a business proposal, it is frequently this entrepreneurial belief in the core technology driving the business idea that they find most compelling.

Major candidates for high technology technical entrepreneurship are scientifically qualified staff that have "spun off", either from public sector research establishments (including universities) or existing (usually large) industrial firms (Mason, 1979; Freeman, 1982; Harvey, 1994). Thus, given the above observations on the importance to success of balancing business skills, a continuing challenge for policy makers is to develop training that adds balancing business skills to existing technical knowledge. However, the United Kingdom government has only recently accepted that the key to a higher *quantity and quality* of technical entrepreneurial "spin outs" from universities is improved business training for new and prospective faculty and student technical academic entrepreneurs (Cm. 2250; Cm. 4176: Mukhtar et al., 1999; Oakey et al., 2002). Previously poor provision for the management needs of technical entrepreneurs is illustrated by the fact that those charged with the development of university science parks in the United Kingdom over the past twenty years have strongly promoted the *technical link advantages* that new high technology firms might enjoy when located adjacent to university science departments on a university science park (Cambridge Science Park Directory, 1985) (which have often not materialized (Oakey, 1985; Westhead and Cowling, 1995)). However, given the obvious initial technical skills bias evident in most technical entrepreneurs, the potentially far more useful management skills locally available in university business schools have rarely been "sold" as a key reason for a university-based Science Park location, with which to *balance* previously acquired technical skills (Oakey and Mukhtar, 1999).

Part of the blame for this rather illogical uncoordinated approach to the promotion of technical entrepreneurship derives from the attitude of senior physical scientists towards social science in general, and management science in particular. For these individuals, management science is often considered a contradiction in terms. This attitude derives from the somewhat irrational view that "social science" is either not real science, or that it is a rather intellectually sub-standard "poor relative" of physical science (Popper, 1966: Harvey, 1973). A sense of this rift between intelligence as represented by "literary intellect" on the one hand, and mathematics-based physical sciences on the other, was observed by C. P. Snow in the 1950s, when he tellingly noted a widening gulf emerging between physical scientists and "other literary intellectual forms of reasoning" (Snow, 1959).

A belief in the superior value of the physical sciences can be more practically observed in the way that many heads of university physical science departments continue to be reluctant to surrender space in their curricula for management teaching, an activity to which they often accord an almost *extracurricular* status, similar to language teaching or sport. Indeed, in the past, management education frequently has been seen as almost irrelevant. The tendency to believe that management training is of marginal importance also stems from an assumption that management skills are "instinctive" or can be "picked up as you go along". Although this paper will accept that successful management is *partly* instinctive, there is a growing body of management research to confirm the importance of management education in *improving* entrepreneurial performance, particularly for those academics and industrial researchers previously with only physical science expertise (Reitan, 1997; McMullan and Gillin, 1998; Cosh et al., 1998). In most cases, effective entrepreneurship by scientists and engineers is not possible without use of management skills involving personnel management, financial accounting, marketing knowledge, and strategic awareness; management skills that clearly assist entrepreneurial success (Chell and Allman, 2002).

Growth Options and the Technical Entrepreneur

While management training can assist the technical entrepreneur to *both* set and achieve strategic goals for the firm, it would be simplistic to assume that such stated aspirations always reflect traditional economic profit maximisation motives. Work by behavioural scientists has conclusively indicated that entrepreneurs often sacrifice economic rationality for other non-financial rewards (Simon, 1955; Cyert and March, 1963; Pred, 1965). For example, empirical studies of high technology small firm founders, most of which are established by technical entrepreneurs, have produced consistent evidence that a substantial number of these individualists cite *independence* (Oakey, 1984a, 1995; Deakins and Philpott, 1994) and/or a physically attractive location (Greenhut and Colberg, 1962) as of equal (or greater) importance to that of pure profit maximisation as a key goal for their businesses. Moreover, they are perfectly willing to substitute these objectives for financial gains, short of becoming insolvent (Oakey and Cooper, 1989).

Indeed, with regard to independence, the technical entrepreneur also may be prepared for his enterprise to either remain static, or grow slowly on the basis of retained profits rather than access external funds (Deakins and Philpott, 1994). While surrendering equity for capital, or taking bank loans, might allow the firm to grow faster, the danger that the involvement of external actors might cause a dilution of the founder's control over the firm often renders this option unattractive. This has been an observed strong imperative for many entrepreneurs, in both the United Kingdom *and* the United States (Oakey, 1984b). Since many new firm founders "spin out" from large public or private sector bureaucracies, a major attraction of founding a new small firm is the organisational freedom that such independence engenders. Indeed, if freedom was attributed the financial value it clearly holds for many entrepreneurs, its maximisation might not be considered economically sub-optimal when judged in terms of "rational" economic behaviour (Marris, 1964). However, in all the above circumstances, the "rational economic" definition of "profit" would need to be broadened to include such psychic factors as "peace of mind", "job satisfaction", "a pleasant work environment" and "independence", rather than simple financial gain.

The Mix of Technical Entrepreneurial Attributes, and the Key Role of Control

The Case of the Lone Entrepreneur

While a "multiple founders" variant to the classical archetype of the lone entrepreneur will be considered below, single entrepreneurship is initially discussed here, both since he or she remains a common occurrence, and because the subsequently considered values of joint-entrepreneurship may be profitably contrasted to this initial consideration of the single form. Much folklore surrounds the individual entrepreneur and, from Henry Ford to Richard Branson, media interest has been intense. This is partly because such individuals appear to personify in the public mind expressions of tenacity, risk, confidence in the face of doubt, and ultimately success; attributes to which individuals naturally aspire. However, public perceptions of entrepreneurship are ambiguous and often contradictory, fluctuating wildly between a (politically right-wing) positive view elaborated above, to an equally broadly held converse view of entrepreneurs which is strongly negative, and partly stems from the (politically left wing) socialist stance that has, from the time of Karl Marx, viewed entrepreneurs as unethical exploiters of the economic system (to achieve selfish goals) in general, and the workers they employ, in particular (Popper, 1966; Magee, 1973).

Distaste for entrepreneurship also partly stems from a belief that the pursuit of personal financial gain is, at worst, simply unethical and, at best, at odds with "the common good". This is currently well illustrated by the long running (but latterly intensifying) controversy over attempts to patent discoveries in the field of medicine in general, and the biotechnology area in particular. Here, the motives of capital gain, through attempts to appropriate Intellectual Property Rights (IPR) for new medical discoveries (and *existing* knowledge over which ownership is under dispute), rather than following the traditional course of sharing medical discoveries for the common good, can be cited as a victory of financial gain over ethics (Macdonald and Lefang, 1998). Moreover, entrepreneurship is more fundamentally feared because of a paradox inherent in the nature of entrepreneurial behaviour. Because, in order to be successful, entrepreneurs need to insist that they prevail, there is a tendency for them to become tyrannical and consequently *addicted* to the winning of arguments, even in cases where they prove to be wrong. As will be discussed below, entrepreneurs who seek independence, mainly in order to exercise *control* over their newly independent firm, per se, can present major management problems for their enterprise as it grows (Oakey et al., 1988).

Figure 15.1 represents the interaction of three key factors (namely Motivation, Technical Management Skills, and Business Management Skills) that characterise the performance of technical entrepreneurs, both singularly, and through their interaction. This is particularly the case where motivational factors shape business management and technical management skills through the "control mechanism" (see Figure 15.1). Significantly, the following discussion of technical entrepreneurship extends what would exist under conditions of "normal entrepreneurship" by adding the technical management skills of the founder, that can *either* enhance or constrict overall entrepreneurial performance. These three areas will be discussed in turn below, beginning with the critical strategic driver of Motivation.

Motivation

Motivation is the *key* strategic driver of the model depicted in Figure 15.1 in that it shapes the *attitude* of the technical entrepreneurial founder towards his chosen mix of technical management and business management skills, the manner in which they are deployed within the firm, the amount of external resources accessed (e.g. capital; management expertise), and the level of personal control that he or she exercises on the "day to day" running of the business. Three major motives for beginning a new business are acknowledged in Figure 15.1, comprising "independence" "wealth" and "exploitation". Most importantly, the desire for independence is divided into two, sharply different, driving sub-motives; namely "freedom" and "control". While the desire for freedom frequently derives from a need to escape the stifling bureaucracy of previous employment in large public or private sector bodies and pursue a personal (often research) agenda, the control motive is a more complex psychological driver.

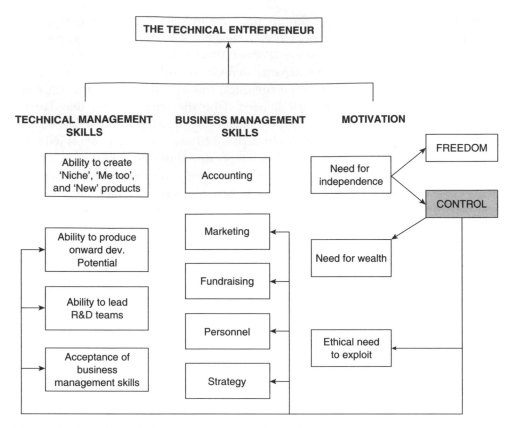

Figure 15.1 *The technical entrepreneur at formation.*

This complexity derives from the paradox that some technical entrepreneurs did not wish to escape control per se when they "spun off" from a large bureaucratic organization. Instead, their problem was that *they* did not exercise this key function! For such entrepreneurs the main attractiveness of beginning their own new firm lies in *their* ability to exercise autocratic and independent control over all aspects of the new enterprise. As Figure 15.1 graphically illustrates, when technical entrepreneurs have a desire for complete control of the firm, this fundamental motivation strongly influences most of the other functions. Such pervasive control influences *both* technical and business management aspects of the enterprise, and critically, shapes the attitude of the owner to many aspects of management, ranging from the conducting of research, through fundraising, to the hiring of new staff.

The particular market segment in which the high technology small firm operates may also influence the viability of specific motivational tendencies. As Figure 15.1 indicates, firms may be established in "niche", "me too" or "new" areas of high technology production. For the first two of these categories (i.e. "niche" and "me too"), it is more likely that autocratic control may be safely maintained because both these activities are slower areas of technology change, where consequent risks and rewards also gradually accrue. The niche producer, perhaps manufacturing in batches (for example) a specialist gas detection instrument, will need to technically improve this product only slowly, while large firm competition in such a low volume "niche" area of production rarely occurs. Similarly, "me too" firms tend to operate in generic, often sub-contract, areas of high technology where, although price competition is strong, R&D costs are low, while a "known" core technology means that barriers to entry are also low (e.g. printed circuit board making; component insertion). In both these instances, lower levels of risk and reward make it easier for an entrepreneur, keen on internal autocratic control, to maintain a "slow growth" introspective management style (Oakey, 1995). However, for technical entrepreneurs developing "new production" in the form of high technology products, with mass market potential (e.g. a "world beating" new treatment in the biomedical area), the scope for maintaining long-term autocratic control is much reduced. This is mainly because the propensity to develop financial problems associated with either R&D cost over-runs and/or later production "scale up" costs are both very high as strong market demand and technically-based competition "pulls" the firm into rapid (often uncontrollable) growth. Interestingly, in *both* these cases of rapidly escalating costs, a sudden and unavoidable need for a rapid external injection of capital is engendered (Oakey, 1995). As will be discussed in detail below under "business management skills" this eventuality may trigger the unavoidable involvement of external investors (e.g. venture capitalists), thus causing a conflict between the imperative of autocratic independence and the urgent need for investment funds, a scenario that independently minded entrepreneurs have every reason to fear (see "business management skills" below).

Technical Management Skills

Clearly, the technical skills of an entrepreneur strongly *determine* the product or service that he or she offers in the market place. For highly gifted scientists, a new product might be developed at the leading edge of technology (e.g. in biomedicine—which would equate to "new" in Figure 15.1), while, as noted above, "me too" and "niche" potential offerings to the market constitute product types of lesser technological sophistication, that none the less, may remain viable vehicles for firm formation and growth. The ability to develop and manage a *team* of researchers, as the firm grows, is a skill that the technical entrepreneur might not readily possess, as noted in the introduction with regard to William Shockley (Cardullo, 1999). This observation leads to a key point concerning a major competence that a technical entrepreneur *must possess*. This is an ability to see the key functional relevance of complementary business management skills in support of technical innovation as part of the overall "success equation". Although this key insight would be implicit to entrepreneurs with *balanced* technical and business management skills, the previously noted prejudice of physical scientists towards social science in general, and an unwillingness on the part of technically qualified scientific entrepreneurs to understand the key relevance of, for example, marketing to product innovation success, is a well documented "blind spot" (Moenart and Souder, 1990; Oakey, 1991).

Neglect of marketing is partly caused by technical entrepreneurs who have a "technology push" view of invention in which technical elegance is often valued more than customer need. Marketing staff, however, who constantly deal with customers, often irritate technical entrepreneurs because of a contradictory "demand pull" view of innovation in which customer requirements are seen as paramount. However, the ultimate value of marketing expertise is witnessed by the fact that, even in cases where there is no customer demand for a new product because it has not previously appeared in the marketplace (i.e. an invention push example—e.g. word processors; personal computers), marketing experts can play a key role in *creating new markets* that previously did not exist. This is often termed educating the market "ahead of itself".

The enthusiasm of Steve Wozniak for the help provided to Apple Computers by Regis McKenna in developing the personal computer market out of a hobbyist "niche" into a mass-market is convincing proof of how important marketing can be. The critical point here, however, is that technical entrepreneurs, in order to be successful (as in the case of Wozniak), must be able to embrace best practice technical management techniques themselves, and be willing to hire or take advice from specialist experts in all areas of business management as the firm grows. Critically, this is the major distinction between the motivations of "freedom" and "control" in Figure 15.1. "Freedom" implies a willingness to use the new enterprise to create a learning organization in which an "open minded" view of entrepreneurship is taken, while "control" in based upon a greater tendency towards introspection and a "not invented here" denial of alternatives.

Business Management Skills

A major factor that encourages technical entrepreneurs to believe that business management skills can be self taught is the frequent reality that businesses, when begun by technical entrepreneurs, initially survive because the founder takes on *all* the business functions illustrated in Figure 15.1 out of necessity (i.e. accounting, marketing, fund raising, personnel management, and strategy). This arrangement has a major early advantage of low cost and, congruity of purpose (since one person performs all functions). However, as the firm grows these key individual tasks become increasingly important and will progressively suffer from not receiving adequate attention if the founder does not delegate to "hired in" specialists.

Given that technical entrepreneurs often have primary responsibility for R&D, it is critical that other business management support, when rapid growth occurs is provided particularly in the finance, marketing and personnel areas. As the firm expands, technical entrepreneurs can either adopt an enlightened attitude to such specialist needs (and make the necessary appointments), or the inadequate performance of such functions will become a "bottleneck" to growth (Oakey et al., 1988). Indeed, when external venture capital *has been* taken "on board" in exchange for equity, the original technical entrepreneur may clash with external investors if he or she is unwilling to allow the development of formal management structures. In extreme cases, external investors may remove such founders, or "side line" them to work as a technical expert, while management is handed to professional managers (Bullock, 1983; CBI, 1997; Oakey, 1984b). Significantly, however, it is fear of such an eventuality that is a major reason why technical entrepreneurs are often unwilling to involve external investors, since such involvement is seen as a "slippery slope" towards a total loss of independence (or control), which (as noted above) may have been the founder's main motive for beginning a business (Figure 15.1). It is certainly true that technical entrepreneurs who refuse to *consider* external involvement are behaving sub-optimally, at least in a strategic sense, in that they are *not* seriously evaluating the *full range* of options open to them. Also, myopic and introspective technical entrepreneurs who resist external involvement during the early life of the firm, perversely, often do not have the experience with which to handle external involvement when they are *forced*, during a crisis of rapid growth *or* decline, to negotiate with (originally unwanted) external partners (Oakey and Mukhtar, 1999).

Joint Entrepreneurship

It is advantageous to pursue the above arguments on the deficiencies of the lone entrepreneur, particularly where they relate to autocratic tendencies and an inability to delegate key tasks, in the context of joint acts of entrepreneurship. There are at least as many instances of joint entrepreneurship as there are examples of individual entrepreneurship although, as noted above, the media often prefer the lone example (Oakey et al., 1988). However, it is clear that venture capitalists are often more comfortable with funding a *team* of founding entrepreneurs who jointly seek to establish a new high technology venture; typically in high technology small firms, a scientist, production engineer and salesman (Bank of England, 2001).

In terms of Figure 15.1, joint entrepreneurship achieves most of the benefits of 'freedom', while the danger of damaging autocratic control is reduced, from the outset, by multiple ownership of the firm. However, because each owner may have differing views on what the firm should seek to achieve (e.g. either grow fast to sell or grow slowly by remaining strongly independent), there may be no *agreed* view on strategy. None the less, in general terms, joint owners tend to have a greater propensity to view the firm, from the outset, in terms of ways in which their shares can be made to rapidly maximise returns (usually implying a "grow to sell" approach), than do individual entrepreneurs. This may be a more "healthy" stance when judged in terms of the future of the firm, since external involvement may become unavoidable. As noted above, it is certainly an attitude that venture capitalists would applaud, since share value appreciation and a safe "exit route" is a motive that they strongly share (Murray and Lott, 1995). Most importantly, multiple-ownership may more often encourage a consideration of the future of the firm that involves, from the outset, an aggressive "grow to sell" approach in which maximum added value is necessary in order to reward *multiple* owners of the firm. Indeed, most successful high technology small firms are eventually absorbed into large global giant firms of any given sector (Granstrand and Sjolander, 1990; Oakey, 1993).

Forward Planning

Strong Control and the Problem of Succession

A final consideration for this paper on the role of technical entrepreneurs in the functioning and growth of high technology small firms concerns various aspects of the forward planning process. First at a most simple level, a major weakness in the above-noted frequently *strong* desire for control among many firm founders is their own mortality. Given that the most usual age among founders for the formation of a high technology small firm is between thirty-five and forty years old, his or her involvement in the firm (assuming it survives) is between twenty five and thirty years. While at the point of formation retirement might appear remote, it will become a major forward planning problem after fifteen to twenty years. For example, should the owner seek external finance during this latter period, the management succession issue will be of critical concern to potential lenders or investors.

Moreover, unlike many small firms where the technology involved is simple and generic (e.g. baking; furniture making; delivery services), technical entrepreneurs may find it difficult to pass on their business, either within the family or to others, because in complex areas of high technology manufacture, other potential managers of the firm (e.g. family members) often do not have the core technical skills of the technical entrepreneur founder. Put simply, the "brain" of the founding entrepreneur is often the firm's main asset. Thus, perversely, if the high technology small firm entrepreneur achieves his or her goal of remaining in independent control of the firm for several years, including remaining the sole source of its technical competence as a technical innovator, severe problems can arise when this individual *approaches* retirement. Despite the above caveats, while it is always possible that he or she could seek to sell the business, at or near retirement as a "going concern", it probably would make better sense (and this is a *key strategic point* to be drawn from this paper), for an entrepreneur with a strong tendency for autocratic control, to temper this tendency and seek to share responsibility with others *from the outset*, both within the firm, and externally.

However, retirement is only one simple example of an exit crisis. Because this eventuality can hardly be described as a strategic choice (and although it can be planned for), it would be a contradiction in terms to describe coping with this eventuality as an exit "strategy". None the less, the succession problem implies that efficient firm owners should *constantly* consider the merits of continuing autonomously against various shared management and/or exit options *throughout the life of the firm*. Indeed, such efficient "exit" considerations might even *precede* the existence of the firm in that a potential technical entrepreneur (e.g. an academic) could decide directly to sell intellectual property he or she has developed (e.g. in a university department) to a large existing firm *before* formation, thus negating the need to found a new business. However, once begun, a technical entrepreneur founder of a firm in the "new" product category of Figure 15.1 with a "world beating" technology, will be constantly approached with offers of part or total ownership of the nascent enterprise by large firm competitors (Oakey et al., 1990).

Deciding on whether to sell or continue is a consideration for the remaining parts of this section on forward planning.

Exit Strategies

For many technical entrepreneurs who begin new firms, stability of demand for their products or services and a good "living wage" is sufficient. In the slower moving "niche" and "me too" areas of production, noted in Figure 15.1, problems associated with "new product" technological developments, by definition, rarely apply since such firms occupy relatively low-risk low-reward areas of high technology production. While issues of price and quality (which also involve elements of avoiding obsolescence) provide constant challenges to firms competing at the "leading edge" of technology, competition in these more generic areas of technology is less onerous (Oakey, 1984b, 1995). Therefore, because in these "niche" and "me too" areas of technology the value of companies are generally lower and stable, issues surrounding possible exit strategies are less acute.

However, in the "new product" technology instances of Figure 15.1, where technologies of extremely high *potential* worth are in the process of development, often within a new high technology small firm, the perceived value of an evolving technology might fluctuate widely in circumstances where comparatively long lead times on R&D development are common (i.e. up to ten years) (Oakey, 1995), depending on scientific progress, competition, government regulations, intellectual property protection problems, and the ill-informed whims of non-scientifically informed investors (Rothwell and Zegveld, 1981). This problem is also common to large pharmaceutical firms in instances where their share prices can be radically influenced by a rumour in the financial press that development of a key new drug is not progressing well.

As noted above, although entrepreneurs in such elite areas of technological development *may* be emotionally inclined towards autocratically maintaining control over a new business that they have established to exploit a "leading edge" technology, in most cases, the power of the technology under development will attract strong external competitive interest (Oakey et al., 1990). Such interest may be direct in that a large competitor company might offer to buy the new firm in question, or it might be indirect in cases where a large firm will deliberately infringe any intellectual property protection enjoyed by the new firm, and effectively illegally acquire the technology concerned by purchasing examples and "reverse engineering" a competing product (Macdonald and Lefang, 1998). Faced with such extreme competition from a large, often multi-national competitor, for most technical entrepreneur founders of new firms, it is not a case of *"if"* to sell out, but more importantly, *"when"* to sell in order to maximise the value of any surrendered intellectual property embodied in the nascent enterprise.

This dilemma for the high technology small firm is expressed in diagrammatic form in Figure 15.2. This diagram expresses the strong functional relationship between the value of any given technology under development and "confidence" in its ability eventually to technically perform efficiently (and by implication) sell in the competitive

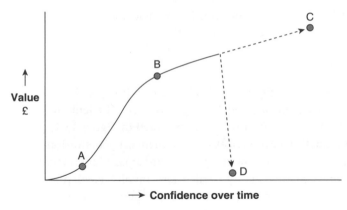

Figure 15.2 *Value versus confidence product life cycle.*

marketplace over time. The key strategic risk for any technical entrepreneur developing such a technology is that he or she cannot be sure that further development of the concept will guarantee further success (and implied value). Various scenarios expressed in Figure 15.2, ranging from options A–D, are discussed in turn.

Scenario A is similar to the strategic option discussed above in which an inventor of a new concept sells the new idea at a very early stage. Unlike the above case, however, where an inventor did not even begin a new firm, in case A the technology is sold at a very early stage after formation, possibly providing funds for the development of another product idea within this nascent enterprise. The main problem with such an approach is that, as indicated in Figure 15.2, the value acquired by the firm is far less than would have been achieved had the product been further developed and sold when development had reached a point further up the development curve (e.g. points B or C). Such observations imply the potential for both possible positive or negative correlations respectively between risk and reward as a product is (or is not) successfully developed.

The position of point B can be simply described as better than A but not as good as C. While the technology concerned has undergone value-adding development that, through a reduction in technical uncertainty, has increased its worth to a potential buyer, the attractiveness of further developing the new technology to point C might render selling out at point B a wasteful strategy. However, as noted in the discussion above, increasing certainty over the potential of a new technology development is a very fragile phenomenon in that there are many technical (e.g. the technology proves dangerous or unreliable) and/or economic (e.g. price and competition) factors that may destroy improving confidence "over night". Thus, in seeking to reach point C on the product development curve, an aggressive entrepreneur might, for the above reasons, cause the demise of his whole business by arriving at point D, following a collapse in confidence that would have a sudden disastrous impact on the value of the technology (and the firm) under development. Clearly, in the absence of a "crystal ball", the key problem for the technical entrepreneur is that future progress cannot be predicted at any given point reached on the growth curve. Further development of any given technology might either prove that it is a new "world beating" approach or a technical "dead end". Unfortunately, *in both cases*, substantial amounts of R&D development investment are necessary to reach *either* points C or D in Figure 15.2. The only personal attributes of the entrepreneur (or entrepreneurs) that might reduce risk and increase confidence in technical entrepreneurs taking strategic decisions in this area are technical excellence, either existing or acquired management expertise, and luck!

Conclusions

This paper must conclude that, although the tendency for technical entrepreneurs to take an independent, or perhaps myopic, approach to high technology small firm management is understandable, in virtually all the instances discussed above, such behaviour is misguided. The failure of a physical scientist with technical management success to acquire business management training is clearly a sub-optimal approach to business development and control. In particular, an unwillingness to hire specialist business management skills, as the business grows, is also likely to inhibit the survival of the enterprise concerned in the medium term, particularly if external financial assistance become an unavoidable need. In cases where both individual and joint entrepreneurship are involved, a flexible approach to the often conflicting merits of internal or external solutions to internal resource bottlenecks, in which *both* options are seriously considered, must lead to a safer business development strategy, and a more democratic work environment in which tasks are determined on the basis of the best (either internal or external) business solution, rather than being driven by the personal prejudices of the technical entrepreneur owner.

Much the same can be concluded regarding exit strategies. Whether to continue or to sell a business should be a *constant* consideration for the technical entrepreneur (or entrepreneurs) from the first day of trading. While the desire to be independent *if possible* can be built into any strategic equation designed to determine whether to continue to own or sell a business, it should not be allocated an unreasonably high value such that it overwhelms or has a veto over all other options. As Figure 15.2 implies, the best time to sell a business depends on many factors that are difficult to determine in advance. However, Figure 15.2 also implies that the right time to sell might occur *at any time* during the life of the firm. To only consider an exit strategy when it is too late to do anything else is, in a strategic sense, a contradiction in terms.

This is not to imply that making strategic decisions regarding undertaking management training, seeking external advice, or selecting the correct exit strategy are simple tasks. Rather, it is reasonable to assert that if the technical entrepreneur opens his or her mind to this full range of intellectual, human and financial resources available to assist management from an early stage in the new high technology small firm's life, on balance, decisions made under this more expansive management regime will be more efficient and likely to succeed. It should be a key role for policy makers at both regional and national levels within the United kingdom to encourage, often reluctant, technical entrepreneurs to embrace management training. The development of such management skills can prove a powerful and valuable adjunct to technical expertise when applied in a business context, where they can provide a balance that, on average, is likely to reduce introspection, increase acceptance of external resources, and consequently lead to better success.

References

Bank of England, 2001. Financing Technology-based Small Firms, Domestic Finance Division, Bank of England, London.

Bullock, M., 1983. According Enterprise, Industrial Innovation, and the Development of High Technology Financing in the United States, Brand Brothers and Co, London.

Cambridge Science Park Directory, 1985. Trinity College Cambridge, November.

Cardullo, M.W., 1999. Technological Entrepreneurism. Research Studies Press Ltd, Baldock, Herts.

Chell, E., Allman, K., 2002. The development of high technology enterprise from HEIs: some methodological considerations. In: Oakey, R.P., During, W.E., Kauser, S. (Eds.), New Technology-Based Firms in the New Millennium, vol. 2., pp. 71–93.

Command Paper 2250. Realising Our Potential: A Strategy for Science, Engineering and Technology, HMSO, London.

Command Paper 4176. Our Competitive future: Building the Knowledge Driven Economy, HMSO, London.

Cooper, A.C., 1970. The Palo Alto experience. Industrial Research May, 58–60.

Cosh, A., Duncan, J., Hughes, A., 1998. The impact of training on business performance: an empirical analysis of UK SMEs 1987–95. Assessing the Impact of Training on the Performance of SMEs. ESRC and Warwick Business School, March.

Confederation of British Industry, 1997. Tech Stars, February, London.

Cyert, R.M., March, J.G., 1963. A Behavioural Theory of the Firm. Prentice Hall, Englewood Cliffs, New Jersey.

Deakins, D., Philpott, T., 1994. Comparative European practices in the finance of new technology entrepreneurs: United Kingdom, Germany and Holland. In: Oakey, R.P. (Ed.), New Technology-based firms in the 1990s. Paul Chapman Publishing, London.

Freeman, C., 1982. The Economics of Innovation. Frances Pinter, London.

Granstrand, O., Sjolander, S., 1990. The acquisition of technology and small firms by large firms. Journal of Economic Behaviour and Organisation 13, 367–386.

Greenhut, M.L., Colberg, M.R., 1962. Factors in the Location of Florida Industry. Florida State University, Tallahassee.

Harvey, D., 1973. Explanation in Geography. Edward Arnold, London.

Harvey, K.A., 1994. The impact of institution intellectual property of the propensity of individual UK universities to incubate NTBFs. In: Oakey, R.P. (Ed.), New Technology-based New Firms in the 1990s. Paul Chapman Publishers, London.

Macdonald, S., Lefang, B., 1998. Patents and policy in the innovation of small and medium sized firms: building on Rothwell. In: Oakey, R.P., During, W.E. (Eds.). New Technology-Based Firms in the 1990s, vol. 5. Elsevier Science Ltd. Oxford, pp. 185–208.

Magee, B., 1973. Popper. Collins Publishers. London.

Marris, R., 1964. Managerial Capitalism. Macmillan, London.

Mason, D., 1979. Factors Affecting the Successful Development and Manufacturing of Innovative Semiconductor Devices, unpublished PhD Thesis. June, SPRU, Sussex University.

McMullan, M.E., Gillin, L.M., 1998. Industrial viewpoint—entrepreneurship education. Technovation 18 (4), 275–286.

Moenaert, R.K., Souder, W.E., 1990. An analysis of the use of extrafunctional information by R&D and marketing personnel: review and model. Journal of Product Innovation Management 7, 229–231.

Mukhtar, S.-M., Oakey, R.P., Kipling, M., 1999. Utilisation of science and technology graduates by the small and medium sized enterprise sector. Education and Training 41 (8), 425–436.

Oakey, R.P., 1984a. High technology small firms: innovation and regional development in Britain and the United States. Frances Pinter, London.

Oakey, R.P., 1984b. Finance and innovation in small independent firms. Omega, International Journal of Management Science 12 (2), 113–124.

Oakey, R.P., 1985. British university science parks and high technology small firms: a comment on the potential for sustained economic growth. International Journal of Small Business 4 (1), 58–67.

Oakey, R.P., 1991. Innovation and the management of marketing in high technology small firms. Journal of Marketing Management 7, 343–356.

Oakey, R.P., 1993. Predatory networking: the role of small firms in the development of the British biotechnology industry. International Small Business Journal 11 (4), 9–22.

Oakey, R.P., 1995. High technology new firms: variable barriers to growth. Paul Chapman Publishing, London.

Oakey, R.P., Cooper, S.Y., 1989. High technology industry, agglomeration, and the potential for peripherally sited small firms. Regional Studies 23 (4), 347–359.

Oakey, R.P., Mukhtar, S.-M., 1999. United Kingdom high technology small firms in theory and practice: a review of recent trends. International Journal of Small Business 17 (2), 48–64.

Oakey, R.P., Rothwell, R., Cooper, S.Y., 1988. The Management Of Innovation in High Technology Small Firms. Frances Pinter, London.

Oakey, R.P., Faulkner, W., Cooper, S.Y., Walsh, V., 1990. New Firms in the Biotechnology Industry: Their Contribution to Innovation and Growth. Frances Pinter, London.

Oakey, R.P., Mukhtar, S., Kipling, M., 2002. Student perspectives on entrepreneurship: observations on their propensity for entrepreneurial behaviour. International Journal of Innovation Management 2 (415), 308–322.

Popper, K., 1966. The Open Society and its Enemies. Routledge, London.

Pred, A.R., 1965. The concentration of high value added manufacturing. Economic Geography 41, 108–132.

Reitan, B., 1997. Fostering technical entreoreneurship in research communities: granting scholarships to would-be entrepreneurs. Technovation 17 (6), 287–296.

Rothwell, R., Zegveld, W., 1981. Industrial Innovation and Public Policy. Frances Pinter, London.

Rothwell, R., Zegveld, W., 1982. Innovation in the Small and Medium Sized Firm. Frances Pinter, London.

Schmookler, J., 1966. Invention and Economic Growth. Harvard University Press, Boston.

Schumpeter, J.A., 1934. The Theory of Economic Development. Harvard University Press, Cambridge Mass.

Saxenian, A., 1985. Silicon Valley and Route 128: Regional prototypes or historic exceptions? In: Castells, M. (Ed.), High Technology, Space and Society. Sage Publications, Beverly Hills and London, pp. 81–105.

Simon, H.A., 1955. The role of expectations in a adaptive behaviouralistic model. In: Bowman, J. (Ed.), Experimentation, Uncertainty and Business Behaviour. SSRC, New York.

Snow, C.P., 1959. The Two Cultures and the Scientific Revolution, Rede Lecture p. 3, University of Cambridge.

Westhead, P., Cowling, M., 1995. Employment change in independent owner-managed high technology firms in Great Britain, Small Business Economics 7 (2), 111–140.

Targeting Innovation and Implications for Capability Development

Dave Francis and John Bessant

Introduction

Since the Palaeolithic period (Curwin, 1954) some, but not all, human societies formed enterprises that created new or improved artefacts, devised 'better' processes, developed new ways of selling and devised alternative models of organising (Diamond, 1997). These enterprises were innovative—they found ways to exploit the latent potential of ideas. Innovation can be defined simply as "the successful exploitation of new ideas" (DTI, 1994). Others have defined innovation more elaborately, but in similar terms; for example (Baumol, 2002) writes that innovation is:

> the recognition of opportunities for profitable change and the pursuit of those opportunities all the way through to their adoption in practice.

Embedded in these definitions is the notion that innovation can be managed. For example, Drucker (1994) argues that innovation is a core process for a firm; he suggests that: "in...a period of rapid change the best – perhaps the only – way a business can hope to prosper, if not survive, is to innovate. This is the only way to convert change into opportunities. This, however, requires that innovation itself be organised as a systematic activity" (Preface 1).

It follows that enterprises that are better able to manage innovation than others and demonstrate a record of successfully exploiting new ideas can be said to possess, at least for a period of time, a superior 'innovation capability'. Developing such capability is an important strategic issue since innovation plays a key role in survival and growth of enterprises. Baumol (op cit) argues that, "virtually all of the economic growth that has occurred since the 18th century is ultimately attributable to innovation". This is also true at the level of the firm. Tidd et al. (1997) in their review of the field conclude that: "Management research suggests that innovative firms—those which are able to use innovation to differentiate their products and services from competition—are on average twice as profitable as other firms".

Source: D. Francis and J. Bessant (2005) *Technovation*, 25: 171–83. Edited version.

The words 'on average' in Tidd et al.'s assessment are important. The contribution of innovation to the profitability of a firm is not straightforward. Some innovation initiatives have proved to be dysfunctional, occasionally leading to catastrophic losses. Even an 'excessive' rate of innovation can be disadvantageous as Yoffie and Cusumano (1999) illustrated when considering the increasing resistance of corporate clients to rapid product developments by Netscape in the mid-1990s (Yoffie and Cusumano 1999). So innovation capability needs to include the ability to make such strategic assessments.

It is reasonable to assume that an innovative firm must generally possess 'innovation capability'—an underlying capacity to gain advantage by implementing more and better ideas than rivals. However, innovation capability may not be a unitary set of attributes—just as physical fitness can be sustained in different ways so different kinds of innovation may require distinctive approaches. Indeed, it may be that the capability needed to support some types of innovation conflicts with that needed to support other types. (For example, this situation is central to the argument surrounding the 'innovator's dilemma' in dealing with both sustaining and disruptive technologies) (Christensen, 1997).

Targeting Innovation

An important aspect of innovation is its functionality—i.e. the uses made of innovation capability. We refer to this as 'targeting'. The well-known case of a Japanese company, Komatsu Ltd., helps us to understand the importance of targeting the exploitation of innovation capability. In the 1960s Komatsu made dumper trucks for the local market. The chairman, Ryoichi Kawai, decided that Komatsu would strive to topple Caterpillar from being the undisputed number one in the EME (Earth Moving Equipment) sector. This statement of strategic intent was called 'Maru-C'—which means, approximately, 'encircle Caterpillar'. The executives at Komatsu did not know how they would achieve their strategic intent, but it provided an overriding direction that guided initiatives in quality management, product design, marketing and so on. Komatsu grew stronger and, in the 1980s, Caterpillar was plunged into severe loss (more than $1 billion over 11 quarters) caused mainly by competition from Komatsu. Ryoichi Kawai took the company through four distinct stages on its path from obscurity to beating Caterpillar in many core markets. The four stages were:

- improve quality
- reduce costs
- develop innovative products
- devise new methods of sales and financing

These waves of focused innovation were undertaken sequentially. The argument used by Komatsu's management was that undertaking too many initiatives at that same time would fragment effort and permit non-achievement. The Komatsu case demonstrates that it is possible to target innovation capability on firm-specific strategic goals and that these vary over time.

The Four 'P's of Innovation Targeting

When Komatsu sought to improve quality, reduce costs, develop innovative products and devise new methods of sales and financing they did more than develop new or improved products. They had to improve processes, change their marketing and think about their company in a new way (as a global not Japanese firm). This is typical. Innovation capability is not confined to improving products: it can be targeted in four main ways. Fortuitously, these all begin with a 'P'.

P_1 innovation to introduce or improve *products;*

P_2 innovation to introduce or improve *processes;*

P_3 innovation to define or re-define the *positioning* of the firm or products;

P_4 innovation to define or re-define the dominant *paradigm* of the firm.

These 4Ps are not tight categories: they have fuzzy boundaries. Nor are they alternatives: firms can pursue all four at the same time. There are linkages between them; a firm using innovation capability for positioning, for example, will be highly likely to introduce or improve products. It is possible to define P_3 and P_4 as variations of re-framing—either concerned with what the offerings the organisation provides or what identity it pursues (Tidd et al., 1997). However, the 4Ps provide a structured approach to examining the opportunity space for innovation.

Innovation in Product

New product and service development is an obvious target for innovation capability and can be considered on several dimensions. For example, Wheelwright and Clark (1992) identify criteria that differentiate products including number, timing and rate of change of product platforms, whether they are variations or derivatives, the frequency of intro-duction/refresh rate, relationship with strategy and degree of modularity. They point out that product innovation is influenced by the state of industry maturity:

> In relatively young industries, such as medical instruments, every development effort appears to be a platform effort (to broaden the firm's market coverage), with incremental changes targeted primarily at correcting deficiencies in the platform products.

The resource requirements for product development can vary over time—with the development of product platforms requiring more effort over a sustained period. A firm may be able to plan for several generations of products over a life cycle with derivatives in between. Here, innovation can be seen as strategy-driven and deliberate rather than emergent or serendipitous (Randale and Rainnie, 1996).

Product innovation is also applicable to service firms[1] whose 'products' are, to some extent, created in real time. For example, Singh (1991) notes that in Singapore Airlines, "the innovative spirit gave the travelling public the first slumberettes on Boeing 747 upper decks, jackpot machines to relieve boredom and round-the-world fares".

[...]

The process of new product development can, in itself, be the target of innovation. Arguably the greatest resource in the future for product innovation will be in the use of the internet for accessing customers and, using mass-customisation and agile techniques, it may be possible for firms to devise a distinctive product for each customer (Goldman et al., 1995). Here, the product is presented as an 'envelope of possibilities' rather than a pre-determined entity. This notion presents intriguing challenges; it may become possible for a customer to participate actively in the development of a unique product.

At one level the notion of innovation in products offered is simple. All a firm has to do is to find ways of providing superior functionality and/or price and signal this to the market. It can be argued that any initiative in which the added value exceeds the added cost by an acceptable margin should be undertaken. Such a stance is simplistic—as the following case example of ABC Lighting demonstrates, product development requires making decisions with unknown consequences, making 'bets' and channeling limited resources.

Managing product innovation within ABC Lighting

ABC Lighting[2] in 1990 had more than 8000 products in their catalogue, some of which were slow-moving, lacked competitive advantage or were priced more highly than competitors' offers. An obvious remedy would be to go through the catalogue and determine to innovate with some products and cut out others. Why was this not done? The view of top management was that a pruning of the product list could prove counter-productive as ABC Lighting's strategy was to offer a 'total solution for the building contractor' rather than a partial offer of superior products. Some managers argued that the firm had to offer certain categories of products at low levels of profitability in order to be able to fulfill all the requirements of large contracts that were generally offered to a sole supplier. In addition, each product put through the factory bore a share or burden of the factory's cost overhead. It could be that, if a marginally profitable but large volume product was cancelled, the added burden on other highly profitable lines, perhaps smaller in volume, might be sufficient to propel them into loss.

[...]

Historically, several of the fundamental technological innovations in lighting had been invented by ABC Lighting, including halogen lighting. ABC Lighting had developed the concept, proven it, taken out patents, devised complex

(Continued)

(Continued)

production machines and assessed the potential market as 'huge'. From such a technological base the business question became 'should we develop a halogen light product range?" and, since the ingredients of competitive advantage appeared to be present, the answer was 'yes'.

ABC Lighting's range of halogen lighting products was launched and rapidly became world-leaders. The product found a ready market amongst commercial designers and profit margins were well above average. However, other major players, notably Philips, saw the rapid growth of the halogen lighting market and invested considerable research resources in devising alternative technologies. It was not long before ABC Lighting saw its margins dropping and competitors' products being made in volumes beyond the capacity of ABC Lighting's factories.

The initial reaction of an observer is to say 'well it's a story of a firm that couldn't capitalise on their advantage, but at least they had the benefits of excellent margins at the beginning'. This was true but developing the halogen lighting range absorbed a huge amount of resource from the managing director, the R&D lab, production engineers and marketing staff. It was the focus of a great deal of strategy formulation and problem-solving effort. In effect, the decision to develop the halogen product deprived other products of development resources.[3]

[...]

It can be seen from this example that managing innovation in product can be a complex task in which branding policies, market development trajectories, industry logics, resource availability, technological opportunism, intrapreneurship and other factors influence decisions. Accordingly, it would be incorrect to define product innovation 'merely' as an internal middle-level managed process—rather it is a major element of strategy. Targeting innovation capability on developing new and/or improved products can involve multiple actors engaged in complex and inter-linked processes with a single end in view— creating value at an acceptable cost for the customer.

Innovation in Process

Processes are widely (Clarysse et al., 1998) accepted as a target for innovation initiatives. Processes are sequences of activities, often proceeding horizontally across the organisation, that are transformations.[4] There is considerable scope in improving the operation of existing processes, through taking out waste of various forms and optimising them for high performance. (Gallagher et al., 1997). For example, new technology can add precision, improved training can increase conformance or process mapping can identify time wasted in unnecessary activities (Stalk Jr., 1993). Much of the 'lean thinking' agenda is based on this principle.

[...]

Processes interact, sometimes in complex ways (Heygate, 1996). In a simple organisation, for example a dentist's reception area,[5] there may be processes in place for registering patients, keeping records, stock management, making bookings, arranging rotas, logging staff time, arranging maintenance work, cleaning the waiting room, reminding patients of forthcoming visits and so on. At least some of these processes will be interdependent and core processes like maintaining hygiene will be particularly important. Innovation in processes in this relatively simple environment is unlikely to be coherently managed—different agents will play distinctive roles and ideas for improvement arise from a variety of sources. For example, there is a likelihood that reception staff will notice weaknesses in some processes or see opportunities and take initiatives to bring about improvements themselves without reference to senior personnel (Hummel-Kohler and Kristof, 1997). From time to time, problems or opportunities may occur that require a formal review and changes will be made on a planned basis. The dentists, who have the highest status in the system, will make suggestions or issue instructions—as many patients and suppliers. Moreover, trade journals will contain occasional articles on improving reception services that give inspiration. The dental practice may decide to submit itself to an overarching set of disciplines like ISO 9000.

It can be seen that ownership of innovation in processes in the dentist's reception area is likely to be diffuse, even though there may be a practice manager in a co-ordinating role (Sirkin and Jr, 1990). There are a variety of sources of critical observations and improvement ideas and several ways in which decisions are taken to initiate change. Such complexity in the ownership of process innovation is typical although major processes, like the layout of a new automated production line, will generally be managed using a systematic approach. This is more difficult to achieve where sub-processes evolve in a number of ad hoc ways (McHugh et al., 1995). Those directly involved may be the best people to identify improvement possibilities and effect change (Bessant, 1992). There can be multiple actors dealing with multiple processes in multiple ways.

The diversity of agents playing roles in process innovation means that they tend to develop without an overall coherence. Accordingly, they can be inefficient, patchy and/or inherently contradictory. Approaches such as business process re-engineering (Hammer and Champy, 1993) seek to overcome such weaknesses, identify core processes and subject them to intensive development.

Process innovation can be facilitated by systematic analysis and by comparative benchmarking. Specific techniques include: process mapping, activity analysis, constraints analysis, kaizen, problem analysis, video recording, modelling, time compression, statistical analysis, pilot experimentation, process management, problem-solving fora and cost structure analysis. These techniques have the effect of raising consciousness about problems and opportunities, thereby increasing the probability that innovative initiatives can be undertaken (Burgess, 1994).

Not all process innovations are within firms. Perry et al. (1999) describe a form of process innovation at the level of the value stream or supply chain. In the early 1990s the textile, clothing and footwear industries in Australia were in danger of being overwhelmed by more efficient foreign suppliers. The Australian government funded the 'Quick Response Program' to facilitate increases in speed-to-market. This took the form of a series of workshops that included participants from all components in a supply chain. The results showed improvements of between 74% and 100% on key indicators over four years. Interestingly, the development of mechanisms for open communication was considered just as significant by participants as the adoption of a standard for electronic data interchange.

Processes present a fertile and extensive set of targets for innovation. Multiple small improvements can accumulate into large gains. Major processes can be improved or re-engineered, perhaps incorporating new technologies. All processes, including those at the strategic apex of the firm and within the value stream, are potential candidates.

Innovation in Position

A positional innovation does not significantly affect the composition or functionality of the product[6] but the meaning of the product in the eyes of the potential customer (Kim and Mauborgne, 1999a–c) and/or the market segments selected as targets.

Positional innovation is not mentioned by some commentators on innovation management who prefer to adopt a narrower product-process definition. Nevertheless, the realisation that innovation can be positional is supported by some publications. For example (Guest et al., 1997) point out that, for some products, "success depends on finding innovative ways of bringing to the market products that appeal to potential buyers".

[...]

Most cases of positional innovation relate to firms, brands or products. However, institutions can go through the same process (Irons, 1993). For example, the Labour party successfully positioned itself as 'New Labour' before the 1997 general election in the UK. This required a host of changes in personalities, power-structures, policies and practices, apparently following a similar change model to that adopted by commercial firms.

Product positioning can be summarised as 'what the firm would like typical customers from targeted groups to feel and say about their product (and company)'. There are many examples of successful positioning and re-positioning (Gummesson, 1987). For example, the Daily Mail repositioned itself as the leading newspaper in the UK for women readers in the 1980s, the BBC repositioned itself as a global media corporation in the 1990s, Henley Management College repositioned itself as Britain's largest internet-based provider of MBA degrees between 1987 and 1993 and Manchester United FC positioned itself as a fashion brand in 1994–96.

The central feature of an innovative product positioning strategy is the management of identities, through advertising, marketing, media, packaging and the manipulation of various signals. These topics are extensively discussed in the literature of brand management (Doyle, 1997). Positional innovation can change the characteristics of a market or create a market that does not exist.

An example is the global brand of ice cream—Haagen-Daz (Joachimsthaler and Taugbol, 1995). This brand was developed by Grand Metropolitan, whose marketing specialists[7] noted in the 1980s that ice cream was associated with children or unsophisticated adults. They decided to create a hitherto unknown product—an ice cream for sophisticated adults that fell into the category of an 'affordable luxury'. Many initiatives followed, including product formulation, packaging, advertising, selection of distribution channels and global product standardisation codes. Haagen-Daz has become a global brand of adult ice-cream and tapped a new market. The case suggests that product identity can be as significant as tangible product attributes. Some positional innovations are so radical in thinking that they could be considered to be innovations in paradigm (discussed below)—the development of Haagen-Daz ice cream would be an example, as neither the concept of an adult ice cream, nor the ambition of global branding for ice cream, had been previously developed it required multiple innovations of mind-set to launch and develop the product.

Product positioning includes the four elements of innovation (idea—adoption—application—benefit) and may excel at the first stage (Beatty, 1997). For example, some would use the word 'brilliant' for the notion of associating a leading brand of toilet paper with the gentleness of a puppy or connecting a brand of petrol (perhaps the ultimate commodity product) with the vitality of a tiger. The final element in the innovation process, harvesting benefits, is difficult to evaluate but this can be attempted (Tull and Hawkins, 1993).

Firms can seek to build a distinctive market position by the management of identity. It is a frequent occurrence to hear a person choosing to buy a product as it comes from Sony, Gap or Harrods. In these cases the firm itself can be seen as a brand in itself. Kim and Mauborgne (1999a–c) discuss the case of Southwest Airlines and comment that by:

> "focussing on the key discriminating factors of both flying and driving, and by eliminating everything else, Southwest has inserted itself creatively between airlines and surface transport, thereby creating a new and highly profitable market".

It is significant that the word 'creatively' is used in the assessment of Southwest's strategic processes. Kim and Mauborgne assert that the company's possessed a superior ability to perceive a latent need and devise a business system to fulfil it. This is an example of positional innovation and Southwest's new business model was, arguably, an innovation in paradigm (see below)—demonstrating that the two can be interdependent. More generally, Kim and Mauborgne suggest that it "is in the space between substitute industries that tremendous opportunities exist for creating new markets". If this is correct, the positional innovation is particularly potent from a managerial perspective.

Innovation in Paradigm

This final 'P' is more contentious. Not all scholars support the notion that 'paradigm' is a legitimate target for innovation capability. However, it is not unknown, for example Rickards (1999) observes: "Today the term 'paradigm' has found its way into the vocabulary of organizational management, in such terms as 'paradigm switch' and 'paradigm breakthrough'. The expressions are broadly taken to imply that a traditional belief system—the old paradigm—has been replaced by a new way of understanding, a new paradigm".

The collective mind-set of the organisation, referred to by Yves Doz as the 'organisational orthodoxy',[8] has a sense-making function. But it is not always functional as it can persist beyond the point of relevance. As Grove (1998) points out, there are times ('strategic inflection points') when managers may know that their current approach is failing but may not know what new paradigm to adopt. Here a 'pre-framing' activity can be required that can be termed 'exploration', 'learning' or 'entering a void'.

Innovation in a paradigm includes a requirement for learning, including self-reflection (Kolb, 1983) and/or discourse. In a metaphorical sense it is necessary for actors in an organisation to 'look into the mirror' and see themselves as having adopted just one of several options in the way that they have framed reality and opportunity. Here reflection is a key enabler and the level needs to be deep and, potentially, transmutational (Cooperrider and Srivastva, 1987).

Although there is a significant degree of fuzziness in definition, it is useful to categorise two types of innovation in paradigm. These are:

Type A—innovation in inner-directed[9] paradigms
Type B—innovation in outer-directed paradigms (business models)

Type A—Inner-Directed Paradigms

Type A innovation capabilities targets organisational values and people management policies. Abrahamson (1991) calls these 'administrative technologies'. These can be important as, for example, Steele (1975) asserted "(o)ne of the most important concepts to emerge from behavioural science consulting is, in my opinion, the notion of social invention. This is simply the realisation that social settings do not have to be taken only as they occur by chance".

The significance of changes in inner-directed paradigms is underlined by (Binney and Williams, 1997) who suggest:

> Underlying the patterns of behaviour that define organisations are the mental
> models that people have, the assumptions and frameworks that enable them to
> make sense of the world... it is these mental models or paradigms that
> ultimately organisations have sought to change.

There are cases in which such 'mental models' appear to have changed. In the late 1960s, General Foods (GF) had a low performing dog food plant in Chicago. In 1969 the company decided to relocate the factory on a green-field site in Topeka, Kansas and to use the new plant as a laboratory for innovative forms of work organisation including autonomous work groups, payment for skills, commitment to the quality of work life, operator-led problem solving, participative decision-making and non-authoritarian leadership styles (Ketchum and Trist, 1992). The initiative was led by the factory director, Ed Dulworth,[10] and supported by Professor Richard Walton as a facilitator (Walton, 1977).

This was one of the first experiments in 'innovative work organisations' to be the subject of systematic research and was managed according to a distinctive set of values, many of which were derived from a socio-technical systems framework (Trist,

1978). The socio-technical experiment at Topeka stimulated root-and-branch innovation in the social organisation of a factory. According to Dulworth, in consequence, a wealth of process innovations followed which resulted in superior performance and gave employees an enriched experience of work. The adoption of a new organisational paradigm is more than a process innovation (discussed above) as it requires a shift in values and associated power structures. In the case of the Topeka GF plant, many processes were revolutionised—as Dulworth said in an interview with this researcher, "we challenged all of the givens". The case also highlights another important aspect of innovation. It can service other stakeholders than the management, shareholders and customers. Employees can also benefit (Ketchum and Trist, 1992).

The Topeka case, and similar experiments in organisational form, had innovation as a superordinate goal. This was pointed out by Ketchum and Trist (1992) who was organisation development manager for GF during the 1970s. Ketchum wrote twenty years later:

> equally important is the replacement of a climate of low risk taking with one of innovation. This implies high trust and openness in relations. All of these qualities are mandatory if we are to transform traditional technocrat bureaucracies into continuous adaptive learning systems.

Ketchum and Trist described the origins of the 'new' paradigm in the 1970s, which they termed 'third order diagnosis of problems of organisational performance'. Importantly, industrial plants that adopted this new paradigm were up to 40% more productive than their counterparts (21) at the time when a financial evaluation was conducted. Ketchum and Trist describe these as 'organizational innovations'.

The underlying principle in Ketchum's observation is that bureaucracy is unfriendly to innovation. Somewhat contentiously he, and others (for example Nutt and Backoff, 1997), argue that innovation capability cannot be achieved by the installation of systematic management of new product and process development. Rather, the fundamental social architecture of organisation needs to be rebuilt to be 'innovation friendly' (Hurst, 1995). Equally disadvantageous, in their view, was the alienating and de-humanising effect of working in a bureaucratic form of organisation where individuality was perceived as a threat (see Beynon, 1973 for a vivid description of this form of social setting)

[...]

Type B—Innovation in Outer-Directed Paradigms (Business Models)

Type B innovations of paradigm relate to business models—these are the system of coherent, comprehensive, explicit and/or implicit constructs used by managers to understand their firm and shape its development (Senge, 1992).

This form of innovation in paradigm is outer-directed in the sense that it seeks to provide an organisational formula for thriving in, generally, a competitive environment. Hence, the test of the efficacy of a business model is whether it provides the necessary conceptual architecture for a firm to gain and sustain competitive advantage. As such, it is more extensive than the market-facing positional innovation discussed above.

[...]

(Slywotzky et al., 1999) [...] argue that there are unifying principles around which a firm's activities need to be aligned. It is possible, Slywotzky et al. argue, to identify 30 or so patterns, several of which may be unfolding at the same time. They argue that what is frequently needed is innovation at the level of business design—the structure of thinking shared by the power elite of the firm that determines policy and practice. Describing firms that had found their way out of a profitless position (for example, Swatch) Slywotzky and his co-authors write:

> In each of these cases, business design innovation brought the business back to sustained profitability. In each of these cases, at least one player created a paradigm shift, a change in the rules of the game, in order to create new kinds of value that had not previously existed in the industry.

There can be multiple innovations to be undertaken in pursuit of a new business design, each of which is aligned to the new meta-patterns selected. This raises the interesting issue of how alignment is to be managed of a rapid flow of innovation initiatives in product, process (market) position and (organisational) paradigm.

The choice of business model shapes innovations in product, process and position. The Slywotzky framework provides an intermediate level of analysis between the generic dynamic resource of innovation capability and the specific needs of a particular organisation. Rather than saying, "all organisations are the same" or "all organisations are different" the approach asserts that, "you need to understand what your dominant strategic thrust is and the attributes that firms in your classification need. How effective are you in each of these?"

A change in business model can have revolutionary implications. Keith Todd, then Chief Executive of the IT company ICL (now part of Fujitsu) commented on the extent of change in the company in the following way: "ICL started as a manufacturing company. Now it has no factories—we put together service products. For companies like ours, these are fundamental discontinuities. They're on the scale of the Berlin Wall coming down" (Jackson, 1998).

Sub-systems within organisations can also be the targets for paradigm innovation. Indeed, they are a natural location. For example, a training function may move from promoting a business school-based approach to executive education to running an in-house action learning programme (Ulrich, 1997) or a finance function may move from cost analysis to activity based costing (Srinidhi, 1998). Such paradigm shifts can be the spur for multiple innovative initiatives (Ulrich, 1995).

Perhaps the most dramatic forms of reconfiguration business model follows acquisitions, mergers, joint ventures and alliances. These may be undertaken specifically to provide an appropriate resource base for innovation, as seems, for example, to have been the rationale for the merger between AOL and Time Warner, described (Hill and Waters, 2001) as "revolutionising the way that news, entertainment and the internet are delivered to the home". In this case the Internet distribution capability of AOL was merged with the content provider, Time Warner, following a 'convergence strategy'.

That this can be a risky endeavour is shown by the decline in share values after the merger.

Moving Beyond the Steady State

Up till now we have been considering the 4Ps framework in the context of mapping innovation under what might be termed 'steady state' conditions, in which firms are concerned to 'do what they do, but better'. As we have seen there is considerable scope within this envelope, especially in exploring all of the four target areas. But it is also clear that organisations need to develop the capacity to explore 'outside the box' and identify radical 'do different' options for innovation, again using all of the four dimensions. The danger is that if they do not contemplate such moves—even if they appear to conflict with current portfolio of activities—they risk being usurped by competitors, often new entrants to their marketplace. Such discontinuities can arise through technological changes moving the frontier of possibilities but discontinuity can also emerge on the demand side with the emergence of totally new markets or where the rules of the game are significantly changed within existing markets. Table 16.1 lists some examples of discontinuity and the 'do different' challenge.

The need to consider discontinuities means that the framework of 4Ps needs to be expanded, as shown in Table 16.2, to take account of the whole innovation agenda.

The problem in terms of developing innovation capability is that the set of behavioural routines and accompanying structures and processes to deal with innovation of the 'do better' variety may not be sufficient to deal with the challenges of 'do different'. As Utterback and other commentators point out, under conditions of discontinuity within industries incumbent firms tend to do badly and are sometimes displaced by new entrepreneurial players (Utterback, 1994). At the limit there may be conflict between the routines for 'do better' and 'do different' innovation. For example, as Christensen points out, the 'good practice' model for 'do better' innovation creates a self-reinforcing and virtuous circle in which close working with customers gives insight into their innovation needs which can be translated into better products and services to serve those markets well (Christensen, 1997). But whilst this is extremely effective for dealing with an existing market, it is a powerful filter cutting out signals about new or emerging markets with different characteristics. Consequently even 'good' firms which had been successful in innovation with previous combinations of technology and market find themselves surprised and their markets disrupted by new entrants with a different proposition—and sometimes they make the discovery at too late a stage to respond effectively.

The implications of this are that organisations need to ensure that their 'innovation agenda' covers the entire spread of the 4Ps illustrated in Table 16.2—and that they develop capabilities to deal with each of these areas (Figure 16.1).

Table 16.1 *Examples of discontinuities and their triggers*

Example	Trigger
Transition from valve-based to solid state electronics	Technological change, particularly the development of the transistor and subsequently integrated circuits. Many of the major players in the glass valve industry did not make a successful transition to the new era of solid state, whilst other new players—for example, Texas Instruments—emerged at this time
Deregulation of utilities markets	Old monopoly positions in fields like telecommunications and energy were dismantled and new players/combinations of enterprises emerged. In particular, energy and bandwidth become increasingly viewed as commodities. Innovations include skills in trading and distribution—a factor behind the considerable success of Enron in the late 1990s as it emerged from a small gas pipeline business to becoming a major energy trade (Hamel, 2000). Although Enron failed to capitalise on their innovative business model (financial concerns became apparent in 2001 and the company became insolvent) their re-conceptualisation of business opportunities remains an example of significant innovation in paradigm. The Enron case demonstrates the risks inherent in radical change where bold moves are called for. Without a track record is difficult for prudent decisions to be made—unquantifiable chances may be needed to be taken
Dismantling of political systems	The post-Cold War experience in Eastern Europe or the transition from apartheid in South Africa led to conditions in which new rules of the competitive game applied (Barnes et al., 2001). Incumbent firms in those regions were ill-equipped to jump trajectories and many failed as a consequence
Emergence of new market constituencies	Christensen's work on disk drives suggests that new markets that later become mainstream and set trajectories/define the innovation

Table 16.1   *(Continued)*

Example	Trigger
	envelope begin at the fringes and are often not detected by established players (Christensen, 1997). Under these conditions 'good practice' recipes like staying close to existing customers, whilst effective for 'do better' types of innovation may not be sufficient to help with the transition to new markets and product platforms
Diminishing innovation space within mature industries	Firms in mature industries may seek to escape the constraints of diminishing space for product and process innovation and the increasing competition of industry structures by either exit or by radical reorientation of their business (Baden-Fuller and Stopford, 1995). For example, Preussag's move from primary production (lead and other ore smelting) into a broad based conglomerate and from there into focussed tourism business

Using the 4Ps Approach for Strategic Development

From studying the 4Ps it is clear that it is possible to target innovation capability in different ways. One firm might invest significant sums of money, and a great deal of creativity, into developing a new range of products, perhaps based on the latest technology. Another company may keep its products more or less the same but invest a great deal in trying to change the way that potential customers perceive the firm, as oil companies appear to do. The question arises, 'can the 4Ps help a firm to take better strategic decisions?'

The answer is, we believe, 'yes'. The 4Ps approach helps companies in three principal ways: focussing effort, managing interdependencies and enlarging choice. An example illustrates this point.

Nine innovation activities were listed on the diamond chart (see Figure 16.1 on page 216), including:

- building totally customized products for customer's individual orders (paradigm)
- using sensors in the next generation of lawn mowers to avoid roots and stones (product)
- re-positioning the company's products as female-friendly as more women are keen gardeners (position)
- installing 3D design software in the R&D department (process).

Table 16.2   *The innovation agenda*

	'Do better' innovation	'Do different' innovation
Product/service innovation— change in what is offered	This is incremental product development. For example, the Bic ballpoint was originally developed in 1957 but remains a strong product with daily sales of 16 million units. Although superficially the same shape closer inspection reveals a host of incremental changes that have taken place in materials, inks, ball technology, safety features, etc.	Radical shift to new product concept for the firm, perhaps for the industry as well. An emerging example of this could be the replacement of the incandescent light bulb originally developed in the late 19th century by Edison and Swan (amongst others). This may be replaced by the solid state white light emitting diode technology patented by Nichia Chemical. This technology is 85% more energy efficient, has 16 times the life of a conventional bulb, is brighter, more flexible in application and is likely to be subject to the scale economies associated with electronic component production
Process innovation— change in the ways in which it is created and delivered	These are incremental improvements in key performance parameters/for example, cost reduction, quality enhancement, time reduction, etc. A good example of incremental process innovation can be found in the 'lean production' field where intra- and inter-firm efforts to drive out waste have led to sometimes spectacular performance improvements—but achieved within the same envelope established by the original processes (Womack and Jones, 1997)	These are radical shifts to new process routes for the firm and, perhaps, for the industry as well. For example, the Bessemer process for steel-making replacing conventional charcoal smelting, the Pilkington float glass process replacing grinding and polishing, the Solvay continuous process for alkali production replacing the batch mode Leblanc process, etc.

Table 16.2 *(Continued)*

	'Do better' innovation	**'Do different' innovation**
Position innovation— change in the context in which it is applied	This includes the launching of a product or deployment of a process in a familiar context and redefining the perception of a product for customers. For example, in mobile telephones a shift has taken place from a business tool to a leisure and recreation aid, with considerable associated incremental product and process development (ring tones, cartoon displays, text messaginging) emerging as a result of such positional innovation	This requires creating completely new markets rather than extending and deepening existing segments or incremental brand identity changes. (Moore, 1999) For example, satellite navigation was originally developed for military use but is now used by sailors, motorists, surveyors and even postmen. Christensen's study of the rapid evolution of the hard disk drive industry highlights the ways in which unimagined markets can quickly become the key segment (Christensen, 1997)
Paradigm innovation— change in the underlying models surrounding it	These are evolutionary changes in the way that business activities are undertaken that provide the opportunity for incremental innovation in paradigm or business model. An example might be rethinking the Rolls-Royce motor car business as that of supplying luxury experience, competing with expensive watches, holidays, clothes, etc.—rather than as a transportation mechanism	These are new business or industry models-for example, 'mass production' vs. 'craft production', (Freeman and Perez, 1989). An example of a recent transformational innovation in paradigm was the development of internet solutions to many business areas like banking, insurance, travel, etc. (Evans and Wurster, 2000)

The selection of just nine major innovation initiatives gave focus to R&P's innovation management; the firm considered that 'it is important not to try to do too much at once". Some initiatives, such as re-launching their trimmer as environmentally friendly, require both product and positional innovation. Such interdependencies are clarified by discussion on the placing of an initiative on the

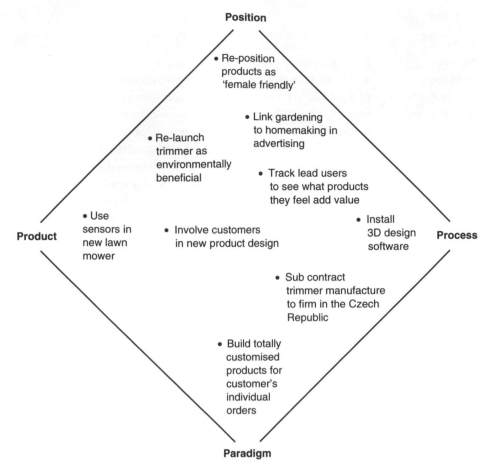

Figure 16.1 *Shows how the approach was applied in a company (R&P Ltd) making garden machinery. The diamond diagram provides an indication of where and how they could construct a board-ranging 'innovation agenda'.*

diamond diagram. Also, the fact that the senior management group had the 4Ps on one sheet of paper had the effect of enlarging choice—they saw the completing the diagram as a tool for helping them think in a systematic way about using the innovation capability of the firm.

[...]

Conclusions

Innovation is widely seen as a critical imperative for survival and growth of firms. But responding to this challenge needs to be balanced against the resource constraints of the organisation in terms of money, skills, time and knowledge base. In this article we have developed a framework for setting a firm's innovation agenda holistically which makes a contribution to thinking about the strategic portfolio of innovation projects undertaken. It also focuses attention on areas which may not be recognized as having innovation potential and on emerging areas in which it may be desirable to explore potential new projects.

Acknowledgements

The authors would like to acknowledge the support of the ESRC/EPSRC Advanced Institute of Management Research for this research.

Notes

1   The distinctive features of a service have been defined as (Irons (1993). Managing Service Companies: Strategies for Success. Wokingham, England, Addison-Wesley): (1) They are transient—leave only memories or promises. (2) Cannot be separated from the person or the provider. (3) They cannot be stored. (4) Standardisation is only partly possible. (5) Constant supervision is almost impossible. (6) The consumer is a participant.

2   Case material drawn from a presentation at INSEAD in March 1994. Certain details have been disguised.

3   During the later stage of this case study ABC Lighting reported a loss on its light source business and sold it.

4   The term 'transformations' is derived from systems theory. Each process in an organisation is conceptualised as a system with defined inputs, transformation processes and outputs. Systems models have been influential since socio-technical systems (Trist (1978). On Socio-Technical Systems, Sociotechnical Systems: A Sourcebook. J.J. Sherwood. San Diego, University Associates: 43–57) began to be articulated in the 1950s and open systems planning was conceptualised in the 1960s (McWhinney (1972). Open Systems and Traditional Hierarchies. International Conference on the Quality-of-Working-Life, Arden. Institute for Developmental Organization). At the strategic level Porter ((1985). Competitive Advantage: Creating and Sustaining Superior Performance. New York, The Free Press) used the underlying philosophy in his concept of the value chain. A more recent iteration of organisational analysis using the systems metaphor is re-engineering (Hammer and Champy (1993). Reengineering the Corporation: A Manifesto for Business Revolution. London, Nicholas Brealey Publishing).

5   This example was suggested by comments by Roper (1996). Explaining Small Business Growth and Profitability, NIERC, Belfast.

6   Product attributes may be changed but these are minor compared with the revised marketing stance.

7   Additional information regarding this case was gathered from an ex-marketing manager of Haagen-Daz in confidence by the first author.

8   Personal communication to the first author.

9   The concept of inner-directed and outer-directed is adapted from Riesman et al. (1953). The Lonely Crowd: A Study of the Changing American Character. New York, Doubleday.

10   Two tape recorded interviews between Ed Dulworth and the first author (made in 1973 and 1975) were consulted in preparation for this section of the article.

References

Abrahamson, E., 1991. Managerial fads and fashions: the diffusion and rejections of innovations. Academy of Management Review 16(3), 586–612.

Baden-Fuller, C. Stopford, J., 1995. Rejuvenating the Mature Business, Routledge, London.

Barnes, J., Bessant, J., et al., 2001. Developing manufacturing competitiveness in South Africa. Technovation 21(5).

♣Baumol, W.J., 2002. The Free-Market Innovation Machine: Analyzing The Growth Miracle Of Capitalism, Princeton University Press, Woodstock, Oxon.

Beatty, S.G., 1997. HP Goes in for a Marketing Makeover. Wall Street Journal. New York, B6.

Bessant, J., 1992. Big bang or continuous evolution: why incremental innovation is gaining attention in successful organisations. Creativity and Innovation Management 1(2), 59–62.

Beynon, H., 1973. Working for Ford. Penguin, Harmondsworth, UK.

Binney, G., Williams, C., 1997. Leaning into the Future: Changing the Way People Change Organizations, Nicholas Brearley Publishing Ltd, London.

Burgess, T.F., 1994. Making the leap to agility: defining and achieving agile manufacturing through business process redesign and business network redesign, Journal of Operations and Production Management 14(11), 23–34.

Christensen, C., 1997. The Innovator's Dilemma, Harvard Business School Press, Cambridge, MA.

Clarysse, B., Utterhaegen, M. et al. (1998). Inside the Black Box of Innovation: Strategic Differences between SMEs. People in Small Firms, Commonwealth Institute, London, Teaching Company Directorate.

Cooperrider, D.L., Srivastva, S., 1987. In: Pasmore, W.A., (Ed.), Appreciative Inquiry into Organizational LifeResearch in Organizational Change and Development, JAI Press, Greenwich, CT, pp. 129–169.

Curwin, E.C., 1954. The Archaeology of Sussex, Methuen and Co Ltd, London.

Cusumano, M.A., Selby, R.W., 1996. Microsoft Secrets, HarperCollins, London.

Diamond, J., 1997. Guns, Germs and Steel, Jonathan Cape, London.

Doyle, P. 1997. Twelve Marketing Case Studies: The contribution of marketing to the Innovation Process, The Marketing Council.

DTI (1994). Winning, DTI (Warwick Manufacturing Group).

♠Drucker, P., 1994. Innovation & Entrepreneurship. Harper & Row, New York.

Evans, P., Wurster. T., 2000. Blown to bits: How the New Economics of Information Transforms Strategy, Harvard Business School Press, Cambridge, MA.

Freeman, C., Perez, C., 1989. In: Dosi, G., (Ed.), Structural Crises of Adjustment: Business Cycles and Investment Behaviour. Technical Change and Economic Theory, Frances Pinter, London.

Gallagher, M., Austin, S., et al., 1997. Continuous Improvement in Action, Kogan Page, London.

Goldman, S.L., Nagel, R.N., et al., 1995. Agile competitors and virtual organizations. Manufacturing Review 8(1), 59–67.

Grove, A.S., 1998. Only the Paranoid Survive: How to Exploit the Crisis Points that Challenge Every Company and Career, Doubleday. New York.

Guest, D., Storey, J., et al., 1997. Innovation: Opportunity Through People. IPD, Wimbledon.

Gummesson, E., 1987. The New Marketing–Developing Long Term Interactive Relationships. Long Range Planning 20(4), 10–20.

Hamel, G., 2000. Leading the Revolution, Harvard Business School Press, Boston, MA.

Hammer, M., Champy, J., 1993. Reengineering the Corporation: A Manifesto for Business Revolution, Nicholas Brealey Publishing, London.

Heygate, R., 1996. Why are we bungling process innovation? The McKinsey Quartely 2, 130–141.

Hill, A., Waters, R., 2000. Media Titans in $327bn Merger. FT. London, 1.

House, C.H., Price, R.L., 1991. The Return Map: Tracking Product Development Teams. HBR (January–February), 92–100.

Hummel-Kohler, V., Kristof, R., 1997. Acting instead of talking: how to develop a fractal hospital. Agility and Global Competition 1(2), 19–37.

Hurst, D.K., 1995. Crisis and Renewal: Meeting the Challenge of Organizational Change, Harvard Business School Press, Boston.

Irons, K., 1993. Managing Service Companies: Strategies for Success, Addison-Wesley, Wokingham, England.

Jackson, T., 1998. Melding of minds to master the intangibles. FT. London, 15.

Joachimsthaler, E.A., Taugbol, P., 1995. Haagen-Daz's Ice Cream (A): The Making of a Global Brand, IESE, Barcelona.

Ketchum, L.D., Trist, E., 1992. All Teams are Not Created Equal: How Employee Empowerment Really Works. Sage, Newbury Park, CA.

Kim, W.C., Mauborgne, R., 1999a. Coffee Blended with Emotion, FT, London.

Kim, W.C., Mauborgne, R., 1999b. How to Discover the Unknown Market. FT, London.

Kim, W.C. Mauborgne, R., 1999c. Southwest Airlines' Route to Success, FT, London.

Kolb, D.A., 1983. Experiential Learning, Prentice Hall, London.

McDonald. J., 1963. Strategy in Poker, Business and War, Norton and Company, New York.

McHugh, P., Merli, G., et al., 1995. Beyond Business Process Engineering: Towards the Holonic Enterprise, Wiley, Chichester.

McWhinney, W. (1972). Open Systems and Traditional Hierarchies. International Conference on the Quality-of-Working-Life, Arden, Institute for Developmental Organization.

Moore, G., 1999. Crossing the Chasm; Marketing and Selling High-tech Products to Mainstream Customers, Harper Business, New York.

Nutt, P.C., Backoff, R.W., 1997. Facilitating Transformational Change. JABS 33(4), 490–508.

Perry, M., Sohal, A.S., et al., 1999. Quick Response supply chain alliances in the Australian textiles, clothing and footwear industry. International Journal on Production Economics 62, 119–132.

Porter, M.E., 1985. Competitive Advantage: Creating and Sustaining Superior Performance, The Free Press, New York.

Randale, K., Rainnie, A., 1996. Managing Creativity, Maintaining Control: a Study in Pharmaceutical Research. Human Resource Management 7(2), 32–46.

Rickards, T., 1999. Creativity and the Management of Change, Blackwells Publishing Ltd, Oxford.

Riesman, D., Glazer, N., et al., 1953. The Lonely Crowd: A Study of the Changing American Character, Doubleday, New York.

Roper, S., 1996. Explaining Small Business Growth and Profitability, NIERC, Belfast.

Senge, P.M., 1992. The Fifth Discipline, Random House, London.

Singh, K., 1991. In: Harrison, J., (Ed.), Successful strategies: the story of Singapore Airlines The Manager's Casebook of Business Strategy, Butterworth Heinemann, Oxford, pp. 157–167.

Sirkin, H., Jr, G.S., 1990. Fix the process, not the problem. HBR(July–August), 26–33.

Slywotzky, A.J., Morrison, D., et al., 1999. Profit Patterns: 30 Ways to Anticipate and Profit from Strategic Forces Reshaping Your Business, Wiley, Chichester, UK.

Srinidhi, B., 1998. Needed: Agile Accounting to Match Agile Organizations. Agility and Global Competition 2(1), 41–55.

Stalk, G. Jr., 1993. Time and Innovation. Canadan Business Review 20(3), 15–19.

Steele, F., 1975. Consulting for Organizational Change, University of Massachusetts Press, Amhurst.

Tidd, J., Bessant, J., et al., 1997. Managing Innovation, Wiley, Chichester, UK.

Tregoe, B.B., Zimmerman, J.W., 1982. Top Management Strategy, John Martin Publishing, London.

Tregoe, B.B., Zimmerman, J.W., et al., 1989. Vision into Action: Putting a Winning Strategy to Work, Simon and Schuster, London.

Trist, E.L., 1978. In: Sherwood, J.J., (Ed.), Socio-Technical Systems: A Sourcebook, University Associates, San Diego, pp. 43–57.

Tull, D.S., Hawkins, D.I., 1993. Marketing Research: Measurement and Method, Macmillan, New York.

Ulrich, D., 1995. Strategic and Human Resource Planning: Linking Customers and Employees. Strategic and Human Resource Planning 15(2).

Ulrich, D., 1997. Human Resource Champions, Harvard Business School Press, Boston, MA.

Utterback, J., 1994. Mastering the dynamics of innovation, Harvard Business School Press, Boston, MA.

Walton, R.E., 1977. Work innovations at Topeka: after six years. JABS 13(3), 422–433.

Wheelwright, S.C., Clark, K.B., 1992. Revolutionizing Product Development: Quantum Leaps in Speed, Efficiency and Quality, The Free Press, New York.

Womack, J., Jones, D., 1997. Lean thinking, Simon and Schuster, New York.

Yoffie, D.B., Cusumano, M.A., 1999. Judo Strategy: the competitive dynamics of internet time. Harvard Business Review(January–February), 71–91.

Part 5

Leadership

It is perhaps not immediately obvious why there should be a Part called Leadership in a book about innovation and change, but without the right sort of leadership, neither would be possible. Western culture (and Anglo cultures in particular) has long been obsessed with strong leadership on the somewhat dubious premise that 'strong leadership is good leadership'. A stereotypical strong leader has a vision and communicates this across the organization: so far so good. Followers then assist the leader with the achievement of his/her goals. The immediate danger is that the goals are now associated with the leader, rather than the organization. Worse, the leader has to have all the brains, and needs to make all the crucial decisions. Doesn't sound very plausible, does it? If you want to make all the decisions, you may soon find yourself surrounded by people who will happily let you. What then happens if something changes and you don't notice? Decisions exist to be challenged, so that only those revealed as robust will survive and evolve. The flipside of empowerment (see the earlier article by Bowen and Lawler, Ch.13) is that good folk will demand an increasing say in what goes on; not just at the level of everyday working conditions, but more and more about relatively strategic issues such as the direction and values of the organization. This should be a sign of strength; good leaders need to promote an organization and a culture that will endure without them, not one in which their presence is indispensable.

Mercifully there is now an increasing body of literature which offers an enlightened take on leadership. The first chapter in this Part, by **Hartley and Allison**, is set in the UK public sector but its findings have much wider resonance. It describes the sort of leadership appropriate for diffuse, multi-agency, multiple-stakeholder organizations where single point authority is unlikely to be either available or even desirable. Importantly, it concludes that traditional, static, hierarchical leadership, concentrated in a single individual, appears increasingly less relevant compared with emergent, dynamic, contingent and distributed forms. The authors also note that while organizations themselves are waking up to such new realities, their taskmasters, whether politicians or shareholders, may still hold an attraction towards more primitive kinds of leader.

The chapter by **Collins** builds upon the findings of an earlier study[1] and develops a thesis regarding the sort of leadership that correlates with sustained excellent performance. The domain is now very much corporate America, but the arguments are persuasive and should resonate in any complex undertaking. In essence, Collins' Level 5 leaders are more interested in building something enduring than feeding their own egos. They ultimately try for an organization that will prosper even without them at the helm, and this requires building capability in terms of people, in terms of expertise, in terms of standards and in terms of imagination. Their 'strength' lies in revealing and developing these capabilities, rather than in micro-management. The correlation of Level 5 with personal humility is perhaps the most fascinating finding of the piece. The very real danger is that many still regard a major ego as a necessary prerequisite to promotion to Levels 3 and 4, thereby dooming the organization to, at best, intermittent success.

Leaders are, almost by definition, marked out by having a disproportionate influence on culture. Although such influence stops well short of control – culture is far too deep and complex for that – their behaviour is widely noted and hugely significant. In a fast-changing world, their attitude towards mistakes is crucial. According to an old English proverb, a mistake is evidence that someone has at least tried to do something; thus there exists an easy way to avoid them! Mistakes are also an essential part of the learning process, but only if they are acknowledged as such. The chapter by **Farson and Keyes** emphasizes the need for managers to *engage* with people, even to adopt a little of the humility advocated by Jim Collins in order to send out the message that mistakes are not necessarily always to be avoided. Furthermore, the distinctly non-macho management style that results encourages good ideas by increasing the number of avenues through which they can emerge. Perhaps unsurprisingly the 'think-on-their-feet, prepared-to-speak-up-at-meetings' types do not have a monopoly on good ideas, even if many of our systems tend to assume that they do. If you want to lead an operation that really performs, avoiding mistakes really does not seem to be a good starting point.

At first glance, the final chapter by **Gittell** might not appear to be concerned with leadership, but a closer reading suggests otherwise. The author offers a comparison of two very different organizations in the same industry, American Airlines and Southwest Airlines. Whereas American might be taken as representative of the traditional big player in the US industry, Southwest emerged as distinctly different. Not only widely credited with having invented the concept of the low-cost airline, Southwest was also the first airline to simultaneously top customer satisfaction ratings for best on-time record, best baggage handling, and fewest customer complaints; clearly they are doing something right. Conventional management wisdom currently argues for flat structures and individual accountability; the first casualties of such a regime are the supervisors. However, the author points to a rather more enlightened role for supervisors; less to do with monitoring performance and more to do with 'adding value through coaching and feedback'. The comparison offered by Gittell is revealing; not for its details but for the totality. Supervision at Southwest is part of a wider framework – customer service, teamwork, learning and a no-blame culture. So is it about culture? The author claims not, but nevertheless argues *'culture comes from somewhere [and] it is powerfully driven by the choices that leaders make'*. Which reminds me of the old maxim attributed to Lao Tzu:

People don't trust a leader who doesn't trust them.

The best leader says little, but when they speak people listen and when they are finished with their work, the people say we did it ourselves.

Note

1 Collins, J.C., and Porras, J.I. (1997) *Built to Last: successful habits of visionary companies*. New York: Harper Business.

The Role of Leadership in the Modernization and Improvement of Public Services

Jean Hartley and Maria Allison

'Leadership' is a common word in recent policy and academic papers on the modernization and improvement of public services. It is in the title of two recent Consultation Papers—*Modernizing Local Government: Local Democracy and Local Leadership* (DETR, 1998a), and *Local Leadership Local Choice* (DETR, 1999a): and it is a key word in the National College for School Leadership, which was announced in the Green Paper, *Teachers Meeting the Challenge of Change* (DTEE, 1998). The debates about new political arrangements for local authorities, including the role of elected mayors, are built on arguments about strong, visible and accountable leadership. Local authorities are to be given new powers and responsibilities for community planning, based on strengthening their community leadership role. To support these developments in political leadership and community leadership, the Improvement and Development Agency is establishing a new Leadership Academy for councillors, to help them develop new roles and capabilities.

It is not just local government which has been charged to show greater leadership in order to modernize public services. In central government, the Sunningdale discussions among permanent secretaries in late 1999 identified leadership as a key theme in aiming for innovation and excellence (Cabinet Office, 1999). In the health sector, there is an increased concern to ensure that managers are also leaders, for example, through the forthcoming NHS Leadership Programme.

Why is leadership seen to be significant in the development of 'modernized' governance and 'improved' public services. Is it simply a mantra or is there some logic to the promotion of leadership in public services? We examine these questions in the context of leadership in local government.

The National Policy Context for Local Government

The Government's modernization agenda argues for an increased role for local authorities in leading their communities and being responsible for the social, economic and

Source: J. Hartley and M. Allison (2000) *Public Money and Management,* 20 (2): 35–40.

environmental well-being of the locality. The White paper *Modern Local Government: In Touch with the People,* notes that 'some councils are actively developing their role as leaders of local communities' (DETR, 1998b, section 2.4).

The consultation paper *Local Leadership, Local Choice* (DETR, 1999a) states that 'councils everywhere need to provide vision and leadership for their local communities, and to deliver high quality services to their local people' (section 1.2). This views local authorities as more than just service providers. They are seen to have a leading role in governing local communities and in facilitating inter-agency partnerships. The White Paper *Modern Local Government: In Touch with the People* reinforced this (DETR, 1998b, section 5.4).

Best Value also emphasises the crucial role of the local authority in leading local choices. *The Local Government Act 1999: Part 1. Best Value,* explains how the leadership role of Best Value will involve the development of community strategies (DETR, 1999b). Such strategies reflect the contribution which the authority and its partners intend to make to the well-being of the locality. Networks, such those arising through the Better Value Development Programme initiated by the Local Government Centre at Warwick University, aim to disseminate better practice and promote continuous improvement in the implementation of Best Value, which requires a leadership as well as a management approach to Best Value (Allison and Hartley, 2000).

The Improvement and Development Agency produced a benchmark of the 'ideal' local authority, with a set of criteria: a 'fully effective local authority recognizes its community leadership role and the distinction between commissioning and providing services, listens, analyses community needs and takes appropriate steps to meet unmet needs, forming partnerships with other bodies where necessary to achieve this (IDeA, 1999, section 1.2). Leadership is the first of the three core competencies of the ideal local authority (IDeA, 1999, section 3 and 5).

The determination to develop 'strong leadership for communities' is part of the reasoning by central government for new political structures in *Local Leadership, Local Choice* (DETR, 1999a). Thus, a clearly identified and separate political executive is proposed in order to 'give leadership and clarity to decision-taking' (section 3.1).

Leadership is proposed as significant for modernization and improvement, but is often alluded to without definition. There are at least two levels of analysis in the concept of leadership. In the first, leadership is the behaviours and actions of individuals, sometimes acting in concert but primarily as solo figures. For example, the proposal that an elected mayor or a head teacher will bring about 'strong' leadership is based on this. The second approach has the local authority organization as the unit of analysis. Here a focus on community leadership is by the local authority as a whole, working with other agencies in the locality, and having particular responsibility for voicing and addressing the needs and aspirations of local communities. This approach includes the role of individuals, but as part of organizational functioning.

Leadership and Influence

What is leadership? First, we distinguish the concept of leader from that of leadership. It is helpful to distinguish between the person, the position and processes. These may in practice co-exist, but it is important to distinguish them conceptually.

The Person

There has been a lot of academic research on the personal characteristics of leaders (see Yukl, 1994 for a review). It tends to focus on skills, abilities, personality, styles and behaviours (for example Avolio, 1999; Burns, 1978) of individual leaders. The role of individuals in shaping events and circumstances at certain times is clear. A difficulty can be that such approaches can lionize individuals, assuming that they have pre-eminent capacity and power. This ignores both so-called 'followers' and also organizational and community constraints.

The Position

Leadership is sometimes used to refer to a formal position in an organization for example, Leader of the Council or Chief Executive. Some commentators (for example Rost, 1998) argue that such formal positions give authority, though not necessarily leadership. Leadership requires more than holding a particular office or role. Heifetz (1996) distinguishes formal from informal leadership, arguing that each may tackle issues through different processes.

The Processes

A third approach is to regard leadership as a set of processes or dynamics occurring among and between individuals, groups and organizations. Here, leadership is concerned with motivating and influencing people, and shaping and achieving outcomes. Burns (1978) distinguishes between transformational and transactional leadership and this has been widely used in conceptualizing leadership. The approaches are complementary. Transformational leadership is characterized by inspirational motivation (the ability to create and build commitment to goals): challenging current reality and established patterns of thinking: and individualized consideration (fair but individual treatment of group members). Nadler and Tushman (1990) describe these as envisioning, energizing and enabling. Transactional leadership, on the other hand, is concerned with embedding actions in a substantial way through the use of systems and rewards which support the objectives.

The idea of leadership as a set of processes concerned with influencing people and achieving goals and outcomes is reflected in the key definition of leadership by Heifetz (1996) as 'mobilizing people to tackle tough problems'. This is very different from the conventional view of leadership of providing solutions to problems. The role of leadership is to work with people to find workable ways of dealing with issues for which there may be no known or set solutions (Heifetz and Sinder, 1988).

Benington (1997) argues that community leadership is based upon three inter-related assumptions. Each has an impact on conceptions of leadership:

- The first is that the purpose of a local authority is not simply to deliver, manage and/or commission services but also to govern and lead the local community. This includes not only representing the needs but also developing the diverse voices and interests in the local community. Leadership in local government therefore includes capacity building, empowerment and representation.

- Second, the local council cannot govern the local community on its own, but needs to do this in partnership with the public, private and voluntary sectors. This requires not just leadership and management of local authority staff, budgets and services but also leadership beyond the boundaries of the organization. This may have to be through influence, persuasion, negotiation and coalition-building, as well as through command.

- Third is the recognition that within such inter-organizational partnerships and networks, the local authority has a unique and distinctive role to play because of its democratic mandate to reflect and represent the needs of the whole community rather than just its diverse and separate parts. In addition, it needs to plan for the needs of future generations as well as current users. Here, the role of political leadership in balancing competing interests is particularly important. But leadership has to mobilize and involve local communities and grain their active consent. Political leadership has to be won not only through the ballot box, but also through policies, actions and development processes in which local communities have reasonable confidence.

Consortium Research on Leadership and the Management of Influence

Our research on leadership and the management of influence has been conducted with the Warwick University Local Authorities Research Consortium, as part of the Local Government Centre's research programme on organizational and cultural change. The research aims to build knowledge about how leadership and influence are exercised in the pursuit of key changes by local authorities, and to transcend traditional models of leadership (which tend to focus on individual action and are often applied without question from the private sector).

The research is based on case studies in four local authorities (here referred to as Eastern County, Western County, Metropolitan, and District). The case studies were chosen as local authorities which are innovating in ways of leading their local communities. Each is engaged in major organizational and cultural change aiming at strengthening democratic local governance or to achieve more citizen-centred services. Our case studies therefore concentrate particularly on the community leadership role, and the use of influence across internal boundaries and across inter-organizational networks.

The case studies cover a variety of organizational change:

- Using information and communication technologies to develop citizen-centred services.
- Developing a community information programme for economic and social regeneration.

- Restructuring the organization to enhance responsiveness to local communities.
- Developing and strengthening relationships between country and district councils.

The four cases include different types of authority (county, metropolitan and district): include primarily rural, primarily urban and mixed geographical areas: range from large to small: and have varied political control (Liberal Democrat, Labour, Conservative and no overall control).

The research team, consisting of both academics and practitioners using co-research methodology (Hartley and Benington, 2000), visited each organization for two days to conduct interviews. These were undertaken with a range of stakeholders so that the different contributions to and perceptions of leadership by political leaders, senior officers, managers, staff, trade union representatives, and community, voluntary and private sector partners could be examined. In total, 75 in-depth interviews were carried out and five focus groups with staff. Observations and documentation were also included in the analyses.

Key Findings

There is clearly a leadership role for particular individuals in shaping visions of the future and encouraging the local authority to look beyond immediate pressures. These were primarily, but not exclusively financial (in the wake of local government reform), economic decline and social exclusion. In each of the case studies, we can discern key individuals who act as leaders, shaping debates and actions about change.

However, there are two interesting features. First, it was not always the person at the political and/or managerial apex. While the role of political leaders and chief executives is clearly crucial, we found that they do not always lead from the front but that some empower nominated others to foster and promote change in the organization. They also create a climate of innovation. Innovation is nurtured rather than mandated. Leadership which 'grows' development, rather than 'pulls levers', was commented on among those we interviewed. This is either a different kind of leadership or a different dimension of leadership than is sometimes assumed from the debates about 'strong' leadership, which often imply more of a command and control approach to leading organizations.

The second interesting issue about individuals is that there is a temporal dimension to leadership which can mean that the leadership role is passed from one individual to another in different time periods with their different leadership challenges. For example, in Metropolitan, leadership has spread out from the corporate centre and is now also being carried by some middle managers and staff.

Leadership may also, from our case studies, provide a different approach to 'the vision', (traditionally an achievement of leaders). The local authorities were concerned to develop transformational change, but much of this cannot be clearly specified in advance. For example, the establishment of the community information programme in Metropolitan, or electronic access to services in Eastern County, requires working with private sector partners on advanced information and communication technologies where the social and organizational implications and outcomes cannot be fully predicted. The customizing of Internet technologies and software by and with people with learning difficulties at a day centre in Metropolitan was not foreseen at the outset of the change. Another example took place in Western County where the vision for greater joined-up working between the District and the County led to the development of partnership committees, although this has taken quite different trajectories in the seven committees.

Each of the case study local authorities was addressing complex, shifting changes, which were dynamic. Both the political and managerial leaderships addressed this not only by plans and schedules but by creating a framework and a vision, within which new developments can be encouraged and sustained to grow organically. Leadership in part may involve empowerment of staff within the organization to take forward change and to work with communities to achieve this. For example, in District Council organizational restructuring has led to the development of a strategic team to address key cross-cutting priorities for the locality. This is about providing the conditions for citizen-centred services rather than specifying them through command and control (through there is still a place for this in some services and some circumstances).

Leadership is therefore no longer (if it ever was) solely about command and control from the 'top' of the organization. Many interviewees reported the role of politicians and managers in encouraging the active engagement of others at all levels and locations in the organization. We observed in our case study research where the active engagement among some groups of politicians, managers and staff contributed to community leadership, helping the authority to exert influence beyond its boundaries. If leadership is taken to be helping people to mobilize resources (Heifetz, 1996), then this is evident at several levels. For example, the library assistants in Metropolitan see themselves as outreach workers, leafleting cafés and talking to people in the street in order to encourage poorly educated people to 'have a go' with computers to access information and jobs. The front-line professional, such as social workers, educational managers and internal consultants in Eastern County, who have carefully examined current procedures among approximately 17 different departments and agencies who work with children with disability. They have constructed alliances, support systems and a collaborative culture for inter-agency working. We describe such initiatives as distributed leadership, because it is dispersed across the organization.

Leadership and influence at the corporate and strategic level (by both elected members and managers) have been concerned not only with the organization (the local authority) but also with leadership between organizations. Here, leadership is concerned with building alliances, links and networks with and between several organizations to achieve synergies, integration and joint outcomes. This may be with the private sector (Metropolitan and Eastern County), with district councils (Western County and Eastern County), with health agencies (Western county, Eastern County) and/or with the voluntary sector (all case studies).

Inter-organizational leadership, however, is a further challenge. As an example, Western County is a local authority with dispersed and diverse communities, which has established and is nurturing seven partnership committees with other levels of local government (district and in some cases parishes), and with some other agencies. This requires not only understanding the context of each organization but also their complex inter-relationships and changing dynamics. Such complexity is taken for granted by some politicians but is a major challenge for political and managerial leaders, even where they are well steeped in local conditions and contexts. From our interviews, it requires responsiveness to changing conditions as well as deep understanding of histories.

Leadership is not only about influence. The role of formal power through a directive style can also be important. The role for politicians, managers and project directors to unlock sticking points through the use of authority and power at times was also evident. For example, a project director at Eastern County explored engaging the local districts and other agencies in using the capacity of the call centre and told them all when the opportunity to join the project with potential private sector contractors would close.

The existence of both influence-based leadership and authority, through formal structures and positions, created some tensions in all four case studies. The use of lateral influence and networks (across services, across departments, across organizations, drawing in appropriate partners according to contribution rather than position) is different from the vertical, hierarchical relationships which are fostered in structured organizations providing services on a large scale. Not everyone finds the interface between the lateral and vertical modes of organizing easy. For example, in Western County there were seen to be two organizational logics of formal and informal authority, centralized and decentralized budgets, resources and power, and lateral as well as vertical systems of influence. In addition, in all the organizations there were differences between those who were engaged in new forms of organizing across boundaries and those who felt shut out or switched off. Trade unions also report finding it hard to organize around citizen-centred services and joined-up government, given that their membership base and organization is largely departmental.

Leadership through influence means that a larger number of politicians and managers work in boundary locations. Managers are no longer buried inside the organization but like politicians, have to work in multiple arenas, locations and with groups with different identities, cultures and histories. We still do not know enough about how to organizationally support politicians, managers and staff in these roles, which are at the points of intersection between different arenas—partly inside and partly outside the organization, working with elected members and with officers, with staff and with communities, within the local authority and with other agencies.

Conclusions

Overall, the four case studies have provided a rich picture of inter-organizational leadership and influence. The role of leadership and influence in such complex networks of inter-relationships between organizations moves beyond traditional models of leadership, which tend to emphasise individual action. The case studies highlight both the potential and the risks of distributed leadership throughout the organization and the importance of inter-organizational leadership. All four case studies also demonstrate the immense changes in internal work organization, cultures, behaviours and processes which are needed for community leadership.

The implications for the debates about modernization and improvement of public services and local governance are substantial. First, the case studies demonstrate distributed leadership throughout the organization, from apex to front line. By contrast some of the implementation of the new political arrangements can be read in terms of concentrating political leadership at the apex of the organization. Although new political arrangements are intended to strengthen community representational roles, much of the intellectual and emotional focus from politicians concerns the role of the executive. To what extent are distributed and concentrated leadership roles compatible, and if so, in what ways? How can they be combined?

Second, much of the debate about modernization and improvement is focused on internal leadership to achieve change. Yet, community leadership takes place not only in the organization but also at the cross-roads of different cultures and organizational forms—for example, at the crossroads between political and managerial activities, with local groups as well as with the internal organization, in different geographical areas, working with senior managers and frontline staff. The modernization debate has taken insufficient account of this complexity and its consequences for roles, structures, cultures, accountabilities, training and development.

Third, the emphasis from central government has often been about individual leaders (head teachers, elected mayors, chief executives), occasionally about collective leadership (cabinets or corporate teams) but rarely about organizational leadership other than in very broad terms. Our research shows that inter-organizational leadership is complex and requires developmental and influence skills, as well as traditional hierarchical skills.

Fourth, we defined our research in terms not only of leadership, but also the management of influence, to emphasise that the skills of shaping directions, shifting resources and achieving outcomes requires directive types of leadership together with the subtle skills of influencing and negotiating. This implies a different model of leadership.

Finally, leadership of modernization and improvement is taking place in conditions of increasing complexity and uncertainty, where outcomes cannot always be specified in advance. Leadership therefore is not about directing a steady state organization where the problems and the solutions are largely known, but leadership takes place in a context of change, flux and uncertainty (Hartley, 2000). This requires an approach which is not only about 'implementation' of pre-specified policies but the 'enactment' (Weick, 1995), or emergence, (Allison and Hartley, 2000) of outcomes. Innovation cannot be pre-specified and therefore part of the role of leadership is to provide a framework and to observe, nurture, shape and reflect as well as to implement. Models of leadership in the UK public sector urgently need updating to reflect this.

References

Allison, M. and Hartley, J. (2000). *Generating and Sharing Better Practice: Reports of the Better Value Development Programme Workshops* (DETR, London).

Avolio, B. (1999). *Full Leadership Development* (Sage, Thousand Oaks).

Benington, J. (1997). New paradigms and practices for local government: capacity building within civil society. In Kraemer, S. and Roberts, J. (Eds). *The Politics of Attachment* (Free Association Press, London).

Burns, J. M. (1978). *Leadership* (Harper and Row, New York).

Cabinet Office (1999). *Report to the Prime Minister from Sir Richard Wilson, Head of the Home Civil Service* (Cabinet Office, London).

DETR (1998a). *Modernizing Local Government: Local Democracy and Local Leadership* (The Stationery Office, London).

DETR (1998b). *Modern Local Government: In Touch with the People* (The Stationery Office, London).

DETR (1999a). *Local Leadership, Local Choice* (The Stationery Office, London).

DETR (1999b). *Local Government Act 1999: Part I. Best Value* (The Stationery Office, London).

DTEE (1998). *Teachers Meeting the Challenge of Change* (The Stationery Office, London).

Hartley, J. (2000). Leading and managing the uncertainty of strategic change. In Flood, P., Carroll, S., Gorman, L. and Dromgoole, T. (Eds). *Managing Strategic Implementation* (Blackwell, Oxford). pp. 109–122.

Hartley, J. and Benington, J. (2000). Co-research: a new methodology for new times. *European Journal of Work and Organizational Psychology* (in press).

Heifetz, R. (1996). *Leadership without Easy Answers* (Harvard University Press, Cambridge. MA).

Heifetz, R and Sinder R (1988) Political leadership. In Reich R. (Ed). *The Power of Public Ideas* (Harvard University Press, Cambridge. MA).

Improvement and Development Agency (1999). *Benchmark of the 'Ideal' Local Authority* (IDeA, London).

Nadler, D. and Tushman, M. (1990). Leadership for organizational change. In Mohrman, A., Mohrman, S., Ledford, G., Cummings, T. and Lawler, E. (Eds). *Large-Scale Organizational Change* (Jossey Bass, San Francisco).

Rost, J. (1998). Leadership and management. In Hickman, G. (Ed). *Leading Organizations: Perspectives for a New Era* (Sage, Thousand Oaks).

Weick, K. (1995). *Sense-Making in Organizations* (Sage, Thousand Oaks).

Yukl, G. (1994). *Leadership in Organizations* (3rd edn). (Prentice Hall, London).

18

Level 5 Leadership: The Triumph of Humility and Fierce Resolve

Jim Collins

In 1971, a seemingly ordinary man named Darwin E. Smith was named chief executive of Kimberly-Clark, a stodgy old paper company whose stock had fallen 36% behind the general market during the previous 20 years. Smith, the company's mild-mannered in-house lawyer, wasn't so sure the board had made the right choice – a feeling that was reinforced when a Kimberly-Clark director pulled him aside and reminded him that he lacked some of the qualifications for the position. But CEO he was, and CEO he remained for 20 years.

What a 20 years it was. In that period, Smith created a stunning transformation at Kimberly-Clark, turning it into the leading consumer paper products company in the world. Under his stewardship, the company beat its rivals Scott Paper and Procter & Gamble. And in doing so, Kimberly-Clark generated cumulative stock returns that were 4.1 times greater than those of the general market, outperforming venerable companies such as Hewlett-Packard, 3M, Coca-Cola, and General Electric.

Smith's turnaround of Kimberly-Clark is one the best examples in the twentieth century of a leader taking a company from merely good to truly great. And yet few people – even ardent students of business history – have heard of Darwin Smith. He probably would have liked it that way. Smith is a classic example of a *Level 5 leader* – an individual who blends extreme personal humility with intense professional will. According to our five-year research study, executives who possess this paradoxical combination of traits are catalysts for the statistically rare event of transforming a good company into a great one. (The research is described in the box "One Question, Five Years, Eleven Companies.")

"Level 5" refers to the highest level in a hierarchy of executive capabilities that we identified during our research. Leaders at the other four levels in the hierarchy can produce high degrees of success but not enough to elevate companies from mediocrity to sustained excellence. (For more details about this concept, see the box "The Level 5 Hierarchy." on page 239) And while Level 5 leadership is not the only requirement for transforming a good company into a great one – other factors include getting the right people on the bus (and the wrong people off the bus) and creating a culture of discipline – our research shows it to be essential. Good-to-great transformations don't happen without Level 5 leaders at the helm. They just don't.

Source: J. Collins (2001) *Harvard Business Review*, 79 (1): 67–76.

One Question, Five Years, Eleven Companies

The Level 5 discovery derives from a research project that began in 1996, when my research teams and I set out to answer one question: can a good company become a great company and, if so, how? Most great companies grew up with superb parents – people like George Merck, David Packard, and Walt Disney – who instilled greatness early on. But what about the vast majority of companies that wake up part-way through life and realize that they're good but not great?

To answer that question, we looked for companies that had shifted from good performance to great performance – and sustained it. We identified comparison companies that had failed to make that sustained shift. We then studied the contrast between the two groups to discover common variables that distinguish those who make and sustain a shift from those who could have but didn't.

More precisely, we searched for a specific pattern: cumulative stock returns at or below the general stock market for 15 years, punctuated by a transition point, then cumulative returns at least three times the market over the next 15 years. (See the Figure below.) We used data from the University of Chicago Center for Research in Security Prices, adjusted for stock splits, and all dividends reinvested. The shift had to be distinct from the industry; if the whole industry showed the same shift, we'd drop the company. We began with 1,435 companies that appeared on the *Fortune* 500 from 1965 to 1995; we found 11 good-to-great examples. That's not a sample; that's the total number that jumped all our hurdles and passed into the study.

Those that made the cut averaged cumulative stock returns 6.9 times the general stock market for the 15 years after the point of transition. To put that in perspective, General Electric under Jack Welch outperformed the general stock market by 2.8:1 during his tenure from 1986 to 2000. A dollar invested in a mutual fund of the good-to-great companies in 1965 grew to $470 by 2000 – compared to $56 in the general stock market. These are remarkable numbers, made all the more so by the fact that they came from previously unremarkable companies.

For each good-to-great example, we selected the best direct comparison, based on similarity of business, size, age, customer, and performance leading up to the transition. We also constructed a set of six "unsustained" comparisons (companies that showed a short-lived shift but then fell off) to address the question of sustainability. To be conservative, we consistently picked comparison companies that, if anything, were in better shape than the good-to-great companies were in the years just before the transition.

With 22 research associates working in groups of four to six at a time from 1996 to 2000, our study involved a wide range of both qualitative and quantitative analyses. On the qualitative front, we collected nearly 6,000 articles, conducted 87

(Continued)

(Continued)

interviews with key executives, analyzed companies' internal strategy documents, and culled through analysts' reports. On the quantitative front, we ran financial metrics, examined executive compensation, compared patterns of management turnover, quantified company layoffs and restructurings, and calculated the effect of acquisitions and divestitures on companies' stocks. We then synthesized the results to identify the drivers of good-to-great transformations. One was Level 5 leadership. (The others are described in the box "Not by Level 5 Alone.", page 240)

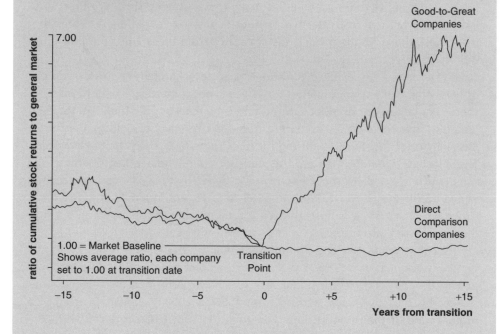

Since only 11 companies qualified as good-to-great, a research finding had to meet a stiff standard before we would deem it significant. Every component in the final framework showed up in all 11 good-to-great companies during the transition era, regardless of industry (from steel to banking), transition decade (from the 1950s to the 1990s), circumstances (from plodding along to dire crisis), or size (from tens of millions to tens of billions). Additionally, every component had to show up in less than 30% of the comparison companies during the relevant years. Level 5 easily made it into the framework as one of the strongest, most consistent contrasts between the good-to-great and the comparison companies.

Not What You Would Expect

Our discovery of Level 5 leadership is counterintuitive. Indeed, it is countercultural. People generally assume that transforming companies from good to great requires larger-than-life leaders – big personalities like Iacocca, Dunlap, Welch, and Gault, who make headlines and become celebrities.

Compared with those CEOs, Darwin Smith seems to have come from Mars. Shy, unpretentious, even awkward, Smith shunned attention. When a journalist asked him to describe his management style, Smith just stared back at the scribe from the other side of his thick black-rimmed glasses. He was dressed unfashionably, like a farm boy wearing his first J.C. Penney suit. Finally, after a long and uncomfortable silence, he said, "Eccentric." Needless to say, the *Wall Street Journal* did not publish a splashy feature on Darwin Smith.

But if you were to consider Smith soft or meek, you would be terribly mistaken. His lack of pretense was coupled with a fierce, even stoic, resolve toward life. Smith grew up on an Indiana farm and put himself through night school at Indiana University by working the day shift at International Harvester. One day, he lost a finger on the job. The story goes that he went to class that evening and returned to work the very next day. Eventually, this poor but determined Indiana farm boy earned admission to Harvard Law School.

He showed the same iron will when he was at the helm of Kimberly-Clark. Indeed, two months after Smith became CEO, doctors diagnosed him with nose and throat cancer and told him he had less than a year to live. He duly informed the board of his illness but said he had no plans to die anytime soon. Smith held to his demanding work schedule while commuting weekly from Wisconsin to Houston for radiation therapy. He lived 25 more years, 20 of them as CEO.

Smith's ferocious resolve was crucial to the rebuilding of Kimberly-Clark, especially when he made the most dramatic decision in the company's history: sell the mills.

To explain: shortly after he took over, Smith and his team had concluded that the company's traditional core business – coated paper – was doomed to mediocrity. Its economics were bad and the competition weak. But, they reasoned, if Kimberly-Clark was thrust into the fire of the *consumer* paper products business, better economics and world-class competition like Procter & Gamble would force it to achieve greatness or perish.

And so, like the general who burned the boats upon landing on enemy soil, leaving his troops to succeed or die, Smith announced that Kimberly-Clark would sell its mills – even the namesake mill in Kimberly, Wisconsin. All proceeds would be thrown into the consumer business, with investments in brands like Huggies diapers and Kleenex tissues. The business media called the move stupid, and Wall Street analysts downgraded the stock. But Smith never wavered. Twenty-five years later, Kimberly-Clark owned Scott Paper and beat Procter & Gamble in six of eight product categories. In retirement, Smith reflected on his exceptional performance, saying simply, "I never stopped trying to become qualified for the job."

The Level 5 Hierarchy

LEVEL 5 LEVEL 5 EXECUTIVE
Builds enduring greatness
through a paradoxical combination
of personal humility plus professional will.

LEVEL 4 EFFECTIVE LEADER
Catalyzes commitment to and vigorous pursuit
of a clear and compelling vision; stimulates
the group to high performance standards.

LEVEL 3 COMPETENT MANAGER
Organizes people and resources toward the effective
and efficient pursuit of predetermined objectives.

LEVEL 2 CONTRIBUTING TEAM MEMBER
Contributes to the achievement of group
objectives; works effectively with others in a group setting.

LEVEL 1 HIGHLY CAPABLE INDIVIDUAL
Makes productive contributions through talent, knowledge,
skills, and good work habits.

The Level 5 leader sits on top of a hierarchy of capabilities and is, according to our research, a necessary requirement for transforming an organization from good to great. But what lies beneath? Four other layers, each one appropriate in its own right but none with the power of Level 5. Individuals do not need to proceed sequentially through each level of the hierarchy to reach the top, but to be full-fledged Level 5 requires the capabilities of all the lower levels, plus the special characteristics of Level 5.

Not What We Expected Either

We'll look in depth at Level 5 leadership, but first let's set an important context for our findings: we were not looking for Level 5 or anything like it. Our original question was can a good company become a great one, and, if so, how? In fact, I gave the research teams explicit instructions to downplay the role of top executives in their analyses of this question so we wouldn't slip into the simplistic "credit the leader" or "blame the leader" thinking that is so common today.

But Level 5 found us. Over the course of the study, research teams kept saying, "We can't ignore the top executives even if we want to. There is something consistently unusual about them." I would push back, arguing, "The comparison companies also had leaders. So what's different here?" Back and forth the debate raged. Finally, as should always be the case, the data won. The executives at companies that went from good to great and sustained that performance for 15 years or more were all cut from the same cloth – one remarkably different from that which produced executives at the comparison companies in our study. It didn't matter whether the company was in crisis or steady state, consumer or industrial, offering services or products. It didn't matter when the transition took place or how big the company. The successful organizations all had a Level 5 leader at the time of transition.

Furthermore, the absence of Level 5 leadership showed up consistently across the comparison companies. The point: Level 5 is an empirical finding, not an ideological one. And that's important to note, given how much the Level 5 finding contradicts not only conventional wisdom but much of management theory to date. (For more about our findings on good-to-great transformations, see the box "Not by Level 5 Alone.")

Not by Level 5 Alone

Level 5 leadership is an essential factor for taking a company from good to great, but it's not the only one. Our research uncovered multiple factors that deliver companies to greatness. And it is the combined package – Level 5 plus these other drivers – that takes companies beyond unremarkable. There is a symbiotic relationship between Level 5 and the rest of our findings: Level 5 enables implementation of the other findings, and practicing the other findings may help you get to Level 5. We've already talked about who Level 5 leaders are; the rest of our findings describe what they do. Here is a brief look at some of the other key findings.

First who: We expected that good-to-great leaders would start with the vision and strategy. Instead, they attended to people first, strategy second. They got the right people on the bus, moved the wrong people off, ushered the right people to the right seats – and then they figured out where to drive it.

Stockdale paradox: This finding is named after Admiral James Stockdale, winner of the Medal of Honor, who survived seven years in a Vietcong POW camp by hanging on to two contradictory beliefs: his life couldn't be worse at the moment, and his life would someday be better than ever. Like Stockdale, people at the good-to-great companies in our research confronted the most brutal facts of their current reality – yet simultaneously maintained absolute faith that they would prevail in the end. And they held both disciplines – faith and facts – at the same time, all the time.

Buildup-breakthrough flywheel: Good-to-great transformations do not happen overnight or in one big leap. Rather, the process resembles relentlessly pushing a giant, heavy flywheel in one direction. At first, pushing it gets the flywheel to turn once. With consistent effort, it goes two turns, then five, then ten, building

(Continued)

(Continued)

increasing momentum until – bang! – the wheel hits the breakthrough point, and the momentum really kicks in. Our comparison companies never sustained the kind of breakthrough momentum that the good-to-great companies did; instead, they lurched back and forth with radical change programs, reactionary moves, and restructurings.

The hedgehog concept: In a famous essay, philosopher and scholar Isaiah Berlin described two approaches to thought and life using a simple parable. The fox knows a little about many things, but the hedgehog knows only one big thing very well. The fox is complex; the hedgehog simple. And the hedgehog wins. Our research shows that breakthroughs require a simple, hedgehog-like understanding of three intersecting circles: what a company can be the best in the world at, how its economics work best, and what best ignites the passions of its people. Breakthroughs happen when you get the hedgehog concept and become systematic and consistent with it, eliminating virtually anything that does not fit in the three circles.

Technology accelerators: The good-to-great companies had a paradoxical relationship with technology. On the one hand, they assiduously avoided jumping on new technology bandwagons. On the other, they were pioneers in the application of carefully selected technologies, making bold, farsighted investments in those that directly linked to their hedgehog concept. Like turbochargers, these technology accelerators create an explosion in flywheel momentum.

A culture of discipline: When you look across the good-to-great transformations, they consistently display three forms of discipline: disciplined people, disciplined thought, and disciplined action. When you have disciplined people, you don't need hierarchy. When you have disciplined thought, you don't need bureaucracy. When you have disciplined action, you don't need excessive controls. When you combine a culture of discipline with an ethic of entrepreneurship, you get the magical alchemy of great performance.

Humility + Will = Level 5

Level 5 leaders are a study in duality: modest and willful, shy and fearless. To grasp this concept, consider Abraham Lincoln, who never let his ego get in the way of his ambition to create an enduring great nation. Author Henry Adams called him "a quiet, peaceful, shy figure." But those who thought Lincoln's understated manner signaled weakness in the man found themselves terribly mistaken – to the scale of 250,000 Confederate and 360,000 Union lives, including Lincoln's own.

It might be a stretch to compare the 11 Level 5 CEOs in our research to Lincoln, but they did display the same kind of duality. Take Colman M. Mockler, CEO of Gillette from 1975 to 1991. Mockler, who faced down three takeover attempts, was a reserved, gracious man with a gentle, almost patrician manner. Despite epic battles with raiders – he took on Ronald Perelman twice and the former Coniston Partners once – he never lost his shy, courteous style. At the height of the crisis, he maintained a calm business-as-usual demeanor, dispensing first with ongoing business before turning to the takeover.

And yet, those who mistook Mockler's outward modesty as a sign of inner weakness were beaten in the end. In one proxy battle, Mockler and other senior executives called thousands of investors, one by one, to win their votes. Mockler simply would not give in. He chose to fight for the future greatness of Gillette even though he could have pocketed millions by flipping his stock.

Consider the consequences had Mockler capitulated. If a share-flipper had accepted the full 44% price premium offered by Perelman and then invested those shares in the general market for ten years, he still would have come out 64% behind a shareholder who stayed with Mockler and Gillette. If Mockler had given up the fight, it's likely that none of us would be shaving with Sensor, Lady Sensor, or the Mach III – and hundreds of millions of people would have a more painful battle with daily stubble.

Sadly, Mockler never had the chance to enjoy the full fruits of his efforts. In January 1991, Gillette received an advance copy of *Forbes*. The cover featured an artist's rendition of the publicity-shy Mockler standing on a mountaintop, holding a giant razor above his head in a triumphant pose. Walking back to his office, just minutes after seeing this public acknowledgment of his 16 years of struggle, Mockler crumpled to the floor and died from a massive heart attack.

Even if Mockler had known he would die in office, he could not have changed his approach. His placid persona hid an inner intensity, a dedication to making anything he touched the best – not just because of what he would get but because he couldn't imagine doing it any other way. Mockler could not give up the company to those who would destroy it, any more than Lincoln would risk losing the chance to build an enduring great nation.

A Compelling Modesty

The Mockler story illustrates the modesty typical of Level 5 leaders. (For a summary of Level 5 traits, see the box "The Yin and Yang of Level 5.", page 243) Indeed, throughout our interviews with such executives, we were struck by the way they talked about themselves – or rather, didn't talk about themselves. They'd go on and on about the company and the contributions of other executives, but they would instinctively deflect discussion about their own role. When pressed to talk about themselves, they'd say things like, "I hope I'm not sounding like a big shot." or "I don't think I can take much credit for what happened. We were blessed with marvelous people." One Level 5 leader even asserted, "There are lot of people in this company who could do my job better than I do."

By contrast, consider the courtship of personal celebrity by the comparison CEOs. Scott Paper, the comparison company to Kimberly-Clark, hired Al Dunlap as CEO – a man who would tell anyone who would listen (and many who would have preferred not to) about his accomplishments. After 19 months atop Scott Paper, Dunlap said in *BusinessWeek:* "The Scott story will go down in the annals of American business history as one of the most successful, quickest turnarounds ever. It makes other turn-arounds pale by comparison." He personally accrued $100 million for 603 days of work at Scott Paper– about $165,000 per day – largely by slashing the workforce, halving the R&D budget, and putting the company on growth steroids in preparation for sale. After selling off the company and pocketing his quick millions, Dunlap wrote an autobiography in which he boastfully dubbed himself "Rambo in pinstripes." It's hard to imagine Darwin Smith thinking, "Hey, that Rambo character reminds me of me," let alone stating it publicly.

Granted, the Scott Paper story is one of the more dramatic in our study, but it's not an isolated case. In more than two-thirds of the comparison companies, we noted the presence of a gargantuan ego that contributed to the demise or continued mediocrity of the company. We found this pattern particularly strong in the unsustained com-parison companies – the companies that would show a shift in performance under a talented yet egocentric Level 4 leader, only to decline in later years.

Lee Iacocca, for example, saved Chrysler from the brink of catastrophe, performing one of the most celebrated (and deservedly so) turnarounds in U.S. business history. The automaker's stock rose 2.9 times higher than the general market about halfway through his tenure. But then Iacocca diverted his attention to transforming himself. He appeared regularly on talk shows like the *Today Show* and *Larry King Live,* starred in more than 80 commercials, entertained the idea of running for president of the United States, and promoted his autobiography, which sold 7 million copies worldwide. Iacocca's personal stock soared, but Chrysler's stock fell 31% below the market in the second half of his tenure.

And once Iacocca had accumulated all the fame and perks, he found it difficult to leave center stage. He postponed his retirement so many times that Chrysler's insiders began to joke that Iacocca stood for "I Am Chairman of Chrysler Corporation Always." When he finally retired, he demanded that the board continue to provide a private jet and stock options. Later, he joined forces with noted takeover artist Kirk Kerkorian to launch a hostile bid for Chrysler. (It failed.) Iacocca did make one final brilliant decision: he picked a modest yet determined man – perhaps even a Level 5 – as his successor. Bob Eaton rescued Chrysler from its second near-death crisis in a decade and set the foundation for a more enduring corporate transition.

The Yin and Yang of Level 5

PERSONAL HUMILITY	PROFESSIONAL WILL
Demonstrates a compelling modesty, shunning public adulation; never boastful.	Creates superb results, a clear catalyst in the transition from good to great.
Acts with quiet, calm determination; relies principally on inspired standards, not inspiring charisma, to motivate.	Demonstrates an unwavering resolve to do whatever must be done to produce the best long term results, no matter how difficult.
Channels ambition into the company, not the self; sets up successors for even more greatness in the next generation.	Sets the standard of building an enduring great company; will settle for nothing less.
Looks in the mirror, not out the window to apportion responsibility for poor results, never blaming other people, external factors, or bad luck.	Looks out the window, not in the mirror, to apportion credit for the success of the company – to other people, external factors and good luck.

An Unwavering Resolve

Besides extreme humility, Level 5 leaders also display tremendous professional will. When George Cain became CEO of Abbott Laboratories, it was a drowsy family-controlled business, sitting at the bottom quartile of the pharmaceutical industry, living off its cash cow, erythromycin. Cain was a typical Level 5 leader in his lack of pretense: he didn't have the kind of inspiring personality that would galvanize the company. But he had something much more powerful: inspired standards. He could not stand mediocrity in any form and was utterly intolerant of anyone who would accept the idea that good is good enough. For the next 14 years, he relentlessly imposed his will for greatness on Abbott Labs.

Among Cain's first tasks was to destroy one of the root causes of Abbott's middling performance: nepotism. By systematically rebuilding both the board and the executive team with the best people he could find, Cain made his statement. Family ties no longer mattered. If you couldn't become the best executive in the industry, within your span of responsibility, you would lose your paycheck.

Such near-ruthless rebuilding might be expected from an outsider brought in to turn the company around, but Cain was an 18-year insider – and a part of the family, the son of a previous president. Holiday gatherings were probably tense for a few years in the Cain clan – "Sorry I had to fire you. Want another slice of turkey?" – but in the end, family members were pleased with the performance of their stock. Cain had set in motion a profitable growth machine. From its transition in 1974 to 2000, Abbott created shareholder returns that beat the market 4.5:1, out-performing industry super-stars Merck and Pfizer by a factor of two.

Another good example of iron-willed Level 5 leadership comes from Charles R. "Cork" Walgreen III, who transformed dowdy Walgreens into a company that outper-formed the stock market 16:1 from its transition in 1975 to 2000. After years of dialogue and debate within his executive team about what to do with Walgreens' food-service operations, this CEO sensed the team had finally reached a watershed: the company's brightest future lay in convenient drugstores, not in food service. Dan Jorndt, who succeeded Walgreen in 1988, describes what happened next:

> Cork said at one of our planning committee meetings, "Okay, now I am going to draw the line in the sand. We are going to be out of the restaurant business completely in five years." At the time we had more than 500 restaurants. You could have heard a pin drop. He said, "I want to let everybody know the clock is ticking." Six months later we were at our next planning committee meeting and someone mentioned just in passing that we had only five years to be out of the restaurant business. Cork was not a real vociferous fellow. He sort of tapped on the table and said, "Listen, you now have four and a half years. I said you had five years six months ago. Now you've got four and a half years." Well, that next day things really clicked into gear for winding down our restaurant business. Cork never wavered. He never doubted. He never second-guessed.

Like Darwin Smith selling the mills at Kimberly-Clark, Cork Walgreen required stoic resolve to make his decisions. Food service was not the largest part of the business, although it did add substantial profits to the bottom line. The real problem was more emotional than financial. Walgreens had, after all, invented the malted milk shake, and food service had been a long-standing family tradition dating back to Cork's grandfather. Not only that, some food-service outlets were even named after the CEO – for example, a restaurant chain named Corky's. But no matter, if Walgreen had to fly in the face of family tradition in order to refocus on the one arena in which Walgreens could be the best in the world – convenient drugstores – and terminate everything else that would not produce great results, then Cork would do it. Quietly, doggedly, simply.

One final, yet compelling, note on our findings about Level 5: because Level 5 lead-ers have ambition not for themselves but for their companies, they routinely select superb successors. Level 5 leaders want to see their companies become even more successful in the next generation, comfortable with the idea that most people won't even know that the roots of that success trace back to them. As one Level 5 CEO said, "I want to look from my porch, see the company as one of the great companies in the world someday, and be able to say, 'I used to work there.'" By contrast, Level 4 leaders often fail to set up the company for enduring success – after all, what better testament to your own personal greatness than that the place falls apart after you leave?

In more than three-quarters of the comparison companies, we found executives who set up their successors for failure, chose weak successors, or both. Consider the case of Rubbermaid, which grew from obscurity to become one of *Fortune's* most admired companies – and then, just as quickly, disintegrated into such sorry shape that it had to be acquired by Newell.

The architect of this remarkable story was a charismatic and brilliant leader named Stanley C. Gault, whose name became synonymous in the late 1980s with the company's success. Across the 312 articles collected by our research team about Rubbermaid, Gault comes through as a hard-driving, egocentric executive. In one article, he responds to the accusation of being a tyrant with the statement, "Yes, but I'm a sincere tyrant." In another, drawn directly from his own comments on leading change, the word "I" appears 44 times, while the word "we" appears 16 times. Of course, Gault had every reason to be proud of his executive success: Rubbermaid generated 40 consecutive quarters of earnings growth under his leadership – an impressive performance, to be sure, and one that deserves respect.

But Gault did not leave behind a company that would be great without him. His chosen successor lasted a year on the job and the next in line faced a management team so shallow that he had to temporarily shoulder four jobs while scrambling to identify a new number-two executive. Gault's successors struggled not only with a management void but also with strategic voids that would eventually bring the company to its knees.

Of course, you might say – as one *Fortune* article did – that the fact that Rubbermaid fell apart after Gault left proves his greatness as a leader. Gault was a tremendous Level 4 leader, perhaps one of the best in the last 50 years. But he was not at Level 5, and that is one crucial reason why Rubbermaid went from good to great for a brief, shining moment and then just as quickly went from great to irrelevant.

The Window and the Mirror

As part of our research, we interviewed Alan L. Wurtzel, the Level 5 leader responsible for turning Circuit City from a ramshackle company on the edge of bankruptcy into one of America's most successful electronics retailers. In the 15 years after its transition date in 1982, Circuit City outperformed the market 18.5:1.

We asked Wurtzel to list the top five factors in his company's transformation, ranked by importance. His number one factor? Luck. "We were in a great industry, with the wind at our backs." But wait a minute, we retorted, Silo – your comparison company – was in the same industry, with the same wind, and bigger sails. The conversation went back and forth, with Wurtzel refusing to take much credit for the transition, preferring to attribute it largely to just being in the right place at the right time. Later, when we asked him to discuss the factors that would sustain a good-to-great transformation, he said, "The first thing that comes to mind is luck. I was lucky to find the right successor."

Luck. What an odd factor to talk about. Yet the Level 5 leaders we identified invoked it frequently. We asked an executive at steel company Nucor why it had such a remarkable track record of making good decisions. His response? "I guess we were just lucky." Joseph F. Cullman III, the Level 5 CEO of Philip Morris, flat out refused to take credit for his company's success, citing his good fortune to have great colleagues, successors, and predecessors. Even the book he wrote about his career – which he penned at the urging of his colleagues and which he never intended to distribute widely outside the company – had the unusual title *I'm a Lucky Guy*.

At first, we were puzzled by the Level 5 leaders' emphasis on good luck. After all, there is no evidence that the companies that had progressed from good to great were blessed with more good luck (or more bad luck, for that matter) than the comparison companies. But then we began to notice an interesting pattern in the executives at the comparison companies: they often blamed their situations on bad luck, bemoaning the difficulties of the environment they faced.

Compare Bethlehem Steel and Nucor, for example. Both steel companies operated with products that are hard to differentiate, and both faced a competitive challenge from cheap imported steel. Both companies paid significantly higher wages than most of their foreign competitors. And yet executives at the two companies held completely different views of the same environment.

Bethlehem Steel's CEO summed up the company's problems in 1983 by blaming the imports: "Our first, second, and third problems are imports." Meanwhile, Ken Iverson and his crew at Nucor saw the imports as a blessing: "Aren't we lucky; steel is heavy, and they have to ship it all the way across the ocean, giving us a huge advantage." Indeed, Iverson saw the first, second, and third problems facing the U.S. steel industry not in imports but in management. He even went so far as to speak out publicly against government protection against imports, telling a gathering of stunned steel executives in 1977 that the real problems facing the industry lay in the fact that management had failed to keep pace with technology.

The emphasis on luck turns out to be part of a broader pattern that we came to call *the window and the mirror*. Level 5 leaders, inherently humble, look out the window to apportion credit – even undue credit – to factors outside themselves. If they can't find a specific person or event to give credit to, they credit good luck. At the same time, they look in the mirror to assign responsibility, never citing bad luck or external factors when things go poorly. Conversely, the comparison executives frequently looked out the window for factors to blame but preened in the mirror to credit themselves when things went well.

The funny thing about the window-and-mirror concept is that it does not reflect reality. According to our research, the Level 5 leaders *were* responsible for their companies' transformations. But they would never admit that. We can't climb inside their heads and assess whether they deeply believed what they saw in the window and the mirror. But it doesn't really matter, because they acted as if they believed it, and they acted with such consistency that it produced exceptional results.

Born or Bred?

Not long ago, I shared the Level 5 finding with a gathering of senior executives. A woman who had recently become chief executive of her company raised her hand. "I believe what you've told us about Level 5 leadership," she said, "but I'm disturbed because I know I'm not there yet, and maybe I never will be. Part of the reason I got this job is because of my strong ego. Are you telling me that I can't make my company great if I'm not Level 5?"

"Let me return to the data," I responded. "Of 1,435 companies that appeared on the *Fortune* 500 since 1965, only 11 made it into our study. In those 11, all of them had Level 5 leaders in key positions, including the CEO role, at the pivotal time of transition. Now, to reiterate, we're not saying that Level 5 is the only element required for the move from good to great, but it appears to be essential."

She sat there, quiet for a moment, and you could guess what many people in the room were thinking. Finally, she raised her hand again. "Can you learn to become Level 5?" I still do not know the answer to that question. Our research, frankly, did not delve into how Level 5 leaders come to be, nor did we attempt to explain or codify the nature of their emotional lives. We speculated on the unique psychology of Level 5 leaders. Were they "guilty" of displacement – shifting their own raw ambition onto something other than themselves? Were they sublimating their egos for dark and complex reasons rooted in childhood trauma? Who knows? And perhaps more important, do the psychological roots of Level 5 leadership matter any more than do the roots of charisma or intelligence? The question remains: Can Level 5 be developed?

My preliminary hypothesis is that there are two categories of people: those who don't have the Level 5 seed within them and those who do. The first category consists of people who could never in a million years bring themselves to subjugate their own needs to the greater ambition of something larger and more lasting than themselves. For those people, work will always be first and foremost about what they get – the fame, fortune, power, adulation, and so on. Work will never be about what they build, create, and contribute. The great irony is that the animus and personal ambition that often drives people to become a Level 4 leader stands at odds with the humility required to rise to Level 5.

When you combine that irony with the fact that boards of directors frequently operate under the false belief that a larger-than-life, egocentric leader is required to make a company great, you can quickly see why Level 5 leaders rarely appear at the top of our institutions. We keep putting people in positions of power who lack the seed to become a Level 5 leader, and that is one major reason why there are so few companies that make a sustained and verifiable shift from good to great.

The second category consists of people who could evolve to Level 5; the capability resides within them, perhaps buried or ignored or simply nascent. Under the right circumstances – with self-reflection, a mentor, loving parents, a significant life experience, or other factors – the seed can begin to develop. Some of the Level 5 leaders in our study had significant life experiences that might have sparked development of the seed. Darwin Smith fully blossomed as a Level 5 after his near-death experience with cancer. Joe Cullman was profoundly affected by his World War II experiences, particularly the last-minute change of orders that took him off a doomed ship on which he surely would have died; he considered the next 60-odd years a great gift. A strong religious belief or conversion might also nurture the seed. Colman Mockler, for example, converted to evangelical Christianity while getting his MBA at Harvard, and later, according to the book *Cutting Edge,* he became a prime mover in a group of Boston business executives that met frequently over breakfast to discuss the carryover of religious values to corporate life.

We would love to be able to give you a list of steps for getting to Level 5 – other than contracting cancer, going through a religious conversion, or getting different parents – but we have no solid research data that would support a credible list. Our research exposed Level 5 as a key component inside the black box of what it takes to shift a company from good to great. Yet inside that black box is another – the inner development of a person to Level 5 leadership. We could speculate on what that inner box might hold, but it would mostly be just that, speculation.

In short, Level 5 is a very satisfying idea, a truthful idea, a powerful idea, and, to make the move from good to great, very likely an essential idea. But to provide "ten steps to Level 5 leadership" would trivialize the concept.

My best advice, based on the research, is to practice the other good-to-great disciplines that we discovered. Since we found a tight symbiotic relationship between each of the other findings and Level 5, we suspect that conscientiously trying to lead using the other disciplines can help you move in the right direction. There is no guarantee that doing so will turn executives into full-fledged Level 5 leaders, but it gives them a tangible place to begin, especially if they have the seed within.

We cannot say for sure what percentage of people have the seed within, nor how many of those can nurture it enough to become Level 5. Even those of us on the research team who identified Level 5 do not know whether we will succeed in evolving to its heights. And yet all of us who worked on the finding have been inspired by the idea of trying to move toward Level 5. Darwin Smith, Colman Mockler, Alan Wurtzel, and all the other Level 5 leaders we learned about have become role models for us. Whether or not we make it to Level 5, it is worth trying. For like all basic truths about what is best in human beings, when we catch a glimpse of the truth, we know that our own lives and all that we touch will be the better for making the effort to get there.

19

The Failure-Tolerant Leader

Richard Farson and Ralph Keyes

"The fastest way to succeed," IBM's Thomas Watson, Sr., once said, "is to double your failure rate." In recent years, more and more executives have embraced this point of view, coming to understand what innovators have always known: that failure is a prerequisite to invention. A business can't develop a breakthrough product or process if it's not willing to encourage risk taking and learn from subsequent mistakes.

The growing acceptance of failure is changing the way companies approach innovation. Some build exit strategies into their projects to ensure that doomed efforts don't drag on indefinitely. Others, like the credit card company Capital One, continually conduct large numbers of market experiments knowing that while most of their tests won't pay off, even the failures will provide valuable insights into customer preferences. Still others launch two or more projects with the same goal, sending teams in different directions simultaneously. This approach – called "simultaneous management" by civil engineering professor Alexander Laufer – creates the potential for a healthy cross-fertilization of new ideas and techniques.

While companies are beginning to accept the value of failure in the abstract – at the level of corporate policies, processes, and practices – it's an entirely different matter at the personal level. Everyone hates to fail. We assume, rationally or not, that we'll suffer embarrassment and a loss of esteem and stature. And nowhere is the fear of failure more intense and debilitating than in the competitive world of business, where a mistake can mean losing a bonus, a promotion, or even a job.

During his years leading Monsanto, Robert Shapiro was struck by how terrified his employees were of failing. They had been trained to see an unsuccessful product or project as a personal rebuke. Shapiro tried hard to change that perception, knowing that it hindered the kind of creative thinking that fueled his business. He explained to his employees that every product and project was an experiment and that its backers failed only if their experiment was a halfhearted, careless effort with poor results. But a deliberate, well-thought-out effort that didn't succeed was not only excusable but desirable.

Such an approach to mistake making is characteristic of people we call "failure-tolerant leaders" – executives who, through their words and actions, help people overcome their fear of failure and, in the process, create a culture of intelligent risk taking

Source: R. Farson and R. Keyes (2002) *Harvard Busines Review,* 80 (8): 64–71.

that leads to sustained innovation. These leaders don't just accept failure; they encourage it. We've studied a number of failure-tolerant leaders – in business, politics, sports, and science – and found some common threads in what they do. They try to break down the social and bureaucratic barriers that separate them from their followers. They engage at a personal level with the people they lead. They avoid giving either praise or criticism, preferring to take a nonjudgmental, analytical posture as they interact with staff. They openly admit their own mistakes rather than covering them up or shifting the blame. And they try to root out the destructive competitiveness built into most organizations.

First and foremost, though, failure-tolerant leaders push people to see beyond simplistic, traditional definitions of failure. They know that as long as someone views failure as the opposite of success rather than its complement, that person will never be able to take the risks necessary for innovation.

Move Beyond Success and Failure

Of course, there are failures and there are *failures*. Some mistakes are lethal – producing and marketing a dysfunctional car tire, for example. At no time can management be casual about issues of health and safety. But encouraging failure doesn't mean abandoning supervision, quality control, or respect for sound practices. Just the opposite. Managing for failure requires executives to be more engaged, not less. Although mistakes are inevitable when launching innovation initiatives, management cannot abdicate its responsibility to assess the nature of the failures. Some are excusable errors; others are simply the result of sloppiness. Those willing to take a close look at what happened and why can usually tell the difference. Failure-tolerant leaders identify excusable mistakes and approach them as outcomes to be examined, understood, and built upon. They often ask simple but illuminating questions when a project falls short of its goals:

- Was the project designed conscientiously, or was it carelessly organized?
- Could the failure have been prevented with more thorough research or consultation?
- Was the project a collaborative process, or did those involved resist useful input from colleagues or fail to inform interested parties of their progress?
- Did the project remain true to its goals, or did it appear to be driven solely by personal interests?
- Were projections of risks, costs, and timing honest or deceptive?
- Were the same mistakes made repeatedly?

Distinguishing between excusable and inexcusable failure offers two broad benefits. First, it gives managers a tool to build a non-punitive environment for mistake making while allowing them to encourage thoughtfully pursued projects that, should they fail, will yield productive mistakes. Second, it allows managers to non-judgmentally promote the sort of productive mistake making that is the basis for learning. By revealing what doesn't work – in the lab or in the marketplace – a failure flowing from a carefully designed and executed project provides insight into what will work.

Success can be approached in much the same way. Like mistakes, all successes are not created equal. A success due to a fortunate accident is not the organizational equivalent of one resulting from a thoughtfully pursued project. Thus, successes might be approached with questions similar to those posed about failures. How much was due to good fortune, how much to the hard work of its creators? Were all contributors acknowledged? Did the success move us closer to our goals? Will it actually serve customers' needs or simply merit an award from peers? By taking this perspective and raising such questions, managers can begin to treat success and failure similarly, more like the siblings they actually are.

Some managers may find that idea difficult to embrace. Treat success and failure the same? Shouldn't I reward success? And even if I don't reprimand an employee who fails, shouldn't I at least call attention to the mistake? Well, no. We suggest a different approach.

Get Engaged

The best coaches take victory and defeat in stride. "I didn't get consumed by losses," said the legendary NFL coach Don Shula," and I didn't get overwhelmed by successes." Failure-tolerant leaders in all fields do the same. Rather than pursue success, they focus on increasing their organizations' intellectual capital: the experience, knowledge, and creativity of the workforce. How? Through engagement. These managers take a tangible interest in their employees' projects. Instead of simply evaluating an employee's efforts, they try to understand the work, interpret it, and discover its meaning to the individual. Often, they are in a position to see the work in a larger context, making them the ideal people to discuss a project's history, goals, and larger significance to the organization.

That process is more collaborative than supervisory. Failure-tolerant managers show interest, express support, and ask pertinent questions: What's new with your project? What kinds of problems are you having? Taking the long view, what might the next steps be? Conversations are less about whether the project is succeeding or failing than about what can be learned from the experience. When a manager and employee are deeply engaged in that discussion, both of them enter the same kind of high-performance zone that athletes do when they're operating at their very best. In this zone, evaluation is less relevant than the subject of where to go from here.

Enlightened managers strive to be collaborative rather than controlling. Only through engaged conversations over time can managers create failure-tolerant work environments that invite innovation. This is not to say that a major achievement shouldn't be applauded, or that repeated, avoidable mistakes should be tolerated. But astute managers mark the daily progress of small successes and failures with an even-handed, open curiosity about the lessons learned and the next steps to take.

Listening is more central to this process than talking. Research on workplace creativity shows that it's not the individual employee's freedom as much as managerial involvement that produces creative acts. No incentive can match the obvious appreciation shown by a manager's interest and enthusiasm. Path-breaking leaders such as Thomas Edison, General Motors' Charles Kettering, the Watsons at IBM, and 3M's William McKnight were famous for schmoozing with employees – not second-guessing or criticizing, but engaging in animated discussions about projects. Nothing does more for productivity, morale, and employee retention. "Edison made work interesting," said a machinist and draftsman who spent a half-century working for the inventor. "He made me feel that I was making something with him. I wasn't just a workman."

Don't Praise, Analyze

New ideas are most likely to emerge in the workplace when managers treat steps in the innovation process – those that work and those that don't – with less evaluation and more interpretation. They don't praise or penalize; they analyze.

Less praise? Haven't managers been told not to skimp on compliments? They have indeed. But psychologists who have studied the effects of praise question its value. As with criticism, compliments can actually demotivate people. Recipients may feel manipulated or think too much is expected of them. Research has found that children playing games lose interest once they're rewarded or complimented for their play. In one study, students praised less by their science teachers did a better job of conducting experiments on their own than the ones who were praised more. That is why, in place of perfunctory praise, many educators are shifting to a teaching style in which they ask questions, give feedback, and show interest, but are spare with compliments. "That's great!" gives way to "I see you've decided to use liquid nitrogen in this experiment." Such a specific response shows real interest in a student's work and is appreciated more than repeated praise. In the workplace, praise can become what is called a "dissatisfier." Like a salary, it is less likely to motivate when it's given out than demotivate when it's expected but withheld. So a manager cannot suddenly stop praising an employee who has come to expect it. But when an engaged manager takes a genuine interest in an employee's work, the need for compliments declines.

Genuine engagement, though, can require far more time than the 11 minutes per task that managers spend, on average. Because involvement takes more time than keeping your distance, occasions for doing so must be chosen carefully. Engaging with employees is demanding and risky; it can threaten a manager's authority. The more involved you get with employees, the harder it becomes to reprimand them when necessary. Although not the same as personal friendships, engaged professional relationships resemble them in ways that can hinder the supervisory process. The challenge is to learn how to get closely involved with an employee's work without presuming to be pals.

Managers may be wary of this type of engagement because it can be unpredictable, raising questions they can't answer or might rather avoid. But that's a price worth paying. The open-ended, less formal nature of an engaged relationship can lead to the unexplored terrain where innovation lies.

Earn Empathy

While the notion of encouraging mistakes may seem alien – or at least a little unnerving – to many managers, it has some celebrated champions. When Jack Welch was head of GE, he said, "We reward failure," explaining that to do otherwise would only squelch daring. GM's Kettering, regarded as second only to Thomas Edison as America's leading inventor mogul, liked to say that a good research man failed every time but the last one. "He treats his failures as practice shots," Kettering noted, adding that he himself had been wrong 99.9% of the time. What every educated person needed to learn, he felt, was "that it's not a disgrace to fail, and that you must analyze each failure to find its cause.... You must learn how to fail intelligently. Failing is one of the greatest arts in the world. One fails forward toward success."

Welch and Kettering knew that creating a risk-friendly environment requires demonstrating unequivocally – in deeds more than words – that stumbles on the innovation path are forgiven. How better for managers to achieve this end than by publicizing their own missteps? The late Roberto Goizueta got years of one-liners from the New Coke fiasco that occurred during his tenure. Admitting his mistake conveyed to his employees better than a hundred speeches or a thousand memos that "learning failures," even on a grand scale, were tolerated.

A former Lockheed executive recalled the time CEO Dan Haughton gathered his company's manufacturing heads to discuss his own errors. One notable mistake, Haughton recounted, was when Howard Hughes once called to tell him that Douglas Aircraft was in trouble and that he should get right over there and buy it "before Jimmy McDonnell [did]." Haughton told his managers that not taking Hughes's advice was the biggest blunder he had made in business. Had he bought Douglas Aircraft, Haughton could have consolidated his company's operations in Southern California and avoided costly future moves.

The former Lockheed executive said that he and his colleagues left the meeting with increased respect for Haughton and renewed motivation to take their own risks. Haughton had told them in the most eloquent way possible that losing a gamble wasn't the worst thing that could happen to them. The message they took away: "If Dan Haughton can make mistakes, I guess I can, too."

Similarly, managers at 3M routinely reinforce the company's mistake-tolerant atmosphere by freely admitting their own goofs. Former CEO L.D. DeSimone never hesitated to recount how he repeatedly tried to stop the development of Thinsulate. Luckily, DeSimone failed, and Thinsulate became one of the company's most successful products. By being so candid about his near blunder, DeSimone powerfully conveyed that it's okay to be wrong and to admit it when you are.

Far from revealing weakness, admitting mistakes shows a leader's self-confidence. It helps forge closer ties with employees and colleagues. A blunder admitted is empathy earned. Leaders who don't cover up their errors reveal themselves as human – they become people whom others can admire and identify with.

Think of Ulysses S. Grant, whose success as a military officer grew directly out of his earlier problems in civilian life. Grant's well-known battles with alcoholism made him more sympathetic to other's weaknesses; his struggle to control his addiction helped him understand and deal with lapses of discipline among subordinates. Grant had also failed repeatedly in business, suffering humiliating experiences that made him more humble than other officers. His failures also made him more daring. Grant took more chances during combat than other generals did. Many like General George McClellan, who had led brilliantly successful lives before the war, lost battle after battle during their military careers.

The greatness of many U.S. presidents was also built on a foundation of unremarkable performance early on. Before Valley Forge, Washington failed repeatedly as a military officer and did a so-so job of running his plantation. Lincoln suffered multiple setbacks in business and politics. Franklin Roosevelt – a mama's boy and a mediocre student – was generally considered a political lightweight before he moved into the White House. It's taken for granted by historians that if he hadn't been paralyzed as a young man, Roosevelt would never have developed the grit, depth, and empathy he needed to become one of our best presidents. FDR's successor, Harry Truman – today ranked among our top half-dozen chief executives – didn't go to college, was a mediocre farmer, and failed as a haberdasher. "Most of our better presidents," observed Ronald Reagan's campaign manager John Sears, "learned to empathize through suffering personal tragedy or failure.... There is something about losing and coming back from it that burns character into a man's soul, breeds confidence without arrogance, and makes a man believable when he talks about problems."

Employees do better when they know they're being supervised by human beings, not detached directors. This doesn't mean they spurn self-confident leaders. We all want to believe that our leaders are competent and have exceptional qualities. But we sometimes want a bit of the opposite as well. An inscrutable mask makes it harder to lead. Both vulnerability and transparency are important for leaders and organizations alike.

Collaborate to Innovate

Creating a culture in which people feel comfortable with failure also requires abandoning traditional ideas about personal competition. The idea that achievement is maximized when we go at one another tooth and nail is engraved on our national psyche. But when the road to success requires making others fail, innovation gets left by the wayside. Competition infects coworkers with a desire to win rather than to solve problems and move projects forward. In the process, employees inhibit the free flow of information so vital to innovation. Those who feel their work is being judged on conventional concepts of success and failure, and who feel they're competing with coworkers for the brass ring, will want to protect information rather than share it. This is a textbook way to squelch innovation. Companies become the losers. If 3M's

Spencer Silver had concealed information about the imperfect adhesive he invented with another colleague, Post-it notes might never have been developed.

Prizes for performance are especially effective at undermining teamwork because they place competition above collaboration. A food services company we'll call Comestibles once had a contest that awarded regional offices that posted the best sales records. Those who won got free vacations. This competition produced a few happy winners and lots of disgruntled losers. Winning became such a fetish that Comestibles' employees began hoarding information they might otherwise have shared with one another. Some even fudged their figures to gain an edge. Rather than encourage employees to collaborate and share information, Comestibles' motivational program created an atmosphere of competition that stifled creativity, openness, and honesty.

Meanwhile, some future-mined companies like Royal Dutch/Shell and Monsanto have developed work groups that emphasize collaboration. The main objective of these groups is to exchange information, not hide it, as so often happens in the heat of competition. 3M has encouraged idea sharing for decades, from the coffee-and-donut skull sessions years ago (like the one where Spencer Silver discussed his not-sticky-enough glue) to today's more formal Tech Forums and in-house trade shows.

Failure-tolerant leaders encourage collaboration, understanding that it is the real road to innovation. They see it as the best means for tapping into the imaginations of employees who are not especially competitive but who might have invaluable, innovative ideas. Because such people don't feel the need to win every exchange of ideas, they don't do well in gatherings of colleagues playing verbal king-of-the-mountain. Competition-based cultures can be especially hard on new hires, introverts, minorities, women, and those for whom English is a second language. It's difficult to exaggerate the stifling effect that competitive idea exchange can have on some of these people. That's where communications technologies can help.

Communications technologies have opened the doors for idea sharing. In organizations of all kinds, they have encouraged bottom-up decision making, loosened sticky spigots of information, and become electronic suggestion boxes. Royal Dutch/Shell, for instance, has found that many of its most worthwhile innovations have come from employees via e-mail. Similarly, IBM's rebirth as a more nimble, Web-savvy company began when CEO Lou Gerstner invited employees at all levels to communicate with him by e-mail soon after he arrived in 1993. It did not take long for Gerstner to begin hearing about stalled projects and unsolved problems that were stuck in IBM's many corporate cobwebs.

E-mail, of course, is only the beginning. Communications technologies now extend well beyond basic e-mail into various kinds of both real-time and asynchronous electronic connections. They include chat rooms and news groups; conferencing systems; technologies for surveys, voting, and joint document preparation; distance education; remote control of computers for demonstrations or group graphic designs; and more. As Robert Shapiro once said, many of these technological developments "just rip through hierarchy."

Electronic communications are ideal for involving creative people who might be shunned or perceived as marginal in organizations that rely too heavily on face-to-face idea exchange. The asynchronous nature of many of today's communications tech-nologies gives employees the opportunity to edit and dig deeper into what they really want to say; the typical pressures of face-to-face meetings – of having to speak up and be aggressive with ideas – are reduced. What's more, use of electronic communications often means that an employee's age, gender, ethnicity, physical appearance, and per-sonality quirks no longer determine how his suggestions are received. The result is that companies are better able to retain unconventional, creative employees who may be bad at office politics but good at generating fresh ideas.

Give the Green Light

At Royal Dutch/Shell, innovation teams fielded suggestions e-mailed by fellow employees. Using a method devised by the consulting firm Strategos, six-person "GameChanger" teams met weekly to assess ideas. As Gary Hamel, the head of Strategos, reported in his article "Bringing Silicon Valley Inside" (HBR September 1999), the GameChanger teams assessed 320 proposals during their first two years of operation. The proposals were evaluated not only on the basis of what Shell stood to lose by pursuing the suggestion, but also what it could lose by *not* doing so. Of Shell's five top innovations in 1999, four bubbled up through GameChanger meetings. One of these was the company's Light Touch method of using laser sensors to discover hydrocarbon emissions of oil deposits. Among the most striking discoveries of the GameChanger process was how many ideas came from employees who weren't thought to be innovative. It turned out that most had never had opportunities to express their ideas.

Failure-tolerant leaders emphasize that a good idea is a good idea, whether it comes from Peter Drucker, *Reader's Digest,* or an obnoxious coworker. This approach blunts the group's natural disposition to squelch imaginative, though difficult, participants. Psychologist Michael Kahn suggests running meetings using what he calls "barn raising," a model based on the way pioneers pitched in as a community to help one another construct outbuildings. According to this model, rather than engage in one-upmanship, members are encouraged to listen carefully to each person's idea, then add their thoughts to see if they can build that idea into a more valuable contribution. Such an atmosphere of exploration lets group members search diligently for value in ideas that might otherwise have been discarded. They also feel comfortable knowing that their suggestions will receive the same treatment.

Like Shell's GameChanger groups, Kahn's barn-raising techniques are an effective catalyst for innovation. So, too, is a gathering known as a "community of practice," or a small group of employees within an organization that meets regularly to discuss common interests. The value of these communities goes far beyond information exchange. In their article "Communities of Practice: The Organizational Frontier" (HBR) January–February 2000), management consultants Etienne Wenger and William Snyder refer to these gatherings as "petri dishes for entrepreneurial insights." The way these groups arrive at ideas is similar to brainstorming: Members suspend judgment and allow others to toss out suggestions in an atmosphere of cooperation and support rather than competition and criticism. Unlike skunk works, these groups are ad hoc gatherings of people from many parts of an organization; their collective attitudes can often infuse an organization's culture as a whole, particularly an attitude of daring. As the member of one Indiana community of practice told Wenger and Snyder, "I took a risk because I was confident I had the backing of my community – and it paid off."

What's really going on in these groups is courage enhancement. By creating an atmosphere of safety and reducing the pressure to succeed, the groups give people the confidence to share their ideas. Employees who once felt inhibited suddenly feel free to express their thoughts, frequently contributing to the innovations that drive the company.

Failure-tolerant leaders send clear messages to their organizations that constructive mistakes are not only acceptable but worthwhile. Employees feel that they have been given the green light to set out and explore, no longer thinking in terms of success or failure but instead in terms of learning and experience. And that's the key to coming up with breakthrough products and processes: viewing mistakes for the educational tools they are and as signposts on the road to success.

Paradox of Coordination and Control

Jody Hoffer Gittell

Whether in the production of goods or the delivery of services, coordination among front-line employees helps organizations achieve high performance outcomes. When front-line employees coordinate directly with each other, problems can be resolved on the spot in a collaborative and timely way, without referral up the hierarchy for resolution by their superiors. Horizontal coordination is particularly valuable in turbulent settings where there is a premium on achieving rapid response to unpredictable changes in operating conditions.

How should horizontally coordinated organizations ensure that the actions taken by its front-line employees are consistent with organizational goals? To achieve control in such organizations, much of the current organizational literature suggests that supervision should be replaced with systems of accountability and performance measurement. In flat organizations, employees can focus on the work itself and on their customers rather than on the chain of command.[1] However, the effectiveness of this approach for achieving coordination and control is questionable. My research in the airline industry shows that supervisors can *support* coordination among front-line employees.[2] Contrary to popular belief, coordination benefits from strengthening the role of supervisors while weakening the role of accountability and performance measurement. Of particular interest is the finding that systems of accountability and performance measurement, rather than being ideal for horizontally coordinated organizations, actually have unintended *negative* consequences. Supervision on the other hand has unexpected *positive* consequences.

This article explores the relationship between coordination and control in the context of two major U.S. airlines—American and Southwest. Although the story of Southwest has been told, important aspects have been neglected, perhaps because they do not "fit" our common wisdom about how organizations should achieve high performance.

The Performance Challenge

The flight departure process is one of the most complex processes that an airline performs on a daily basis. Repeated hundreds of times daily in dozens of locations, its

---

Source: J.H. Gittell (2000) *California Management Review*, 42 (3): 101–17.

success or failure can make or break an airline's reputation for convenience and reliability. A departure is successful from the customer's point of view if it does not involve unnecessary hassles and if it results in the on-time arrival of the customer and his or her baggage. A departure is successful from the airline's point of view if these customer outcomes are achieved in an efficient way—without excess airport staffing or gate time for the airplane. Excess staffing carries obvious costs. Gate time is also costly, because it represents time that the plane is sitting at the gate, not being utilized and not earning passenger revenues. Based on lost revenues alone, the cost of a hypothetical five-minute increase in gate time was estimated at $1.6 billion, or $4,700 per employee, for the ten major U.S. airlines over a one-year period.[3]

To achieve these performance goals, a multitude of tasks must be performed by groups with distinct skills under changing conditions in a limited period of time—between the arrival of a plane and its departure for the next flight. Pilots, flight attendants, gate agents, ticket agents, operations agents, mechanics, caterers, cabin cleaners, ramp agents, baggage handlers, cargo handlers, and fuelers all play significant roles (see Figure 20.1). Given high levels of uncertainty, interdependence, and time constraints, coordination among these groups is critical.

Accountability of Front-Line Employees

American: Functional Accountability

Under Robert Crandall's leadership in the 1980s and 1990s, American increased its focus on accountability. "It helps a lot just to keep score," noted one field manager. "People are naturally competitive. They absolutely need to know the score. Once they know, they will do something about it. Every delay comes to my attention and gets a full investigation … The last thing most of them want is the spotlight on them. I just increased the amount they had to do to keep the spotlight off of themselves." Each time a delay occurred, managers on duty were responsible for figuring our which function caused it. Immediate penalties accompanied delays, in the form of having to explain what happened. If a delay occurred on a flight scheduled to make connections elsewhere, "Crandall wants to see the corpse," said one field manager. "It is management by intimidation."

This system had the unintended effect of encouraging employees to look out for themselves and avoid recrimination, rather than focusing on their shared goals of on-time performance, accurate baggage handling and satisfied customers. "If you ask anyone here, what's the last thing you think of when there's a problem," said a ramp supervisor, "I bet your bottom dollar it's the customer. And these are guys who bust their butts everyday. But they're thinking, how do I keep my ass out of the sling."

American's system of accountability also resulted in a great deal of time spent trying to sort out the cause of delays. "There is so much internal debate and reports and meetings, "said one field manager. "This is time that we could be focusing on the passengers." Another result appeared to be frequent misidentification of the problem. "We have delay codes for when the pope visits, or if there are beetles in the cockpit," said another field manager only half in jest, "but sometimes a problem occurs

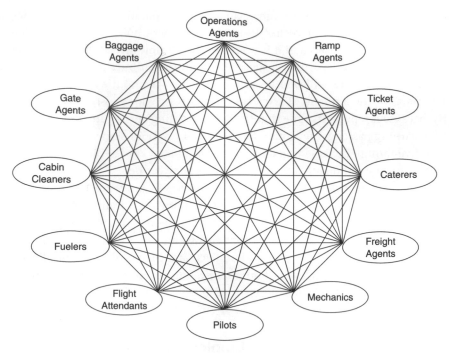

Figure 20.1 *The Flight Departure Process*

routinely and we have no code for it. What usually happens is a communication breakdown, but we have no code for that. So we tag it on the last group off the plane."

Southwest: Cross-Functional Accountability

Determining the cause of a delay was a conflict-ridden process at Southwest, as it was at American, and it often deteriorated from problem solving to finger pointing and blame avoidance. Southwest countered this tendency in the early 1990s by instituting a "team delay" which allowed less precise reporting of the cause of delays, with the goal of diffusing blame and encouraging learning. According to Jim Wimberly, executive vice-president of operations, "We had too many angry disagreements between flight attendants and gate agents about whose delay it was. It was too hard to determine whose fault it was." One of Southwest's chief pilots explained, "The team delay is used to point out problems between two or three different employee groups in working together. We used to do it [in the following way]: if people were still in the jetway at departure time, it was a station delay. If people were on-board at departure time, it was a flight crew delay. But now if you see everybody working as a team, and it's a team problem, you call it a team delay. It's been a very positive thing."

The reduced precision of performance measurement did not appear to concern Southwest leaders. "We could have more delay categories," said Wimberly. "But we only end up chasing our tail."

Accountability of Field Managers

American: Focus on Measurement

As part of the focus on accountability at American, field managers were given performance standards, called Minimum Acceptable Performance Standards (MAPS), for on-time performance, baggage handling, and customer complaints. This led to what a field manager called being "harassed on a daily basis ... Headquarters has a performance analysis department that is looking at my MAPS every day, analyzing the station's performance. Failure to meet MAPS is perceived to result in punitive action."

Another field manager gave his perspective on the new regime of accountability: "The hardest part ... has been changing the way I manage. I have grown a lot as a manager over this past year, but it has not been easy," he explained. "It is scary to delegate, especially here, where there is a very strong company culture toward accountability. This is fine, but the penalties that go along with that accountability make people afraid to take risks—afraid to let go of their control. To push decision making and responsibility down, you have to be willing to let others make mistakes and learn from them."

Managers noted that there was a split between the field and headquarters, and that the information flow between them was based largely on the numbers. For some field managers, their reaction to the split between field and headquarters was bitterness, "Better communication clearly matters at the station level, but it doesn't make a bit of difference what they do at headquarters," according to one field manager. "In this company, accountability is statistical," said a human resources manager. "The field manager is judged on the numbers and not on how he got them. He could have used a club for all it matters to his rewards." An employee relations manager concurred: "All that matters is the numbers; how you achieve them is secondary. This is part of the culture of fear." Information in the form of numbers went from the field to headquarters for evaluation, but there was little discussion—and little learning.

Southwest: Focus on Learning

At Southwest, the role of headquarters appeared to be supportive rather than punitive. The relationship between field and headquarters was characterized by a two-way flow of information and a focus on learning. Field managers were vague about how their performance was assessed. "I don't know," was one typical response, given with a laugh. "I'll hear about it if I'm not doing a good job. I get free rein if I do OK." "It is watched, but there is no fear factor," said another field manager. "I know what the relationship [between headquarters and the station] is usually like," according to another field manager, "because I worked at Eastern for 20 years. It's usually an entrenched bureaucracy between the station manager and headquarters. Its nothing like that here." "We do what we think is right, and talk directly to our executive vice presidents and Herb," said his assistant manager. " They are just a phone call away. If they question something we did today, they will call tomorrow."

Colleen Barrett, executive vice president of customers, suggested that this learning approach was particularly valuable when performance was lagging. "There is one station we're real concerned about right now," she said. "We've sent in a team of managers from other stations for a couple of months to help them turn things around. We made it clear to [the station manager] that we're here to help. We are talking every day."

Supervision

American: Large Supervisory Spans of Control

Along with the focus on accountability under Crandall at American came a dramatic reduction in supervisory staffing, leaving one supervisor for each 30 to 40 front-line workers. Because front-line workers were held accountable through measurement of functional performance, supervisors were thought to be redundant. Monitoring occurred through impersonal measurement rather than through the personal intervention of supervisors.

However, supervisors had been engaged in more than monitoring. Their roles had also included coaching and feedback to front-line employees. Reducing the number of supervisors reduced their ability to carry out these other roles. As one supervisor put it, "[Now] we only have time to focus on the bad apples."

Southwest: Small Supervisory Spans of Control

Unlike American, Southwest had not attempted to increase the supervisory span of control. They had one supervisor for every 8 to 9 front-line employees, rather than one for every 30 to 40 as at American. The nature of the supervisory relationship appeared to be understood differently at American and Southwest. Supervisors at Southwest told me that the people who reported to them were their internal customers and that their job was to help these people do their jobs better. "We are responsible for what the agents do," explained one supervisor. "It is very difficult sometimes, because it's such a family-oriented company. You might feel like a sister to one of the [front-line workers], then you have to bring discipline. You have to step back and put the friendship aside and say, 'I don't agree with what you just did.' But the [front-line workers] are also our customers. We are here to help them do their jobs."

The supervisory role at Southwest was not primarily to monitor front-line employees: "If there is a problem like one person taking a three-hour lunch, they take care of that themselves for the most part. Peer pressure works well." In addition, supervision was not just about telling people what to do: "You could just point to this and that. But you don't have to—everybody knows what to do."

The supervisor's role was primarily to facilitate learning. "I would be personally offended if their only drive was that if the plane didn't leave on time, they'd come in to my office to—you know, the threats," said a field manager. "I don't feel they're afraid of me and that means a lot. If there's a delay, we find out why it happened. We get ideas from them on how to do it better next time. If you've got that kind of relationship then they're not going to be afraid.

"Say there was a ten-minute delay because freight was excessive. If I'm screaming, I won't know why it was late. They'll think, 'He's an idiot, if only he knew.' Then they'll start leaving stuff behind or they'll just shove it in, and I won't know. If we ask, 'Hey what happened?' then the next day the problem is taken care of. We move the freight, we re-route the freight to where it's less damaging. You have to be in that mode every day. There's no one person who can do it. We all succeed together—and all fail together. You have to truly live it."

Employee Selection

American: Selection Without Regard to Teamwork

At American, hiring decisions for front-line employees tended to focus on technical skills, as well as interpersonal skills for those who dealt directly with customers. However, there was no explicit concern reflected in hiring practices with how potential employees would work with each other across functional lines. In the case of airport employees, said one supervisor, "the work groups are so well-defined that … we don't look for that. It would cause problems." The hiring of flight attendants was viewed similarly. "We would not ask how this person would interface with other groups," said a human resource manager.

When hiring pilots, "we look for command presence, the most self-assured arrogant people we can possibly find," said an employee relations manager. Problems arose from these selection criteria. Pilots were frequently reported not to show a great deal of respect for their colleagues in other functions. "There is a certain amount of hostility that pilots face from the other employee groups," said another manager. "The personality of the pilot generates that hostility." This personality was not inherent to pilots, however, but rather was an artifact of the selection process.

Southwest: Selection for Teamwork

Southwest, on the other hand, placed a great deal of importance on hiring people who were inclined toward teamwork. According to Ann Rhodes, former vice president of people, one of the important unwritten rules at Southwest was that "you can't be an elitist."[4] "We get mutual respect partly from the selection process," said a chief pilot. "We really try to select people with the right attitude. We evaluate the impact they will have on internal and external customers." The emphasis on selection was due to a belief that certain critical attitudes could not be readily taught. According to a field manager: "One thing we cannot teach is attitudes toward peers or to other groups. There's a code, a way you respond to every individual who works at Southwest. The easiest way to get in trouble at Southwest is to offend another employee. We need people to respond favorably. It promotes good working relationships."

Airport employees were selected through a time-consuming process designed to identify the desired characteristics. "The entire process starts with an interview," said a ramp manager. "I'm very involved with that. Something we look at is people who are very team-oriented from prior work experiences. We use target selection. In answering this question, take an incident from your prior work and walk us through it. Do they limit themselves to the job, or go above and beyond? We don't just look at work history. We've turned away people with 15-16 years of airline experience in favor of people with none. The concept of teamwork is tough. You really don't know if a person will be able to cross over from his or her primary responsibility and do other things. We get a feel for people who will go above and beyond."

Even when hiring pilots, Southwest explicitly sought people who lacked an attitude of superiority and who seemed likely to treat coworkers with respect, in addition to being highly skilled in their profession. A story circulated around industry pilot circles that a pilot came to interview at Southwest and treated an administrative assistant with disrespect. "He didn't get the job," the story concludes.

Conflict Resolution

American: Minimal Conflict Resolution

At American, conflict resolution was largely designed to address grievances that employees filed with managers, rather than conflicts among peers in different departments. Field managers claimed that resolving conflicts among employees was a relatively unimportant part of their jobs. Their performance evaluation system was based on results, they claimed, and it mattered little to their rewards how those results were achieved. Though "supporting good working relationships" was included in their job descriptions, that item was allocated zero weight in the formal system of performance measurement that governed relationships between field managers and headquarters at American.

Southwest: Proactive Conflict Resolution

At Southwest, by contrast, resolving conflicts between functional groups was taken quite seriously. "What's unique about Southwest is that we're real proactive about conflict," said a field manager. "There is a lot of stress when the plane is on the ground," said Wimberly. "Inevitably some conflict will arise. All employees know, particularly operational employees, how things are supposed to go. If something happens out of the ordinary, if you feel someone didn't handle something correctly, you fill out a report."

"We are trying to push resolution of these conflicts and problems down to where they actually occur," Wimberly explained. "When the senior managers get the final report, we decide if a meeting is needed, if it looks like they haven't resolved it. We tell them this is not a disciplinary meeting ... We'll leave the room if you like. We are just moderators; the focus is between employees and on how important teamwork is."

It is sometimes difficult to get employees together, for example if the conflict involves a pilot who is based in Baltimore and a gate agent who is based in Phoenix. Convening these sessions can also be intimidating, even for experienced managers. "You never know how it will turn out," said one. "Sometimes it blows up in your face."

Still the results were usually worth the trouble, he said. According to Barrett, "it is wonderful to see the lights go off in people's eyes when they understand the other person's point of view."

Alternative Systems of Coordination and Control

These two case studies show that there are alternative systems for achieving coordination and control of the flight departure process. These alternative systems are summarized in Table 20.1. Both are internally consistent and self-reinforcing, but one appears to be more effective than the other. One system achieves control through functional accountability, measuring performance "by the numbers," and assigning outcomes to individual departments. Because control in such an organization is based on objective performance evaluation, which can be carried out from a distance, supervisory functions can be minimized. Such an organization can therefore become quite flat in the field operation. Systems of functional accountability thus achieve control in a fairly efficient way. However, systems of functional accountability tend to produce weak coordination. Control is achieved in a way that undermines rather than supports coordination.

This system is exemplified by American Airlines. American's design was premised on control through "the numbers." Empowerment meant intensifying accountability of managers in the field and extending accountability to front-line employees, in both cases using "the numbers" rather than traditional supervisory relationships to transmit performance information. However, this reliance on the numbers had the effect of exacerbating the functionally oriented character of accountability, reinforcing front-line employees' inclination to focus on their own piece of the process and ignore downstream consequences. American's functional orientation was not conducive to cross-functional coordination. When American's field managers tried to empower front-line workers, their efforts were hampered by the narrow functional perspective of front-line employees.

Southwest's system, by contrast, was premised on the need for coordination. Over time, Southwest's leaders developed a way to achieve control without undermining coordination. They created the concept of a "team delay" to reduce the precision of

Table 20.1 *Alternative Systems for Achieving Coordination and Control*

	American	Southwest
Control Mechanisms	Functional Accountabilty	Cross-Functional Accountability
	Larger Supervisory Span of Control	Small Supervisory Span of Control
Human Resource Practices	Selection for Functional Skills	Selection for Cross-Functional Teamwork
	Minimal Cross-Functional Conflict Resolution	Proactive Cross-Functional Conflict Resolution

performance measurement, in order to reduce unproductive blaming. They staffed supervisory positions adequately to allow supervisors to play a coaching role, reinforcing a focus on learning, and allowing for richer communication across levels of the organization than could be captured by "the numbers" alone. Likewise in the relationship between headquarters and the field, they took the approach of active feedback delivered in a non-punitive way, resulting in richer two-way communication than could be captured by quantitative measures alone. To further support this system of cross-functional accountability, they hired people based on their potential for engaging in cross-functional teamwork. They established a process to resolve conflicts between the functions and to build a common understanding of the departure process.

American's system allows it to operate with a relatively low level of trust: indeed it is virtually guaranteed to produce low trust by setting up conflicts over who is responsible for problems. However, in areas that require high levels of coordination, like the flight departure process, it is less effective than the alternative. Southwest's system is conductive to coordination of flight departures, but it is far more vulnerable to the loss of trust. Employees are not as easily evaluated and motivated according to clearly delineated functional goals. Good performance is not so easily defined. Often, it is "doing whatever is needed to get the job done." Such performance goals cannot be measured easily "by the numbers." More fine-tuned evaluation is needed. The Southwest model achieves control instead through practices that emphasize the rich flow of information up and down the organization. The span of control is much smaller, to allow a more fine-tuned interaction between supervisors and front-line employees.

These two cases suggest several propositions for achieving control in a way that supports rather than undermines coordination; these are presented in Table 20.2.

Broader Support for Propositions

Based on simple correlations between organizational practices and outcomes at the original nine sites (two from American Airlines, two from Continental Airlines, two from Southwest Airlines and three from United Airlines), we see broader evidence to suggest that different systems for coordinating and control can lead to significantly different outcomes (see Table 20.3). Greater cross-functional accountability, smaller supervisory spans of control, greater selection for teamwork, and more active cross-functional conflict resolution are associated with more frequent communication, stronger shared goals, greater shared knowledge, and higher levels of mutual respect among employees in different functions. The same set of organizational practices is associated with higher quality performance and greater efficiency of the flight departure process.

Theorists Disagree about Accountability

Contrary to these findings, classical organizational theorists argued that functional accountability is an effective way to achieve control.[5] They recognized risks of

Table 20.2   *Propositions*

Control Mechanisms	Cross-Functional Accountability	Shared accountability across functional lines diffuses blame and finger pointing, encourages shared goals, and improves quality and efficiency performance.
	Supervisory Span of Control	Small supervisory spans of control allow coaching and feedback across levels of the organization, improving shared goals and shared knowledge among employees, as well as quality and efficiency performance.
Human Resource Practices	Selection for Teamwork	Selecting for teamwork identifies people who will treat their counterparts in other functions with respect, and who will take responsibility for outcomes beyond their own functions, improving both quality and efficiency performance.
	Cross-Functional Conflict Resolution	Cross-functional conflict resolution resolves misunderstandings as they emerge, and creates a better shared understanding of the overall process and its participants, improving both quality and efficiency performance.

functional accountability: that employees would focus on functional goals at the expense of organizational goals and that they might therefore fail to cooperate across functional lines. Still, they argued, the gains achieved from control out-weighed these risks.

Proponents of TQM took a strong position against functional accountability, arguing that efforts to achieve control through functional accountability have detrimental effects on information sharing and learning.[6] Preoccupation with functional accountability leads to blaming, which in turn causes information to be distorted or to go underground.[7] "Accounting and reward systems [should be] designed to *diffuse* blame for problems and thus to encourage collective efforts to identify and rectify their sources."[8] Organization and work design theorists have also argued for shared accountability. If participants in a process are responsible for overall process outcomes and not just their own piece of the process, they are more likely to do what is necessary to get the job done.[9]

A handful of organizational theorists have gone farther, arguing that quantiative performance measurement inevitably generates some level of dysfunctional behavior, due to the impossibility of designing performance measures that encompass all

Table 20.3 *Organizational Practices and Outcomes (n=9)*

Organizational Practices[a]	Outcomes[b]					
	Frequent Communication	Shared Goals	Shared Knowledge	Mutual Respect	Quality Performance	Efficiency Performance
Control Mechanisms						
Cross–Functional Accountability	.746** (.021)	.860** (.003)	.800** (.010)	.735** (.024)	.958** (.000)	.927** (.000)
Supervisory Span of Control	–.616** (.077)	.668** (.049)	–.620** (.075)	–.582+ (.100)	–.638+ (.065)	–.748 (.021)
Human Resource Practices						
Selection for Teamwork	.632* (.068)	.811** (.008)	.781** (.013)	.768** (.016)	.924** (.000)	.902** (.001)
Cross–Functional Conflict Resolution	.567+ (.105)	.913** (.001)	.821** (.007)	.868** (.002)	.845** (.004)	.820** (.007)

+ p < .15   * p < .10   ** p < .05.

a. Cross-functional accountability is measured as the number of functions that can be held accountable for a given flight departure delay. Supervisory span of control is measured as the number of front-line employees per supervisor. Hiring for teamwork is measured as the number of functions for which teamwork is an important hiring criterion. Cross-functional conflict resolution is measured as the importance of such conflict resolution to a field manager's job, as perceived by that manager, on a one to five scale. See Jody Hoffer Gittell. "Organizing Work to Support Relational Coordination." *International Journal of Human Management.* 11 (3): 517–539.

b. frequent communication, shared goals, shared knowledge, and mutual respect are measured using a survey of employees. Questions are asked with respect to each respondent's ties to each of the 12 functional groups involved in the flight departure process. Quality and efficiency performance are based on archival data. Quality performance is a reverse-coded index of late arrivals, baggage mishandling and customer complaints. Efficiency performance is a reverse-coded index of turnaround time per departure and staffing per passenger, adjusted for product complexity. Jody Hoffer Gittell, "Organizing Work to Support Relational Coordination. *International Journal of Human Resource Management.* 11 (3): 517–539: Jody Hoffer Gittell, "Relational Coordination and Flight Departure Performance," Harvard Business School Working Paper.

desirable behaviors and outcomes.[10] This problem suggests that systems of quantitative performance measurement need to be supplemented by qualitative performance feedback,[11] something that arguably can be provided by front-line supervisors.

Theorists Disagree about Supervision

However, theorists have also differed on the proper role of supervisors. Many have argued, for example, that supervision is ineffective for motivating discretionary effort.[12] Others have gone farther, suggesting that supervisory monitoring is particularly ineffective in highly interdependent processes.[13] Because such processes are not programmable, supervisors cannot readily monitor employee compliance with them. Participants in highly interdependent processes are therefore more effectively controlled through shared goals, a form of control presumed to be inconsistent with supervision. Some empirical studies have supported this negative view of supervision.[14]

However, others have argued that supervisors can and do play a positive role. Supervisors are in a position to transmit organizational goals to front-line employees through daily interaction with them.[15] Small spans of control give supervisors the ability to observe behaviors and outcomes and to provide useful feedback, roles that are particularly valuable when managing complex, interdependent work processes.[16] Empirical studies have found positive effects of supervision in work settings where supervisory monitoring is clearly not the driving force behind performance—where supervisors are more likely to add value through coaching and feedback.[17]

Alternative Perspective on Control

The strongest systems are those that rely on cross-functional accountability, supplemented by supervisors who are staffed sufficiently to engage in an ongoing dialogue about how to achieve effective performance, rather than simply measuring performance relative to a set of pre-established behaviors or goals.

The evidence presented here supports this perspective. American Airlines chose to reduce supervision and to increase the emphasis on performance measurement through functional accountability. These choices were mutually reinforcing. Less supervision was needed for the purpose of monitoring if front-line employees were to be held accountable for performance through detailed systems of measurement. However, neither of these choices was conducive to coordination. Functional accountability reduced cooperation and learning across functional boundaries, while broad spans of control reduced the potential for supervisors to support coordination through coaching and feedback.

Southwest chose instead to increase supervision and to reduce the emphasis on performance measurement by adopting cross-functional accountability. These choices were mutually reinforcing. With a system of performance measurement that offered less detailed information about performance, more supervisors were needed for coaching and feedback. Both of these choices were also conducive to coordination. Cross-functional accountability increased cooperation and learning across functional boundaries, while narrow spans of control allowed supervisors to engage actively in supporting coordination through coaching and feedback.

There are of course other potential explanations for the observed differences between American and Southwest. Let us consider the two explanations that are most commonly offered: differences in overall strategy, and differences in organizational culture.

Does Strategy Make a Difference?

Perhaps American developed a weaker capability for coordination because its strategy is fundamentally different from that of Southwest. Being a hub and spoke carrier, rather than a point-to-point carrier, quick turnarounds are arguably less relevant to American. American's hubs generate pricing power that counterbalances the inherent costs of the hub and spoke system. According to American's senior vice president of planning, a hub generates up to 20 percent more revenue per plane than a comparable point-to-point flight.[18] Southwest, on the other hand, as a point-to-point carrier, has neither hubs nor pricing power. Southwest has instead used a quick turnaround strategy, and the high aircraft utilization inherent in this strategy, to offer low cost air travel to consumers. The quick turnaround strategy requires a simple product and a configuration of assets— aircraft, routes, and maintenance facilities—that is very different from that of a hub and spoke operation. It clearly required high levels of coordination.

Even American, however, with its more traditional strategy, can benefit from improving coordination of the departure process. The key, contrary to current industry belief, is not whether or not one has adopted Southwest's quick turnaround strategy, complete with its simple product and a particular arrangement of its physical assets. The key is reducing turnaround time and staffing, not absolutely, but relative to the complexity of the product that one offers. A forty minute turn for a more complex flight— longer, with more passengers, more connections, and more freight and mail—can require just as much coordination as a twenty minute turn for a simpler flight.

Some leaders at American clearly recognized the benefits to be gained from improvements to the departure process. "We view Southwest as a different product," said Donald O'Hare vice president of field services at the time. "But teamwork is just as essential to us." Indeed, a more complex process like American's should benefit even more from the kind of coordination at which Southwest excels. Organization design theorists agree that coordination is *more* valuable the more complex the process to be coordinated.[19]

Does Culture Make a Difference?

Perhaps American has a weaker capability for coordination because its culture is fundamentally different from that of Southwest. Rather than the explanations offered here regarding systems of accountability, supervision, employee selection, and conflict resolution, perhaps these two organizations simply have very different cultures, such that none of these other factors really matters in the end.

Indeed, these two organizations do have very different cultures, as the data presented here and elsewhere clearly suggest.[20] However, culture comes from somewhere, after all, and the evidence presented here suggests that it is powerfully driven by the choices that leaders and others make about how to measure performance, how to supervise, how to select employees, how to resolve conflicts, and so on. It is important to go beyond the observation that "culture matters" to identify organizational practices that shape the culture of an organization, as reflected in the beliefs and behaviors of its employees.

Conclusion

Organizations can achieve control through means that are highly supportive of coordination, or through means that undermine it. Contrary to current thinking, the best way to achieve coordination is not to create a flat organization based on performance measurement and little supervision. Rather it is better, particularly in turbulent settings such as the one in which flight departures occur, to build an organization based on cross-functional accountability to diffuse blame, with adequate supervisory staffing to provide coaching and feedback.

Acknowledgements

I thank Teresa Amabile, Rob Austin, George Baker, Amy Edmondson, Steve Spear, and Leigh Weiss for useful discussions regarding ideas in this article. I also thank reviewers at *California Management Review* for their comments and suggestions. Last but not least, I thank the managers and front-line employees of American and Southwest Airlines for sharing their experiences with me.

Notes

1. Michael Piore and Charles Sabel, *The Second Industrial Divide* (New York, NY: Basic Books, 1984); Richard Walton, "From Control to Commitment in the Workplace," *Harvard Business Review*, 63/2 (March/April 1985): 76–84 (1995); James Womack, D. Jones, and Daniel Roos, *The Machine that Changed the World: The Story of Lean Production* (New York, NY: HarperCollins, 1991); Peter Doeringer (ed.), *Turbulence in the American Workplace* (New York, NY: Oxford University Press, 1991); Charles Heckscher and Anne Donnellon, eds., *The Post-Bureaucratic Organization: New Perspectives on Organizational Change* (Thousand Oaks, CA: Sage, 1994); Eileen Appelbaum and Rosemary Batt, *The New American Workplace* (Ithaca, NY: ILR Press, 1994); Lynda Applegate, "In Search of a New Organizational Model: Lessons from the Field," in G. DeSanctis and J. Fulk, eds., *Shaping Organization Form: Communication, Connection and Community* (Newbury Park, CA: Sage 1998).

2. This study examined four major airlines—American, Southwest, Continental, and United—at nine individual airport sites. Early in the study, I interviewed managers at these sites and at their headquarters to understand the formal organizational practices in place at each site. I later surveyed 356 employees across the nine sites about their communication and relationships with each other functional group involved in the flight departure process. I also measured quality and efficiency performance of the flight departure process at these sites, and differences in product complexity. Comprehensive results from this study are reported in Jody Hoffer Gittell, "Organizing Work to Support Relational Coordination," *International Journal of Human Resource Management* 11 (3): 517–539; Jody Hoffer Gittell, "Relational Coordination and Flight Departure Performance," Harvard Business School Working Paper.

3. Jody Hoffer Gittell, "Cost/Quality Tradeoffs in the Departure Process? Evidence from the Major U.S. Airlines," *Transportation Research Record*, 1480 (1995): 25–36. Figures reported here are adjusted for inflation.

4. Roger Hallowell and James Heskett, "Southwest Airlines," Teaching Case, Harvard Business School Publishing, 1993.

5. Max Weber, *Economy and Society* (Berkeley, CA: University of California Press, 1978); Frederick W. Taylor, *Principles of Scientific Management* (New York, NY: Harper and Row, 1911); Chester Barnard, *Functions of the Executive* (Cambridge, MA: Harvard University Press, 1938); James March and Herbert Simon, *Organizations* (New York, NY: Wiley, 1958); Albert Chandler, *Strategy and Structure* (Cambridge, MA: Massachusetts Institute of Technology Press, 1989).

6. J. Edward Deming, *Out of the Crisis* (Cambridge, MA: Massachusetts Institute of Technology Press, 1986); Robert Cole, "Different Quality Paradigms and their Implications for Organizational Learning," presented at the conference "Japan in a Global Economy: A European Perspective," Stockholm School of Economics, 1991; Robert Grant, Rami Shani, and R. Krishnan, "TQM's challenge to Management Theory and Practice," *Sloan Management Review*. 35/2 (Winter 1994): 25–35.

7. Amy Edmonson, "Learning from Mistakes is Easier Said Than Done: Group and Organizational Influences on the Detection and Correction of Human Error," *Journal of Applied Behavioral Science*, 32/1 (March 1996).

8. Davis Jenkins, "Learning-Intensive Work Organization," Doctoral Thesis, Carnegie Mellon University, 1994.

9. Richard Hackman, "The Design of Work Teams," in Jay Lorsch, ed., *Handbook of Organizational Behavior* (Englewoods Cliffs, NJ: Prentice-Hall, 1987); Susan Albers Mohrman, Susan Cohen, and Allan Mohrman, *Designing Team-Based Organizations: New Forms for Knowledge Work* (San Francisco, CA: Jossey-Bass, 1995); Jay Galbraith, *Competing with Flexible Lateral Organizations* (Reading, MA: Addison-Wesley, 1995); Ann Majzrchak and Qui Wang, "Breaking the Functional Mind-Set in Process Organizations," *Harvard Business Review*, 74/5 (September/October, 1996): 92–99; Ruth Wageman and George Baker, "Incentives and Cooperation: The Joint Effects of Task and Reward Interdependence on Group Performance," *Journal of Organizational Behavior*, 18/2 (1997).

10. V.F. Ridgway, "Dysfunctional Consequences of Performance Measurements," *Administrative Science Quarterly*, 1/2 (September 1956): 240–247; Robert Austin, *Measuring and Managing Performance in Organizations* (New York, NY: Dorset House Publishing, 1996).

11. George Baker, Robert Gibbons, and Kevin Murphy, "Subjective Performance Measures in Optimal Incentive Contracts," *Quarterly Journal of Economics*, 109/4 (November 1994): 1125–1156.

12. Richard Hackman and Gregory Oldham, *Work Redesign* (Boston, MA: Addison-Wesley, 1980); Richard Walton, "Establishing and Maintaining High Commitment Work systems," in John Kimberly, Robert Miles and Associates, eds., *The Organization Life Cycle: Issues in the Creation, Transformation and Decline of Organizations* (San Francisco, CA: Jossey-Bass, 1980); Richard

Mowday, Lyman Porter, and Richard Steers, *Employee-Organization Linkages* (New York, NY: Academic Press, 1982); Richard Walton and Richard Hackman, "Groups Under Contrasting Management Strategies," in Paul Goodman and Associates, eds., *Designing Effective Work Groups* (San Francisco, CA: Jossey-Bass, 1986).

13. William Ouchi, "A Conceptual Framework for the Design of Organizational Control Mechanisms," *Management Science*, 25/9 (1979): 833–848.

14. R.I. Beekun, "Assessing the Effectiveness of Sociotechnical Interventions: Antidote or Fad?" *Human Relations*, 47 (1989): 877–897; N. Brewer, C. Wilson, and K. Beck, "Supervisory Behavior and Team Performance Amongst Police Patrol Sergeants," *Journal of Occupational and Organizational Psychology*. 67/1 (1994): 69–79; Susan Cohen, G.E. Ledford, and G.M. Spreitzer, "A Predictive Model of Self-Managing Team Effectiveness," *Human Relations*, 49/5 (1996): 643–676.

15. Douglas McGregor, *The Human Side of Enterprise* (New York, NY: McGraw-Hill, 1960); Rensis Likert, *New Patterns of Management* (New York, NY: Wiley, 1961); Arnold Tannenbaum, *Control in Organizations* (New York, NY: McGraw, 1968).

16. Peter Blau, "Interdependence and Hierarchy in Organizations," *Social Science Research*, 1 (1972): 1–24.

17. L.W. Fry, S. Kerr, and C. Lee, "Effects of Different Leader Behaviors Under Different Levels of Task Interdependence," *Human Relations*, 39 (1986): 1067–1082; Deborah Ancona, "Outward Bound: Strategies for Team Survival in an Organization," *Academy of Management Journal*, 33/2 (1990): 334–365; J.C. Henderson and S. Lee, "Managing I/S Design Teams: A Control Theories Perspective," *Management Science*, 38/6 (1992): 757–777; Y. Kim and B. Lee, "R&D Project Team Climate and Team Performance in Korea: A Multidimensional Approach," *R&D Management*, 25/2 (1995): 179–196; Kathleen Eisenhardt and B.N. Tabrizi, "Accelerating Adaptive Processes: Product Innovation in the Global Computer Industry," *Administrative Science Quarterly*, 4 (1995): 84–110.

18. Howard Banks, "A Sixties Industry in a Nineties Economy," *Forbes*, May 5, 1994.

19. Andrew Van de Ven, Andre Delbecq, and Robert Koenig, Jr., "Determinants of Coordination Modes Within Organizations," *American Sociological Review*, 41 (1976); Jay Galbraith, *Organization Design* (Reading, MA: Addison-Wesley, 1977).

20. Jeffrey Pfeffer, *Competitive Advantage Through People: Unleashing the Power of the Work Force* (Boston, MA: Harvard Business School Press, 1996); James Heskett, Earl Sasser, and Leonard Schlesinger, *The Service Profit Chain: How Leading Companies Link Profit and Growth to Loyalty, Satisfaction, and Value* (New York, NY: The Free Press, 1997).

Index

Index compiled by Indexing Specialists
    (UK) Ltd